GRADE 1

2008–2009 YEARBOOK

The Education Center, Inc.
Greensboro, North Carolina

The Mailbox® 2008–2009 Grade 1 Yearbook

Managing Editor, *The Mailbox* Magazine: Amy Erickson

Editorial Team: Becky S. Andrews, Diane Badden, Kimberley Bruck, Karen A. Brudnak, Pam Crane, Lynn Drolet, Sarah Foreman, Pierce Foster, Margaret Freed (COVER ARTIST), Tazmen Hansen, Marsha Heim, Lori Z. Henry, Debra Liverman, Kitty Lowrance, Jennifer Nunn, Tina Petersen, Mark Rainey, Greg D. Rieves, Hope Rodgers, Eliseo De Jesus Santos II, Rebecca Saunders, Donna K. Teal, Rachael Traylor, Sharon M. Tresino, Zane Williard

ISBN10 1-56234-922-8
ISBN13 978-1-56234-922-6
ISSN 0199-6045

Printed in the United States of America.

The Education Center, Inc.
P.O. Box 9753
Greensboro, NC 27429-0753

Contents

Math Units

Seasonal Units

Arts & Crafts

Arts & Crafts

Student Look-Alikes

These projects are so cute, you'll want to show them off! Display them with students' names or photos during open house.

Materials for one project:
oval template (face)
skin-toned sheet of paper
lengths of yarn (hair)
kidney beans (eyebrows and hair)
pasta twists (hair)
scissors
crayons
glue

Steps:

1. Trace the oval on the paper. Cut out the tracing.
2. To make a self-likeness, draw your face on the cutout. Then glue yarn, kidney beans, and/or pasta twists to the cutout to add hair and any other desired details.

Sheila Criqui-Kelley, Lebo Elementary, Lebo, KS

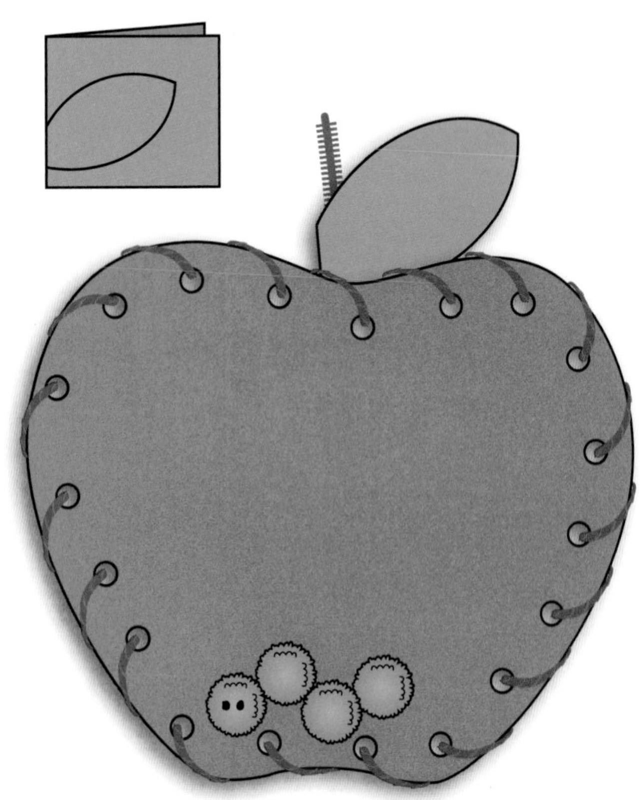

Apple and Friend

For easy lacing, dip a few inches of one yarn end in white glue and then allow it to dry. The result will be a sturdy lacing tip that doesn't fray!

Materials for one apple project:
2 large identical apple cutouts with holes punched along the edges
piece of tissue paper
green construction paper scraps
3" brown pipe cleaner
length of yarn
4 small green pom-poms
scissors
glue
tape
black marker

Steps:

1. Fold a piece of green paper in half. Draw a leaf on the fold as shown. Cut it out.
2. Unfold the leaf, place the pipe cleaner on the crease, and then glue the leaf closed. Tape the pipe cleaner to one apple to make a stem.
3. Begin lacing the two apples together with yarn so the taped end of the pipe cleaner is on the inside. When the apples are almost entirely laced, gently stuff them with crumpled tissue paper. Then finish lacing the apples.
4. Glue the pom-poms on the apple to make a worm. Draw two eyes on the worm.

Amy Melisi, Peaslee Elementary, Northboro, MA

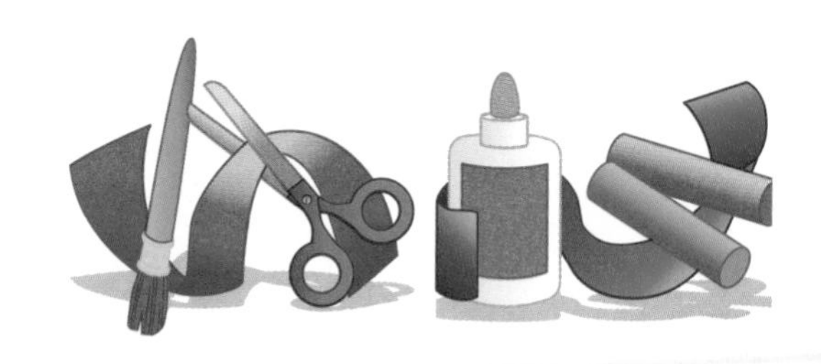

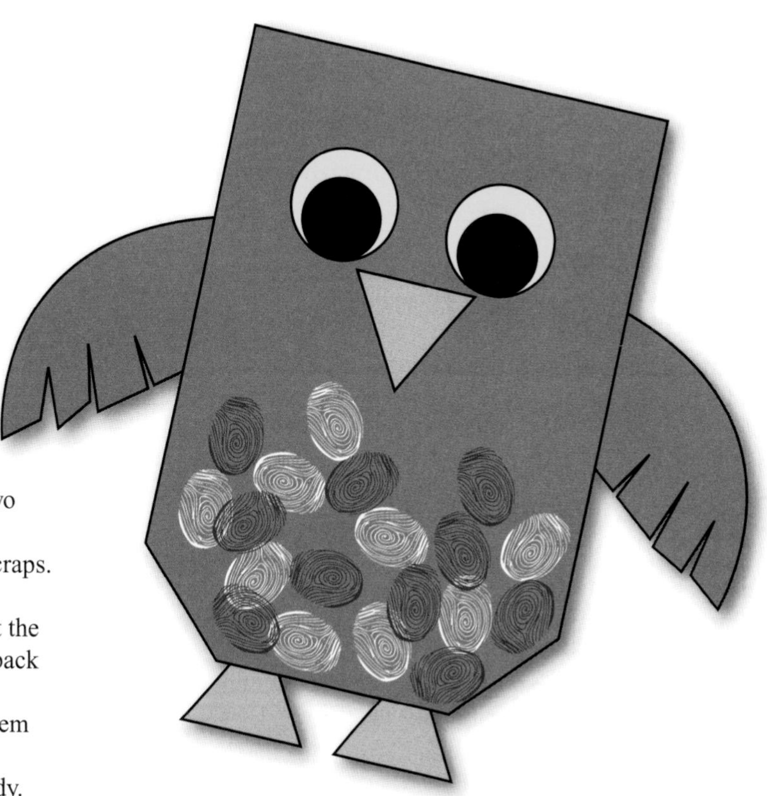

Quick and Easy Owl

No patterns are needed for this project!

Materials for one owl:
6" x 9" brown construction paper
two 3" x 6" brown construction paper rectangles
yellow, black, and orange construction paper scraps
white and brown paint in shallow containers
scissors
glue

Steps:

1. Vertically position the 6" x 9" paper. Cut off the two bottom corners as shown.
2. Cut two eyes, two pupils, and a beak from paper scraps. Glue them in place.
3. Cut a wing from each 3" x 6" rectangle. Fringe-cut the straight edge of each wing. Glue the wings to the back of the owl.
4. Cut two triangles (feet) from paper scraps. Glue them in place.
5. Use the paint to make fingerprints on the owl's body.

Sweet Sheep

This adorable idea is perfect to use with a farm unit or *Russell the Sheep* by Rob Scotton.

Materials for one sheep:
1½" x 2" gray construction paper oval
gray construction paper scraps
2 wooden clothespins
cotton balls
craft stick
black marker
scissors
glue

Steps:

1. Draw hooves on the clothespins as shown.
2. Clip the clothespins to the craft stick to make the project self-standing.
3. Draw a sheep face on the gray oval. Cut two ears from gray paper scraps and then glue them to the oval. Glue the oval to one end of the craft stick.
4. Stretch out cotton balls. Glue them to the sheep's head and body.

Heather Moseley, Carver Kindergarten, Lockhart, TX

Speedy Fire Truck

This project is a perfect token of appreciation for your local firefighters!

Materials for one truck:
4½" x 10" red construction paper rectangle with a slit in one long side as shown
white and black construction paper scraps
length of yarn
scissors
glue

Steps:
1. Cut a window and two wheels from black paper. Glue them in place.
2. Cut two long strips and several short strips from white paper. Glue them on the truck to make a ladder.
3. Squeeze some glue on the truck where you want the hose to be. Then arrange the yarn to make the hose.

Cute Cat

Sticky dots make it simple for students to make the eyes on this adorable feline.

Materials for one cat:
2 black circles, one 6" and one 8"
black construction paper scraps
black pipe cleaner
2 green sticky dots
pom-pom
orange yarn cut into short lengths
yarn or ribbon bow
masking tape
glue
black marker
white crayon

Steps:
1. Fold the pipe cleaner in half and twist it to make a tail. Tape the ends of the pipe cleaner to the eight-inch circle. Place the circle taped-side down.
2. Glue the six-inch circle to the eight-inch circle as shown.
3. Cut two ears from black paper. Glue them in place.
4. Put the two sticky dots on the head to make eyes. Draw black pupils.
5. Glue the pom-pom to the head to make the nose. Glue lengths of orange yarn to the cat to make whiskers. Draw a mouth with the white crayon.
6. Glue the bow below the head.

adapted from an idea by Beth Dillie
Markesan Elementary
Markesan, WI

Pumpkin Puzzle

Since each of these pumpkins is unique, this idea is great to pair with a discussion about individuality and *The Legend of Spookley the Square Pumpkin* by Joe Troiano.

Materials for one pumpkin:
pumpkin cutout without a stem
black sheet of paper
green and yellow construction paper scraps
scissors
glue
ruler (optional)
pencil (optional)

Steps:

1. Cut the pumpkin into several vertical strips and then reassemble it on the black paper. (For an easier version, use a ruler and a pencil to divide the pumpkin into several vertical sections. Lightly number the sections before you cut them apart.) Glue the strips to the paper, leaving space between them.
2. Cut a stem from green paper. Glue it in place.
3. Cut facial features from yellow paper. Then glue them to the pumpkin.

Sarah Bajema
White Pine Academy
Lansing, MI

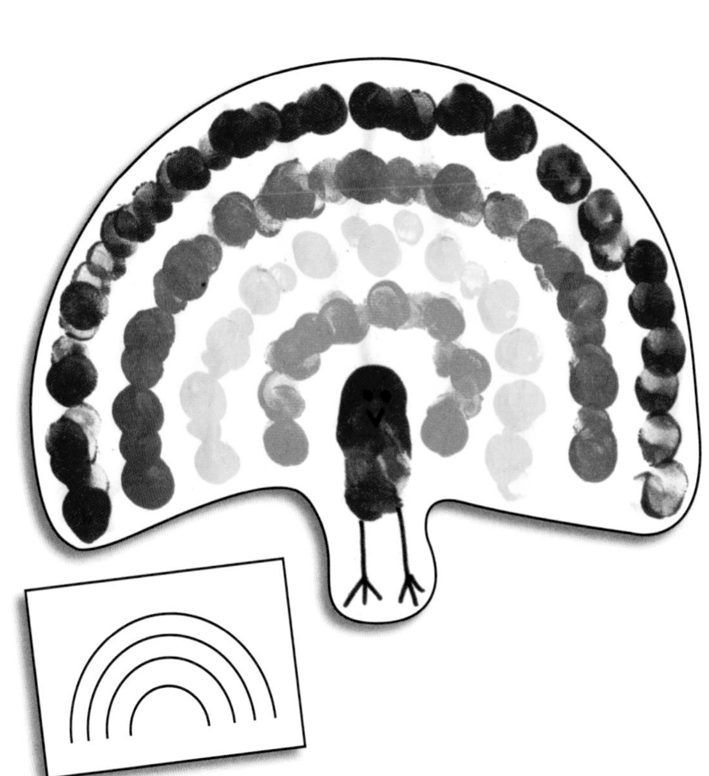

Fingerprint Gobbler

Set out wet wipes to make it easy for children to clean their fingers between rows of prints.

Materials for one turkey:
paper labeled with four arcs, like the one shown
white paper
paint in the following colors: brown, orange, yellow, and red
black marker
scissors

Steps:

1. Place the blank paper atop the paper with the arcs.
2. Using the paper with the arcs as a placement guide, make a thumbprint (turkey body) with brown paint as shown. Then make fingerprints in four arcs around the turkey's body, using a different color of paint for each arc. Allow the paint to dry.
3. Draw two eyes, a beak, and two legs. Then trim the paper as desired.

Kelly Kramer
Rivercrest Elementary
Bartlett, TN

Holiday Garland

For best results, encourage students to carefully crease their papers to make sharp fold lines.

Materials for one garland:
copy of the patterns on page 17, cut out
various colors of construction paper
length of yarn
scissors
glue
craft materials such as cotton, curling ribbon, and glitter glue

Steps:
1. Fold a piece of paper in half. Place a pattern on the fold and then trace it. Cut out the tracing, keeping the fold intact. Make a desired number of additional cutouts as described.
2. Stretch out the yarn horizontally. Open each cutout and slide the yarn inside it.
3. Glue the cutouts closed. Decorate them as desired.

Cindy Barber
Fredonia, WI

Dapper Doily Mobile

Since glue might drip through a doily, protect each student's work surface with a nonstick covering, such as waxed paper.

Materials for one mobile:
8-inch white paper doily
three 12-inch white crepe paper streamers
5" x 8½" hat cutout
four 1½" x 6" paper rectangles (scarf)
white, black, and orange paper scraps
glue
scissors
black marker
tape
hole puncher
string
glitter

Steps:
1. Glue the hat to the doily.
2. To make eyes, cut out two small white circles and two slightly larger black circles. Draw black pupils on the white circles. Glue all the circles to the doily as shown.
3. Cut a nose and mouth from scrap paper. Glue them in place.
4. Glue one rectangle to the bottom of the doily. Tape the streamers to the rectangle and then glue another rectangle atop the streamers so the rectangles are aligned. Fringe-cut the remaining rectangles and glue them to the project as shown.
5. Punch a hole in the hat. Thread string through the hole and tie its ends to make a hanger. Decorate the hat with glitter.

Luz Villarreal
Dr. Green Elementary
El Paso, TX

Sparkly Ornament

To present this ornament as a gift, simply put it in a decorated paper lunch bag, fold down the top of the bag, and punch two holes in it. Then thread a ribbon through the holes and tie it.

Materials for one ornament:
cardboard tube cut into ½-inch rings
waxed paper
glue
white paint
paintbrush
glitter
thread

Steps:

1. Arrange several cardboard rings on the waxed paper so they resemble a snowflake. Glue the rings together. Allow the glue to dry.
2. Paint the snowflake and sprinkle glitter on it while the paint is wet. Then let the paint dry.
3. Tie thread to the snowflake to make a hanger.

Melanie Rishel
Pippi's Playskool
Lindsborg, KS

Swirled Snowballs

For a holiday variation, make this textured painting on the front of a construction paper greeting card.

Materials for one painting:
6" x 9" blue paper
cotton ball
shallow container of white paint
construction paper scraps, including black and brown
scissors
glue
black marker

Steps:

1. Dip the cotton ball in the paint. Then gently swirl the cotton ball on the blue paper to make three circles, as shown, reloading the paint as needed. Allow the paint to dry.
2. Cut a hat, a nose, two arms, a scarf, and any other desired items from scrap paper. Glue them in place.
3. Complete the snowpal with marker details.

Andrea Selking
Lantern Farms School
Fishers, IN

Arts & Crafts

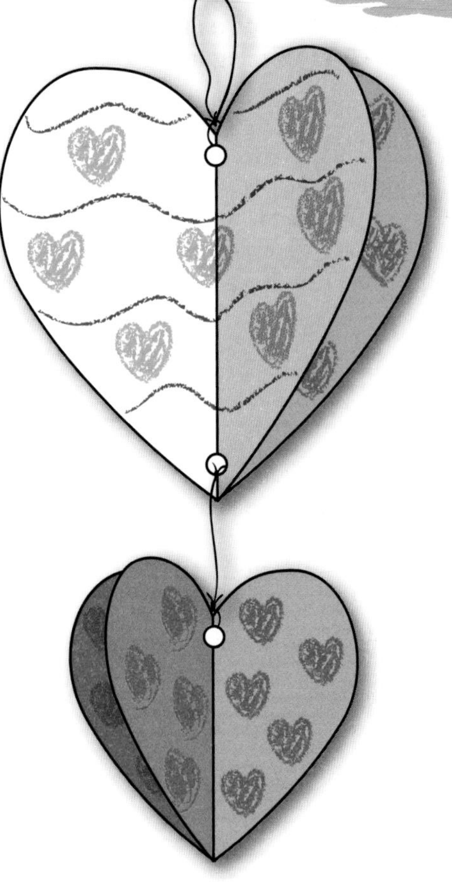

Heart Trios

Cutting the hearts from folded paper makes it easier to assemble the mobile.

Materials for one mobile:
large and medium heart-half templates
construction paper
scissors
crayons
glue
hole puncher
string

Steps:
1. Make three large hearts and three medium hearts by folding construction paper in half, tracing the templates on the fold, and then cutting out the tracings.
2. Unfold the hearts. Use crayons to decorate them. Then refold the hearts.
3. Glue the hearts together, as shown, to make two 3-D hearts.
4. Punch holes in the hearts and connect them with string. Tie a string to the top of the mobile to make a hanger.

Diane L. Flohr-Henderson
Kent City Elementary
Kent City, MI

Fingerprint Fun

Plan for students to complete this project over two days to allow plenty of time for the paint to dry.

Materials for one card:
4" x 5" white construction paper
4½" x 12" colorful construction paper
red paint in a shallow container
fine-tip markers
glue

Steps:
1. Dip the top third of your pointer finger in red paint. Make two overlapping prints on the white paper to create a heart. Make additional prints, dipping your finger in the paint as needed. Allow the paint to dry.
2. Use fine-tip markers to decorate the hearts.
3. Fold the colorful construction paper in half to 4½" x 6". Glue the painted paper to the front of the folded paper. Write a message in the resulting card.

Heather E. Graley
Grace Christian School
Blacklick, OH

Wild and Woolly

When you dye the macaroni noodles, add a drop or two of rubbing alcohol to the food coloring for a more vibrant color.

Materials for one lion and one lamb:

yellow copy of the lion face pattern and black copy of the lamb face pattern from page 18
uncooked macaroni noodles, dyed orange
3' length of white curling ribbon, curled
four 1½" x 2½" black rectangles
small red heart cutout
two 6" white paper plates
scissors
black marker or crayon
glue
cotton swab
white paint

Steps:

1. Cut out the patterns.
2. To make a lion, draw a face on the lion face cutout. Glue the cutout to a plate. Then glue the macaroni around the cutout.
3. To make a lamb, glue the lamb face cutout and the black rectangles to a plate as shown. Cut the curling ribbon into short pieces. Glue them around the face. Glue the heart to the lamb. Use a cotton swab and white paint to make two eyes.

Sue Fleischmann
Mary Queen of Saints Catholic Academy
West Allis, WI

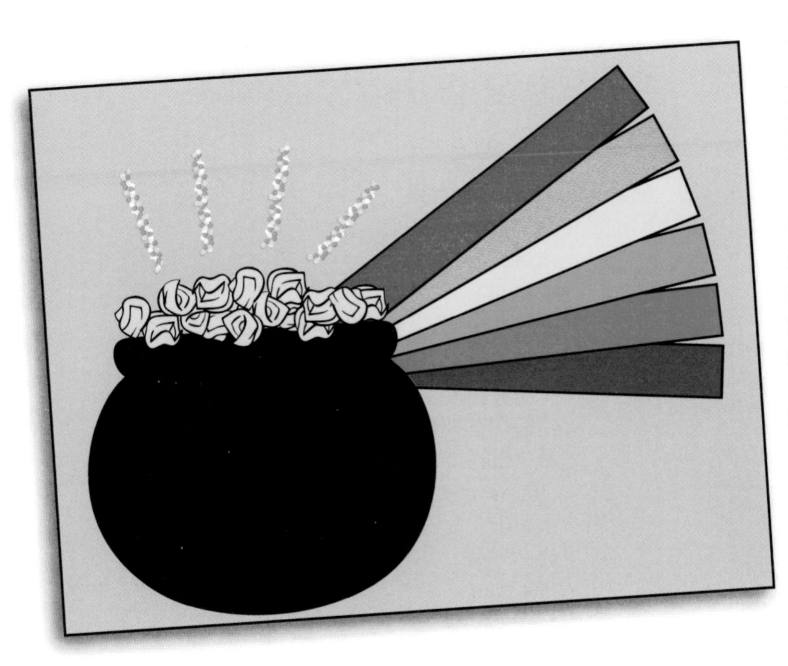

Rainbow's End

This colorful project is a perfect paper topper for March writing.

Materials for one project:

black pot cutout (patterns on page 18)
¾" x 6" paper strip in each of the following colors: red, orange, yellow, green, blue, purple
6" x 8" blue paper
small yellow tissue paper squares
stapler
glue
gold glitter

Steps:

1. Stack the paper strips in the order listed above so the red strip is on top. Fan out the strips to make a rainbow. Then staple the strips together at the narrow end of the rainbow.
2. Glue the rainbow and pot to the blue paper as shown.
3. Crumple the tissue paper squares. Glue them along the top edge of the pot so they resemble gold coins.
4. Glue glitter above the coins as shown.

Arts & Crafts

Fuzzy Chick

Since the thread is taped rather than tied, students can make this mobile with little adult assistance.

Materials for one mobile:
white construction paper copy of the chick and egg pattern from page 19
small piece of a kitchen sponge
cotton ball
thread
scissors
shallow container of yellow paint
black marker
glue
clear tape

Steps:
1. Cut the egg pattern along the outer and inner edges. Cut out the chick pattern. Discard the shaded part of the pattern.
2. Sponge-paint both sides of the chick yellow. After the paint dries, draw an eye on each side of the chick.
3. Pull apart the cotton ball and glue a small amount of cotton on each side of the chick.
4. Tape one end of a length of thread to the top of the chick and then tape the thread to the egg, as shown. Then loop the thread and tape the loose end to the egg to make a hanger.

Jeanette Jonas
Rainbow Child Care Center
Bakersfield, CA

Speckled Frog

This adorable amphibian is made mainly with three circles!

Materials for one frog:
two 4" green circles
6" green circle
black scrap paper
2 white pom-poms
scissors
glue
black marker
sticky dots

Steps:
1. Fold the four-inch circles in half. Then unfold the circles and cut them along the fold lines.
2. To make legs, glue two half circles to the back of the intact circle (frog body) as shown. To make feet, glue the two remaining half circles to the front of the frog.
3. Glue the pom-poms to the frog so they resemble eyes. Cut out two black pupils and glue them in place.
4. Draw a mouth on the frog and details on the feet.
5. Embellish the frog with sticky dots.

Bunny Bag

This Easter project can be easily modified for different-size bags.

Materials for one bunny:

5" x 9¾" white paper bag
cellophane grass
two 3" x 4½" white rectangles
5" white circle
2½" white circle
cotton ball
scissors
pink crayon
glue
black marker

Steps:

1. Fold each rectangle in half. Draw half an ear on each folded paper as shown. Cut out the tracings. Color the inner part of each ear pink.
2. Glue the ears to the five-inch circle. Draw a bunny face on the circle.
3. Cut the top four inches from the bag. Then open the bag and glue the bunny head to it.
4. Cut the 2½-inch circle in half so the halves resemble paws. Draw details on them, as shown, and then glue them in place.
5. Glue the cotton ball to the back of the bag so it resembles a tail.
6. Put cellophane grass in the bag.

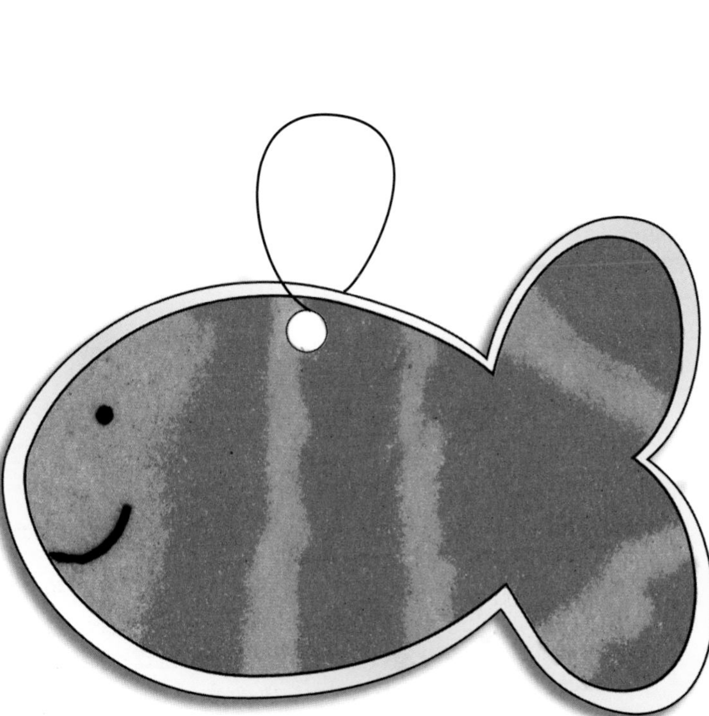

Fancy Fish

Suspend a school of these eye-catching fish in a window or on a bulletin board.

Materials for one fish:

fish pattern from page 19, cut out
craft sand of various colors
clear Con-Tact covering
thread
sheet of paper to use as a work surface
scissors
black permanent marker
hole puncher

Steps:

1. Trace the fish pattern on the backing of a piece of clear Con-Tact covering. Cut out the tracing. Remove the backing and put the cutout sticky-side up on a sheet of paper.
2. Sprinkle craft sand on the cutout. Shake off the excess sand.
3. Cover both sides of the fish with clear Con-Tact covering. Trim the covering, leaving a border.
4. Draw a face on each side of the fish.
5. Punch a hole in the top of the fish and then tie thread through it to make a hanger.

Jennifer Jantausch
New Morning School
Bedford, NH

Arts & Crafts

Paper-Cup Posy

For a smaller project, use a 3-ounce cup and adjust the size of the leaves and stem accordingly.

Materials for one posy:
5-ounce decorative paper cup
1" x 12" green paper strip
two 3" x 6" green paper rectangles
12" x 18" sheet of paper
small yellow tissue paper squares
glue
scissors
stapler

Steps:
1. Glue the paper strip to the sheet of paper so the strip resembles a stem.
2. Make several cuts in the cup from the top to the bottom. Fan out the resulting strips. Staple the cup to the paper as shown.
3. Crumple tissue paper squares and glue them to the base of the cup.
4. Fold each 3" x 6" rectangle in half. Cut a leaf on each fold. Unfold the leaves and glue them to the stem.

What a Whale!

The curve on the head pattern makes it easy for youngsters to glue a smile to the project.

Materials for one whale:
copy of the whale patterns from page 20, cut out
5-inch white circle
9" x 12" sheet of black paper
length of red yarn
2 white paper reinforcers
scissors
glue
glitter

Steps:
1. Use the patterns and black paper to make one head, one tail, and two flippers.
2. Glue the head to the white circle as shown. Glue the tail to the back of the head. Glue the flippers in place.
3. Stick the paper reinforcers to the head so they resemble eyes.
4. Glue the yarn to the whale as shown.
5. Glue glitter to the tail so it looks like water spraying.

Sue Fleischmann
Mary Queen of Saints School
West Allis, WI

Garland Patterns

Use with "Holiday Garland" on page 10.

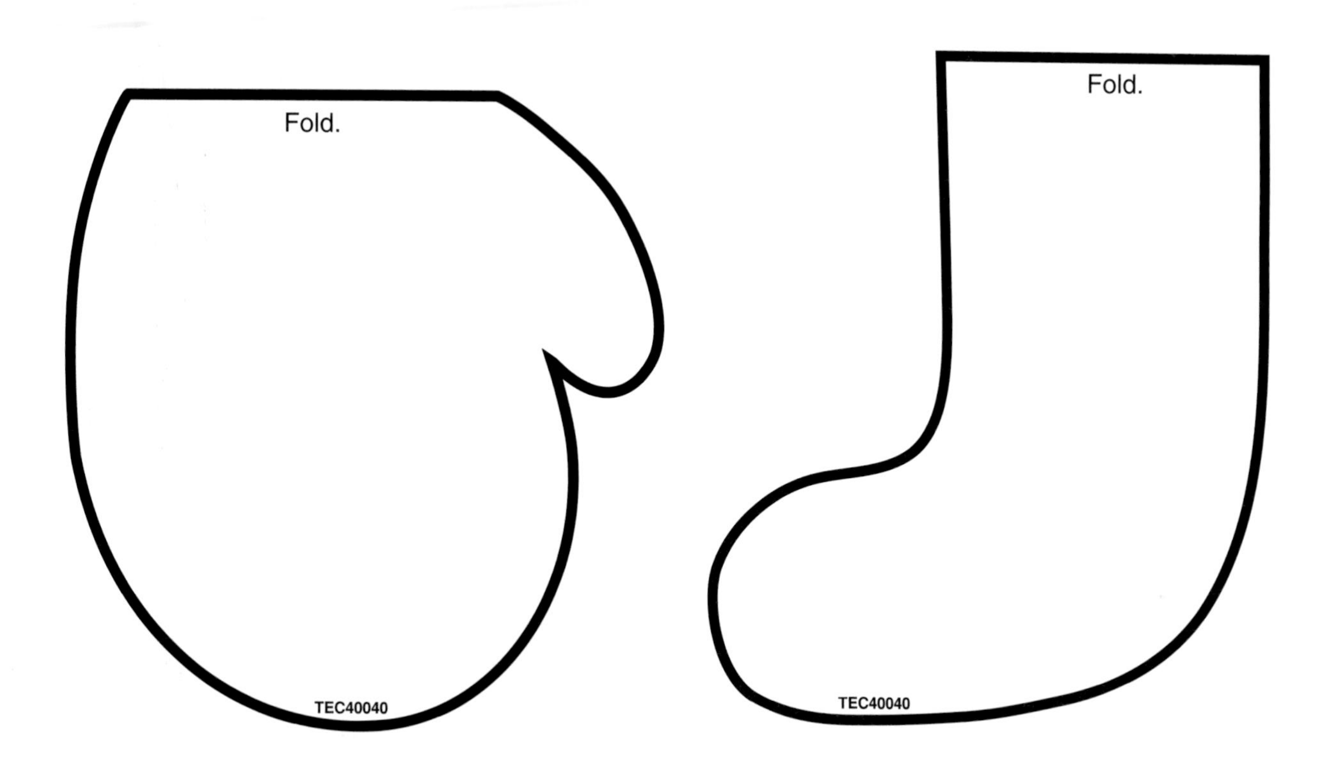

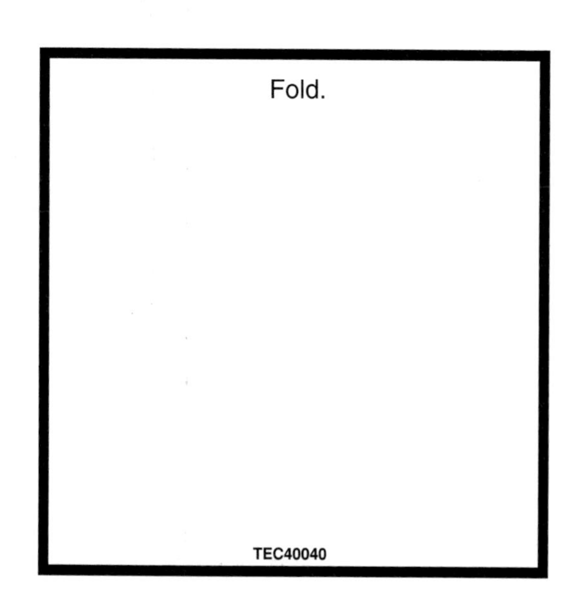

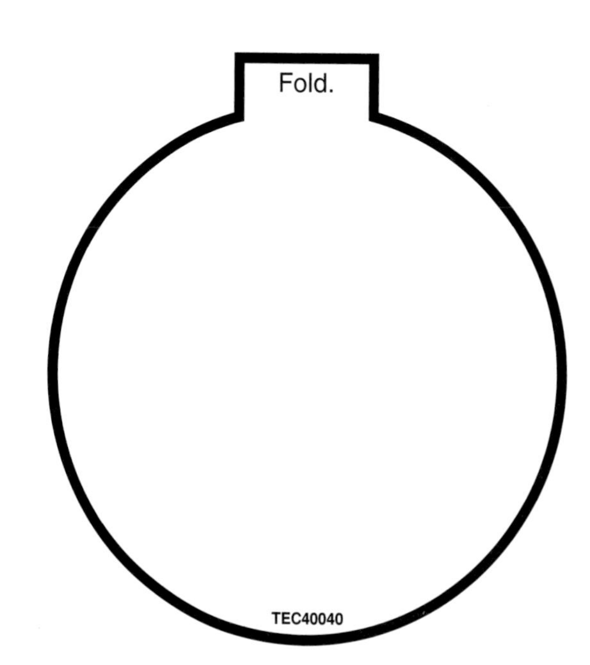

Face Patterns

Use with "Wild and Woolly" on page 13.

Pot Patterns

Use with "Rainbow's End" on page 13.

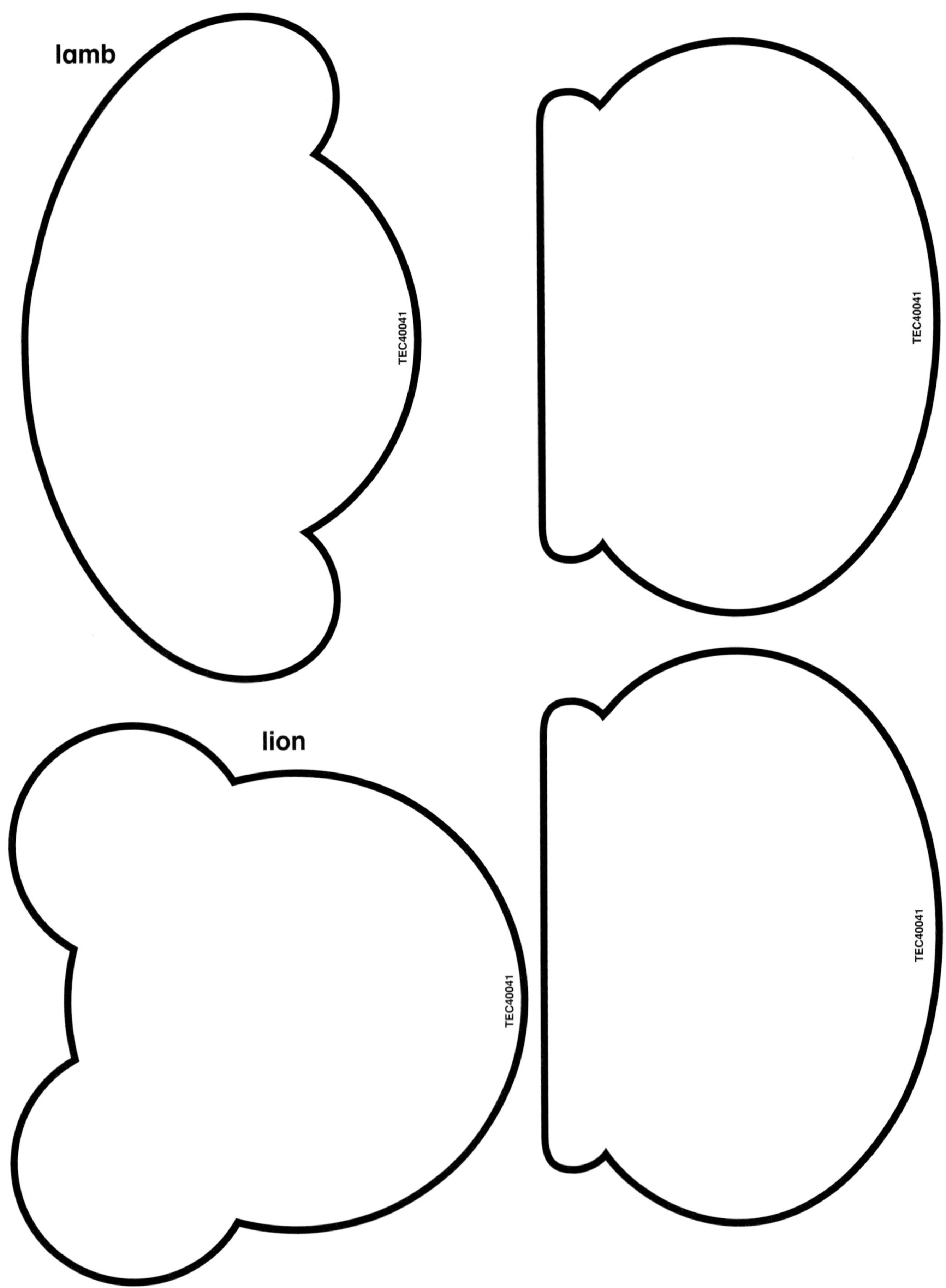

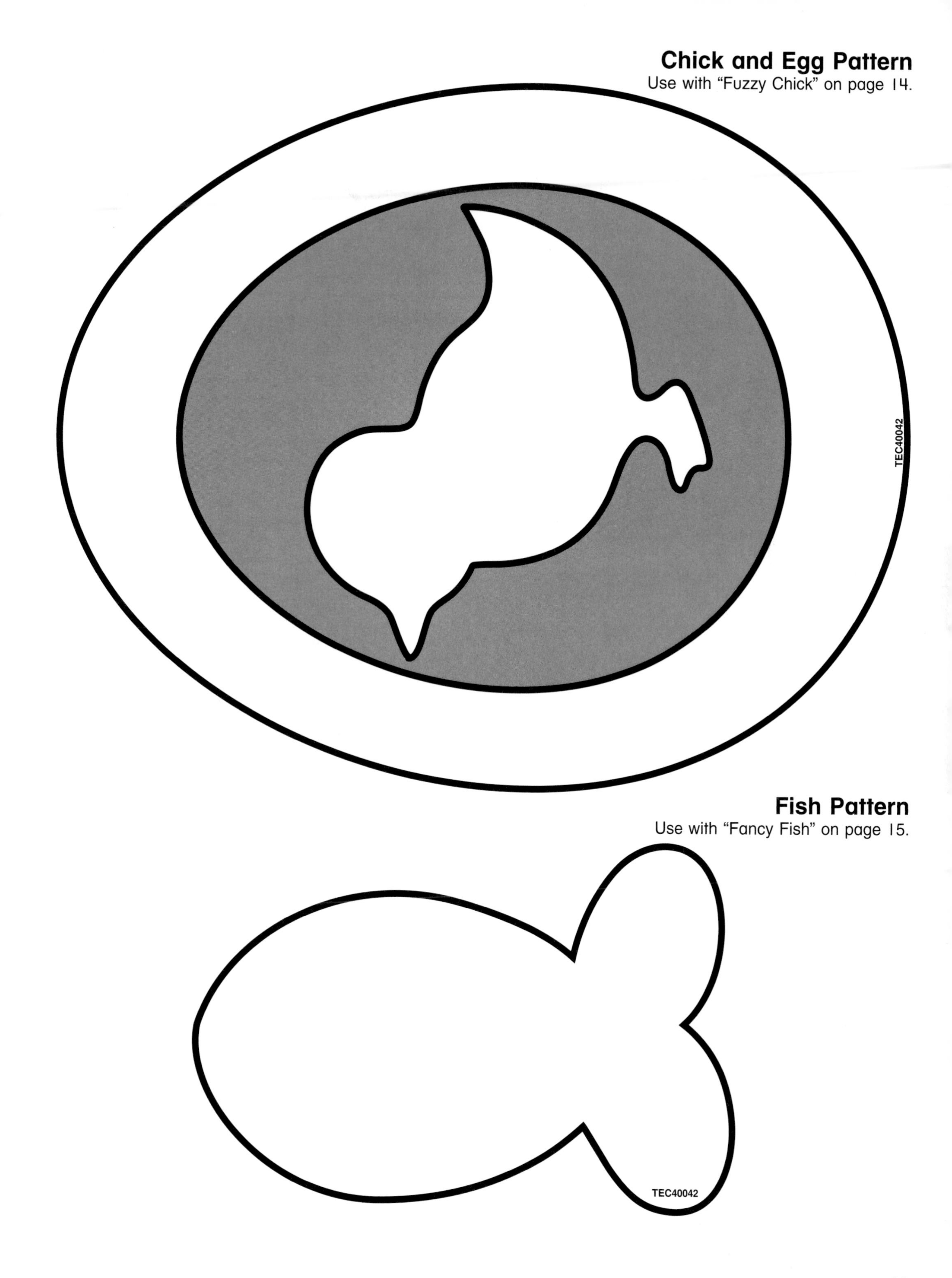

Chick and Egg Pattern

Use with "Fuzzy Chick" on page 14.

Fish Pattern

Use with "Fancy Fish" on page 15.

Whale Patterns

Use with "What a Whale!" on page 16.

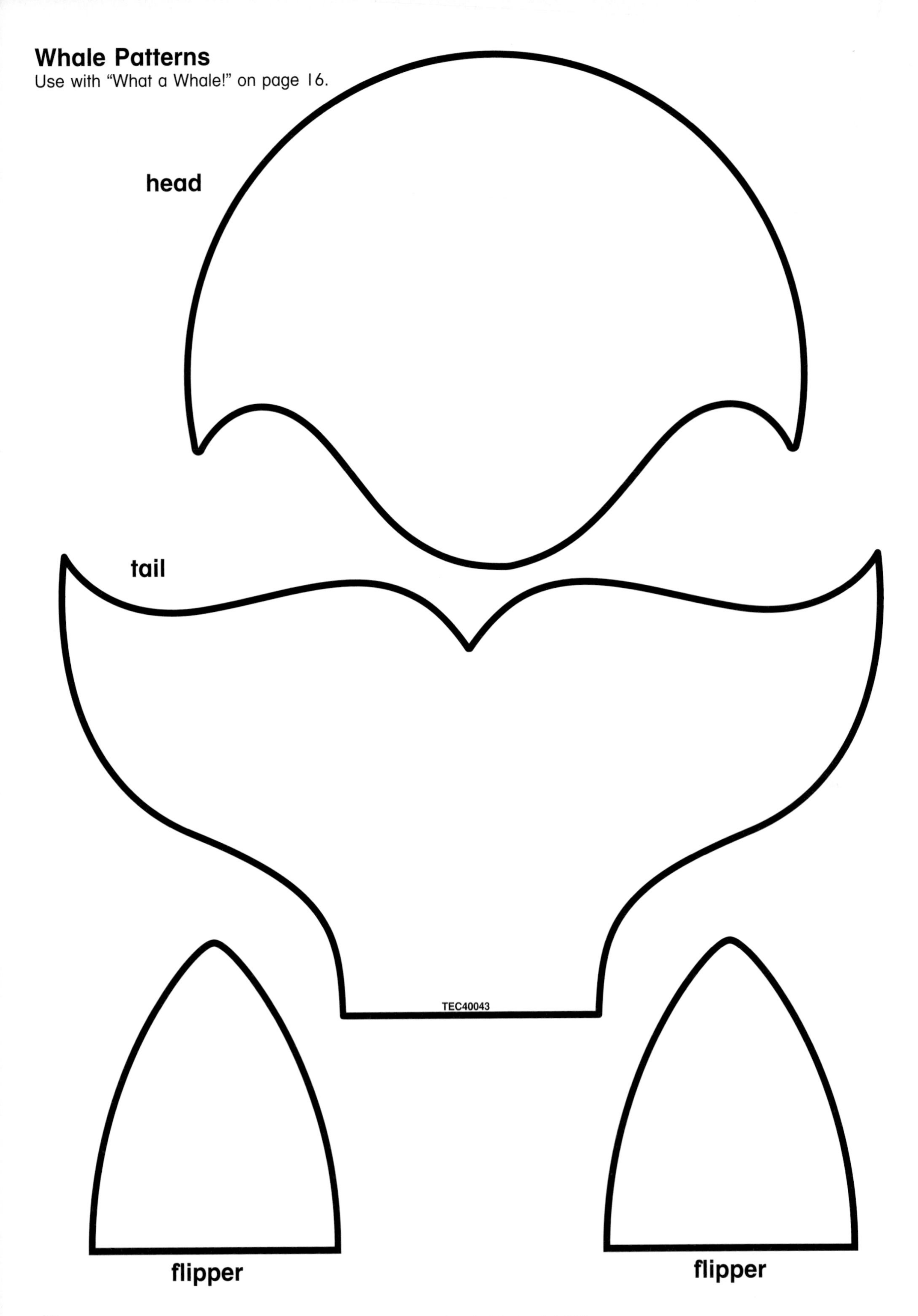

THE BOOK CORNER

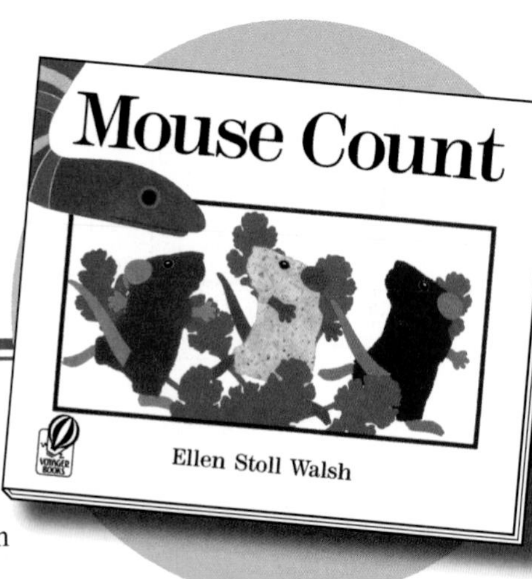

Mouse Count

by Ellen Stoll Walsh

An overhead projector makes these follow-up ideas a hit among young students! Gather ten dried kidney beans (mice), a clear plastic cup (jar), and a rubber snake. Turn on an overhead projector and then choose from the options below.

Retelling: Have students use the cup, beans, and snake to act out the story on the projector.

Counting backward: Place the snake near the projector. Put the mice in the cup and then spill them out onto the projector. Have students count backward from ten as you set aside each mouse, in turn.

Addition combinations: Put the snake near the projector. Then place the cup on the projector and set out a number of mice equal to a chosen sum. Guide students to model corresponding addition combinations by putting some mice in the cup and the rest of the mice beside it. List the combinations on the board.

Sheila Criqui-Kelley
Lebo Elementary
Lebo, KS

Song and Dance Man

Written by Karen Ackerman
Illustrated by Stephen Gammell

This selection is a perfect choice near National Grandparents Day (the first Sunday after Labor Day). After you read the book aloud, ask students to imagine they each have a trunk like Grandpa does. Invite them to tell what mementos they would put inside. Next, give each youngster a copy of the trunk patterns from page 30. Instruct him to write his name on the line. Have him color the lid and the bottom part of the trunk and then cut out the patterns. Staple the lid to the trunk as shown. Then ask the youngster to open the trunk and illustrate items that remind him of a special time. Encourage him to write a caption or dictate a caption for you to write. ***Making connections***

Go Away, Big Green Monster!

By Ed Emberley

Here's a monstrously fun approach to describing words! Read the book to students. Then instruct each child to use a green circle and provided arts-and-crafts supplies to make a monster head on a black sheet of paper. After each child finishes her artwork, revisit the book and draw students' attention to the describing words. Then invite each child to show her monster to the group and use describing words to tell about it. **For more advanced students,** have each youngster write a brief description of her monster. ***Describing words***

Jill Tittsworth, Chief Joseph Elementary, Meridian, ID

My monster has big orange eyes. It has blue hair. It looks funny.
Natasha

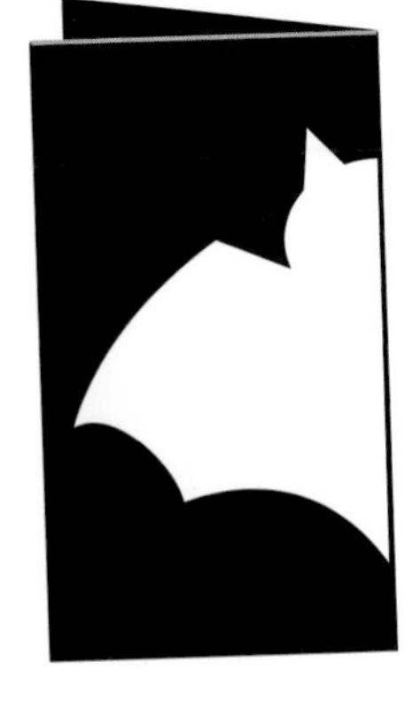

Bat Jamboree

Written by Kathi Appelt
Illustrated by Melissa Sweet

To prepare this estimating activity, make a number of bat cutouts appropriate for your students' math skills. (For easy preparation, trace a pattern like the one shown on folded black paper.) After you read the book to students, draw on the board a triangle just large enough to hold the cutouts. Tell students that you will make a bat pyramid. Then loosely tape one cutout to the bottom left corner of the triangle. Encourage students to think about the size of the cutout as they estimate how many bats will fit in the triangle. After you record students' estimates, loosely tape the bats to the board to fill the triangle. Then have students compare the actual number of bats with the estimates. ***Estimating quantities***

Angie Kutzer, Garrett Elementary, Mebane, NC

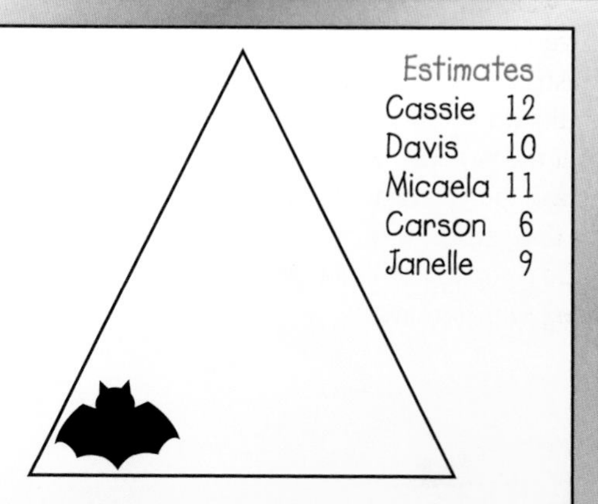

Duck for President

Written by Doreen Cronin
Illustrated by Betsy Lewin

After you share the book with students, suggest that the class have an election for a new boss of the barnyard. Have students recall the different types of animals in the story; then list the animals on the board to identify the election candidates. Over a few days, encourage each youngster to make a poster for his favorite candidate and ask each of several students to tell the group why he thinks his chosen candidate is the best. On a designated day, have each youngster vote for his favorite candidate by secret ballot. Count the votes with students and record the results on the board. (If there is a tie, determine how to resolve it with student input.) Declare the top vote-getter the boss of the barnyard! ***Participating in a mock election***

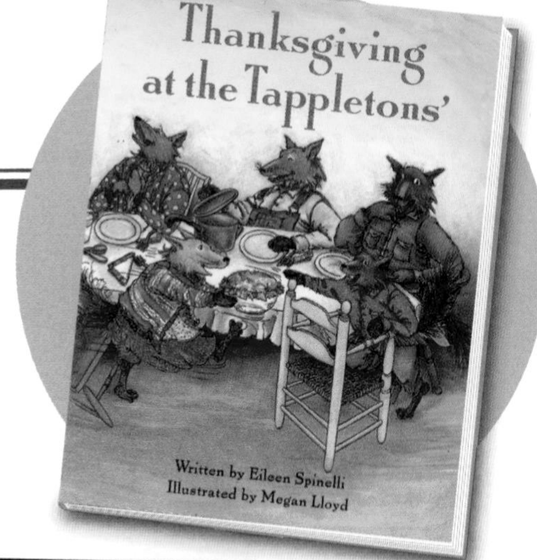

Thanksgiving at the Tappletons'

Written by Eileen Spinelli
Illustrated by Megan Lloyd

The Tappletons don't serve up turkey with all the trimmings. Instead, they serve up a reminder of what Thanksgiving is about! After your students are familiar with the story, give each youngster a paper plate. Have her illustrate it to show one or more things for which she is thankful. Invite her to add labels or dictate labels for you to write. Then instruct her to attach the plate, a napkin, and a plastic fork to a sheet of paper and label the paper with her name. Display students' resulting place settings with the title "We Give Thanks!" ***Making connections***

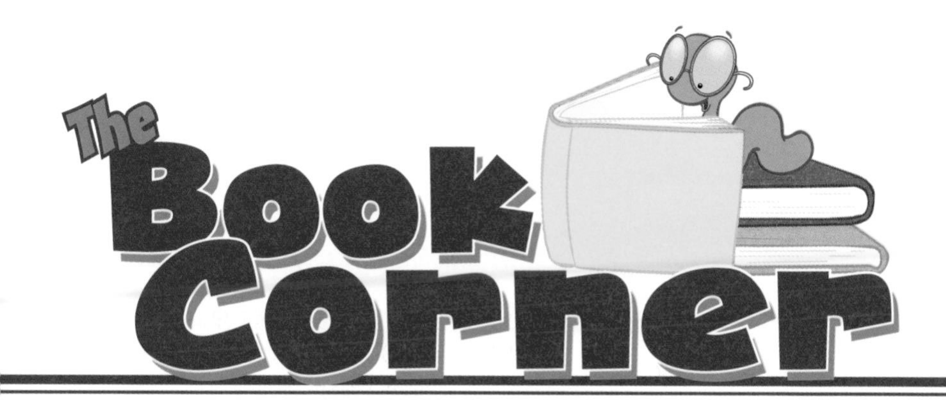

The Mitten

adapted and illustrated by Jan Brett

This follow-up activity reviews story details as well as parts of sentences! Ask each youngster to write a sentence about a story event on a piece of scrap paper. Then draw a large T chart on the board. Label the first column "Naming Part" and the second column "Telling Part." Ask a volunteer to read aloud his sentence. Have students identify the naming and telling parts of the sentence; then write them on the chart.

After you record a few sentences, give each youngster two labeled mitten cutouts like the ones shown. Instruct him to write the naming and telling parts of his sentence on the appropriate mittens. Then punch a hole in each mitten and connect the mittens with yarn. Display students' completed work on a board titled "Read About *The Mitten!*" ***Naming and telling parts of sentences***

Antoinette Griffin
John G. Shedd Branch School
Chicago, IL

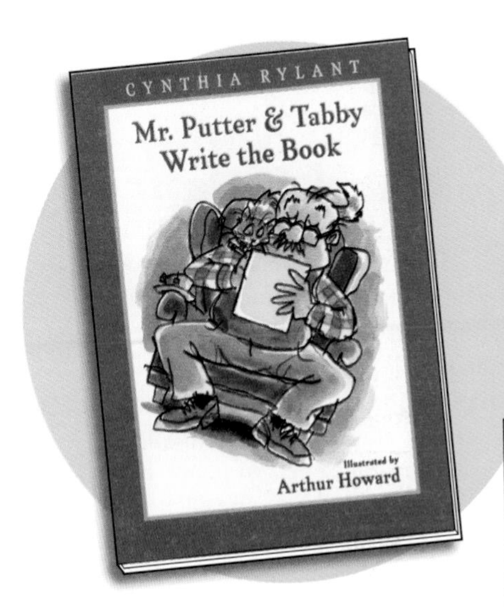

Mr. Putter & Tabby Write the Book

Written by Cynthia Rylant
Illustrated by Arthur Howard

Mr. Putter discovers that it's a challenge for him to write about an unfamiliar topic, but it's much easier for him to write about things he knows and loves. Surely, that's true for your students too! After you share the book with students, have each youngster complete a copy of the graphic organizer from page 31. Then invite her to write on provided paper about one of the topics she listed. Once she finishes her writing, ask her to keep the graphic organizer in a writing folder for future reference. The next time she writes, she'll have several just-right topics at her fingertips! ***Using a graphic organizer***

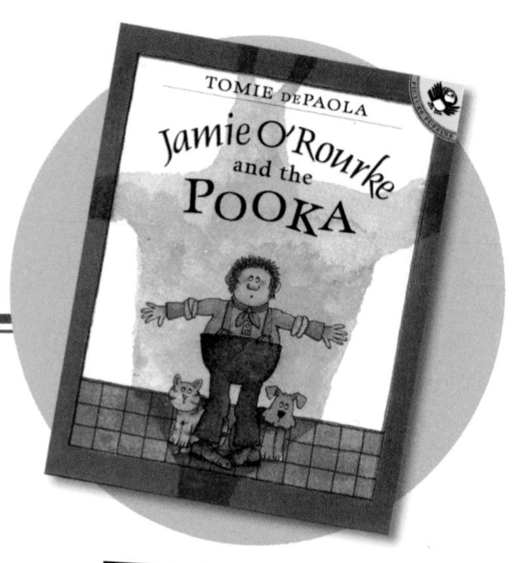

Jamie O'Rourke and the Pooka

by Tomie dePaola

Choose from the ideas below to pair this Irish tale with skill reinforcement.

Prior knowledge: Before reading the book aloud, write the word *lazy* on the board and have students define it in their own words. Tell students that the main character is lazy. Then invite them to describe what they expect a lazy character to do or say.

Character analysis: After you share the book with students, post the code shown and give each student a list of the adjectives on this page. Have him use the code to match the characters with the words that describe them. After students complete their work, ask volunteers to tell who they listed with each adjective and why.

Character Code
J = Jamie
F = Jamie's friends
P = the pooka

lazy	J F
hardworking	P
selfish	J F
grumpy	J
helpful	P
friendly	J F P

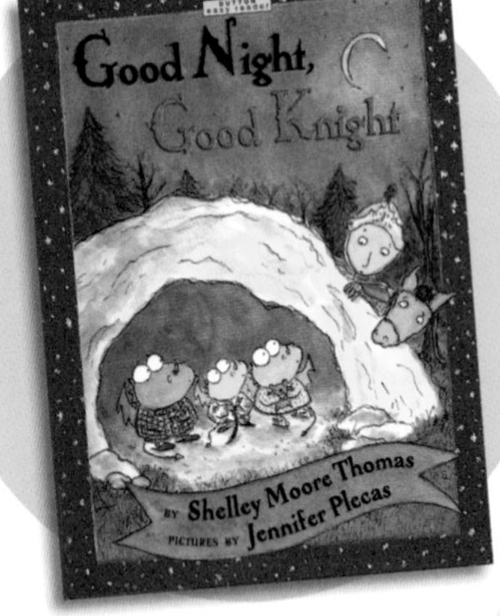

Good Night, Good Knight

Written by Shelley Moore Thomas
Illustrated by Jennifer Plecas

To follow up this adorable story, back a bulletin board with black paper. Post a moon cutout and a large castle cutout labeled as shown. Pair students. Give each twosome a yellow star labeled with a homophone word pair and two sheets of paper. Have the students in each twosome each write a sentence with a different word from their word pair. Then ask youngsters to illustrate their work. Display on the board each pair of papers with the corresponding star.
Homophones

Homophones
ate, eight
be, bee
eye, I
one, won
sail, sale
sea, see
son, sun
some, sum
to, two

Junie B., First Grader: Boss of Lunch

Written by Barbara Park
Illustrated by Denise Brunkus

Since this lunch bag journal has pages and pockets, it has lots of skill-boosting possibilities! For each child, staple several white paper strips (8½" x 11" paper cut in half lengthwise) between two brown paper lunch bags so the bag openings are on the right-hand side. Trim the excess paper. Have each youngster title and illustrate the front cover of his journal and sign his name. Follow up each chapter with an option below.

Revising sentences: Write sentences from the chapter on the board. Instruct each youngster to write the sentences in his journal, revising them to improve the tone or grammar.

Character analysis: Have each student write two things Junie B. says or does. Then ask him to draw a smiley face beside each positive comment or action and a sad face beside each inappropriate comment or action.

Vocabulary: Ask each youngster to write vocabulary words on separate cards. Review the word meanings as desired and have each student store his cards in his journal.

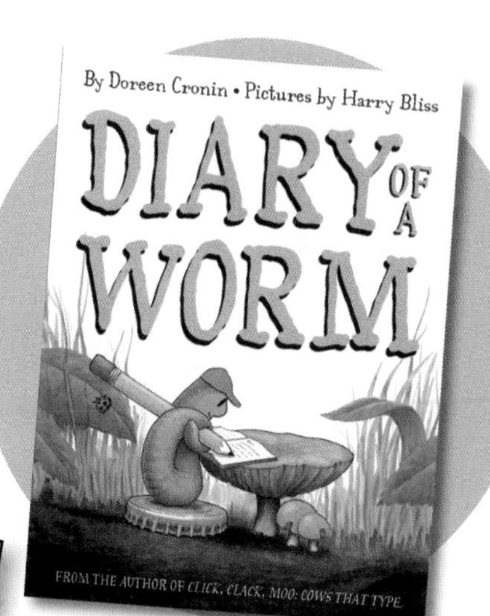

Diary of a Worm

Written by Doreen Cronin
Illustrated by Harry Bliss

After students are familiar with the book, comment that it has characteristics they may want to include in their writing. Revisit the book with students and list on chart paper the characteristics they observe. Next, give each student a blank booklet with construction paper covers and five white pages. Instruct her to title the booklet "Diary of a First Grader." Have her write a diary entry on each of five school days, encouraging her to include several listed characteristics.
Exploring writing styles

Chickens Aren't the Only Ones

by Ruth Heller

This selection presents perfect opportunities for integrating science into reading.

Prior knowledge: Read the title and show students the front cover. Ask them what they think the title means. After students share their ideas, read the book aloud.

Listening for details: During a second reading, have students name the animals that lay eggs. List the animal names on a sheet of chart paper.

Animal classification: Give each child a copy of the classification cards from page 32 and a paper divided into six equal-size boxes. Instruct him to label the first box as shown and cut out the cards. Ask him to glue the cards in different boxes and then illustrate and label corresponding examples.

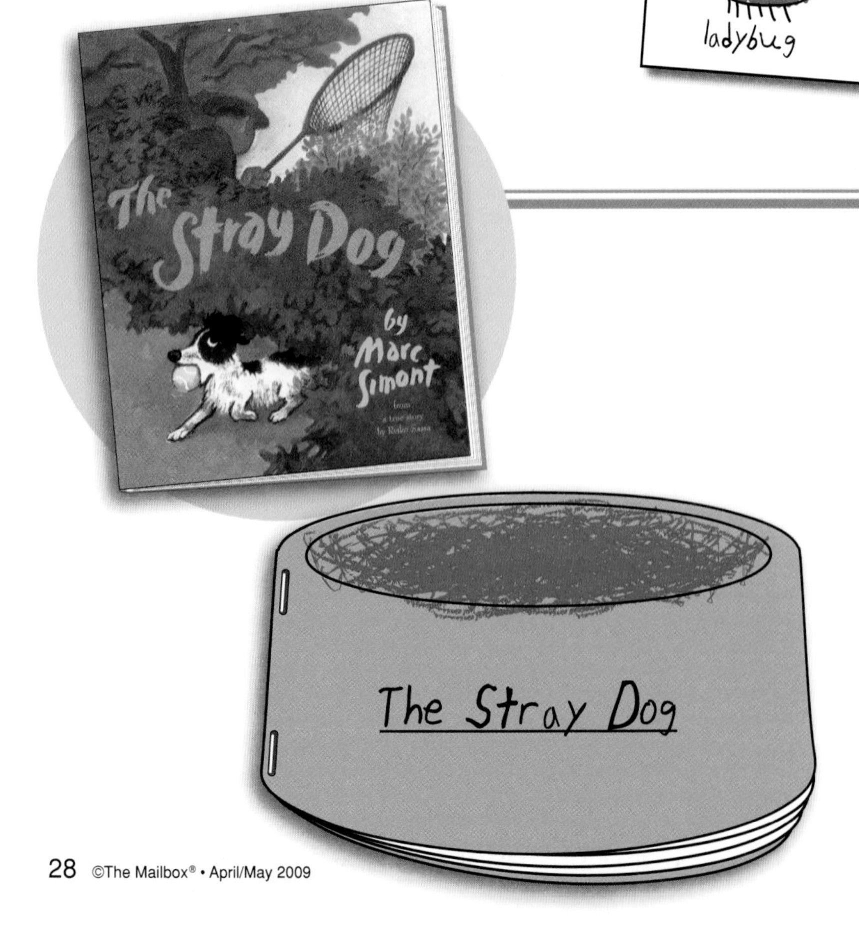

The Stray Dog

retold and illustrated by Marc Simont

Ask students to recap the heartwarming sequence of events with this minibooklet. To begin, have each youngster cut out a colorful copy of the dog bowl pattern from page 284. Next, instruct her to stack three white half sheets of paper (pages) on a colorful half sheet of paper (back cover) and place the dog bowl on the stack. Then staple the stack as shown and ask her to trim the paper.

To complete the booklet, the student colors the front cover and writes the book title on it. She cuts out a copy of the story event cards from page 32, arranges the cards in chronological order, and numbers them accordingly. Then she glues the cards in order on separate booklet pages, using the front and back of each page. ***Sequencing story events***

The Secret Shortcut

by Mark Teague

What better way to follow up this imaginative tale than by encouraging students to use their imaginations? To begin, revisit with students the description of Wendell's shortcut, emphasizing directional words, such as *over, under, across,* and *through.* Next, sit with students in a circle. Begin to tell an imaginative story by saying, "This morning I took a secret shortcut to school. First, I went…" Then ask the student beside you to continue the story, encouraging him to include a directional word. Continue around the circle until each student adds to the story. Then conclude the story. ***Participating in storytelling***

...over a bridge and past a giant fish.

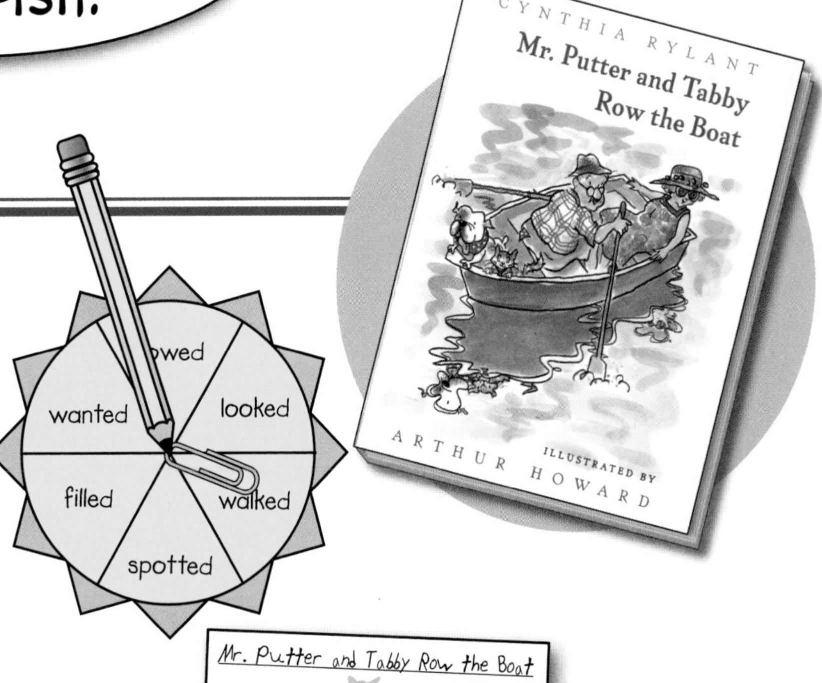

Mr. Putter and Tabby Row the Boat

Written by Cynthia Rylant
Illustrated by Arthur Howard

Words with *-ed:* Make a sun-shaped spinner like the one shown. Write in each section a verb from the story with the inflectional ending *-ed.* Have each student, in turn, use a paper clip and pencil to spin the spinner, read the corresponding word, and use the word in a sentence.

Beginning, middle, and end: Have each child draw waves to divide a sheet of paper into four horizontal sections. Instruct him to write the book title and label the sections as shown. Then ask him to draw a book-related illustration at the top of the paper and write about the beginning, middle, and end of the story in the corresponding sections.

Mr. Putter and Tabby Row the Boat

Beginning
Mr. Putter, Mrs. Teaberry, Zeke, and Tabby are hot.

Middle
They go to the pond. They have fun.

End
They go home and Mrs. Teaberry dumps water on their heads.

Trunk Patterns

Use with *"Song and Dance Man"* on page 22.

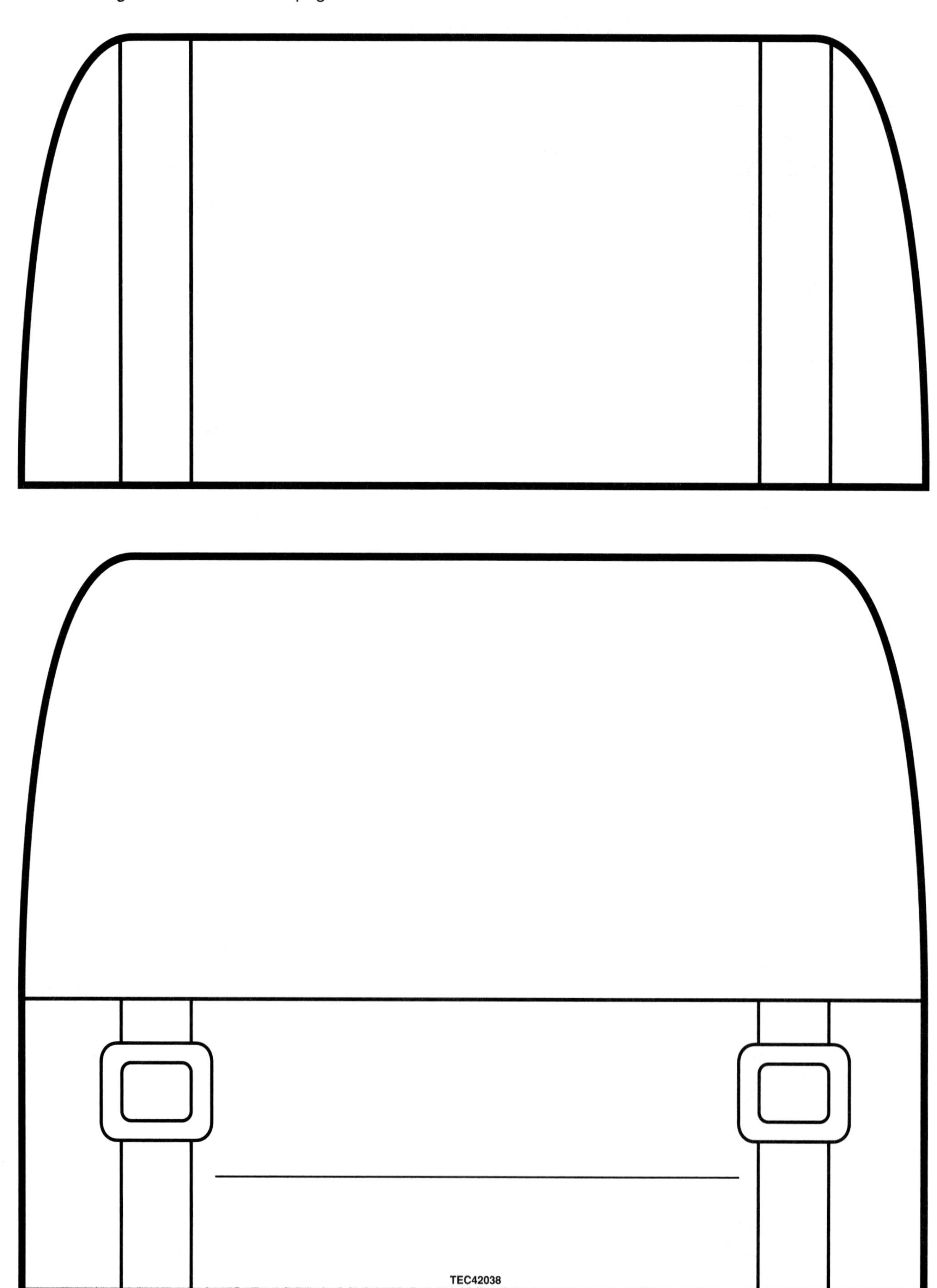

Name ____________________

Good Things

Indoors

1. ____________________
2. ____________________
3. ____________________
4. ____________________
5. ____________________
6. ____________________

Outdoors

1. ____________________
2. ____________________
3. ____________________
4. ____________________
5. ____________________
6. ____________________

Note to the teacher: Use with *"Mr. Putter & Tabby Write the Book"* on page 25.

Classification Cards

Use with *"Chickens Aren't the Only Ones"* on page 28.

birds

TEC40042

reptiles

amphibians

fish

insects

Story Event Cards

Use with *"The Stray Dog"* on page 28.

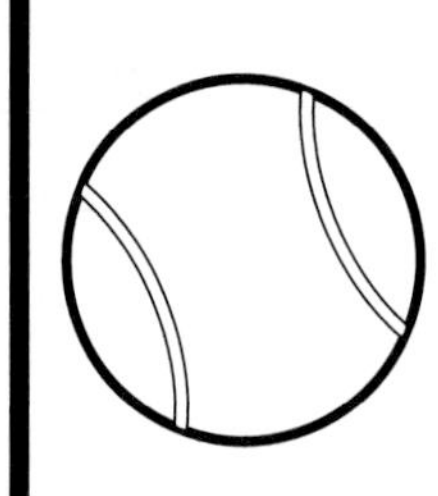

The family goes home without the dog.

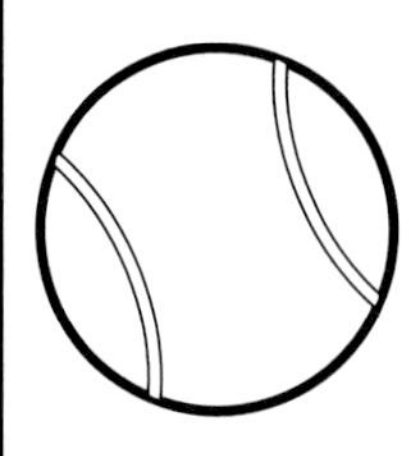

The kids say the dog belongs to them.

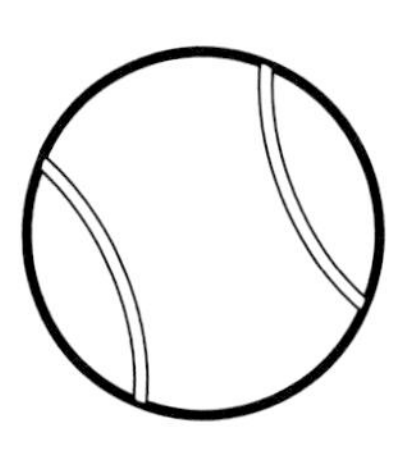

A family sees a dog when they go on a picnic.

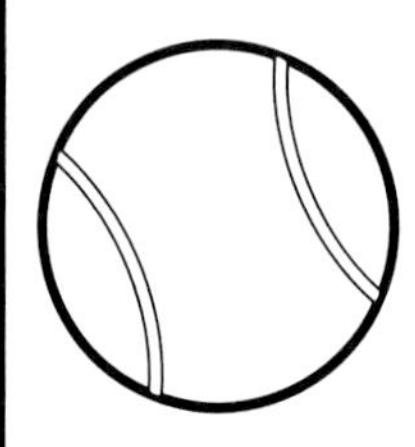

The dog warden chases the dog.

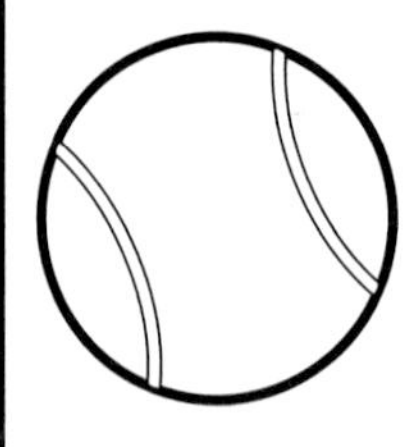

The kids play with the dog. They name him Willy.

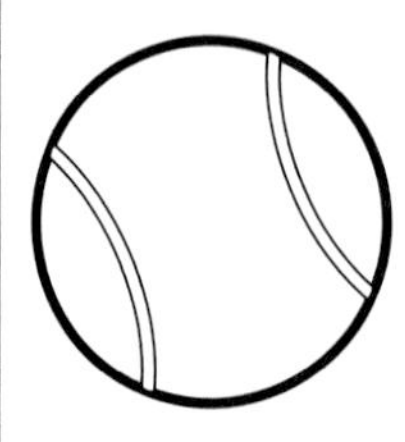

The family takes the dog home.

TEC40042

Building Math Skills

Building Math Skills

Shapely Designs

Patterning

For this assessment idea, make a supply of small cutouts of different colors and shapes. (Use scrapbook punches for quick and easy preparation.) Give each student a copy of page 40. Instruct him to arrange chosen cutouts on the paper to make a shape pattern and a color pattern. After you check his work, have him glue the cutouts in place and invite him to color the illustrations. **For more advanced students,** have students draw the patterns rather than make them with cutouts.

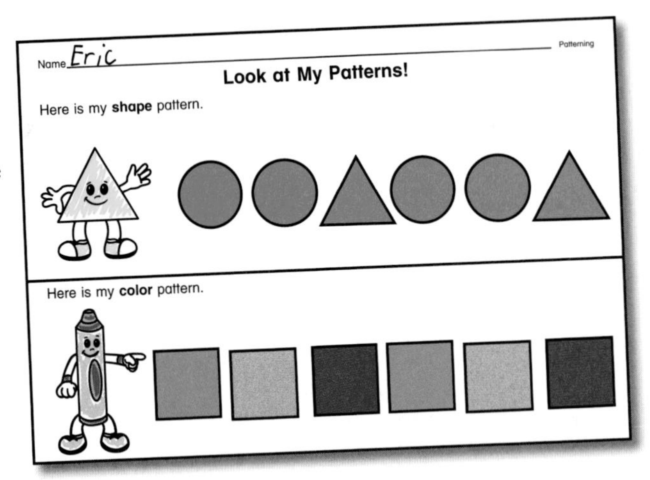
Name Eric Patterning

Look at My Patterns!

Here is my **shape** pattern.

Here is my **color** pattern.

Jessica Dauzat
Lafargue Elementary
Effie, LA

Hidden by Hives

Beginning subtraction

Try this honey of an idea for modeling subtraction stories! For each child, fold a half sheet of paper (5½" x 8½") in half lengthwise. Cut the top layer of the paper to make five flaps. To begin, ask each child to illustrate a hive on each flap. Next, instruct her to lift each flap, in turn, and make a yellow thumbprint below it. After the thumbprints dry, have her illustrate them to look like bees. Then ask her to unfold all the flaps and model relevant subtraction stories.

Donna Pollhammer
Westminster, MD

There were five bees.
Two bees went in hives.
Three bees are left.

Growing Day by Day

Counting

Here's an adorable way to keep track of how many days of school have passed. Display on a classroom wall a large felt circle that you have decorated to look like a caterpillar's head. On the first day of school, help a youngster label a felt square "1" and then post it beside the caterpillar's head to begin creating a body. On the next school day, help a student add to the caterpillar's body a felt square labeled "2." Invite students to make the caterpillar grow in the same manner each school day. Since the felt will stay bright, the display is sure to be a colorful teaching tool you can use all year for counting by ones, counting backward, and skip-counting!

Deborah Provencher
West Brookfield Elementary
West Brookfield, MA

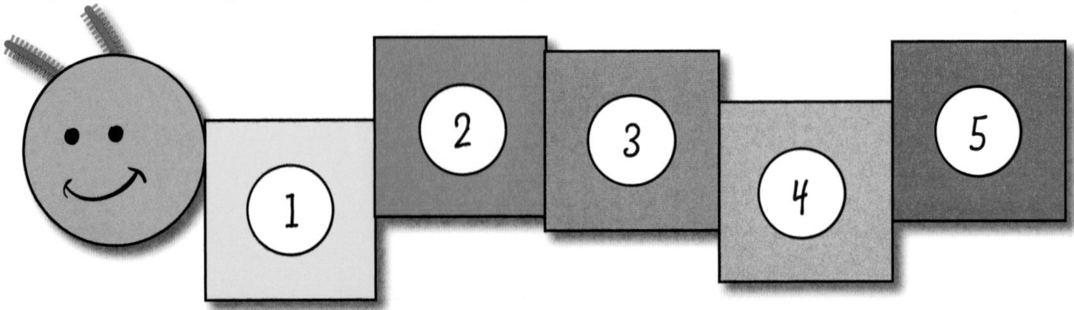

Building Math Skills

Orderly Passengers

Ordinal numbers

For this imaginary train ride, make a train engine cutout and several boxcar cutouts. Write on a separate blank card one ordinal number per cutout, beginning with "1st" and continuing in sequence to match the number of cutouts. Ask a matching number of students (passengers) to sit side by side with the backs of their chairs facing the class. Tape the engine to the back of the first chair and a boxcar to each of the other chairs.

Next, read aloud a chosen ordinal number card. Have students chant "Chug! Chug! Chug!" as a youngster who is not on the train attaches the card to the appropriate train cutout. Then pretend to stop the train and have the passenger in the named seat leave the train. Continue as described until the train is empty.

Linda Edwards
Brinson Memorial School
New Bern, NC

Roll and Sort

Sorting by two attributes

To make dice, cover two cubic boxes with white paper. Then illustrate each side of one box with a different shape and color each side of the other box with a different color. Make a large Venn diagram on the floor with yarn. To play one round, give each child a colorful shape cutout. Invite two students to roll the dice. Then use sticky notes to label the Venn diagram with the shape and color rolled. After each youngster correctly places his cutout on or outside the diagram, discuss the results with students.

Jill Davis
Kendall-Whittier Elementary
Tulsa, OK

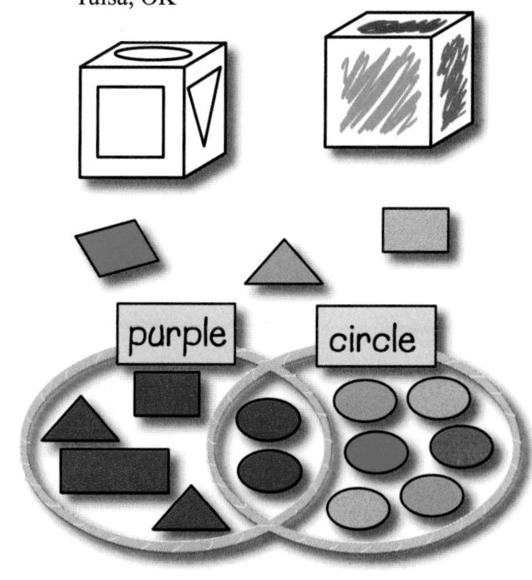

Oops!

Addition

Make a class supply of banana cards (patterns on page 41). Program half the cards with addition combinations and the other half with the corresponding sums so there is one combination or sum per card. To begin, distribute the cards to students at random. Next, have a student with a sum stand and read his card. Then lead the class in saying, "Banana peel, banana peel. Oops, don't fall! Banana peel, banana peel, [sum] in all." Ask each student with a corresponding combination to stand, read it, and then sit with the youngster who has the sum. Help students match the remaining sums and addition combinations in the same manner.

Cathy Wroten
Bear Branch Elementary
Magnolia, TX

Building Math Skills

Number Shuffle

Fact families

Since this activity is such a simple way to reinforce math facts, you'll want to use it often! Remove the aces and face cards from a deck of oversize playing cards. Attach magnetic tape to the back of each number card. To begin, display on a magnetic whiteboard three cards whose numbers belong to a fact family. Have a youngster write an addition or subtraction sentence with the corresponding numbers. Then ask different students to write the rest of the fact family, encouraging them to rearrange the cards to help them identify the appropriate number sentences.

Karen Potter
Red Oak-Sturgeon Elementary
Alberta, VA

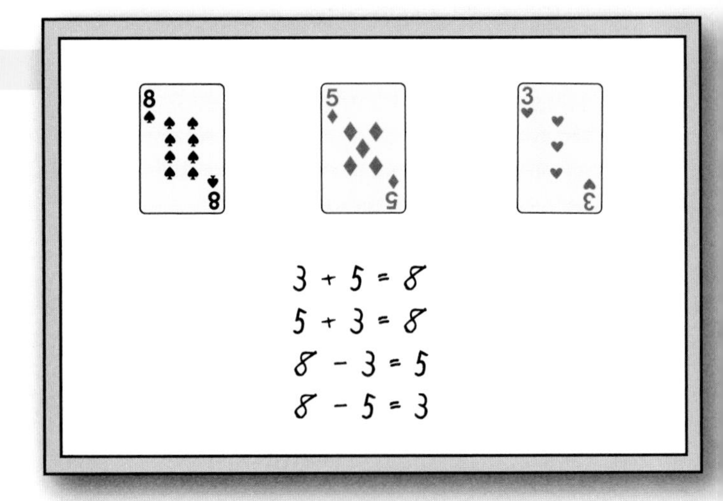

Search!

Number order

On the 100th day of school, hide around the classroom 100 cutouts numbered from 1 to 100. Then, at a chosen time, say, "Number search!" Give students about two minutes to gather any cutouts they find. When the time is up, instruct students to order the cutouts in a large pocket chart in rows of ten, leaving spaces for the missing cutouts. Have brief number searches throughout the day until students find all the cutouts and display them in the correct order.

Sheila Criqui-Kelley
Lebo Elementary
Lebo, KS

Prehistoric Patterns

Odd and even numbers

Give each youngster a copy of page 42. Have him continue the number pattern to 18 and then color the even numbers yellow. Next, guide students to realize that even numbers end with 0, 2, 4, 6, or 8. Then ask each youngster to write on the dinosaur's sign three even numbers that are not already on the paper. Invite him to finish coloring the illustration as desired. For reinforcement, name various numbers and ask students to tell whether they are odd or even.

adapted from an idea by Reba Vuncannon
Cedar Park Elementary
Trumann, AR

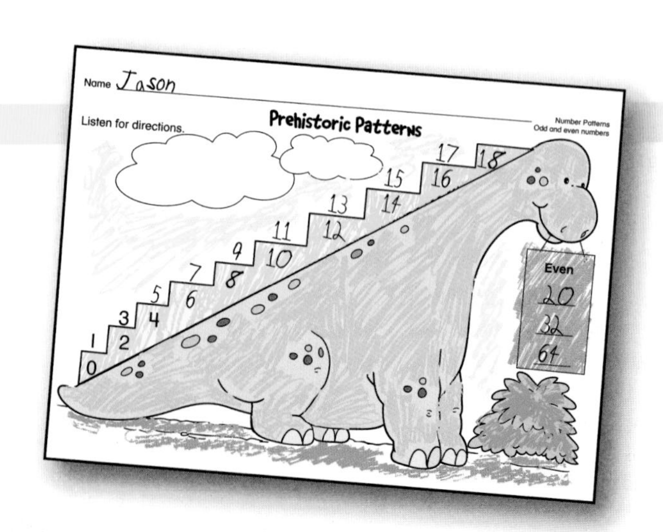

Building Math Skills

Far-Out Facts

Subtraction

Your students will love the grin-inducing results of this creative review! Give each child a list with subtraction problems like the one shown. After he solves the problems, instruct him to draw a large shape on a separate sheet of paper to make the body of an alien. Ask him to draw the listed body parts in quantities that correspond with the matching math problems. Then have him color the alien and add background details.

Carmen Giovenco
Cedar Road Elementary
Chesapeake, VA

heads: 11 – 9 = 2
hairs: 17 – 8 = 9
eyes: 13 – 6 = 7
mouths: 12 – 9 = 3
arms: 13 – 9 = 4
fingers: 15 – 7 = 8
legs and feet: 13 – 8 = 5

Timely Tales

Elapsed time

Spark students' interest in math with fairy-tale word problems! Give each child a copy of page 44. Read the first problem aloud. Then show the corresponding start time on a demonstration clock. Instruct each child to draw clock hands on her paper to show the answer to the problem and have her write the matching digital time where indicated. Then invite a volunteer to show the end time on the demonstration clock. After each child checks her work and makes any needed corrections, read the next problem to continue.

Joyce McRae
Richmond Primary School
Hamlet, NC

Name Ashley

Timely Tales

Elapsed time

Listen for directions.

The Three Little Pigs start to work at 4:00.
They work for 1 hour.
At what time do they stop working?
5 : 00

Goldilocks takes a nap at 10:00.
She sleeps for 2 hours.
At what time does she wake?
___ : ___

The bean stalk starts to grow at 3:00.
It grows for 2 hours.
At what time does it stop growing?
___ : ___

The Little Red Hen bakes bread at 1:00.
The bread bakes for 1 hour.
At what time is the bread done?
___ : ___

The ball at the castle starts at 8:00.
It lasts for 3 hours.
At what time does the ball end?
___ : ___

Pass It On!

Solid figures

To reinforce geometry vocabulary, divide students into small groups and instruct each group to sit in a circle. Next, give each group a solid figure, varying the types of figures among the groups. (If desired, give the groups familiar objects that are solid figures.) As you play some lively music, ask the students in each group to pass their figure around the circle. Have each youngster identify the solid figure each time she holds it. After a few moments, stop the music to signal the students to stop passing the items. Then ask the students with the solid figures to set them down and trade places with one another. Resume the music to continue.

Jolene Rosploch
Kosciuszko Elementary
Cudahy, WI

Zap It!

Addition or subtraction facts

For this small-group game, write "Zap it!" on one craft stick and an addition or a subtraction problem on each of several different craft sticks. Stand all the sticks in a canister so the programming is not visible. To begin, set a timer for three minutes. Then have each student, in turn, take a stick and say the corresponding math fact. If she takes the stick that says "Zap it!" have her return it along with any other sticks she has. The game continues until time is up. The player with the most sticks wins.

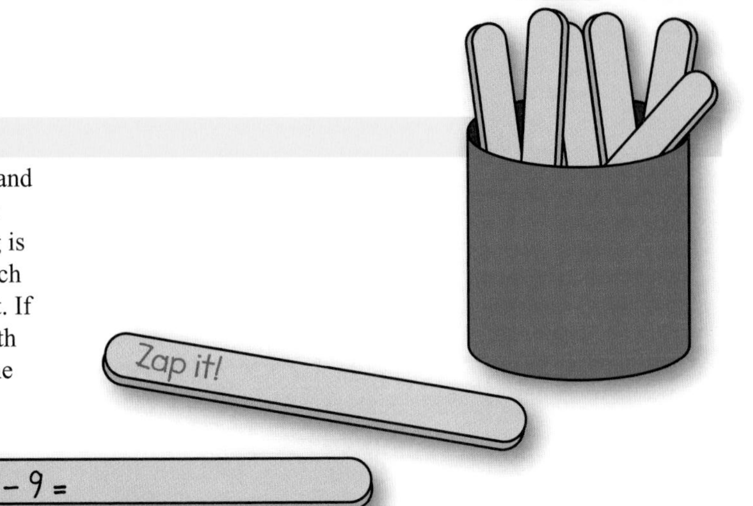

Tracey Harding-Stricker
Lincoln Elementary
Edison, NJ

Pairs Plus

Doubles facts

It's a snap to prepare this partner game! Simply remove the aces and face cards from a deck of playing cards and then shuffle the remaining cards.

The players stack the cards facedown. Player 1 turns over the top two cards and puts them side by side on the playing surface. If the cards show different numbers, his turn is over. If the cards show the same number, he says, "Doubles," names the corresponding sum, and takes the two cards. Next, if no cards remain faceup, Player 2 plays the top two cards from the stack as described. If there are already cards faceup, Player 2 takes only one card from the stack, puts it on a faceup card, and then plays the top card in each pile. The players take turns, reusing the unmatched cards as needed, until time is up or no cards are left in play. The player with more cards wins.

Cathy Wroten
Magnolia, TX

Pick Three!

Coins

To differentiate a review of money skills, give each child a copy of page 45. Have each youngster draw an X on a box in the first row and complete the corresponding activity. Repeat the process with the remaining rows on different days.

Christi Seehase, Tripoli Elementary, Tripoli, IA

Name Angelica

Coins

Three for Me!

Follow your teacher's directions.

1. Write a money ... problem ...	2. Draw coins to show ways to make 25¢.	3. Draw 2 snacks with price tags. Draw coins to match.
4. Write a song or poem about dimes.	5. Write a coin riddle ... three ...	6. Glue coupons on paper. Use coin stamps to show each money amount.
7. Make a poster about a penny, nickel, dime, and quarter.	8. Look at both sides of some coins. Write what you see.	9. Draw 4 coins and ... the total ... Then ... again.

Building Math Skills

Sticker Survey

Collecting and recording data

This easy-to-prepare activity is perfect for a year-end assessment. Give each student a chart with four rows, like the one shown. Ask her to put a different sticker in each row. Then instruct her to ask each classmate, in turn, which sticker he likes best. Have her write each student's name in the appropriate row to record the responses. Over the next few days, guide each youngster to represent the data she collected with a tally table, a pictograph with smiley faces, and a bar graph.

	Tanisha Anthony
	Keira David Joe Abby
	Lexi
	Colin Rachel

Deryl Heflin and Eva Brown
Vaughan Elementary
Powder Springs, GA

Selling Seashells

Counting coins

For this small-group activity, cut out a copy of the coin cards from page 47 and make nine seashell cards. (See the patterns on page 47.) Write each of the following prices on a different seashell card: 41¢, 45¢, 50¢, 52¢, 55¢, 61¢, 65¢, 70¢, and 75¢. Back all the cards with tagboard for durability.

To begin, spread out the coin cards facedown. Designate a volunteer as Sid or Sally. Have the volunteer show the group a seashell card and read the price aloud. Then lead students in saying the tongue twister below. Next, invite a student to turn over a coin card and identify the corresponding money amount. If the amount matches the price, the youngster takes the two cards and becomes Sid or Sally for the next round. If the amount does not match the price, he returns the coin card. Play continues until students pair all the cards.

[Sid] sells seashells by the seashore.
Who will buy this seashell [Sid] sells?

Lynnea DeBernardis, Chesapeake, VA

Eraser Race

Linear measurement

Channel your students' year-end excitement into this kid-pleasing activity! Gather two whiteboard erasers. Designate a starting line on a smooth surface such as a floor or long tabletop. Then ask two students at a time to place the erasers at the line. Have each youngster push an eraser at your signal and then measure the distance each eraser slid.

Marie E. Cecchini, West Dundee, IL

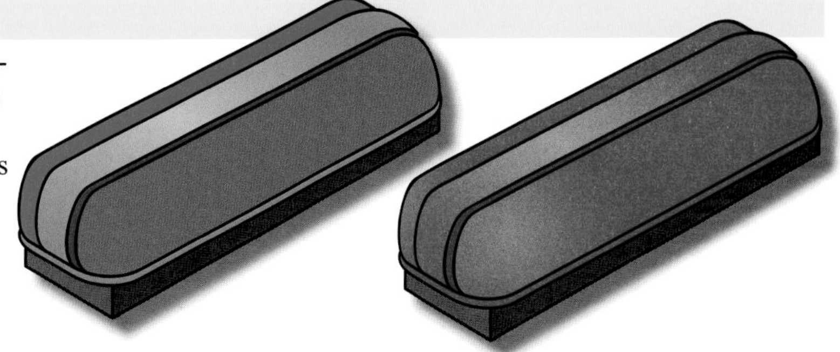

Name ________________________________

Look at My Patterns!

Here is my **shape** pattern.

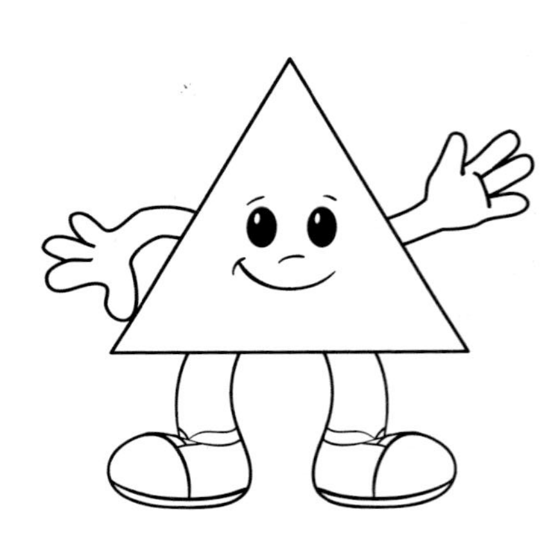

Here is my **color** pattern.

Note to the teacher: Use with "Shapely Designs" on page 34.

Banana Cards

Use with "Oops!" on page 35.

Name ____________________

Prehistoric Patterns

Listen for directions.

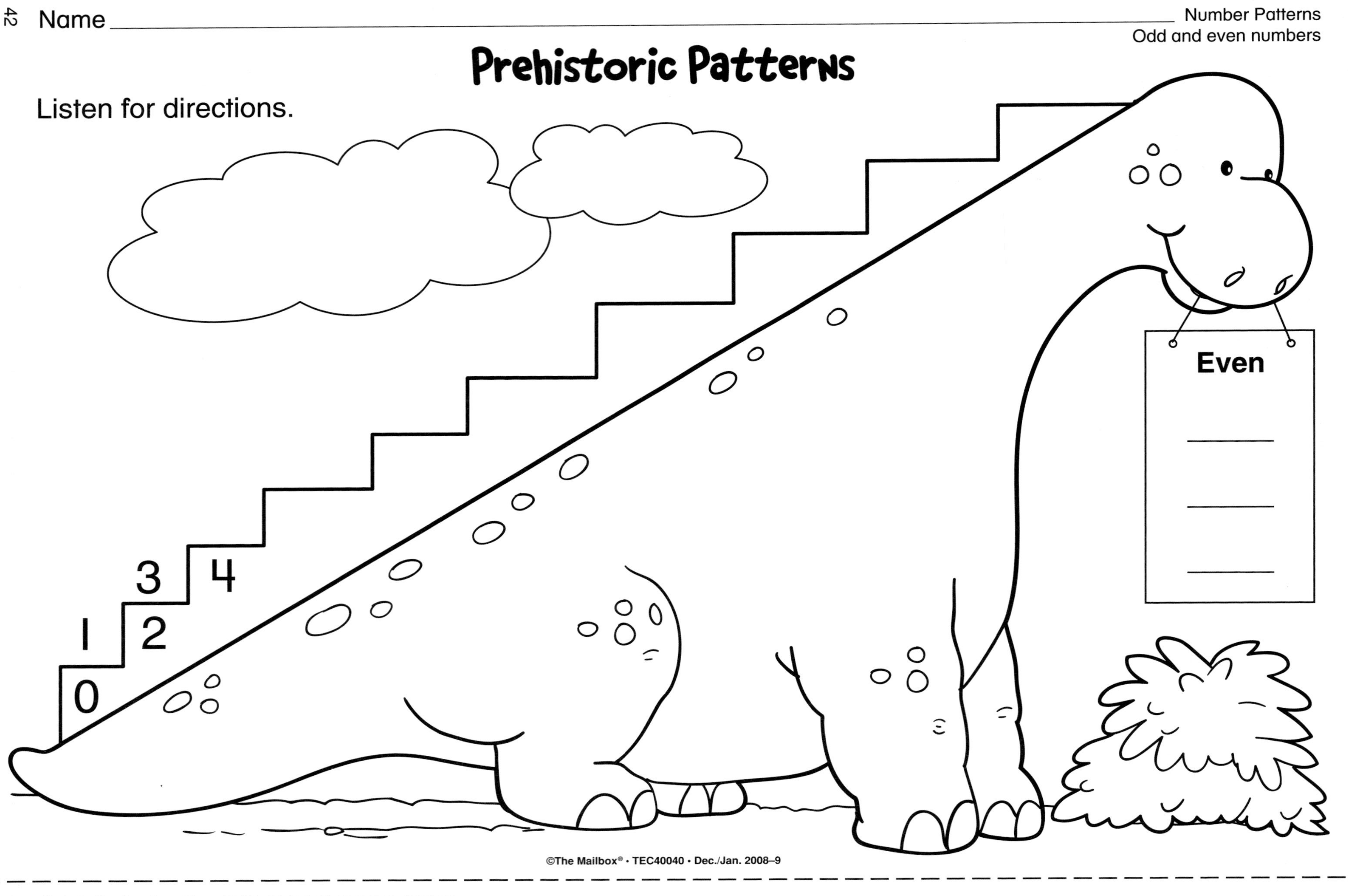

Note to the teacher: Use with "Prehistoric Patterns" on page 36.

Name ______________________

Blast Off!

Write the fact families.

6	4	10

_____ + _____ = _____

_____ + _____ = _____

_____ − _____ = _____

_____ − _____ = _____

3	8	11

_____ + _____ = _____

_____ + _____ = _____

_____ − _____ = _____

_____ − _____ = _____

12	7	5

_____ + _____ = _____

_____ + _____ = _____

_____ − _____ = _____

_____ − _____ = _____

Name ____________________ Elapsed time

Timely Tales

Listen for directions.

The Three Little Pigs start to work at 4:00.
They work for 1 hour.
At what time do they stop working?

____ : ____

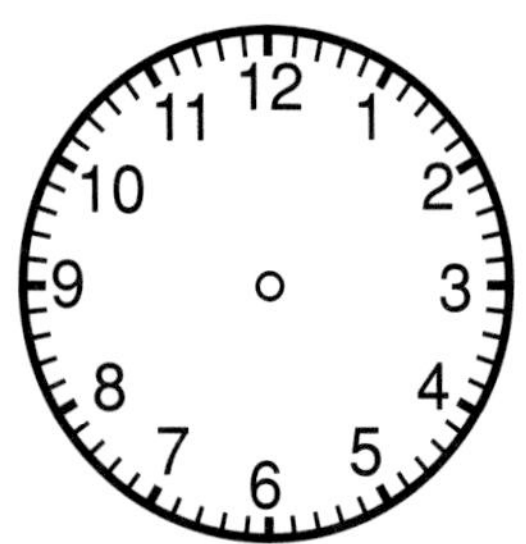

Goldilocks goes to the bears' house at 10:00.
She stays for 2 hours.
At what time does she leave?

____ : ____

The bean stalk starts to grow at 3:00.
It grows for 2 hours.
At what time does it stop growing?

____ : ____

The Little Red Hen bakes bread at 1:00.
The bread bakes for 1 hour.
At what time is the bread done?

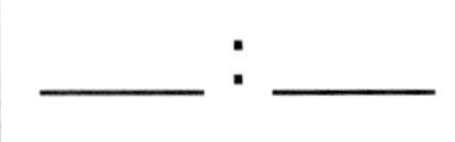

____ : ____

The ball at the castle starts at 8:00.
It lasts for 3 hours.
At what time does the ball end?

____ : ____

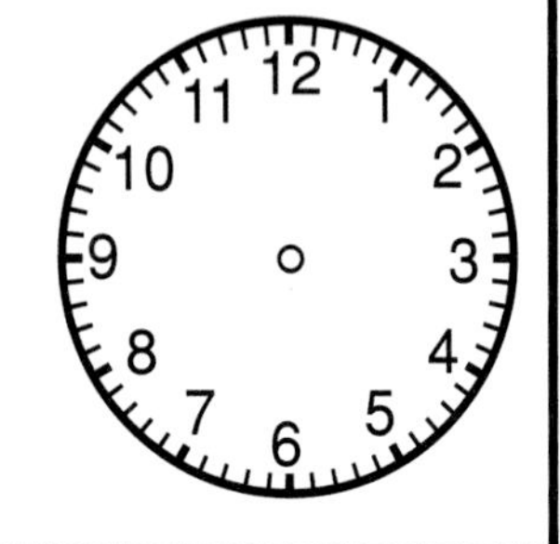

 Note to the teacher: Use with "Timely Tales" on page 37.

Three for Me!

Follow your teacher's directions.

1. Write a money story problem. Show the answer. 	2. Draw coins to show ways to make 25¢. 	3. Draw 2 snacks with price tags. Draw coins to match. 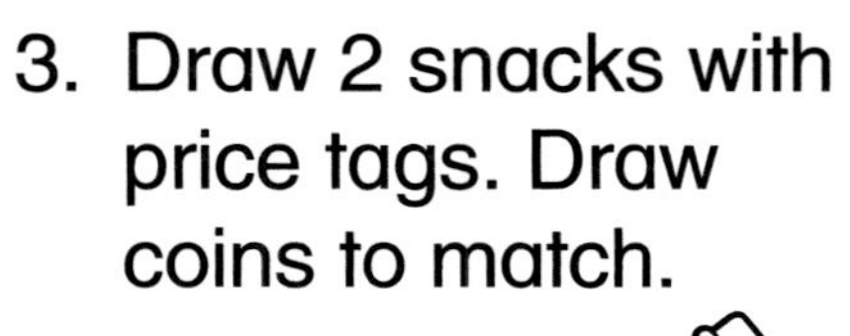 
4. Write a song or poem about dimes.	5. Write a coin riddle with three clues. What am I?	6. Glue coupons on paper. Use coin stamps to show each money amount. 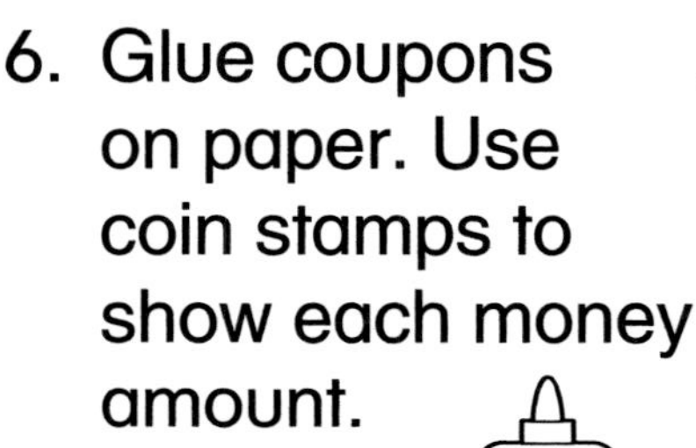 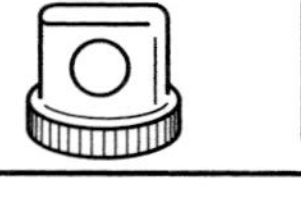 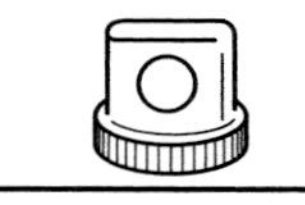   GLUE
7. Make a poster about a penny, nickel, dime, and quarter.	8. Look at both sides of some coins. Write what you see.	9. Draw 4 coins and write the total money amount. Then do it again. 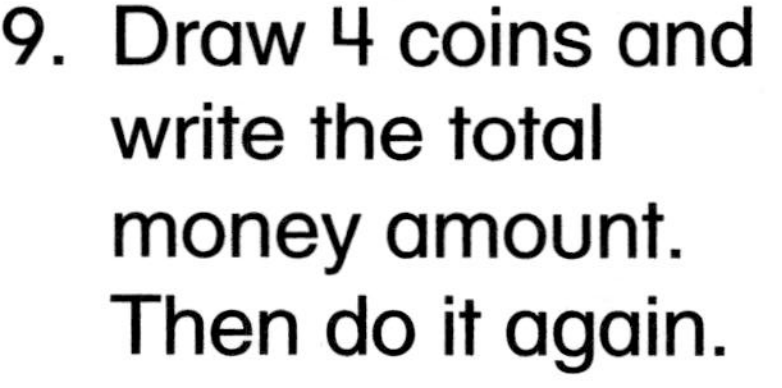   

Note to the teacher: Use with "Pick Three!" on page 38.

Rise and Shine!

For each problem, circle the two numbers you want to add first.
Add. Write.

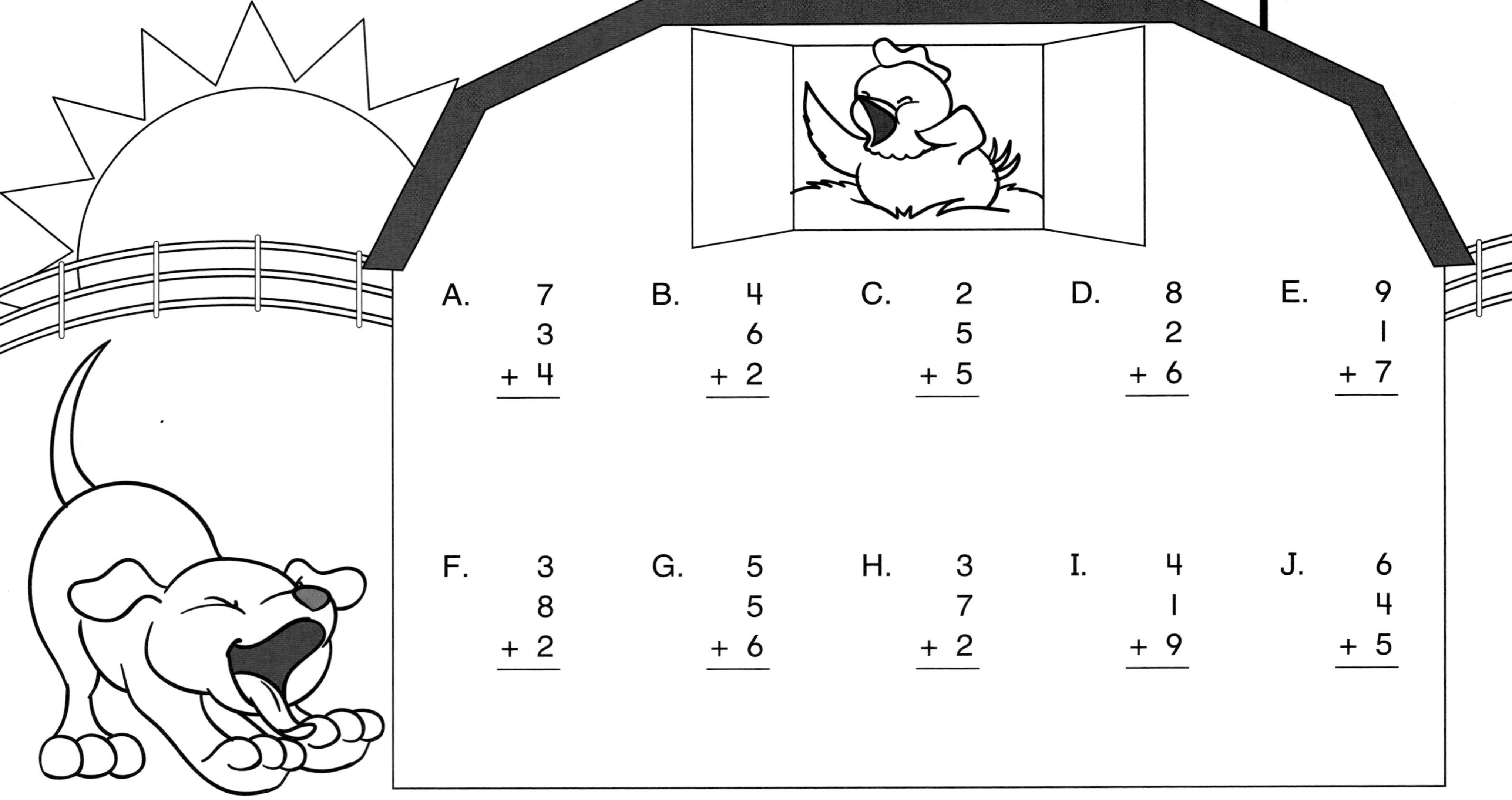

A. $\begin{array}{r} 7 \\ 3 \\ +\ 4 \\ \hline \end{array}$ B. $\begin{array}{r} 4 \\ 6 \\ +\ 2 \\ \hline \end{array}$ C. $\begin{array}{r} 2 \\ 5 \\ +\ 5 \\ \hline \end{array}$ D. $\begin{array}{r} 8 \\ 2 \\ +\ 6 \\ \hline \end{array}$ E. $\begin{array}{r} 9 \\ 1 \\ +\ 7 \\ \hline \end{array}$

F. $\begin{array}{r} 3 \\ 8 \\ +\ 2 \\ \hline \end{array}$ G. $\begin{array}{r} 5 \\ 5 \\ +\ 6 \\ \hline \end{array}$ H. $\begin{array}{r} 3 \\ 7 \\ +\ 2 \\ \hline \end{array}$ I. $\begin{array}{r} 4 \\ 1 \\ +\ 9 \\ \hline \end{array}$ J. $\begin{array}{r} 6 \\ 4 \\ +\ 5 \\ \hline \end{array}$

Coin and Seashell Cards

Use with "Selling Seashells" on page 39.

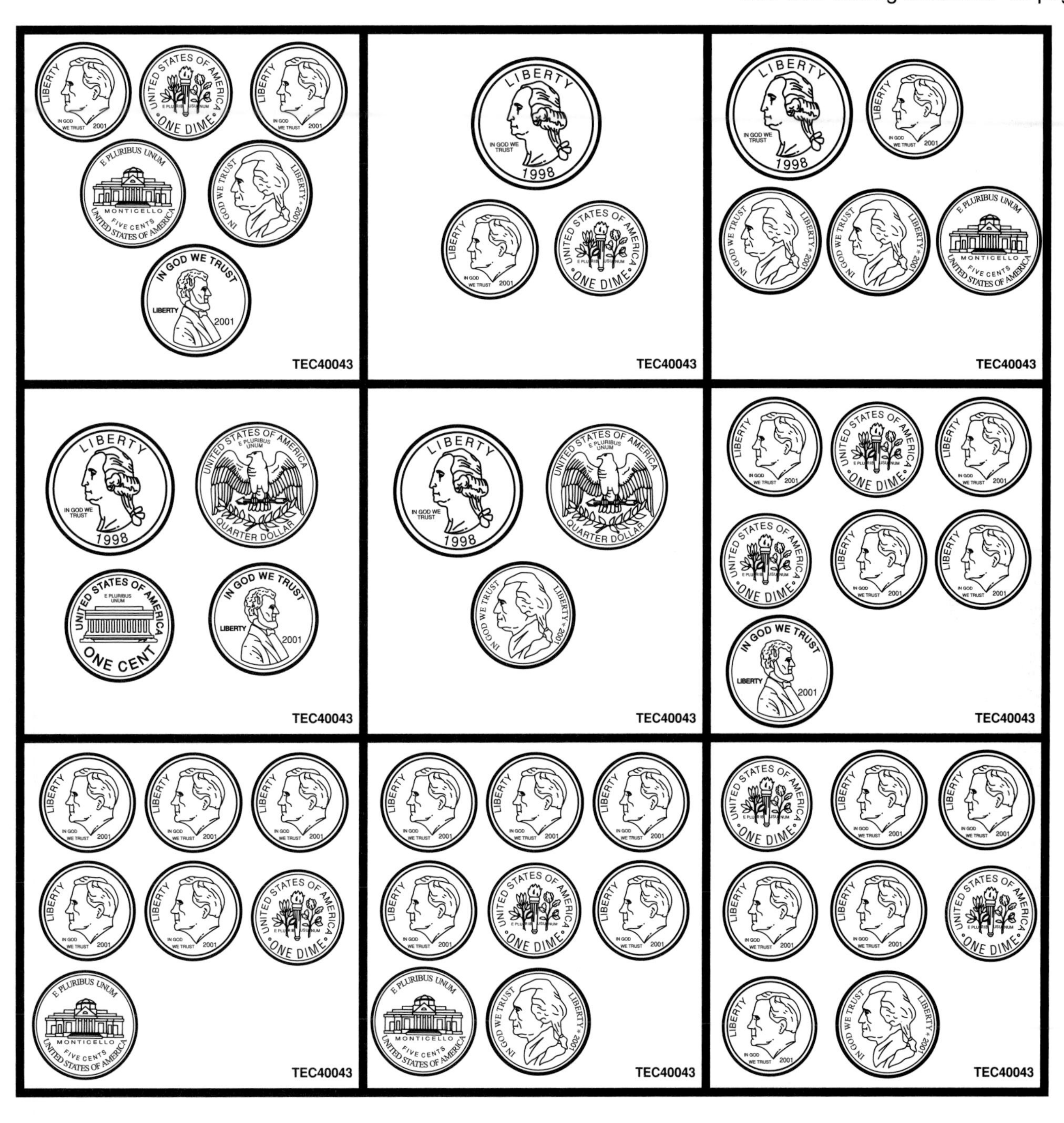

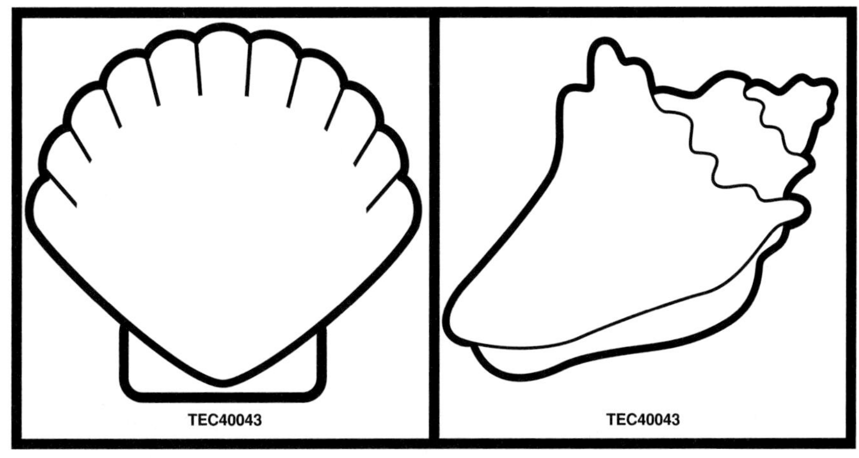

Name____ Problem Solving
Making an organized list

Super Cheese Sandwiches

Each sandwich can have one kind of cheese and bread.

Orange Cheese

Yellow Cheese

White Bread

Brown Bread

Read.

Max has **orange cheese** and **yellow cheese.**
He has **white bread** and **brown bread.**
How many kinds of sandwiches can he make?

Solve.

Write.

Max can make _____ kinds of sandwiches.

Note to the teacher: Give each child a copy of this page. Read and discuss the problem with students. Model one or more ways they can list the four kinds of sandwiches in the provided space. For example, you might draw simple pictures or write pairs of corresponding color words. Then ask each child to complete his paper.

Name____

Flo's Flowers

Read.

Flo sells **1** flower on **Monday.**
She sells **3** flowers on **Tuesday.**
She sells **5** flowers on **Wednesday.**
If the pattern keeps on, how many flowers will she sell on Saturday?

Solve.

Write.

Flo will sell ________ flowers on Saturday.

Note to the teacher: Give each child a copy of this page. Read and discuss the problem with students. Guide them to name ways to determine the answer (*11 flowers*), such as making a table or an organized list. Then have each youngster complete his paper.

Name____ Problem Solving
Using a pattern

Ready, Set, Jump!

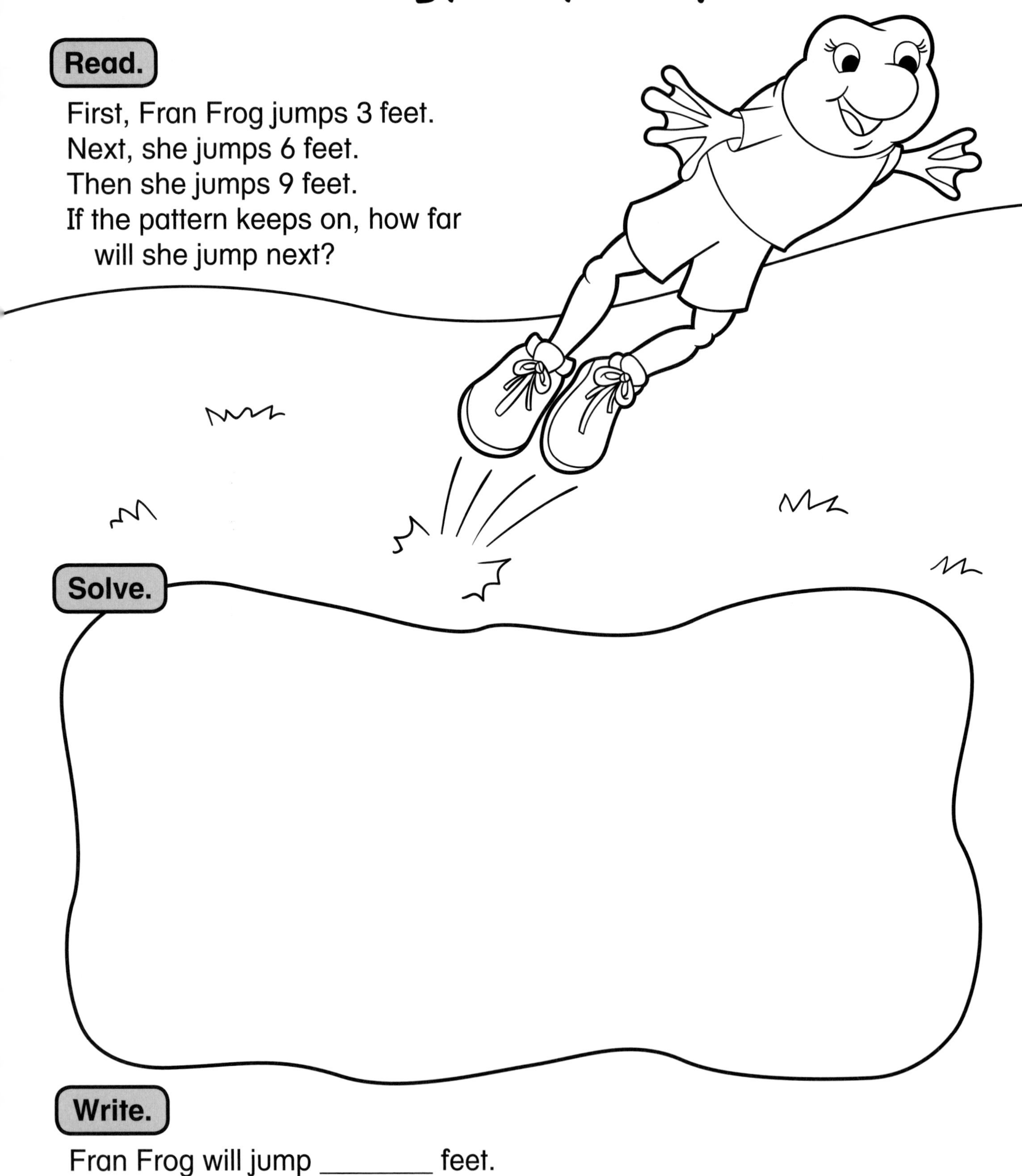

Read.

First, Fran Frog jumps 3 feet.
Next, she jumps 6 feet.
Then she jumps 9 feet.
If the pattern keeps on, how far will she jump next?

Solve.

Write.

Fran Frog will jump ________ feet.

Note to the teacher: Give each student a copy of this page. Read and discuss the problem with students. Then encourage each youngster to represent the pattern in the provided space and determine the answer *(12 feet).*

Reproducible partner game: Use with the directions on page 53.

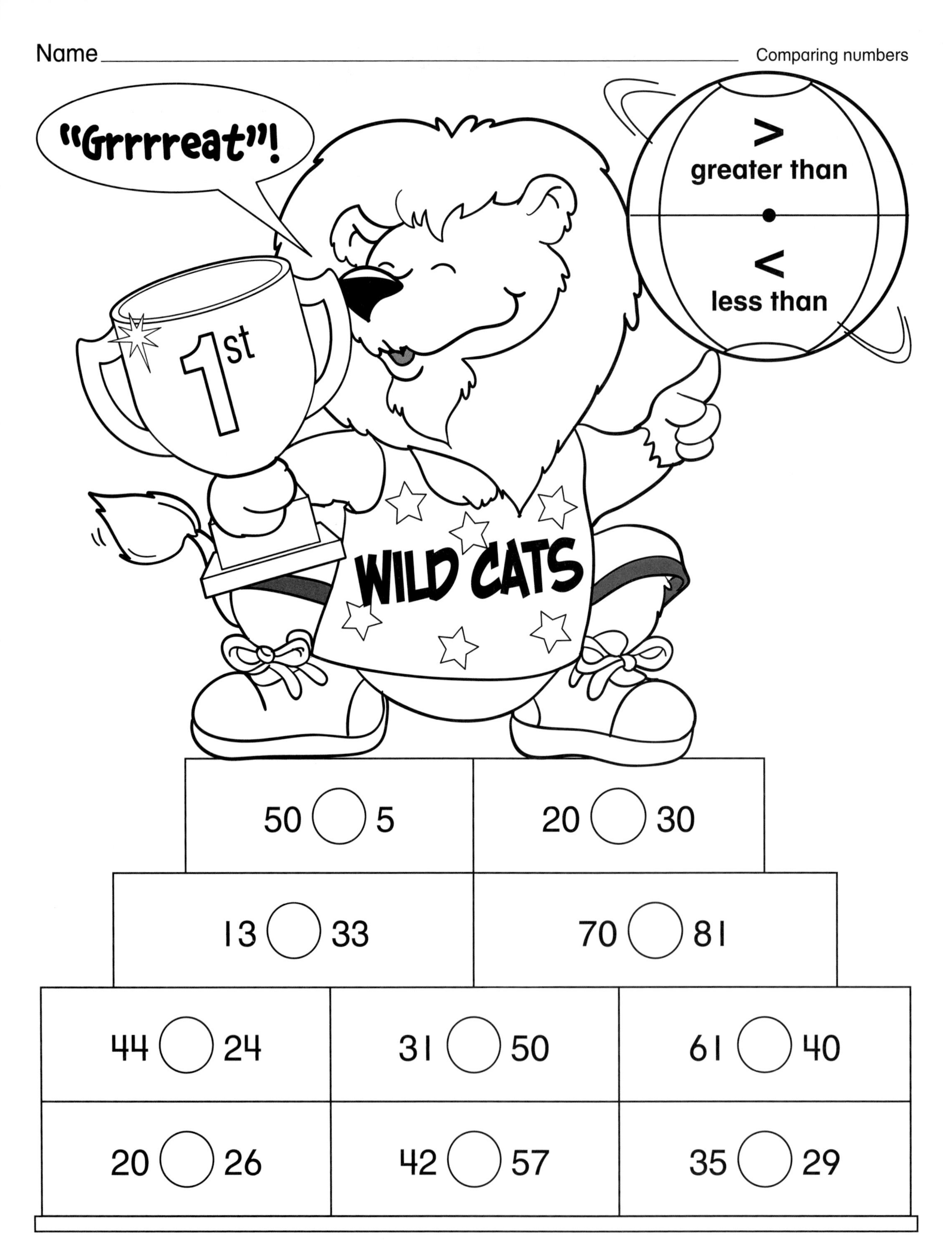

 Reproducible partner game: Use with the directions on page 53.

Twins With Fins

Skill: Addition to 18

What You Need
gameboard
2 game markers
labeled counter 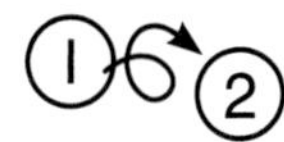

How to play:
1. Play with a partner. Put the game markers on different fish.
2. Toss the counter, in turn, and move your marker.
3. Read the space you land on. Say the sum.
4. The first player to reach FINISH wins.

"Grrrreat"!

Skill: Comparing numbers

What You Need
2 gameboards
paper clip
pencil

How to play:
1. Play with a partner.
2. Spin, in turn, and read the math symbol.
3. Look for a number pair that matches the symbol.
   If you find one, write the symbol.
   If you do not find one, your turn is over.
4. Play until you write > or < in each circle.

Note to the teacher: Use with the gameboards on pages 51 and 52.

Up, Up, and Away!

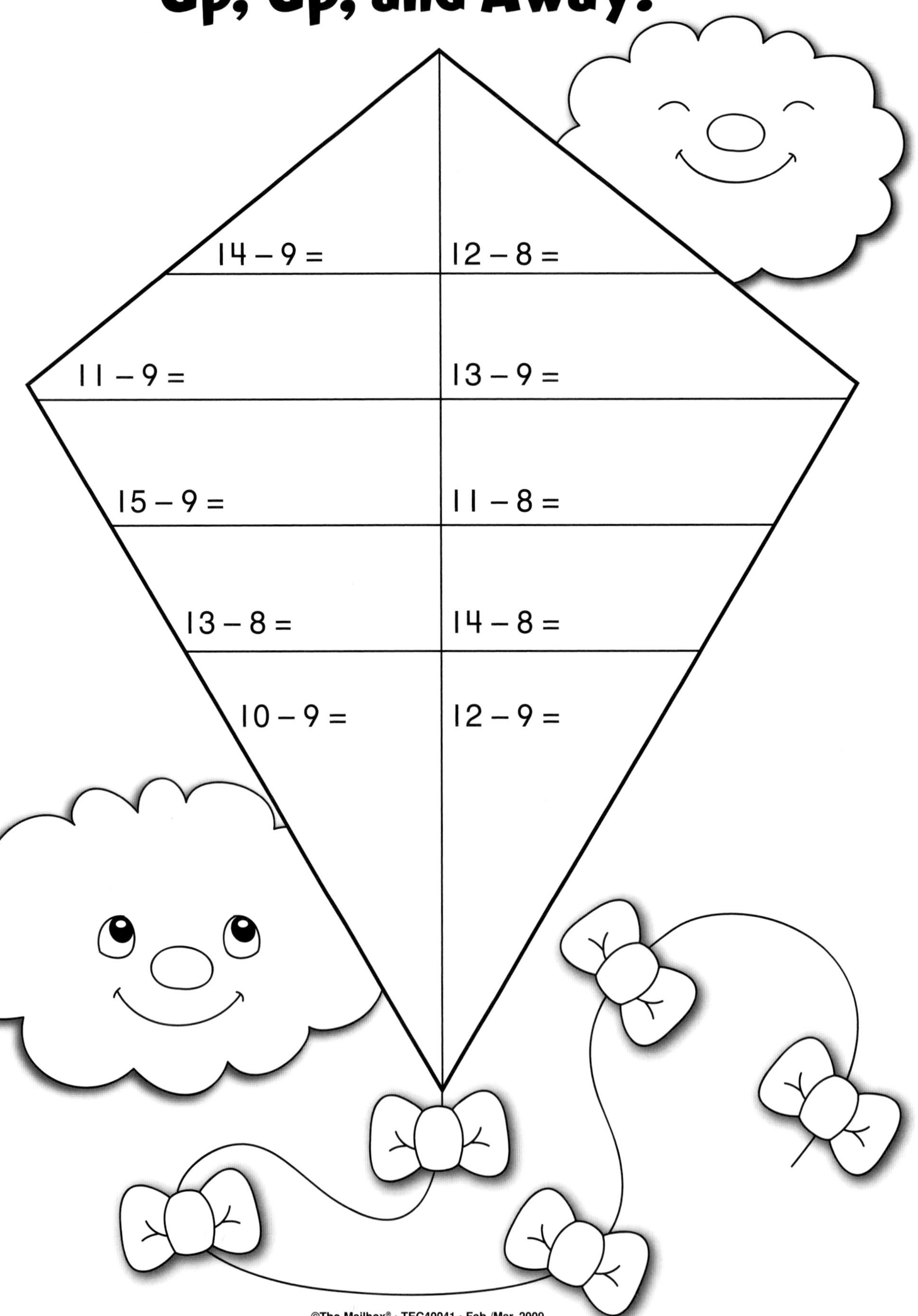

 Reproducible partner game: Use with the directions on page 56.

Cookie Cover-up

Reproducible partner game: Use with the directions on page 56.

Up, Up, and Away!

Skill: Subtraction facts

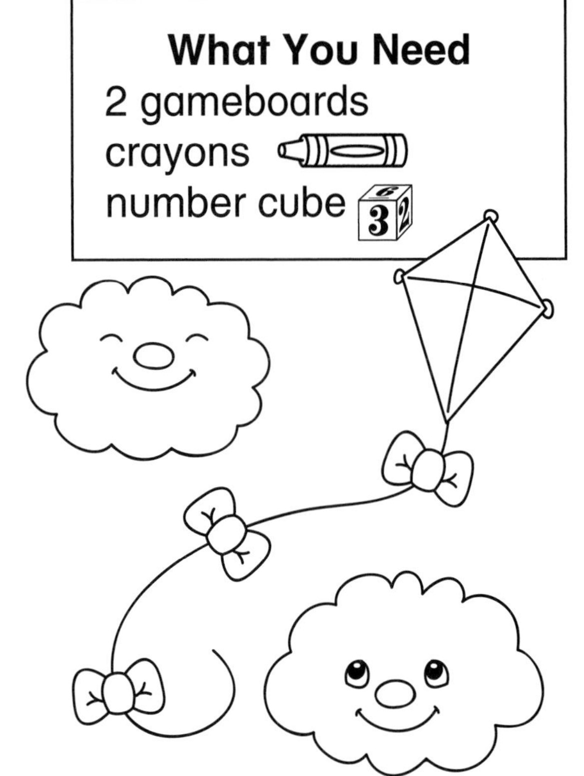

What You Need
2 gameboards
crayons
number cube

How to play:

1. Play with a partner.
2. Write the answer for each problem.
3. Toss the number cube, in turn.
4. Color a kite part with a matching answer and read its number sentence. If there is no matching kite part left to color, color a bow.
5. Play until one player colors all his kite or bows. The player who colors more of his kite wins.

Cookie Cover-up

Skill: Fractions

What You Need
2 gameboards
pattern blocks: 8 □
4 ⏢
6 ▱
paper clip
pencil

How to play:

1. Play with a partner.
2. Spin, in turn, and read the fraction.
3. Put a matching pattern block on the correct cookie. If the cookie is covered, do nothing.
4. The first player to cover all his cookies wins.

 Note to the teacher: Use with the gameboards on pages 54 and 55.

Name ______________________________ Doubles facts

Double Bubbles

Big Bubbles →	2 + 2	7 + 9	9 + 9	8 + 6	Pop!	5 + 9	7 + 7	3 + 3	6 + 6
9 + 5									5 + 5
7 + 7									9 + 6
6 + 8									8 + 8
9 + 9									7 + 8
Pop!	5 + 5	8 + 8	9 + 8	6 + 6	8 + 7	9 + 6	4 + 4	9 + 9	Pop!

Reproducible partner game: Use with the directions on page 59.

Caterpillar Clocks

Reproducible partner game: Use with the directions on page 59.

Double Bubbles

Skill: Doubles facts

What You Need
2 gameboards
2 game markers
die
crayons

How to play:

1. Play with a partner. Put your game marker on the box with the .
2. In turn, roll the die and move your marker.
3. If you do not land on a problem, your turn is over. If you land on a problem, solve it. Then color 2 bubbles if it is a doubles fact. Color 1 bubble if it is not a doubles fact.
4. The first player to color all his bubbles wins.

Caterpillar Clock

Skill: Time to the half hour

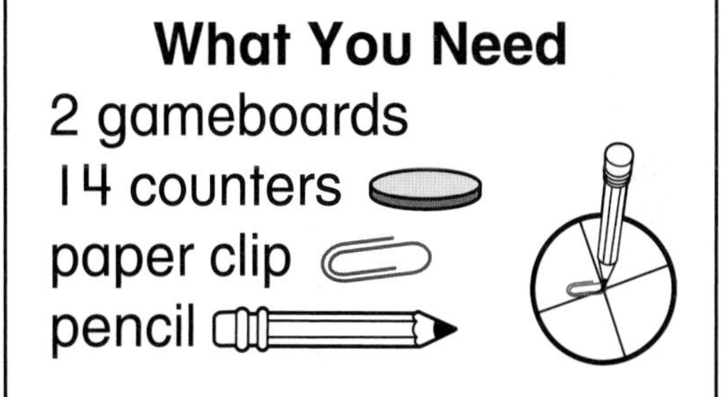

What You Need
2 gameboards
14 counters
paper clip
pencil

How to play:

1. Play with a partner. Spin, in turn.
2. If the spinner lands on "You pick!" read a clock and put a counter on it. If the spinner lands on a time, put a counter on the matching clock if it is not already marked.
3. The first player to put a counter on each clock wins.

Note to the teacher: Use with the gameboards on pages 57 and 58.

Busy Builders

A.

_______ tens + _______ ones = _______

B.

_______ tens + _______ ones = _______

C.

_______ tens + _______ ones = _______

D.

_______ tens + _______ ones = _______

E.

_______ tens + _______ ones = _______

Reproducible partner game: Use with the directions on page 62.

A Triple Treat

Player A ______	
4 + 6 + _____ = _____	
6 + 3 + _____ = _____	
4 + 4 + _____ = _____	
8 + 2 + _____ = _____	
5 + 4 + _____ = _____	
3 + 7 + _____ = _____	
5 + 5 + _____ = _____	
How many ☺?	

Player B ______	
5 + 5 + _____ = _____	
4 + 5 + _____ = _____	
6 + 2 + _____ = _____	
7 + 3 + _____ = _____	
3 + 6 + _____ = _____	
2 + 8 + _____ = _____	
6 + 4 + _____ = _____	
How many ☺?	

Reproducible partner game: Use with the directions on page 62.

Busy Builders

Skill: Place value

What You Need
2 gameboards
paper clip
pencil
cubes

How to play:

1. Play with a partner. Spin, in turn, and write the number in the first blank.
2. Spin, in turn, again and write the number in the second blank.
3. Write the sum. (Use cubes to help you.)
4. If the sum is greater than your partner's sum, circle it. If it is not, do nothing.
5. Solve all the problems. The player with more circled numbers wins.

A Triple Treat

Skill: Addition with three addends

What You Need
gameboard
die

How to play:

1. Decide who will be Player A and B. Write your name.
2. Roll the die, in turn. Write the number on the first line.
3. Write the sum.
4. If the sum is greater than your partner's sum, draw a ☺ in the box.
   If it is not, do nothing.
5. Solve all the problems.
   Write how many ☺ you have. The player with more ☺ wins.

 Note to the teacher: Use with the gameboards on pages 60 and 61.

Classroom Displays

CLASSROOM DISPLAYS

Count on open house guests to go wild over this idea! Help each child make a construction paper animal head and then cut out an oval for the face. Attach a photo of the child to the animal head so the child's face shows through the opening. Showcase the animals with the title shown. During open house, challenge parents to identify their children's photos.

Candy McCormick, Mohawk Elementary, Bessemer, PA

For this year-round display, write each youngster's name and birthdate on a banana cutout. Then arrange the bananas in a bunch hanging from a tree. (See the banana and stem patterns on page 71.) Add a title, a monkey head, and two monkey hands. At the beginning of each month, highlight the upcoming birthdays by attaching the corresponding bananas to the monkey's hands.

Meagan Waters
The Discovery School
Gambrills, MD

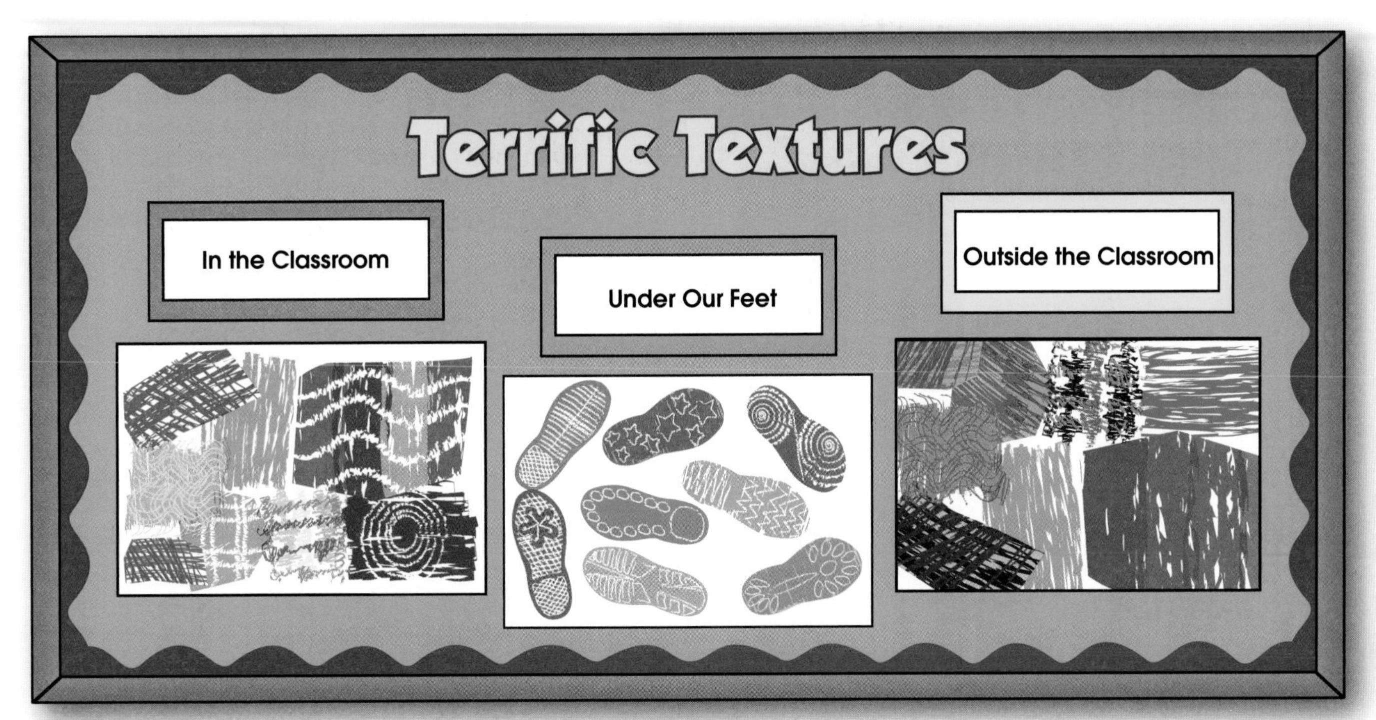

Here's a fun idea to add to your five senses unit. Have students use crayons to do rubbings of various items in the classroom and outside of the classroom. Make a collage of each set of rubbings. Also ask each youngster to do a rubbing of the sole of his shoe, cut out the rubbing, and then mount it on a poster. Display the rubbings as desired.

Diane Awakuni, Koko Head School, Honolulu, HI

To make a horse, tack crumpled tissue paper to a board as shown. Then add strips of tissue paper for the tail, mane, and hooves. Dress a cardboard head-and-torso cutout to make a rider. Position the rider on the horse and add cardboard arms. To complete the display, frame students' photos or names with horseshoe cutouts (pattern on page 71) and post a title.

Donna A. Davidson, B. P. S. Kindergarten, Ringgold, GA

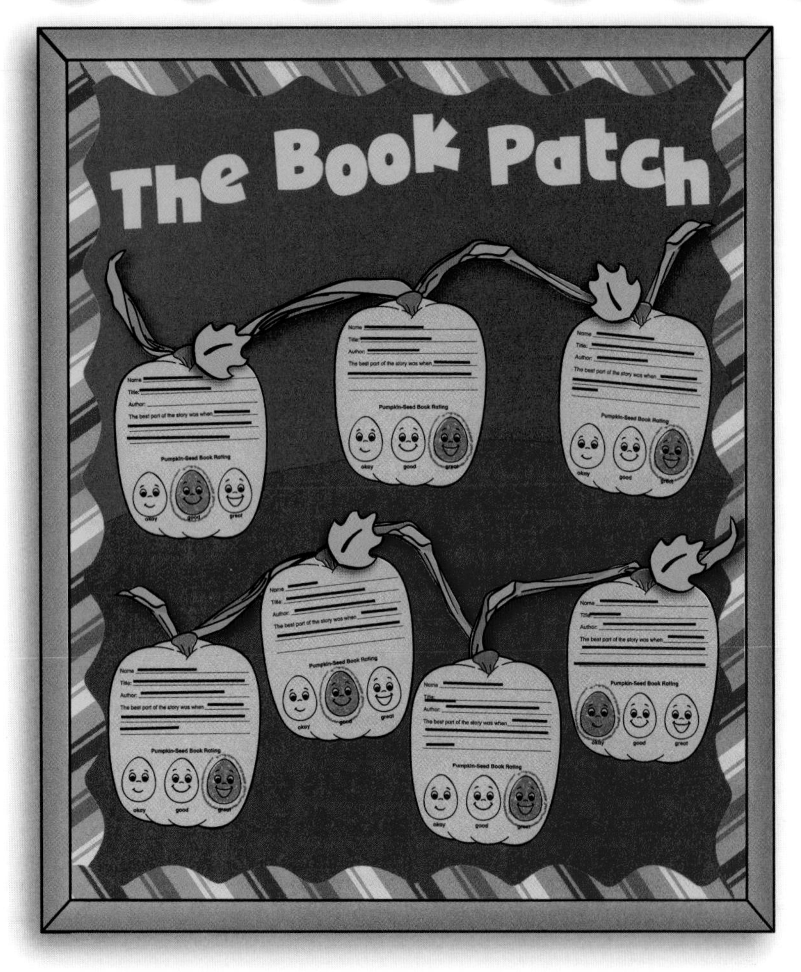

After a student listens to a read-aloud or reads a story, have him complete an orange copy of the book report form from page 72 and color the pumpkin stem. Display youngsters' completed forms with leaf cutouts and crepe paper streamers (vines) as desired. No doubt youngsters will be eager to make the patch of pumpkins grow throughout the fall!

Darlene Martin
South Elementary
Hingham, MA

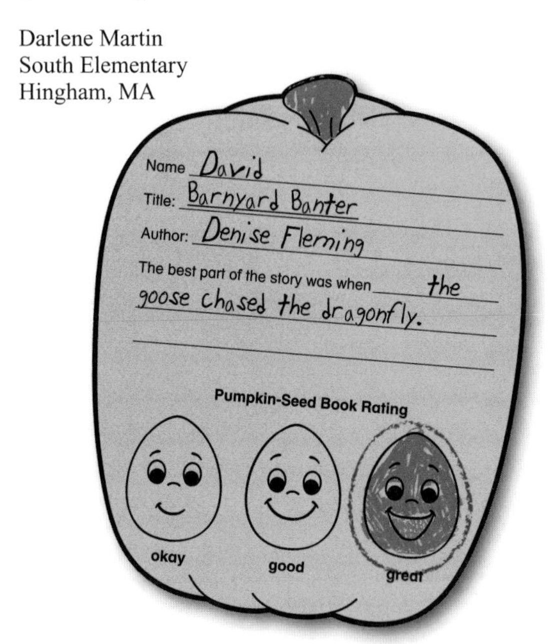

Look What Followed Us to School!

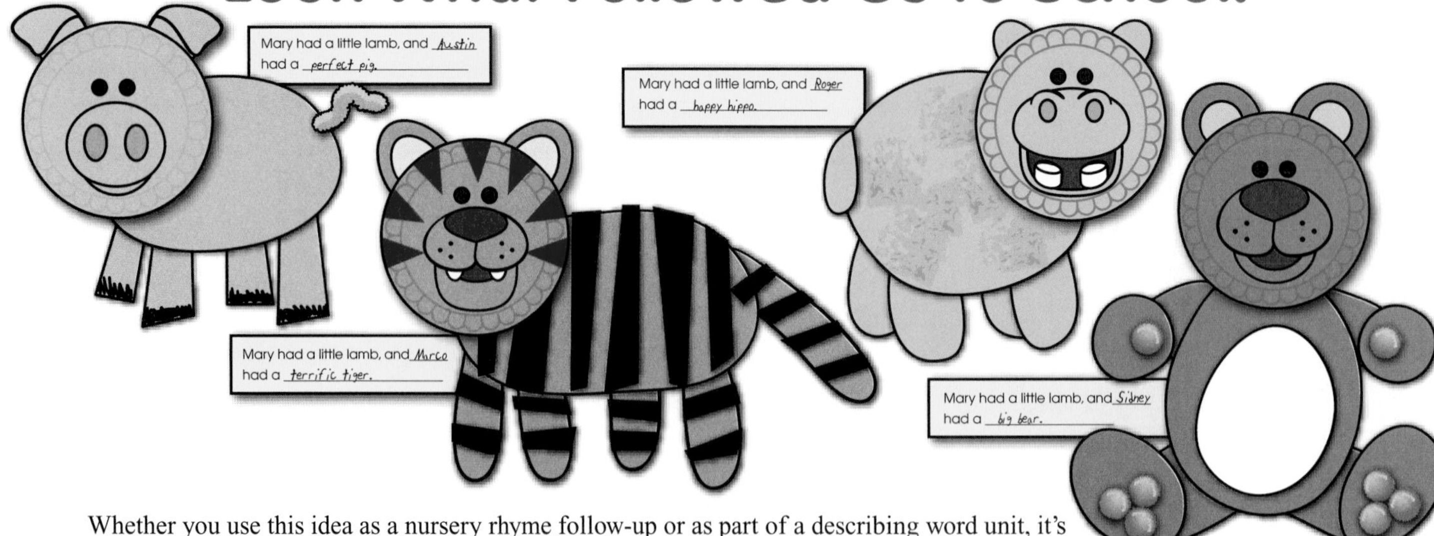

Whether you use this idea as a nursery rhyme follow-up or as part of a describing word unit, it's sure to please! Have each student make an animal using a disposable animal plate and chosen arts-and-crafts supplies. Then help her complete a caption, like the ones shown, with her name and an alliterative animal phrase. Display students' one-of-a-kind critters with the captions and a title.

Cheri Adair, Merkel Elementary, Merkel, TX

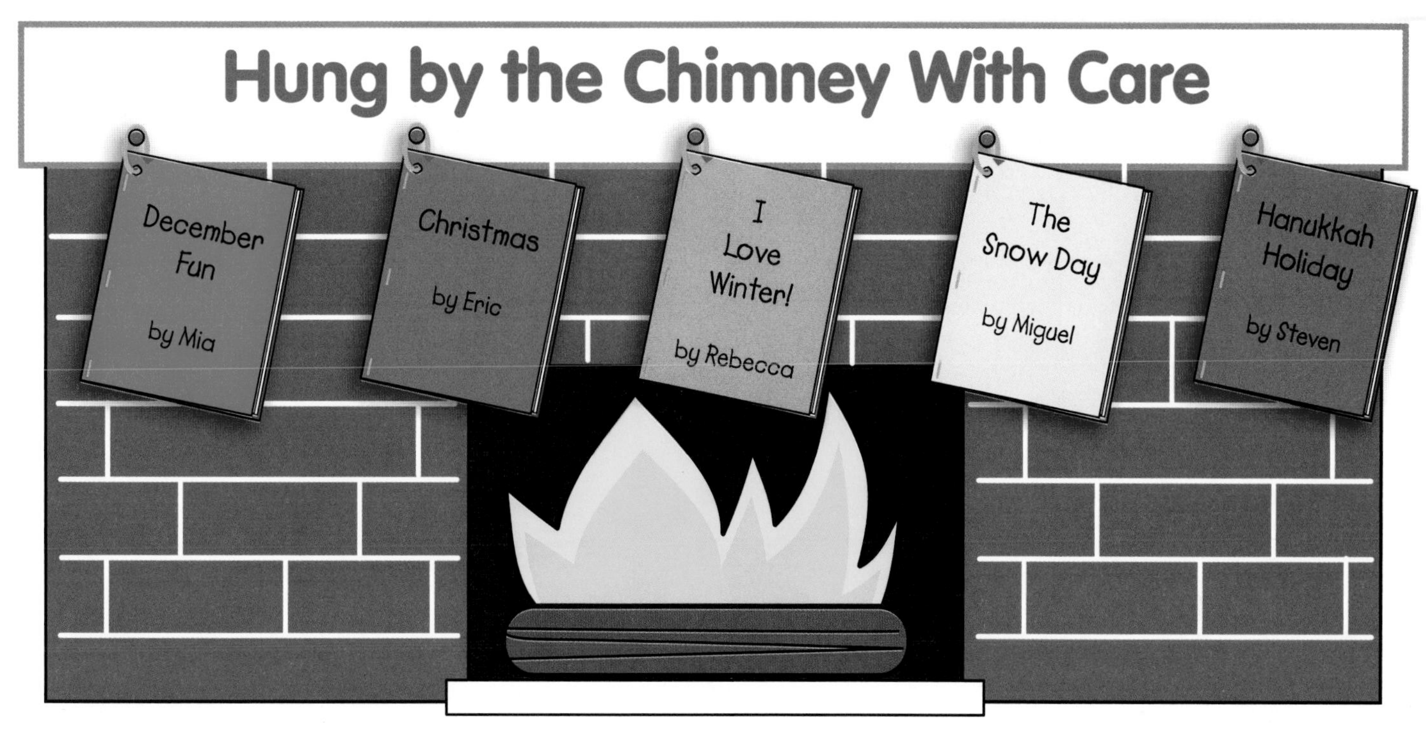

Here's a fun way to showcase students' writing this season. Post a large fireplace cutout with a log and some flames. Have each youngster write a story in a booklet with construction paper covers. Then hang the booklets on the mantle and title the display as shown.

Meredith Garrison, Chester Park Center of Literacy Through Technology, Chester, SC

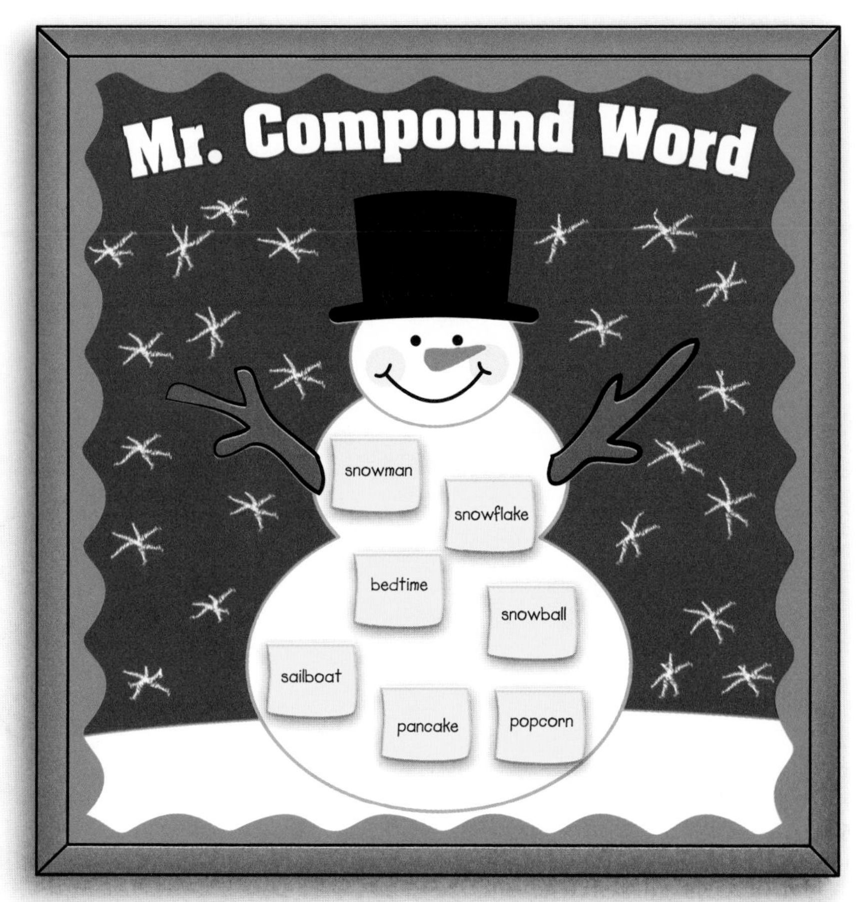

Highlight compound words with this cheery snowpal! Use chalk to draw snowflakes on a prepared bulletin board. Then post a large snowpal and the title shown. Place a supply of large sticky notes nearby. Whenever a student comes across a compound word in her reading, invite her to write the word on a sticky note and attach it to the snowpal.

Cynthia Brown
DeArmanville Elementary
Anniston, AL

Who are the frosty friends that adorn this wintry display? They're smiling students! Have each child attach a photo of his face to a snowpal cutout. Then invite him to decorate the snowpal with arts-and-crafts materials. Display the snowpals on a titled board along with student-made snowflakes.

Amy Kerrigan, Frostick Elementary, Croswell, MI

To make this New Year's Day display, have each child decorate a paper circle to make a self-likeness. Then help her write a holiday resolution on a speech bubble cutout. Display each youngster's artwork with her resolution on a titled board. It's sure to help students keep their goals in mind!

Ada Goren, Winston-Salem, NC

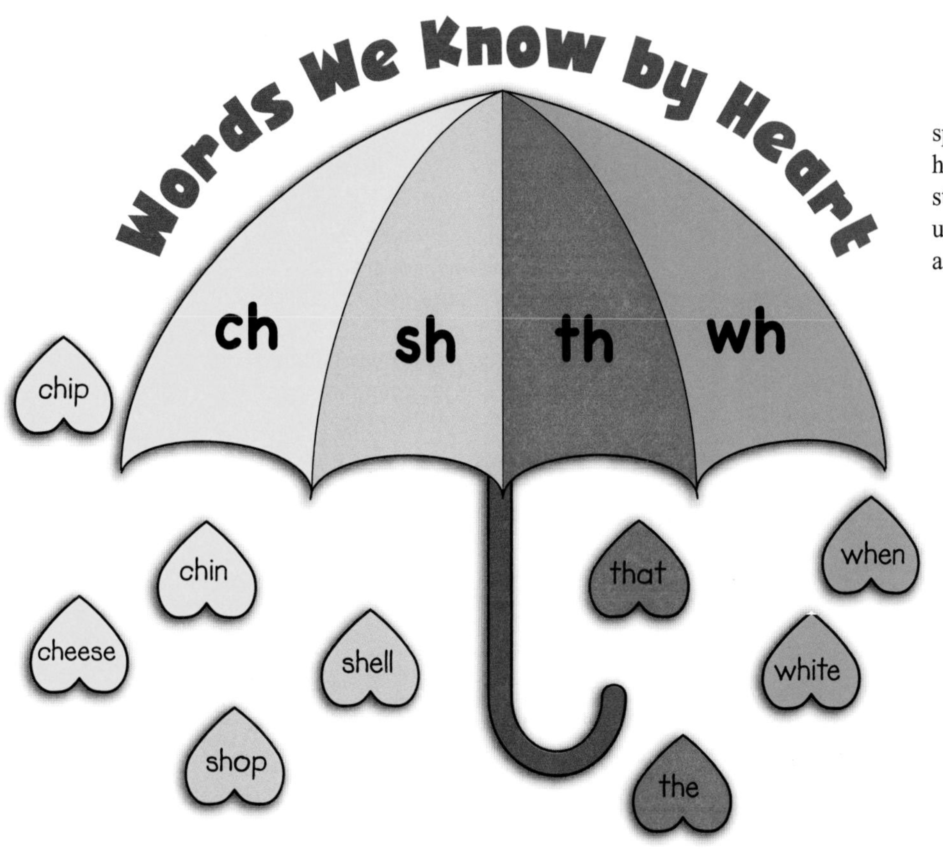

You can use this heart display through spring! Post an umbrella cutout that you have programmed for a skill below. Ask students to label heart cutouts to match the umbrella. Arrange the hearts as desired and add a title.

- Consonant digraphs
- Word families
- Long-vowel and short-vowel words

Have each student use pattern block stamps or cutouts to decorate a paper kite. Then instruct him to attach yarn and two bows. Showcase the kites with clouds and a title. Follow up with the ideas below.

Graphing: Help students make a graph that shows the number of each type of pattern block.

Geometry: Give students shape-related clues about a kite, such as "It has two trapezoids and two hexagons." Then challenge students to identify the kite.

Debbie Hill, Stone Elementary, Crossville, TN

CLASSROOM DISPLAYS

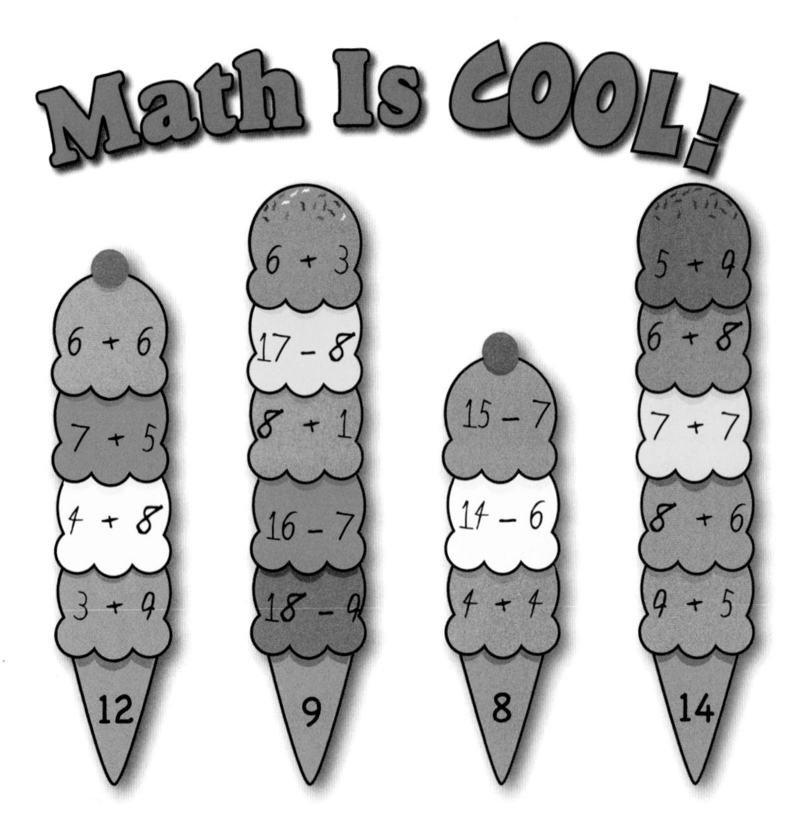

Choose an option below. Have youngsters assemble the ice cream cones and decorate the top scoops. Then showcase students' work with a title.

Literacy: Label cone cutouts with rimes. Ask students to program ice cream scoop cutouts with words that contain the rimes.

Math: Program cone cutouts with numbers (sums or differences). Instruct students to write corresponding math problems on ice cream scoop cutouts.

Neshie Gelbwachs
Lev Bais Yaakov
Brooklyn, NY

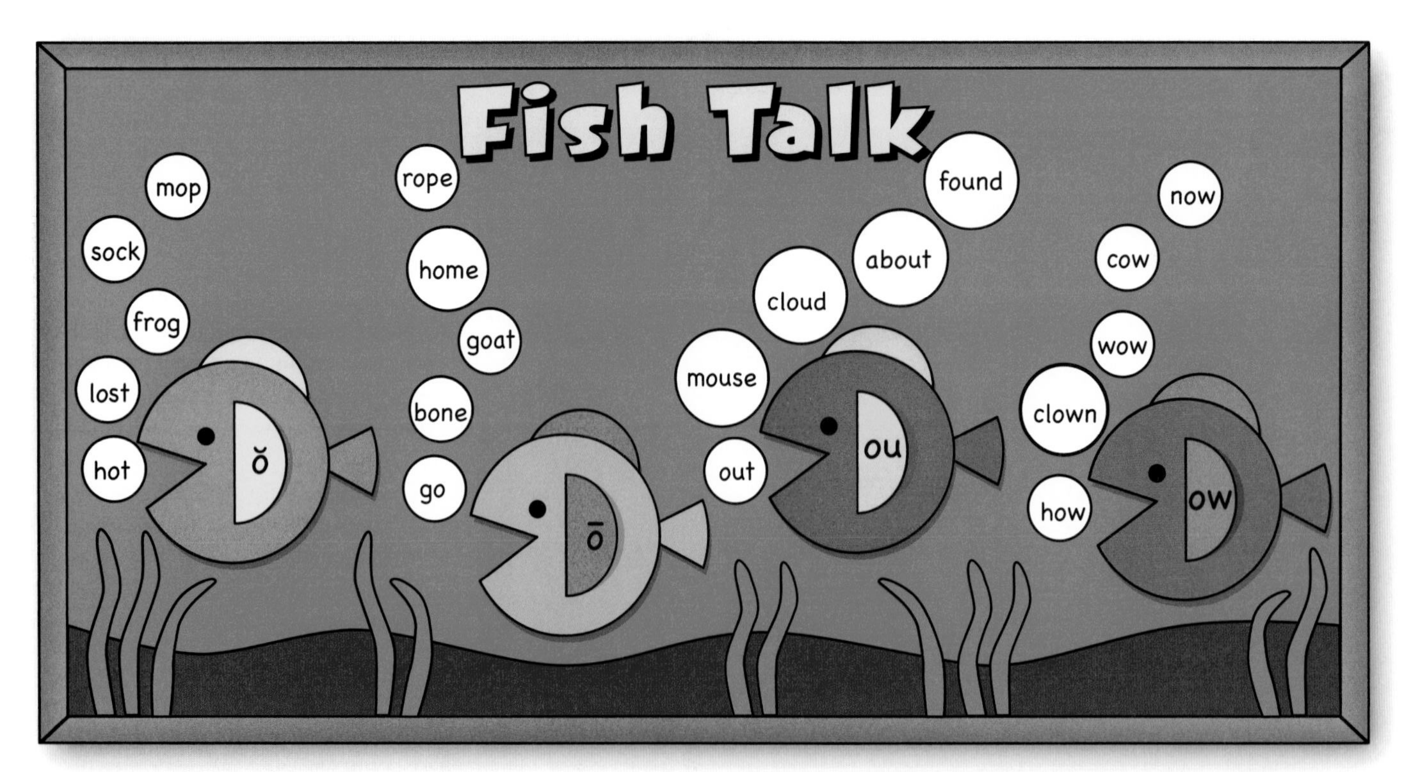

To make a fish for this phonics display, cut a triangle from a circle and then attach it to the opposite side of the circle as shown. Draw an eye. Then glue to the fish two fin cutouts, one of which you have programmed with a phonics element. Display a few fish on an ocean-themed bulletin board. Program white circles (bubbles) with corresponding words and place them in a plastic fishbowl near the display. Then have students post the bubbles near the appropriate fish.

Kathryn Davenport, Partin Elementary, Oviedo, FL

Stem and Banana Patterns

Use with "Birthday Bunch" on page 64.

Horseshoe Pattern

Use with "We're Roping In Great Work!" on page 65.

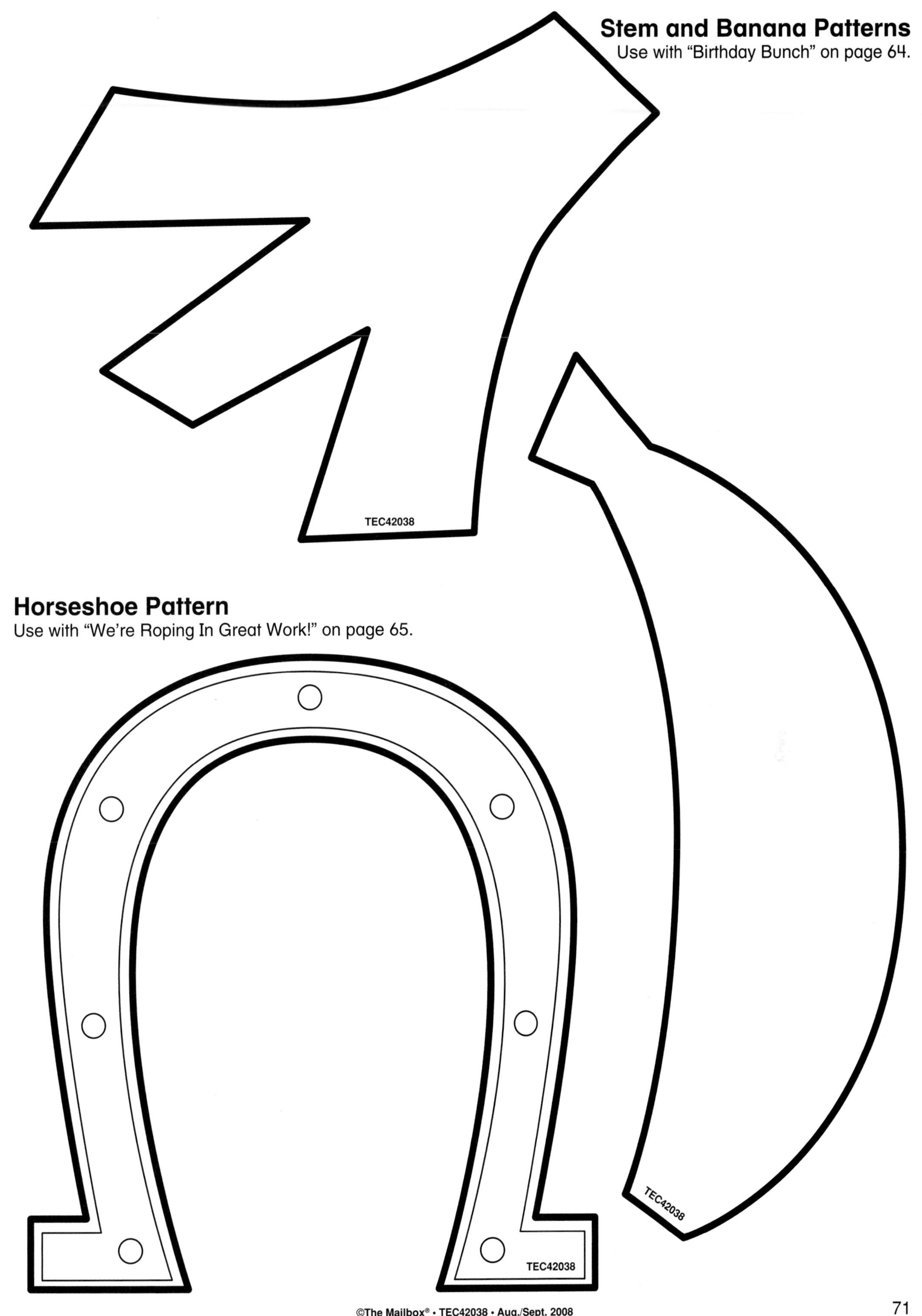

Book Report Form

Use with "The Book Patch" on page 66.

Name ______________________________

Title: ______________________________

Author: ______________________________

The best part of the story was when ______________________________

____

____

Pumpkin-Seed Book Rating

okay **good** **great**

TEC42039

Learning Centers

Namely, Sorting

Literacy Center

To prepare this letter-perfect activity, divide and label a sheet of paper as shown. Place the prepared paper, a class supply of name cards, and a supply of letter cards at a center. To complete the activity, a youngster sets his name card above the labeled paper. Then he sorts the letter cards into the appropriate columns, attending to the uppercase and lowercase forms of the letters. ***Letter recognition***

Jayne E. Jaskolski
21st Street School
Milwaukee, WI

Packaged for Reading

Literacy Center

Show youngsters that they are already readers with this brand-name book! Mount several familiar food labels and box fronts on separate sheets of construction paper. Laminate the papers. Then bind them between two covers and title the resulting book as desired. Invite each center visitor to read the book independently or with a partner. **For more advanced students,** write a chosen letter or word on each page before laminating it. Have students use a wipe-off marker to circle the designated letters and words. ***Environmental print***

Jean Ricotta, Paumanok Elementary, Dix Hills, NY

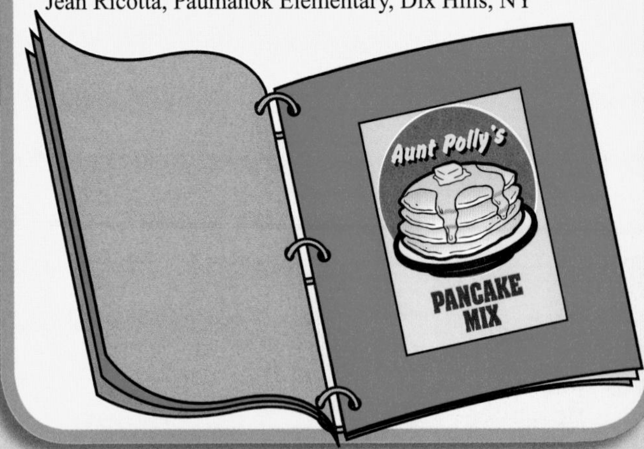

Counting Sheep

Math or Literacy Center

What makes this activity a "shear" delight? It's easy to adapt for different skills! Mount several copies of the sheep cards from page 82 on colorful paper and choose an option below.

Modeling numbers: Write a different number on each sheep. A youngster puts the designated number of cotton balls on each card.

Addition: Write an addition problem on each sheep and set out a supply of paper. A student models the problems with cotton balls and writes each corresponding number sentence.

Phonological awareness: Glue a copy of a picture card from page 82 on each sheep. Write on the back of each sheep card the number of syllables in the corresponding word. A student names each word, claps once for each syllable, and then puts the matching number of cotton balls on the sheep. To check her work, she clears each card, in turn, and flips it.

Tiffini Ann Amato, The Center for Discovery, Harris, NY

Shake It Up!

Literacy or Math Center

Choose an option below and program 12 sticky dots as described. Adhere each dot to a different cup of a sanitized foam egg carton. Then place a pom-pom in the carton and close it. Place the carton at a center stocked with paper. A student shakes the carton and then opens it. After she reads the sticky dot on which the pom-pom landed, she completes the activity as described below.

Letter-sound associations: Write a letter on each sticky dot. A child draws pictures whose names begin with the indicated letter.
Word families: Write a rime on each sticky dot. A child lists words that contain the indicated rime.
Addition: Write a number (sum) on each sticky dot. A child illustrates and writes corresponding addition combinations.

Daina Flores, Sunset Ridge Elementary
Pacifica, CA

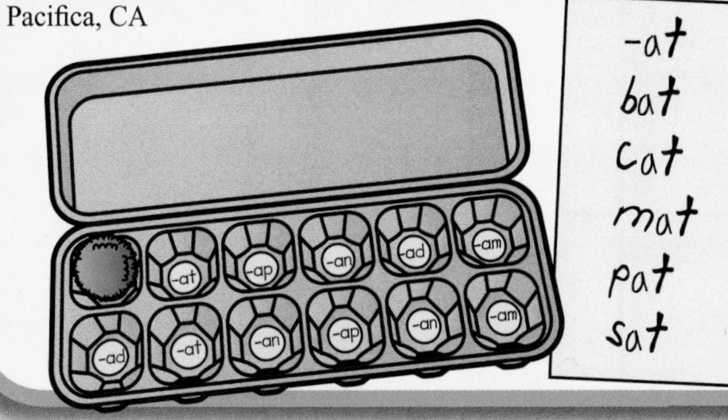

Hands-On Reading

Literacy Center

This activity requires nearly no advance preparation! Place some play dough and two or three vinyl placemats near your word wall. Arrange for two or three students to complete the activity at one time. Have each youngster use the play dough to form words on a placemat and then ask the other students at the center to read them. ***Reading and spelling words***

Beth Kickert
T. C. Cherry Elementary
Bowling Green, KY

Ten-Frame Treasure

Math Center

Here's a kid-pleasing approach to counting sets! Purchase an inexpensive treasure chest or decorate a box to make one. Then put in the chest up to 15 of each of the following items: plastic gems, colorful bow-tie pasta, imitation pennies, paper clips, large buttons, and counters. Place the chest, a piece of felt (workmat), and student copies of page 83 at a center. When a student visits the center, he colors the workmat. Then he sorts the treasures and uses the ten frame on his paper to count them. He writes the corresponding numbers where indicated. ***Counting to 15***

Susan Robinson
North Ridge Primary School
Commack, NY

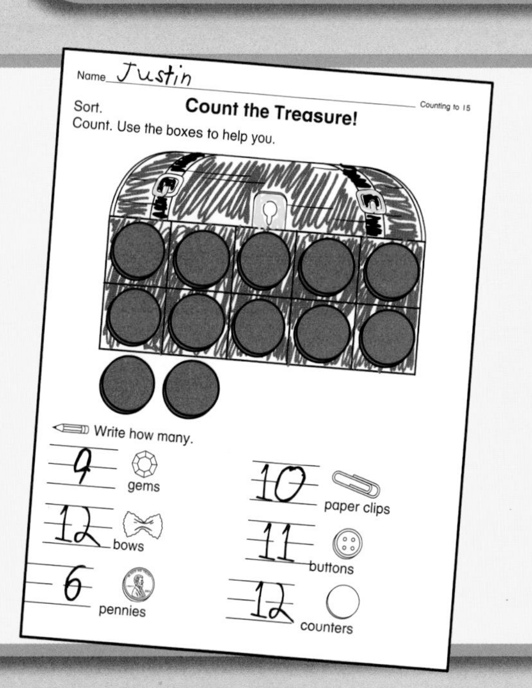

Learning Centers

Stocking Stuffers

Math Center

To prepare this money activity, purchase several small Christmas stockings or make several stocking cutouts. Write a different money amount on each stocking. Then put the stockings and imitation coins at a center. To complete the activity, a child arranges the stockings from the smallest to the greatest money amount. Then she puts coins on the stockings to model the corresponding values. ***Counting coins***

Meagan Naumann
St. Paul's Lutheran School
East Troy, WI

Roll and Write

Literacy Center

Word families are the topic of this activity. Use tape to assemble a copy of the word family cube pattern on page 84. Put the cube and a supply of recording sheets like the one shown at a center. Arrange for one or more students to visit the center at a time. To complete the activity, students roll the cube and then read the rime on its top. Each youngster writes in the corresponding section of his paper a word that contains the rime. Students continue as described until they have written a designated number of different words. Then each student chooses three words he wrote and writes sentences with them on the back of his paper. ***Word families***

Stacy Schriever
Prairie Lincoln Elementary
Columbus, OH

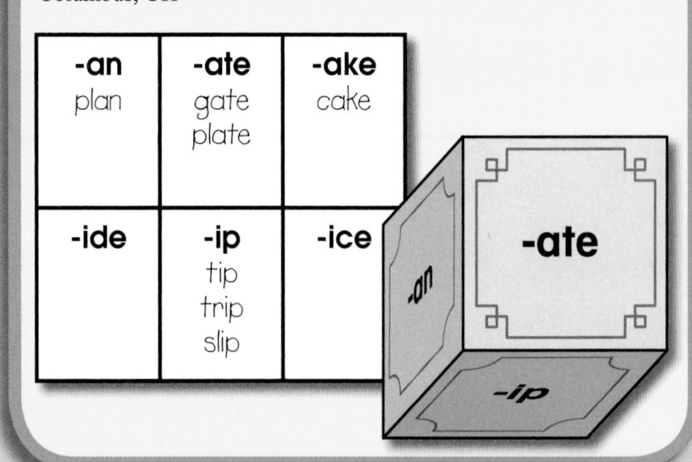

Asking or Telling?

Literacy Center

This editing idea is easy to adapt for different reading levels! Write on each of several sentence strips either a question or a statement, using a lowercase letter for the first word in each sentence and omitting the end punctuation. (Use different-colored markers to distinguish strips for different reading levels.) To make headings, write "Asking Sentences" and "Telling Sentences" on separate blank cards. Place the cards and sentences at a center stocked with writing paper.

A student sets out the two heading cards. She reads the sentences and sorts them below the appropriate headings. Then she writes the sentences on a sheet of paper, using correct capitalization and punctuation. ***Editing sentences***

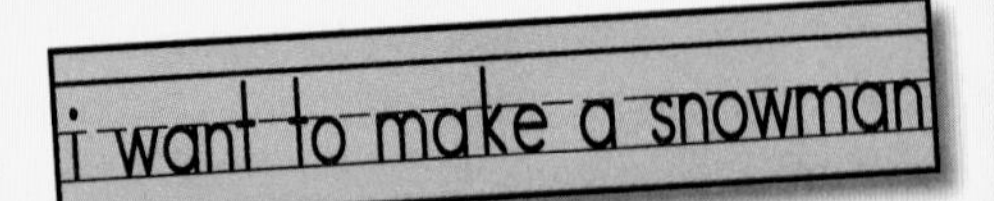

Nicolette Fourman, Cranberry Elementary, North Port, FL

Learning Centers

Which Word?
Literacy Center

For this partner game, make a supply of word cards so each word begins with a different letter. To play, one student deals all the cards. Each player stacks his cards word-side down. Then each player puts his top card faceup on the playing surface and reads the word. The player with the word whose initial letter is closer to the beginning of the alphabet takes both cards and sets them aside. Play continues, with the players reusing cards as needed, until one player has no cards or the allotted time is up. ***Alphabetical order***

adapted from an idea by Terry Fortier
Days of Wonder Learning Day Care Center
Caribou, ME

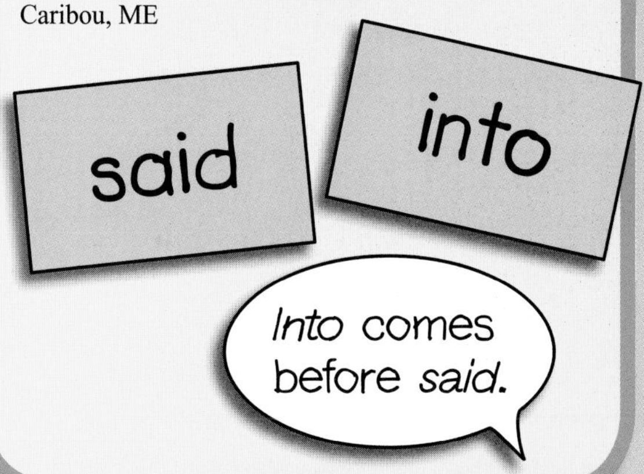

Clocks and Critters
Math Center

Here's a fun way to give students practice with elapsed time! Cut out a copy of the time activity cards on page 85 and mount them on separate blank cards for durability. Write on the back of each animal card the letter of the matching clock. Place the cards and a manipulative clock at a center. To complete the activity, a child spreads out the cards faceup. He reads a chosen animal card, uses the manipulative clock to determine the answer, and then sets the animal card with the matching clock card. After he pairs all the cards in this manner, he flips the cards to check his work. ***Elapsed time***

Sweet Dreams
Literacy Center

Promote the use of transition words with this "purr-fect" sequencing activity! Color a copy of the center mat on page 86 and the activity cards on page 87. Cut out the cards and put each set in a separate resealable plastic bag. Place the mat and cards at a center stocked with writing paper.

A student spreads out one set of cards faceup. She arranges the cards in order on the mat. Then she writes about the pictures, using words such as *first, next,* and *then.* ***Sequencing, writing***

Catherine Broome-Kehm, Melbourne Beach, FL

Learning Centers

Heads or Tails?
Math Center

Count on this partner game to get rave reviews from your students! At a center, place paper and a disposable cup containing several imitation coins. To begin, one player calls "heads" and the other player calls "tails." Next, one player shakes the coins and spills them out. The youngsters sort the coins by heads and tails. Then each player claims his corresponding set of coins. The player with the set of greater value gets one point. If the players have sets of equal value, they each get a point. The players return the coins to the cup for another round of play. The first player to earn five points wins. ***Counting coins***

Shelley Brooks
Crow Elementary
Arlington, TX

Sum Sorting
Math Center

It's a snap to prepare this addition activity. Simply cut out a colorful copy of the math cards on page 88 and then place the cards at a center stocked with paper. To complete the activity, a youngster arranges the star cards side by side in numerical order. She reads each addition problem and places it below the appropriate star card. Then she writes the corresponding addition facts on a sheet of paper. ***Addition to 18***

Marie E. Cecchini
West Dundee, IL

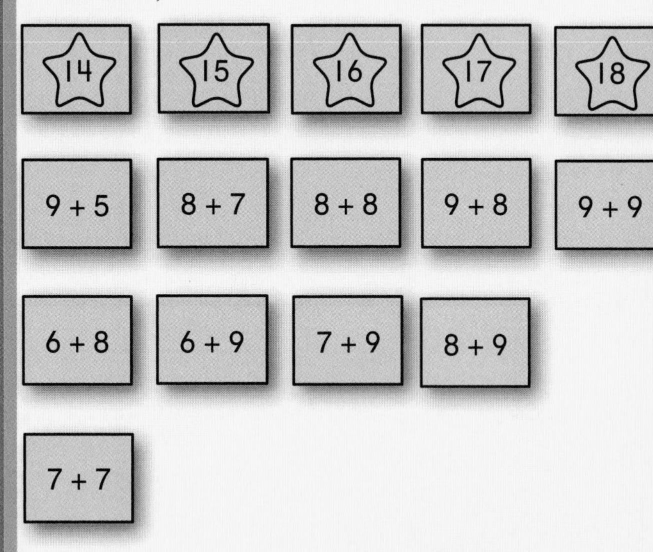

They Go Together!
Literacy Center

To reinforce compound words, gather 12 identical plastic eggs. Write a compound word on each egg so the two words that make up the compound word are on different halves of the egg. Then take the eggs apart. Put the egg halves, a sanitized egg carton, and writing paper at a center. A student puts two egg halves together to form a compound word, writes the word on a sheet of paper, and puts the egg in the egg carton. Then he continues with the remaining egg halves. ***Compound words***

Lisa Vrana
Kate Schenck Elementary
San Antonio, TX

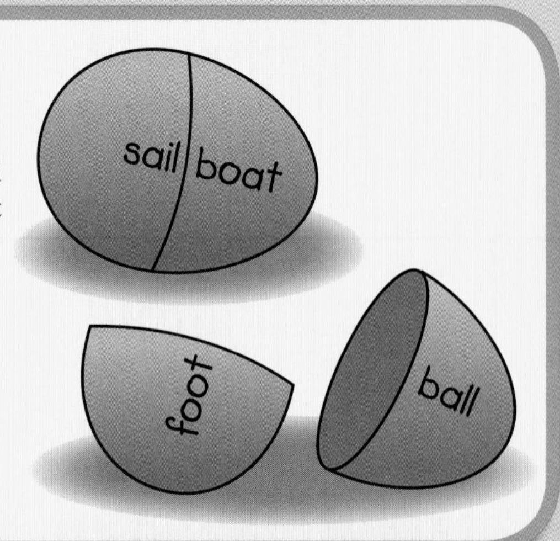

Soda Shop Spelling

Literacy Center

This activity is easy to differentiate for different skill levels. To prepare, gather caps from water or soda bottles. Program the caps with letters that spell several words, writing one letter per cap. (Use different-colored markers to program caps for different spelling lists.) Cut one side from a 12-pack soda carton and then laminate it to make a workmat. Put at a center the workmat, the caps, a list of words, and either restaurant order pads or writing paper. When a child visits the center, she uses the caps to form each word, in turn, and writes it on an order pad or a loose sheet of paper. ***Spelling***

Suzanne Hunter
Mathis Elementary
Hayti, MO

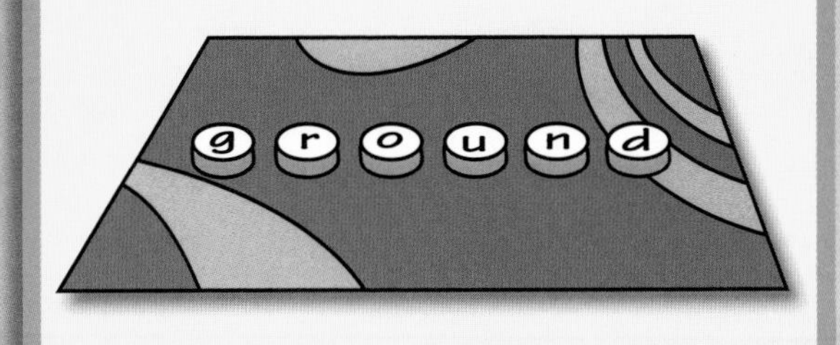

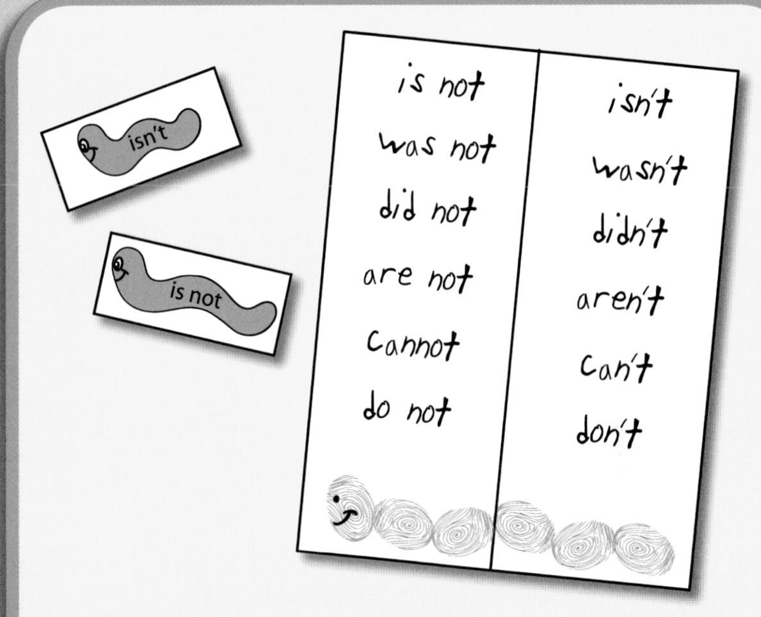

Creepy-Crawly Contractions

Literacy Center

Color and cut out a copy of the word cards from page 89. Scramble the cards. Then put the cards, a washable green ink pad, and a supply of paper at a center. A student pairs the cards to make matching sets of words. Next, he divides a sheet of paper into two columns and lists each set of words as shown. Finally, he uses the ink to make a fingerprint worm below the lists and then draws a face on the worm. ***Contractions***

Lunch for Two

Math Center

For a fun approach to place value, color a copy of the center mat on page 90 and the center cards on page 91. Place the cards and mat at a center. To complete the activity, a student spreads the cards out faceup. Next, she puts a fish card on the mat. She determines what number is represented by the illustration and then puts the corresponding number card on the mat. Then she sets the matching card pair aside facedown. She pairs the remaining cards in the same manner. ***Place value***

Catherine Broome-Kehm
Melbourne Beach, FL

Learning Centers

Play Ball!

Literacy or Math Center

Use the patterns on page 92 to prepare the activities below. Then put the activity materials at a center stocked with paper.

CVC words: Write each vowel on a separate baseball cutout. Write a consonant-vowel-consonant word on each of several bat cutouts, omitting the vowels. A student puts each ball, in turn, on each bat and writes on a sheet of paper the real words he forms.

Comparing numbers: Write the greater than and less than symbols on separate baseball cutouts. Program each of several bat cutouts with two numbers. A student takes each bat, in turn; places the ball with the appropriate math symbol between the numbers; and then writes the resulting inequality statement on a sheet of paper.

Kathryn Davenport, Partin Elementary, Oviedo, FL

Just Hatched

Math Center

Gather several different-colored plastic eggs and put a different set of imitation coins in each egg. To make an answer key for your use, list each egg's color and money amount. Place the eggs at a center stocked with paper and crayons. To complete the activity, a student takes an egg. She draws and colors a matching egg on her paper. Next, she opens the plastic egg. She determines the money amount and writes it beside the egg illustration. Then she closes the plastic egg with the coins inside. She continues with the remaining eggs. ***Counting coins***

Andrea Singleton
Waynesville Elementary
Waynesville, OH

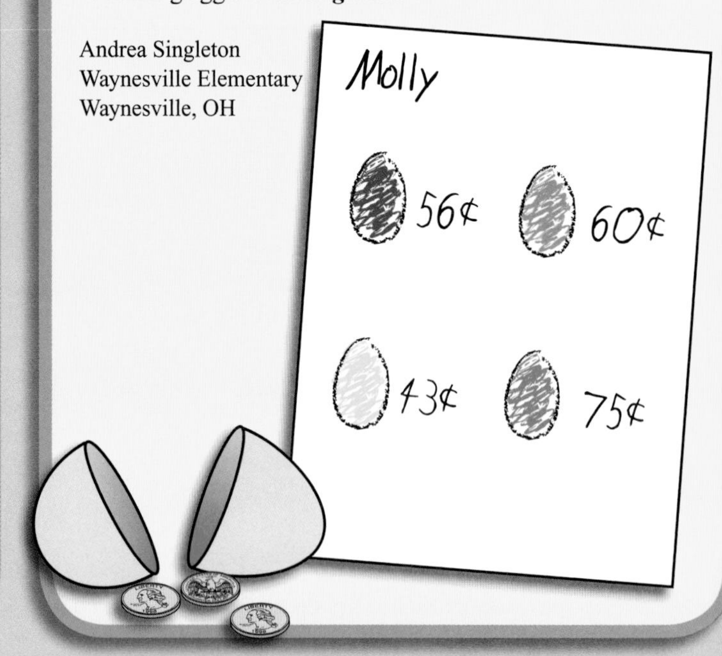

Mark My Words!

Literacy Center

Make a three-by-three grid. Program each grid space with a different reading word. (For easy management, make grids for different reading levels on different-colored paper.) Place the grid at a center with cubes of two different colors. Each player claims a different color cube. The students play as in the traditional game of tic-tac-toe except a player reads the word before marking its space. ***Word recognition***

Erin Taylor, Kennedy Elementary
Terrell, TX

Learning Centers

Blossoming Totals

Math Center

Cultivate students' problem-solving skills with this approach to addition. To prepare, cut out a colorful copy of the flower cards from page 93. Trim several colorful index cards to make flowerpots. Label each flowerpot with a sum of three different digits from 1 to 9. Put the flowerpots and flowers at a center stocked with paper. To complete the activity, a student takes a flowerpot and finds three flowers with a corresponding sum. She puts the flowers on the top edge of the flowerpot. Then she writes the matching addition sentence on a sheet of paper. She continues with the remaining flowerpots, reusing the flowers as needed. ***Addition with three addends***

Count and Connect!

Literacy Center

For this phonemic awareness activity, color and cut out a copy of the picture cards from page 93. Back the cards with tagboard for durability. To make the activity self-checking, write on the back of each card the number of sounds in the corresponding word. Put the cards and Unifix cubes at a center. When a student visits the center, he takes a card and names its picture. Next, he slowly repeats the word as he takes one cube for each sound. Then he connects the cubes and sets them near the card. After he repeats the process with the remaining pictures, he flips the cards to check his work. ***Segmenting words***

Deborah Carlberg
Stewartsville Elementary
Goodview, VA

Four Rolls

Math Center

Your students will want to play this partner game again and again! Set out unlined paper, two dice, and imitation coins. Each player divides her paper into four sections as shown. In turn, each player rolls two dice and then models the corresponding money amount in a blank section of her paper. For example, if a player rolls a six and a four, she may put a dime in the first section. The players continue until they have money in each section of their papers. Then each player trades her coins for equivalent coins of larger denominations and determines her total money amount. The player with the greater amount wins. ***Counting coins***

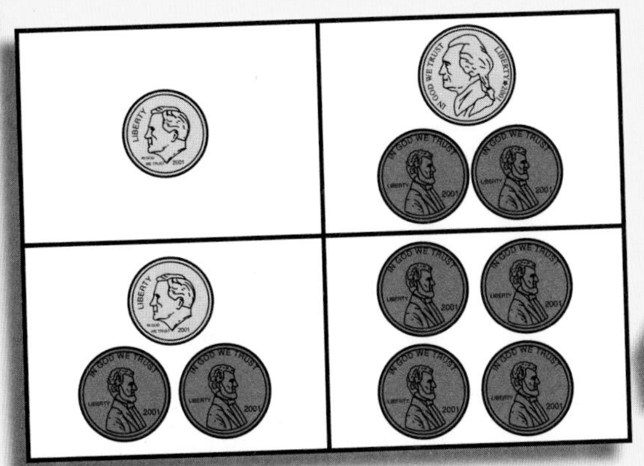

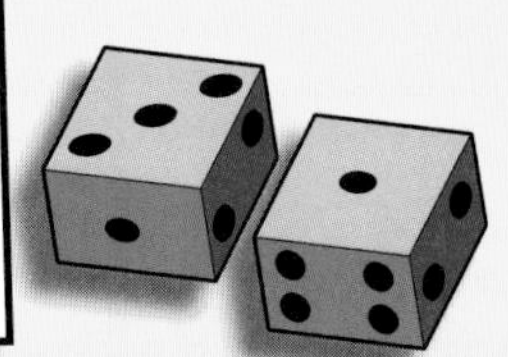

Sheep Cards

Use with "Counting Sheep" on page 74.

Picture Cards

Use with the phonological awareness option for "Counting Sheep" on page 74.

Name______________________________

Count the Treasure!

Sort.

Count. Use the boxes to help you.

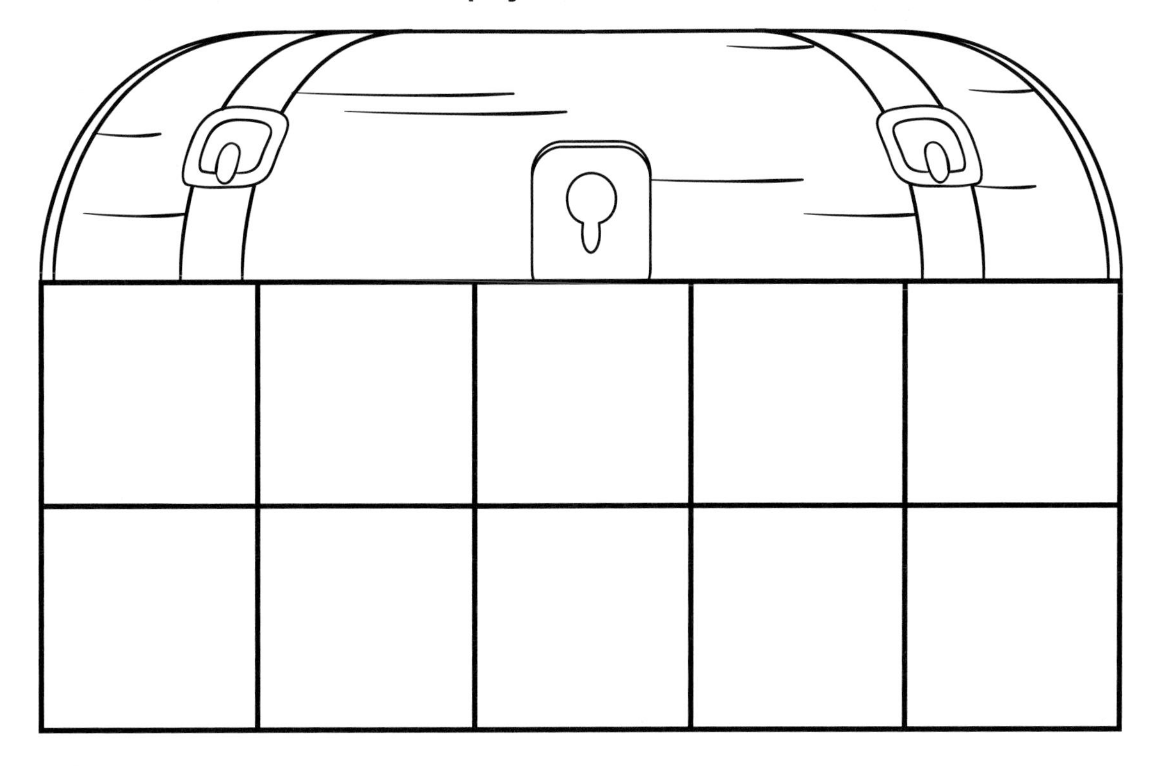

Write how many.

______ gems

______ paper clips

______ bows

______ buttons

______ pennies

______ counters

Note to the teacher: Use with "Ten-Frame Treasure" on page 75.

Word Family Cube Pattern

Use with "Roll and Write" on page 76.

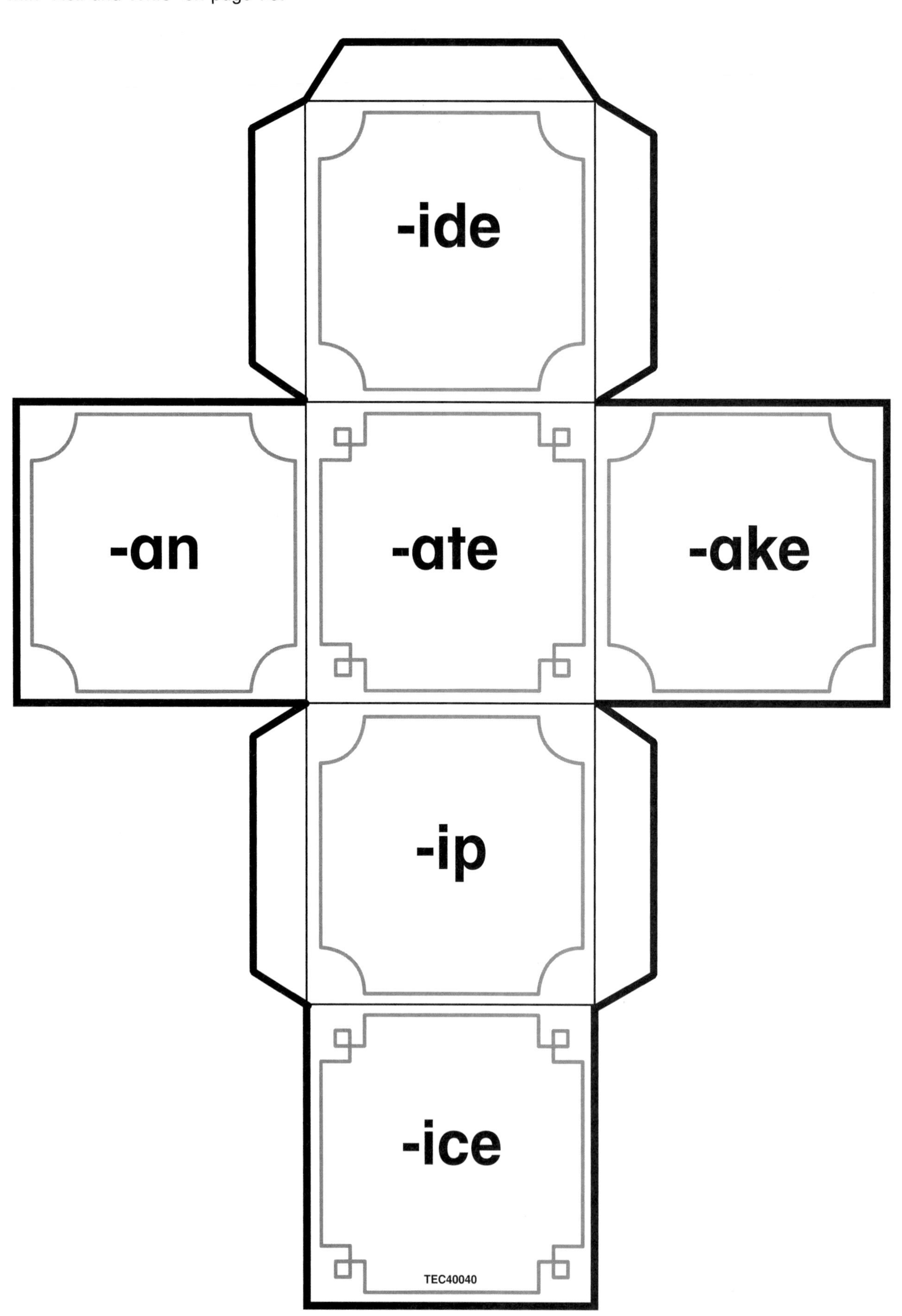

Use with "Clocks and Critters" on page 77.

Sweet Dreams

Put the cards in order. Write.

Center Cards

Use with "Sweet Dreams" on page 77.

Math Cards

Use with “Sum Sorting” on page 78.

TEC40041

7 + 7

TEC40041

9 + 5

TEC40041

TEC40041

6 + 8

TEC40041

6 + 9

TEC40041

TEC40041

8 + 7

TEC40041

7 + 9

TEC40041

TEC40041

8 + 8

TEC40041

8 + 9

TEC40041

TEC40041

9 + 8

TEC40041

9 + 9

TEC40041

Word Cards

Use with "Creepy-Crawly Contractions" on page 79.

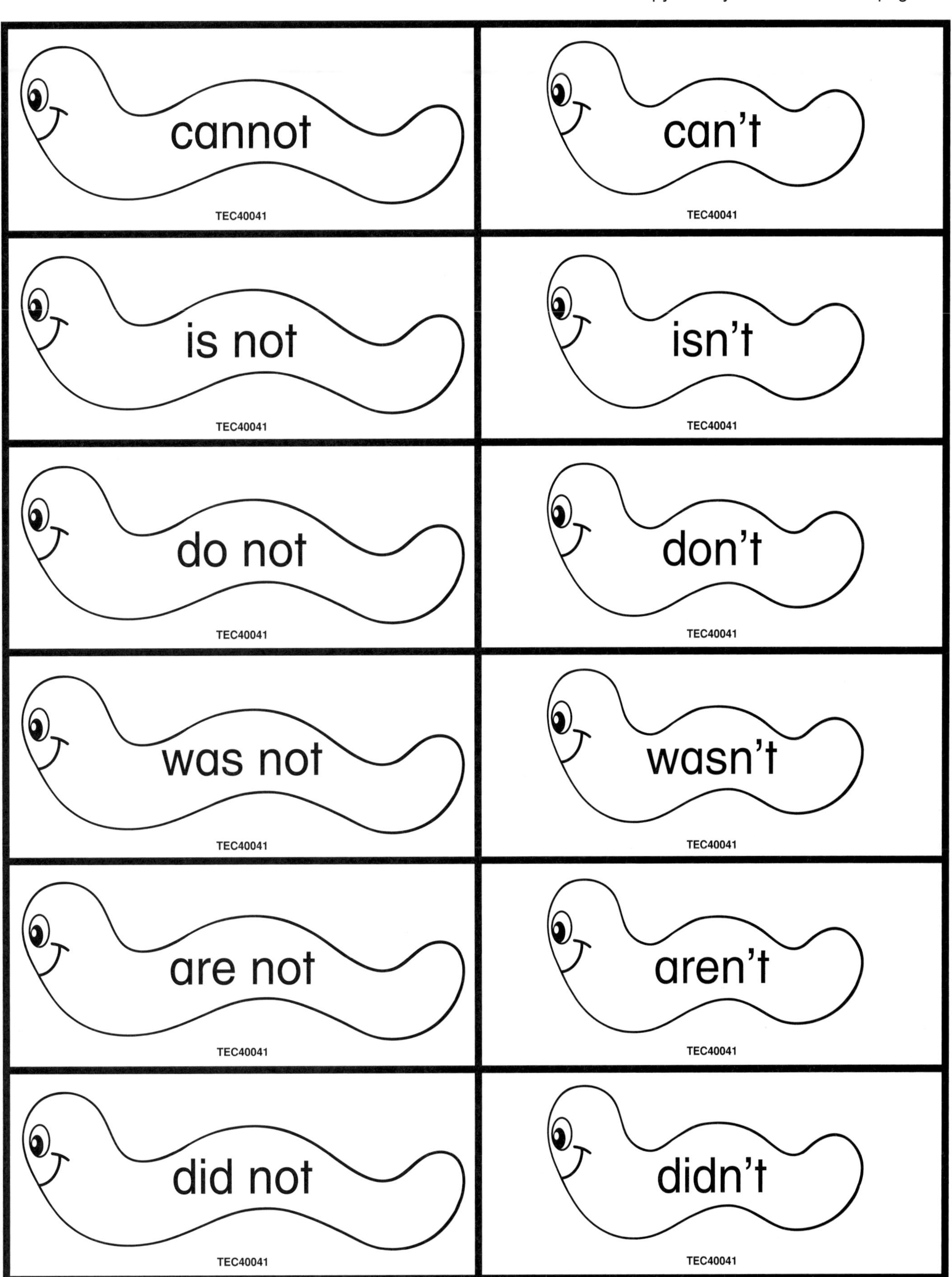

Lunch for Two

Put a fish card.
Put the matching number card.

Center Cards

Use with "Lunch for Two" on page 79.

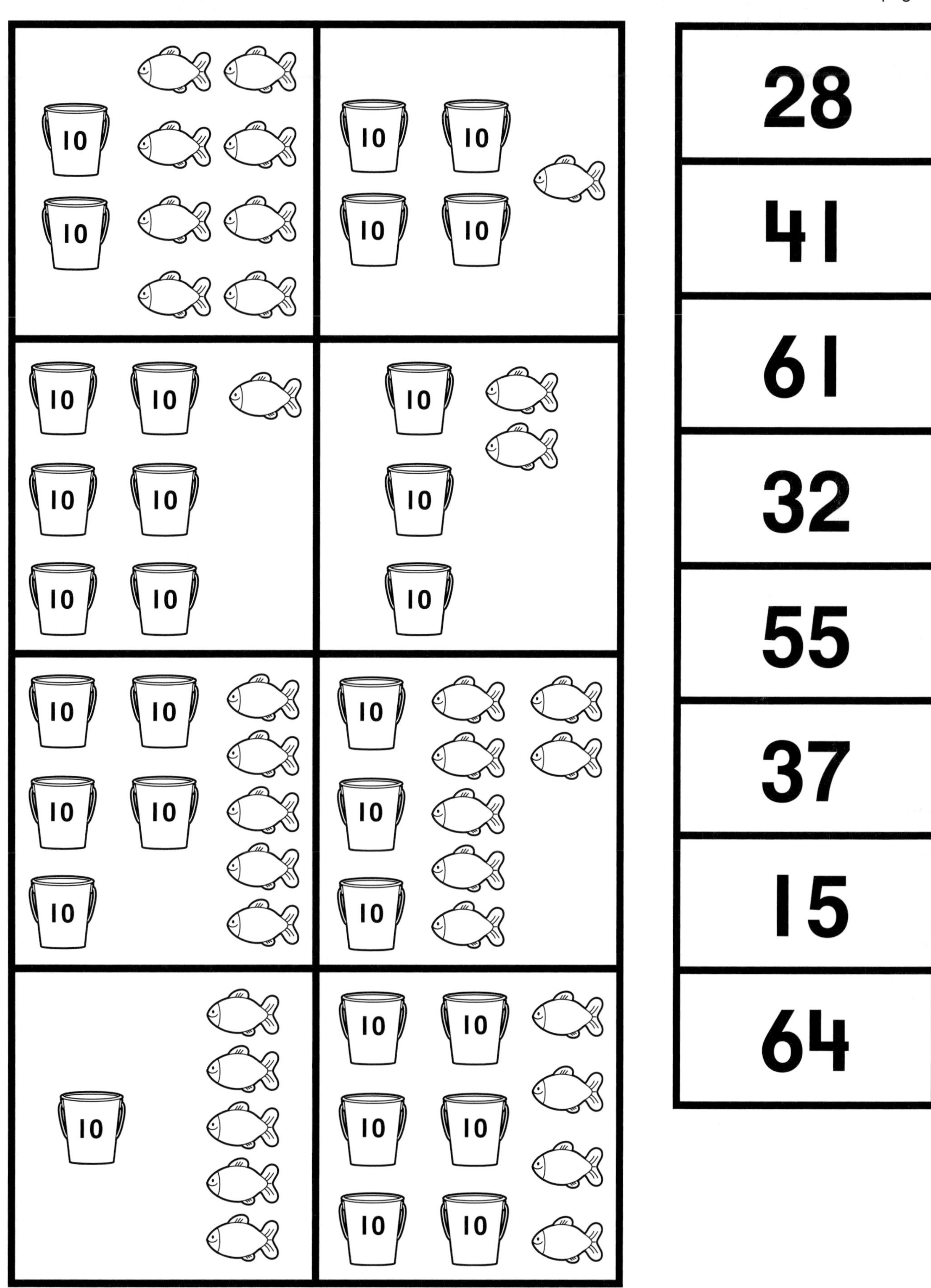

Baseball Bat and Ball Patterns

Use with "Play Ball!" on page 80.

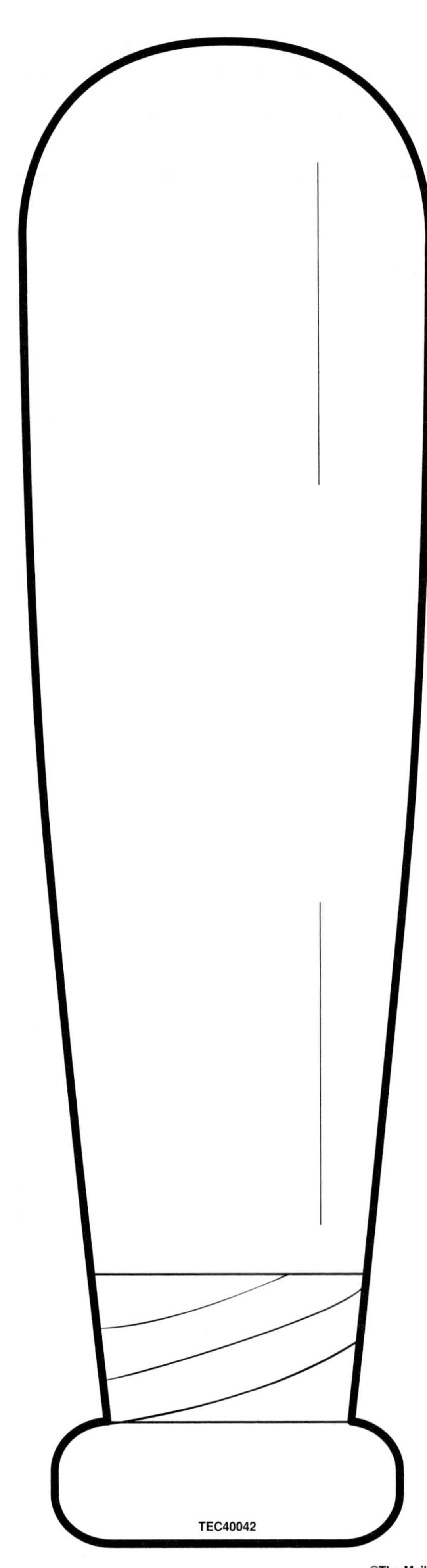

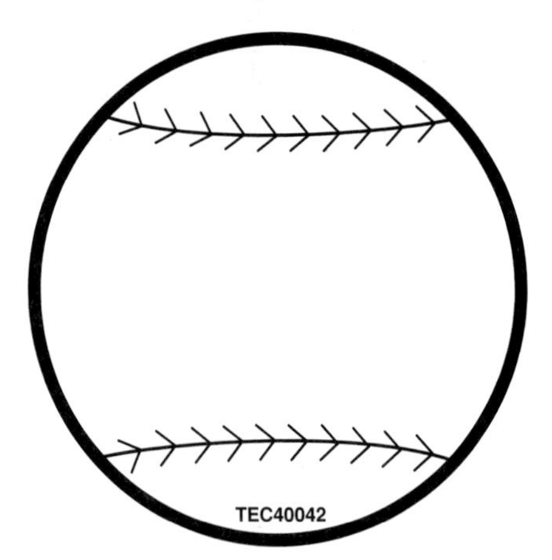

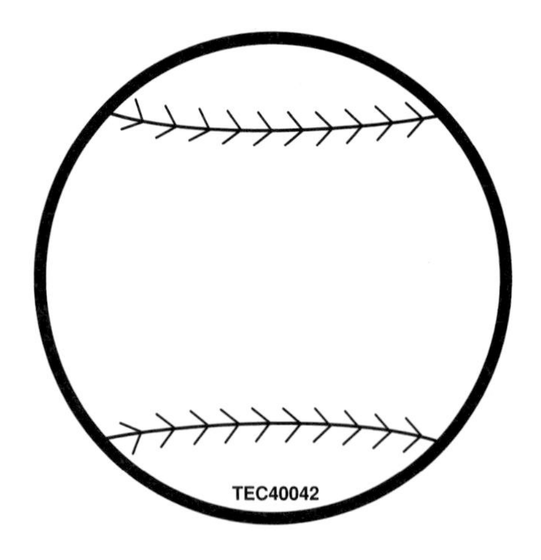

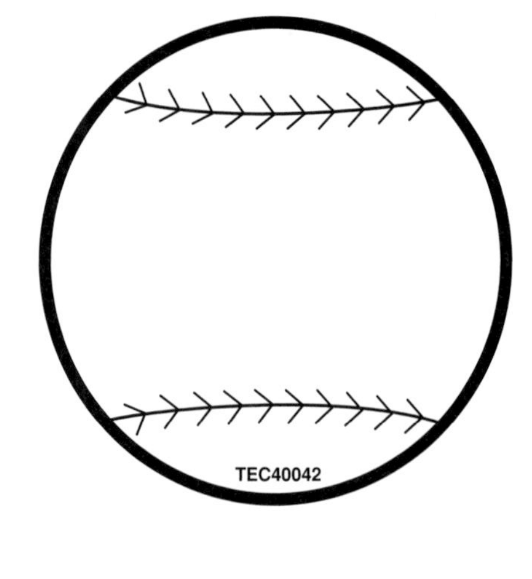

Flower Cards

Use with "Blossoming Totals" on page 81.

Picture Cards

Use with "Count and Connect!" on page 81.

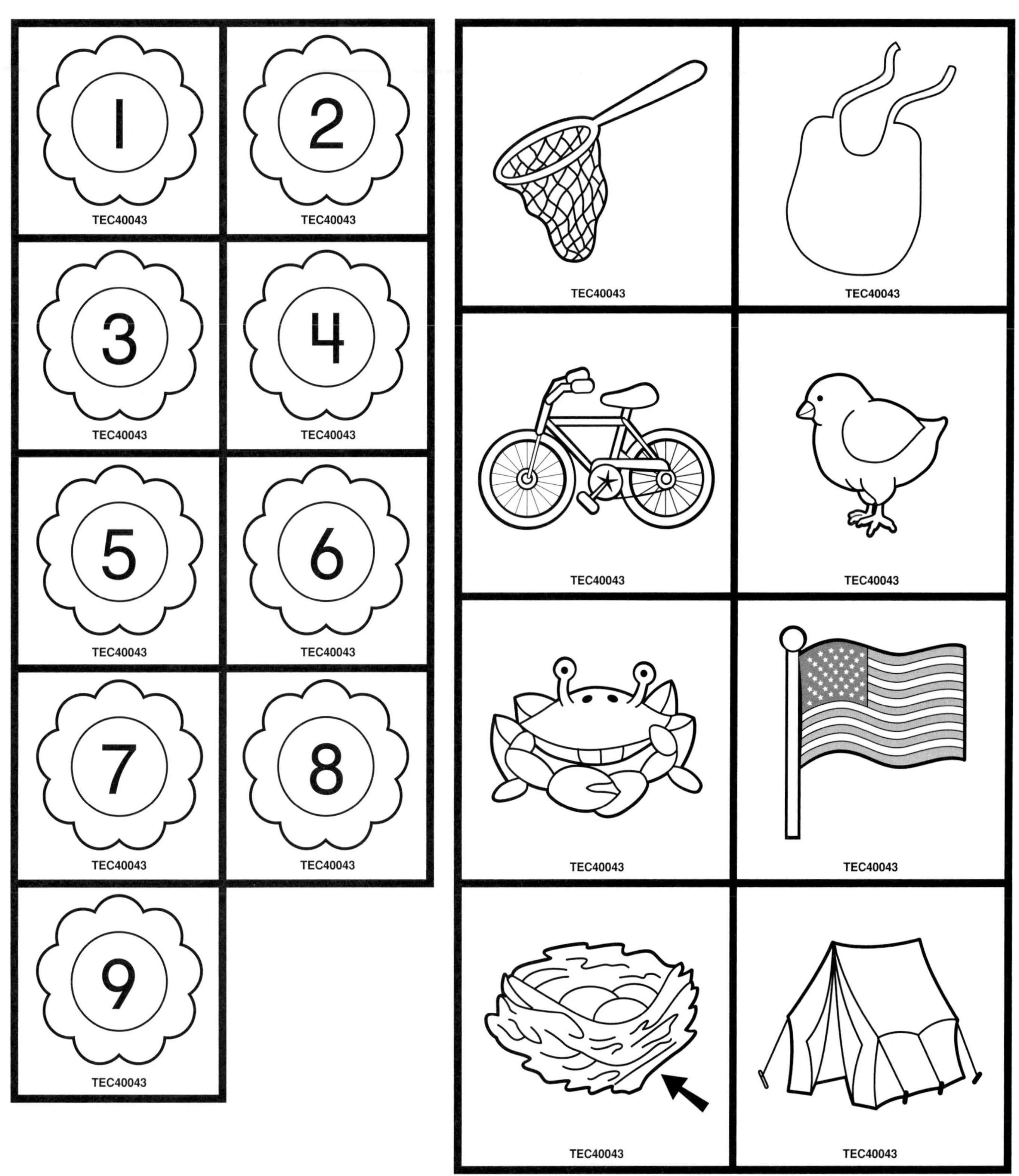

Line Them Up!

What You Need

10 sticky notes
highlighter
paper

What You Do

(1) Draw a line. Number your paper.

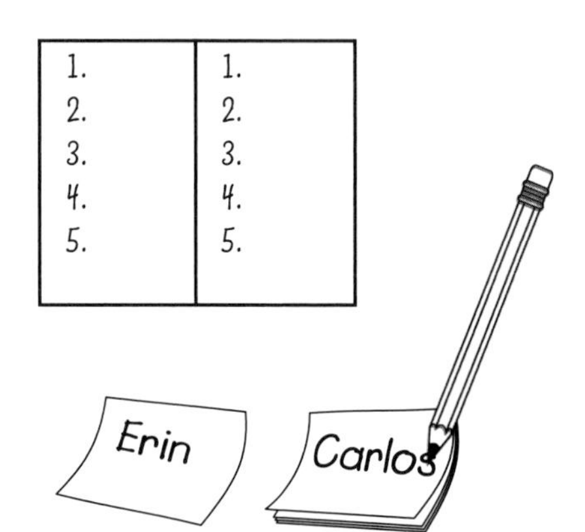

(2) Write a name on each sticky note.
(Each name must start with a different letter.)

(3) Highlight the first letter of each name.

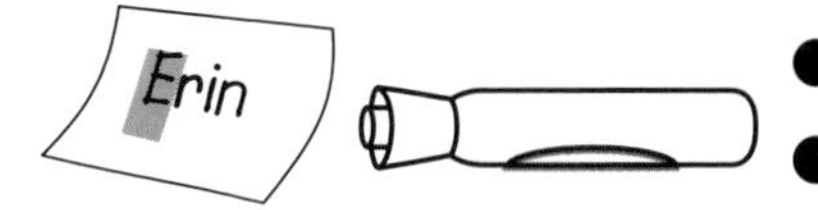

(4) Put 5 names in ABC order.

(5) Write the names in ABC order.

(6) Put the other names in ABC order. Write.

Step-by-step center activity: Put a copy of this activity card in a plastic page protector for durability. Then put the activity card and the needed materials at a center.

Terrific Trios

What You Need

2 number cubes
paper

What You Do

1. Draw two lines and a happy face.

2. Roll the cubes.

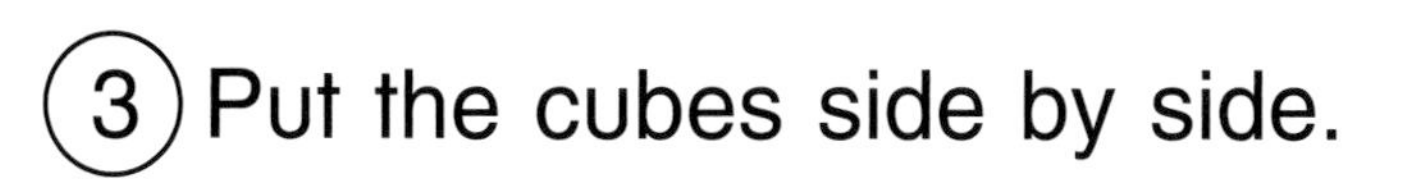

3. Put the cubes side by side.

4. Write the number you made.

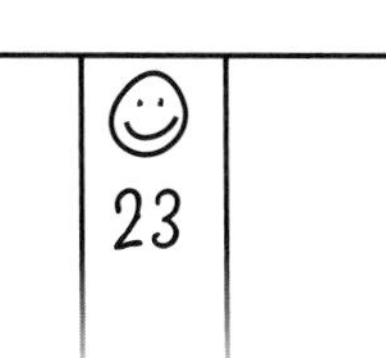

5. Write the number that comes just **before.**

22 | 23 |

6. Write the number that comes just **after.**

22 | 23 | 24

7. Do Steps 2–6 again.

Step-by-step center activity: Put a copy of this activity card in a plastic page protector for durability. Then put the activity card and the needed materials at a center.

Card Columns

What You Need

playing cards (no aces or face cards)
paper

What You Do

1. Take three cards.

2. Put the cards in the order you want to add them.

3. Write the addition problem.

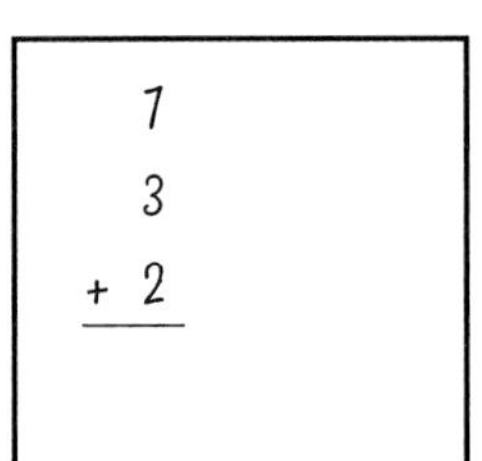

4. Write the answer.

7
3
+ 2
12

5. Do Steps 1–4 again.

Step-by-step center activity: Put a copy of this activity card in a plastic page protector for durability. Then put the activity card and the needed materials at a center.

Let's Do Social Studies!

Let's Do Social Studies!

Necessary or Nice?

Wants and needs

Here's a skill-based way to give students a new perspective on wish lists. Post the color code shown. On each of several days during the winter holiday season, display a wish list that includes both wants and needs. Read the list to students. Then reread each listed item, in turn, and have students draw either a red or green checkmark beside it to categorize it by the code.

Color Code
red—needs
green—wants

Kim Minafo
Dillard Drive Elementary
Raleigh, NC

Dear Santa,
Here is my wish list.
Love,
Rex

- ✔ water
- ✔ bike
- ✔ coat
- ✔ games
- ✔ computer
- ✔ fruit

For the Celebration

Understanding the significance of Kwanzaa

This tiny booklet is a big reminder of Kwanzaa symbols! Have each child color a copy of page 102 and cut out the cover and pages. Then ask her to stack the pages in numerical order and put the cover atop the stack. Staple the stack to make a booklet. Next, explain that Kwanzaa lasts for seven days. Then discuss the information below with students as they follow along in their booklets.

Kwanzaa Symbols and Meanings

mat: tradition
fruits of the harvest: hard work
candleholder: African ancestors
candles: seven principles of Kwanzaa
ears of corn: children and the future
unity cup: family and community unity
gifts: sharing and love

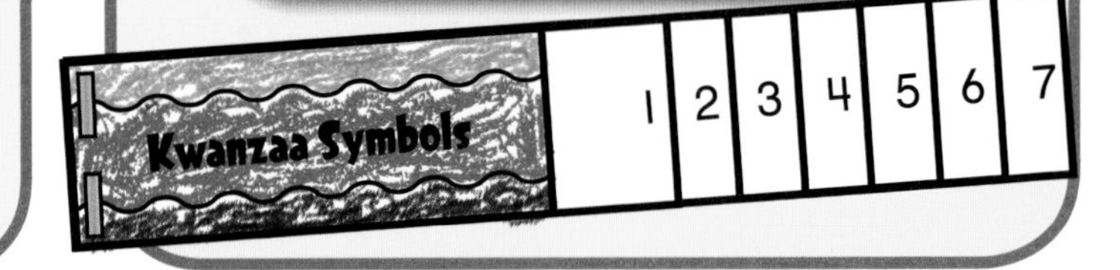

In a Word

Contributions of historic figures

Near Martin Luther King Day, read aloud a book about the civil rights leader, such as *Martin's Big Words* by Doreen Rappaport. Then draw a large circle on the board and label it "Dr. King." Have students name words that describe the historic leader. Write the words around the circle and create a web. Next, give each youngster a sheet of writing paper. Ask him to choose three or more words from the web and use them in sentences about Dr. King. Bind students' completed work between two covers and title the resulting book "Remember Dr. King!"

Let's Do Social Studies!

DC Delivery

Knowing patriotic holidays

This Presidents' Day idea helps you make the most of your time by incorporating writing into social studies. To begin, discuss the holiday and the current president with students. Then have each youngster plan a letter to the president on a graphic organizer like the one shown. After he writes and edits the letter, invite him to decorate it with red and blue stars or stickers. Mail students' letters and a class photo in one large envelope. No doubt youngsters will be thrilled to have their writing sent to the White House!

Joy Barnes
Hellen Caro Elementary
Pensacola, FL

Ms. Barnes' Class

The White House
1600 Pennsylvania Avenue NW
Washington, DC 20500

Letter Planner	
Who is the letter for?	the president
Why am I writing?	to say thank you to wish him a happy Presidents' Day
What can I ask about?	his job the White House his dog

Point the Way!

Cardinal directions

For this lively activity, give each youngster four sticky notes. Have her write the initial for each cardinal direction on a separate sticky note. Then instruct her to put the sticky note with *N* on her head, the sticky note with *S* on one of her feet, the sticky note with *E* on her right hand, and the sticky note with *W* on her left hand. Next, have students stand facing the same direction. Lead them in the song shown, encouraging them to move their heads, feet, or hands when they sing the corresponding cardinal direction.

(sung to the tune of "Head and Shoulders")

North and south, east and west,
East and west.
North and south, east and west,
East and west.
North and south and east and west.
North and south, east and west,
East and west!

Rachel Butler
Oak Ridge, NJ

Who's Who?

Knowing famous Americans

Use this quick activity on each of several days. To prepare, cut out a copy of the clue card from page 103 and have each child cut out a copy of the picture cards from the same page. To begin, have each student spread out his cards faceup. Next, read aloud a pair of clues. Ask each youngster to pick up the card that shows the corresponding person and hold it so the illustration is concealed. Once each child is holding a card, instruct students to turn their cards so you can see the illustrations. Then confirm the correct response. Read different clues to continue.

Karen Potter
Red Oak-Sturgeon Elementary
Alberta, VA

Let's Do Social Studies!

Song of Seven

Identifying the continents

Use these skill-boosting ideas with the song below.

Reading: Give each child a copy of the song. Point to a continent on a map and guide students to name it. Then instruct each youngster to use a crayon of a designated color to underline the continent's name in the song.

Geography: Invite a student to spin a globe as her classmates sing the song. Then have the youngster stop the globe by putting a finger on it. Ask her to name the continent closest to her finger.

adapted from an idea by Joanna Wu
Calahan Street School
Northridge, CA

(sung to the tune of
"Twinkle, Twinkle, Little Star")

Seven continents on the map—
Naming them can be a snap!
North and South America,
Europe, Asia, Australia,
And don't forget Africa
Or, way down south, Antarctica.

To-Do List

Identifying goods and services

For this real-life approach to economics, post a to-do list that involves goods and services. Read the list aloud. Then have student volunteers write an *S* or a *G* beside each errand to show whether it refers to purchasing a good or obtaining a service. To follow up, instruct each youngster to write a similar list, trade lists with a classmate, and then code his classmate's list.

Ms. Carson's To-Do List

S Go to the dentist.
G Buy a new book.
S Take my cat Snowball to the vet.
S Get my car oil changed.
G Buy a birthday cake for my daughter.
G Buy flowers for my patio.

From City to Planet

Understanding geographic locations

This simple booklet is a great visual aid! For each child, stack three vertical half sheets of paper (4¼" x 11"). Slide the top two sheets upward about one inch. Slide the top sheet up one more inch. Then fold the papers forward to create six graduated pages. Staple along the fold. To complete her booklet, a child writes the title and her name on the cover. She labels each page as shown and colors it. Then she writes on each page the name of the corresponding location and adds any desired illustrations. **For more advanced students,** use four half sheets of paper for each booklet and have students include pages for street and county.

Lisa Nelson
Horizons Home Study
Concord, CA

My World
by Chloe
city
state
country
continent
planet

Let's Do Social Studies!

Our Earth

Geography

Use this poetic booklet with a unit on land and water. To begin, give each child a copy of page 104. Read the booklet pages with students. Then have them circle designated words, such as *hills, mountain,* and *desert.* Next, instruct each youngster to use arts-and-crafts materials to illustrate one or more landforms on a horizontal 6" x 8" piece of paper. Ask him to cut out the booklet pages, stack them in order, and then place a 2½" x 8" paper strip atop the stack. After you staple the stack to the illustrated paper, as shown, have the youngster title the resulting booklet and sign his name on the strip.

adapted from an idea by Cindy Dailey
Labelle Elementary
Marietta, GA

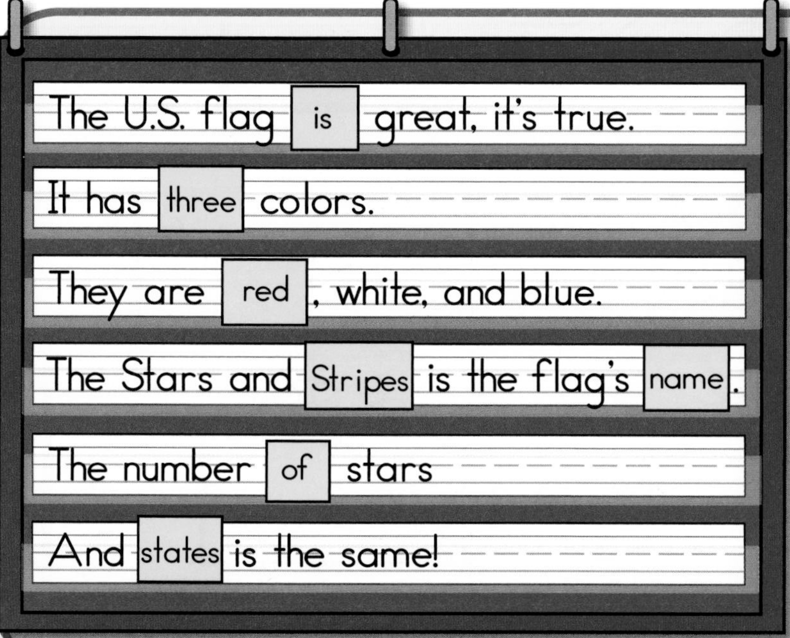

Flag Facts

Patriotic symbol

Pair reading and social studies with this pocket-chart idea. Display the poem shown, drawing blanks in place of several words. Write the missing words on separate cards. Then scramble the cards and display them near the poem. To begin, guide youngsters to use context clues and decoding skills to put each card in the correct place. Next, lead students in reading the poem a few times. Then help them determine how many stars are on the flag and how many states are in the United States.

Tip: If a large pocket chart isn't available, write the poem on chart paper and the missing words on large sticky notes.

Booklet Pages and Cover
Use with "For the Celebration" on page 98.

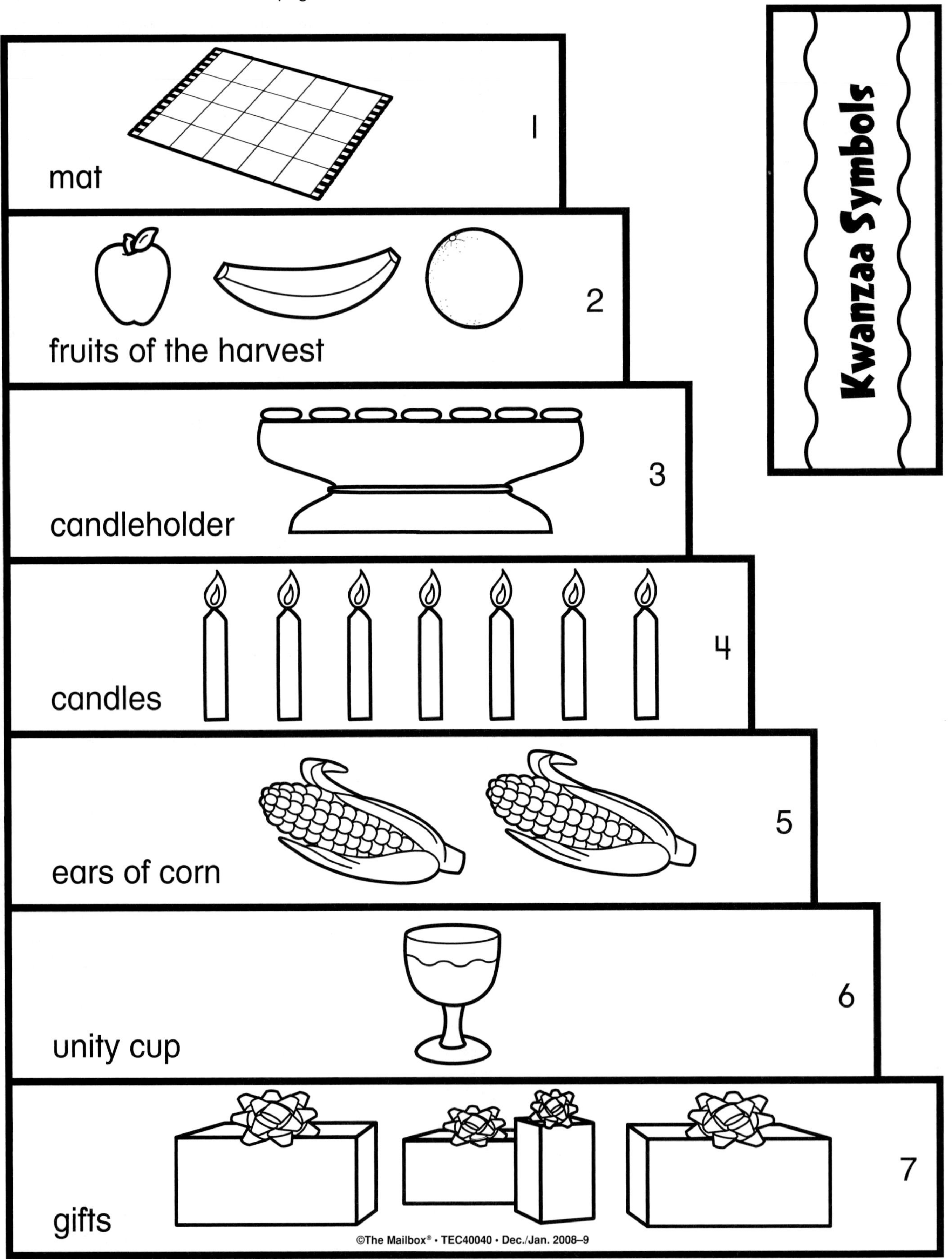

Use with "Who's Who?" on page 99.

Famous Americans

Clara Barton
Nurse for soldiers
Started the American Red Cross

George Washington Carver
Scientist
Made over 300 products from peanuts

Benjamin Franklin
Signed the Declaration of Independence
Inventor who studied electricity

Mae Jemison
Astronaut and doctor
First African American woman to travel in space

Martin Luther King Jr.
Civil rights leader
Gave the famous "I have a dream" speech

Abraham Lincoln
Helped end slavery
16th U.S. president

Rosa Parks
Seamstress
Refused to give her bus seat to a white person

George Washington
"Father of the Country"
First U.S. president

TEC40041

Booklet Pages

Use with "Our Earth" on page 101.

Our Earth is different
From place to place.
There are hills, rocks, and trees
And wide open space.

A mountain is high.
A valley is low.
On top of some mountains,
You will find snow.

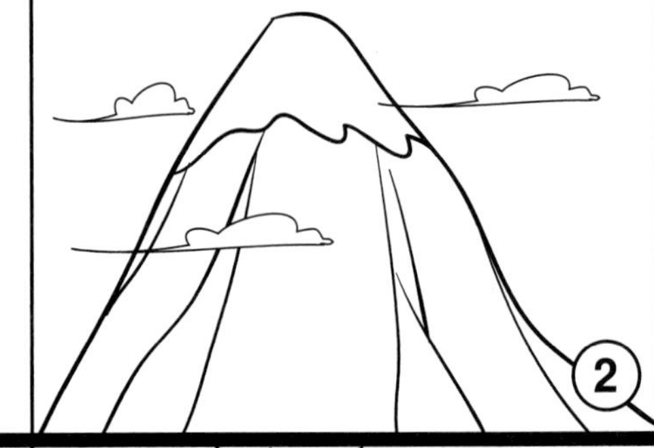

The water in oceans
Is salty and deep.
The coasts can be
Rocky, sandy, or steep.

A desert is dry.
It does not get much rain.
Some low, flat land
Is called a plain.

A plateau is flat,
But it's high, not low.
Our Earth is amazing,
As we all know.

Management Tips & Timesavers

Management Tips & Timesavers

Messages and Reminders

Make lost parent notes a thing of the past! For each child, make a blank booklet for home-school communication. Put the booklet in a personalized pocket folder in which you have fastened a top-loading page protector. Encourage each youngster to take his folder home daily and return it to school the next day. Whenever you write a note to a child's parents, alert them by putting the booklet in the page protector and have them do likewise when they write to you. If you need to give the whole class the same message, simply print the message on adhesive labels and place a label in each journal. *Michelle Morrow, Red Bank Elementary, Lexington, SC*

Handy for Helpers

For each classroom job, glue a corresponding labeled photo or picture to an individual library pocket. (See the picture cards on page 112.) Display the pockets as desired. Then put a personalized craft stick in each pocket to assign the jobs. To reassign the duties, just move the sticks to different pockets! *Katherine Boldt, McKinley Elementary, Appleton, WI*

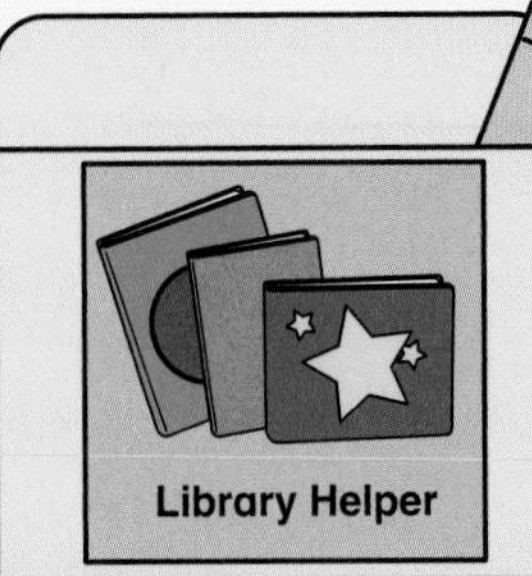

"A-peel-ing" Behavior

Here's a fresh approach to encouraging positive behavior! Trace a large apple cutout on a paper-backed bulletin board. Then draw a leaf and stem. Next, visually divide the back of the cutout into several sections and number them sequentially. Then cut apart the sections. Whenever students exhibit exceptionally good behavior, post an apple section on the board so the pieces are displayed in order. After the entire apple is assembled, reward the students as desired. *Heather E. Graley, Grace Christian School, Blacklick, OH*

Hands, Feet, and More!

This call-and-response chant helps students line up quickly.

Teacher: Hands
Students: Back *(Put hands behind backs.)*

Teacher: Feet
Students: Together *(Put feet together.)*

Teacher: Face
Students: Forward *(Face the front.)*

Teacher: Mouth
Students: Mmm *(Stop talking.)*

Aubrey Brinkmeyer, West End Elementary, Industry, TX

Personal Space

To help each student stay in his own area during floor activities, have youngsters sit on inexpensive vinyl placemats. The placemats clearly define each youngster's space. Plus, they're easy to clean and require little storage space. For added kid appeal, use different placemats throughout the year to correspond with topics of study or the seasons. *Jennifer Weinstein, Trumansburg Elementary, Trumansburg, NY*

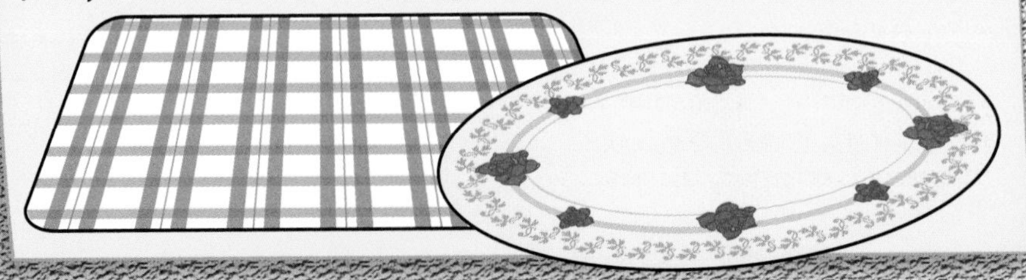

Management Tips & Timesavers

Pleasing Paper Storage

For quick and easy access to different colors of construction paper, label a separate hanging file folder for each color. Store the paper in the appropriate folders in a file cabinet or crate. The paper will stay in good condition, and you'll have the colors you need at your fingertips! *Anna N. Morris, L. B. J. Elementary, Jackson, KY*

Mess-Free Painting

Cleaning paint cups is a snap with this idea! Before you pour paint into a paint cup, place a small resealable plastic bag in the cup and then turn the top of the bag over the edge of the cup. When it's time to clean the cup, simply remove the bag and throw it away. Or, if you want to save unused paint, seal the bag for later use. Either way, you won't have messy paint cups! *adapted from an idea by Laura Boeve, Beverly Elementary, Beverly Hills, MI*

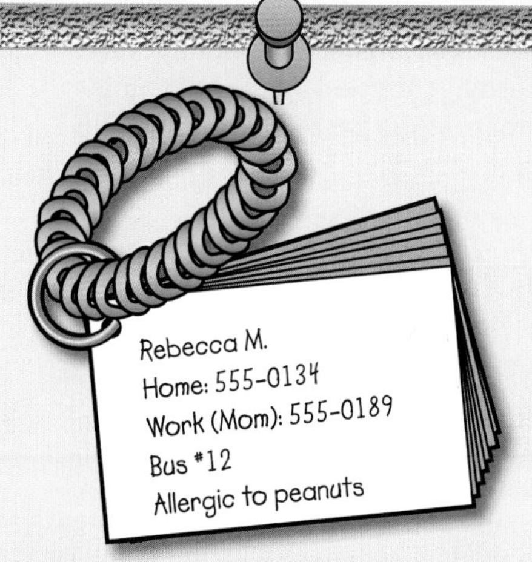

Ready for Emergencies

To keep students' emergency information close at hand, list each child's contact, transportation, and pertinent health information on a separate blank card. Punch a hole in each card and secure the cards on a coil key ring. Keep the key ring near your classroom door. Whenever you and your students leave the room, slip the key ring on your wrist. If there is a fire drill or an emergency when you're away from the room, you'll have the information you need! *Karen Potter, Red Oak-Sturgeon Elementary, Alberta, VA*

Space Dividers

If your students have difficulty staying in their own table space, divide the tops of the tables with colorful electrical tape. The tape clearly defines each student's work area. Plus, if you use different-colored tape for each table, you can identify each group by color! *Laura Chapman, Chapel Glen Elementary, Indianapolis, IN*

Picture Perfect

With this tip, even young students can keep classroom supplies neat and organized! In each classroom area in which students use materials independently, post a photo that shows how the area should look. If desired, color-code the supplies and the shelves or containers where they belong. Not only will students know where to return the supplies, but they will also know how to arrange them! *Melissa Rent, Stonegate Elementary, Zionsville, IN*

Paired in a Jiffy

Here's a quick and easy way to assign partners. Get a class supply of craft sticks of two different colors, ensuring that there is an equal number of each color. Write each student's name on a different stick so the names of students who need more advanced learning buddies are on sticks of the same color. To designate a student pair, simply take one stick of each color. ***Chris Holmstrom, Bristol Elementary, Bristol, WI***

Fuss-Free Lines

Try this letter-perfect approach to having students line up. Ask students to line up alphabetically by their first names on each of several days. On the next several days, have them line up alphabetically by their last names. Then, each following day, designate a line helper and have him decide whether students will line up alphabetically by their first names or their last names. ***Emile Blake, Sherrills Ford Elementary, Sherrills Ford, NC***

Practical Pockets

To keep activities and materials at your fingertips, hang a pocket shoe bag in your classroom. Then stock it with games to use when the class has a few minutes between activities. If desired, also stock pocket shoe bags with art supplies and learning center activities. The pockets keep the materials neat, organized, and easy to access! ***Deanna Calvert, Kendall-Whittier Elementary, Tulsa, OK***

Flashlight Fridays

This bright idea promotes both positive behavior and reading! Display a blank grid with a picture of a flashlight. Whenever your class exhibits exceptionally good behavior, color a grid space yellow. Once the grid is completely colored, schedule a Flashlight Friday. On the designated day, darken the room and use flashlights during storytime. Or pair up with another teacher and arrange for students to take turns reading with flashlights in one classroom while the remaining students listen to a read-aloud in the other classroom. ***Erin Taylor, Kennedy Elementary, Terrell, TX***

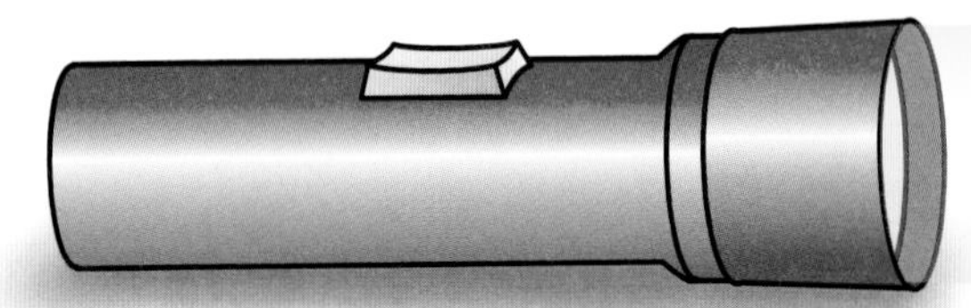

Norman the Name Bear

If your students often forget to put their names on their papers, try this! Put a stuffed bear that you named Norman near where students turn in their papers. Then place a highlighter in the animal's paws. Just before a student turns in a paper, have him highlight his name. If he forgot to write it, no doubt he'll remember to add it when he sees Norman! ***Stacy Musick, St. Thomas Elementary, St. Thomas, PA***

Management Tips & Timesavers

Check It Out!

To keep track of class books and other items students take home on a rotating basis, personalize a tote bag. Then program the front of a blank card with the message shown and the back of it with your class list. Laminate the card and attach it to the bag. Before a youngster takes an item home, ask him to write his name and the name of the item on the board. After he returns the item, cross his name off the class list and have him erase his name from the board. ***Kirsten Parr, Germantown Hills Elementary, Metamora, IL***

Pocket Pal

Keep overhead manipulatives at your fingertips! Simply tie a carpenter's waist apron around an overhead projector and then put the manipulatives in the pockets. ***Reba Vuncannon, Cedar Park Elementary, Trumann, AR***

Rewarding Locations

For this weekly incentive plan, post a laminated coordinate grid. Write each coordinate on a separate piece of paper and put the papers in a container. When a youngster demonstrates exceptional positive behavior or achieves a homework completion goal, ask her to use a wipe-off marker to mark a grid location and label it with her initials. At the end of the week, take a paper from the container and give the youngster who marked the corresponding grid location a reward. (If no one marked the location, draw another paper.) Wipe off the grid to prepare it for another week. ***Danielle Watt, St. Aloysius Gonzaga School, Buffalo, NY***

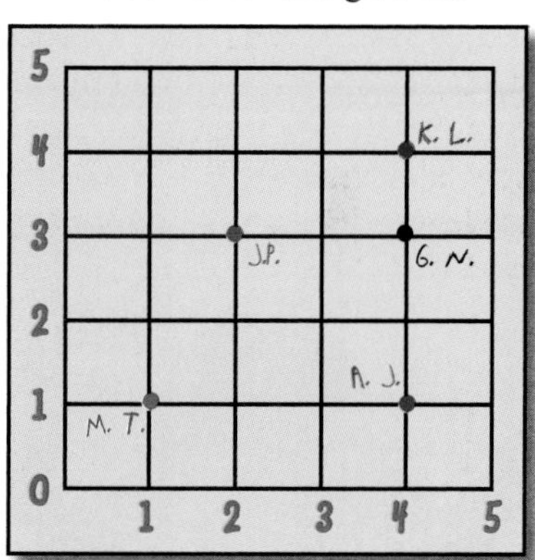

Peer Solutions

Each week designate two youngsters as Problem Solvers. Whenever students have a disagreement, encourage them to enlist the help of the Problem Solvers. The students are sure to come up with creative solutions, and you'll have more time to teach! ***Lu Auer, Ivy Hall Elementary, Buffalo Grove, IL***

Fast Finishers

For each student, make a copy of a list similar to the one shown. Attach the list to a folder for her incomplete or ongoing assignments. Whenever a youngster finishes a task with time to spare, have her work on any assignments in her folder and then do a listed activity. ***Candice Wells, Elias Boudinot Elementary, Burlington City, NJ***

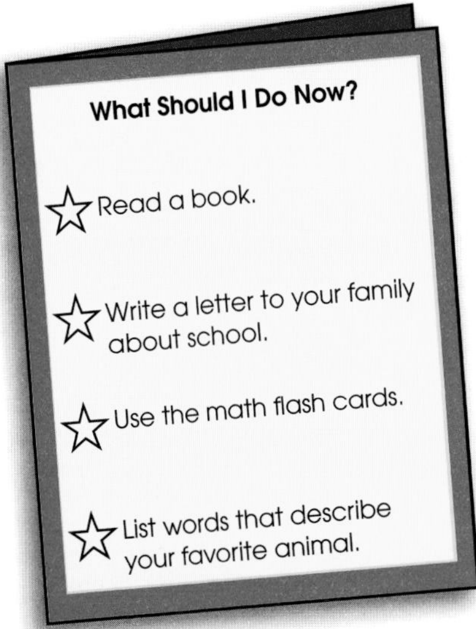

Management Tips & Timesavers

Spotting Good Behavior

For this class incentive, display a large ladybug cutout that has Xs in place of spots. Each time your class exhibits exceptionally positive behavior, attach a black circle to an X with reusable adhesive. After all the Xs are covered, reward students as desired. Then remove the circles to begin another round of the incentive plan.

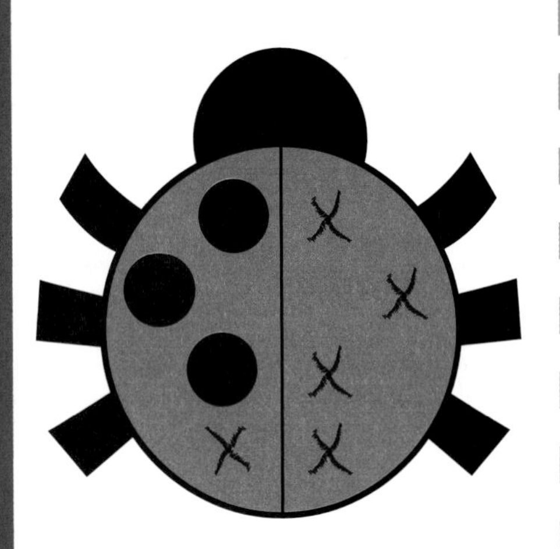

Write and Toss

When you trim laminated classroom materials, save the scrap pieces of laminating film. Use the pieces instead of blank overhead transparencies on an overhead projector and then discard them. Not only will you save money, but you'll also save time since you don't need to wipe the film clean! ***Eileen Miller, Olivet Elementary, Pittsgrove, NJ***

Hall Honor

To motivate students to walk quietly in the hall, put a class supply of personalized craft sticks in a lunch bag. Whenever the class lines up to leave the classroom, secretly remove two sticks from the bag. After the class reaches its destination, read the names on the sticks. Then give each named youngster who walked appropriately a sticker or another reward. ***Ginger Edwards, Wyalusing Elementary, Wyalusing, PA***

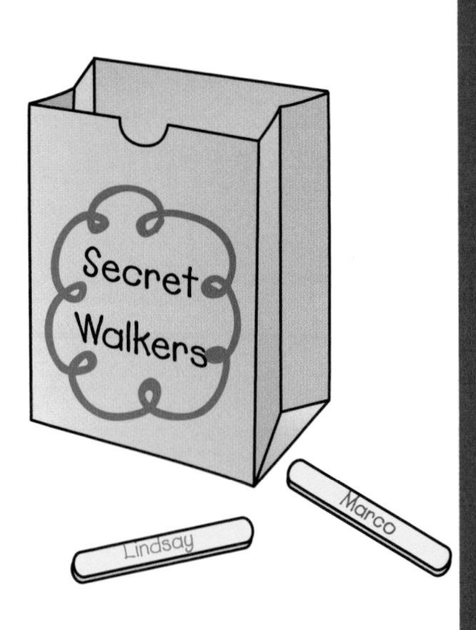

Great for Subs

Count on your substitute teachers to love this handy reference! To prepare, attach a small photo of each student to the inside of a file folder. Then write below each photo the corresponding child's name and information such as any medication or support services he needs. ***Antoinette Lucero, Cesar E. Chavez Community School, Phoenix, AZ***

Check It Off!

Instead of trying to remember the prep work you need to do each week, try this! List the tasks by day and make a copy of the list at the beginning of each week. Throughout the week, check off each task after you complete it. Use the back of the list to jot down information you want to include in your next newsletter. It's a stress-free way to stay organized and gain a sense of accomplishment! ***Shelia Criqui-Kelley, Lebo Elementary, Lebo, KS***

Checklist for the Week of April 20

Monday
✓ Put lesson plans in Mr. Och's box.
✓ Cut out laminated items.
✓ Change center activities.

Tuesday
✓ Type reading words.
✓ File word cards.

Wednesday
___ Update gradebook.
___ Put out Desk Fairy notes.

Thursday
___ Put weekend projects on desks.
___ Write newsletter.

Friday
___ Take five student folders home.
___ Change classroom helpers' chart.
___ Change weekly poem.

Management Tips & Timesavers

Busy Bees

This honey of an idea promotes positive independent work habits. Post a large hive cutout labeled with a number. Whenever you observe students working well independently, illustrate a yellow sticky dot so it resembles a bee and then attach it to the hive. When the number of bees matches the number on the hive, reward the class.

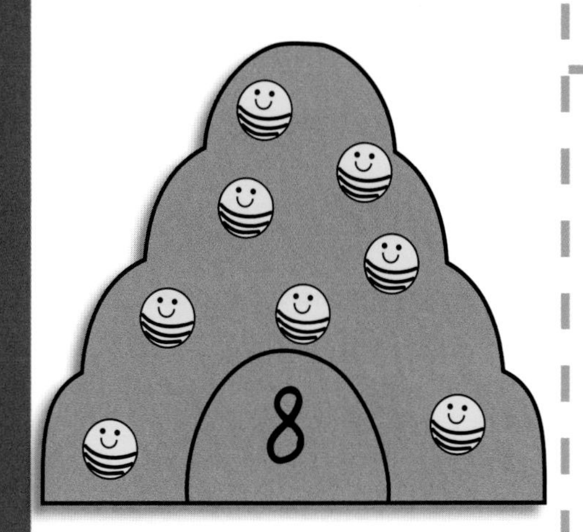

Call on All

Looking for a fresh way to ensure every student has a turn answering questions? Try this! First, assign each child a number and write the numbers on separate clothespins. Put the clothespins in a container and then string a clothesline. To determine who you will call on, select a clothespin without revealing the number. Next, say a math problem whose answer is the number on the clothespin. Once students determine the correct answer, call on the student with the matching assigned number and clip her clothespin to the clothesline. After you have called on each student, return the clothespins to the container. ***Bridgette Cerny, John C. French Elementary, Cuero, TX***

On the Same Page

Keep a craft foam frame or a mat for a picture frame in a top corner of your board. Whenever you instruct students to turn to a particular page in a book, write the page number as shown. If students forget the page number, they can easily find it on the board! ***Tzippora Metzger, Yeshivah of Flatbush, Brooklyn, NY***

Great Group Work

To encourage students to work cooperatively in groups, designate a different color for each group. Put pushpins that match the group colors in a row on a bulletin board so there is one pushpin per group. Then hang a plastic math link or a monkey from a Barrel of Monkeys game on each pushpin to begin a chain. Whenever a group demonstrates good work habits, add a link or monkey to its chain. When a group's chain is a designated length, reward each group member with a sticker. ***Kathi Rogers, Maxwell Air Force Base Elementary, Maxwell Air Force Base, AL***

Field Trip Helpers

Just before you take your class on a field trip, give each chaperone a list of guidelines. It's a simple way to share your expectations and ensure that the adults are tracking with one another! ***Anita Miller, Mease Elementary, Dakota City, IA***

Guidelines for Field Trip Chaperones

1. Remind students to
   - be good listeners
   - keep their hands and feet to themselves
   - walk, not run
2. Praise students who follow directions.
3. Let me know if any discipline problems come up.
4. Have fun!

Picture Cards

Use with "Handy for Helpers" on page 106.

Our Readers Write

Our Readers Write

Picture This!

Here's a kid-pleasing way to introduce yourself to students. Gather a few photos of yourself from when you were about their age. Then display the photos as desired in a prominent classroom location. No doubt youngsters will enjoy seeing that you were once a student just like them!

Mary Beth Pugh
Vance Elementary
Vance, AL

Glue Guidance

To help students use an appropriate amount of glue on projects, I teach them this simple rhyme.

How Much?
Just a little glue will do.
Just a dot, not a lot.

Ina Austin
W. G. Mallet School
Farmington, ME

Pleasing Portfolios

On the first day of school, I have each student draw an illustration on the front of a personalized file folder. Then I collect the folders. Every month I have each youngster choose a sample of his best work for me to put in his folder. At the end of the school year, I return each student's folder and ask him to draw an illustration on the back of it. When students compare their two illustrations and review their work samples, they're sure to be amazed by the progress they made!

Susan Schipper
Charles Street School
Palmyra, NJ

Seasonal Center Signs

My center signs double as classroom decorations. I make large seasonal cutouts and laminate them for durability. For example, I make apples in the fall, snowpals in the winter, and flowers in the spring. I suspend each sign above the corresponding center or supply area. They make my classroom bright and cheery!

Jennifer Farneski, Watsessing School
Bloomfield, NJ

Serving Up Math

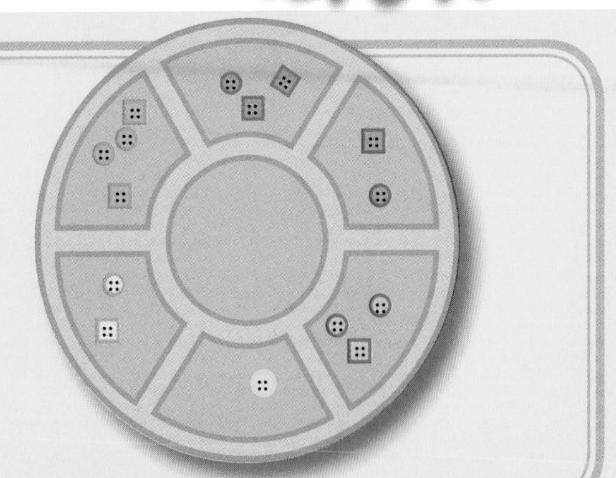

One of the best sorting tools I have is an inexpensive sectioned serving tray. Since the tray has several sections, it's perfect for sorting objects by various attributes, such as size, shape, and color!

Erin Green
Rosewood Elementary
Rock Hill, SC

Center Locations

When it's time to set up your classroom for back-to-school, purchase some inexpensive tablecloths. I use tablecloths to cover center tables and work areas. They not only designate the center areas but also make my room look inviting. I change the tablecloths each season to give my room a fresh look.

Bonnie Lee Gaynor, Franklin Elementary, Franklin, NJ

Word Bird

I love using puppets in my classroom! I named one puppet Word Bird and use it to reinforce word recognition. Each week Word Bird wears selected sight words around his neck. When it is time to review the words, he "chooses" students to read them aloud. Youngsters are always eager to show off their reading skills for Word Bird!

Nancy Aquino
Steele School
Baldwin, NY

Birthdays in Bloom

I make students' birthdays special with this space-saving alternative to a birthday bulletin board. I write each student's name and birthdate on a flower cutout. I decorate each cutout with a birthday sticker and then attach the cutouts to separate birthday pencils. I put floral foam in a labeled plastic window box. Then I stand the pencils in the foam. When it's time to celebrate a student's birthday, I invite her to "pick" her birthday bloom!

Amanda Kaye Bain, Wrights Mill Road Elementary
Auburn, AL

Neat Nametags

Keeping my students' nametags neat and secure on their tables was a challenge until I started using Velcro fasteners. Now I attach the loop side of a Velcro fastener to each student's place at a table and the hook side to the back of his nametag. I can easily detach the nametags, so it's a snap to reassign students' seats!

Molly Lynch
Arundel School
San Carlos, CA

Our Readers Write

Wonderful Weavings

During our spider unit, I tell my students about different types of webs, such as orb, triangular, flat, and tangled webs. Then I have each youngster use rubber bands and a Geoboard to make a model of a web we learned about or a web of his own creation. It gives students a new appreciation for nature!

Kelly Finch
Vaughan Elementary
Powder Springs, GA

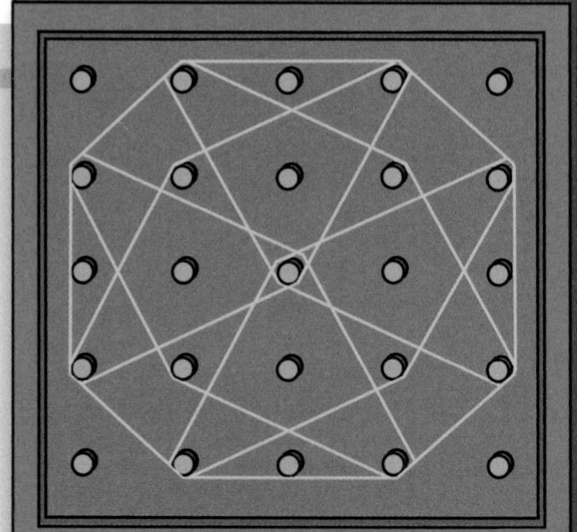

For Parents

Before fall parent-teacher conferences, I showcase on a hallway wall photographs of classroom activities, field trips, and special school events. Then I post captions on leaf cutouts. The display is easy to prepare and it's an excellent way to show parents what their children have been doing at school. After I take the display down, I save the photos in a class scrapbook or send them home with students.

Emily Ryherd
Helen Baker Elementary
Glencoe, MN

Turkey Tune

Here's a cute song that's perfect for a Thanksgiving performance.

(sung to the tune of "I'm a Little Teapot")

I'm a little turkey, *(Place hands on hips.)*
Short and fat.

Here on the farm *(Point down.)*
Is where I've sat.

When it's near *(Cup hands*
Thanksgiving, *around mouth.)*
Hear me shout,

"Open the gate *(Swing arm out.)*
And let me out!"

Stephanie Ives
Deep Springs Elementary
Lexington, KY

Seasonal Reading Sticks

After my colleagues or I make seasonal cutouts with a die-cut machine, I laminate several castoffs. Then I attach each castoff to a separate ruler to make reading sticks. My students and I use the sticks to frame letters, numbers, and sight words. Youngsters also use the sticks when they "read" the room!

Linda Tavares
Clara Macy Elementary
Bellingham, MA

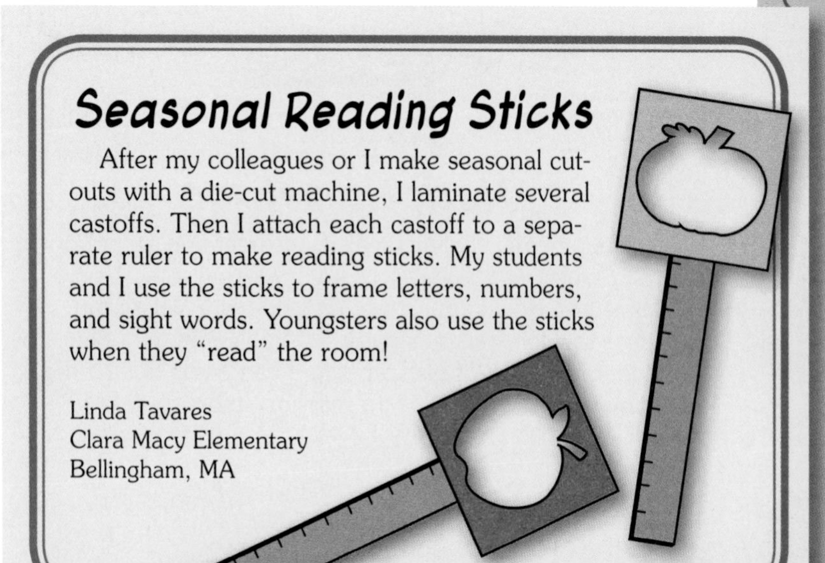

Clever Countdown

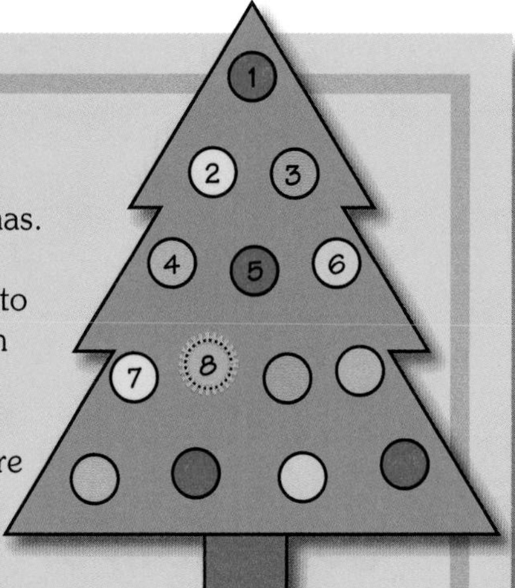

My students love this display because it builds their anticipation for Christmas. I love it because it reinforces counting backward! I make one circle for each school day before the holiday. I number the circles and use reusable adhesive to post them on a tree cutout. Then I put a ring of garland around the circle with the greatest number. To start the countdown, a student removes the garland, turns over the corresponding circle, and then moves the garland to the next greatest number. Students update the display each day until all the numbers are turned over.

Tina Ellis
Divide Elementary
Lookout, WV

Switcheroo

Since my students don't get much outdoor physical activity in the winter, I use this idea to add movement and excitement to the day. During a chosen paper-and-pencil task, I say, "Switcheroo!" Then, as I count to ten, each child quickly takes his paper and goes to another seat to finish his work. My students get a kick out of sitting at someone else's place!

Lisa Coppola
Blessed Sacrament School
Syracuse, NY

Reading Chains

I channel students' holiday enthusiasm into sight word practice. Each youngster writes a sight word on each of several holiday-colored paper strips. Then he forms a paper chain with the strips so the colors create a pattern and the words face outward. We display the chains around the classroom for several days before students take them home and use them as holiday decorations.

Bonnie Cazer
Canandaigua Primary
Canandaigua, NY

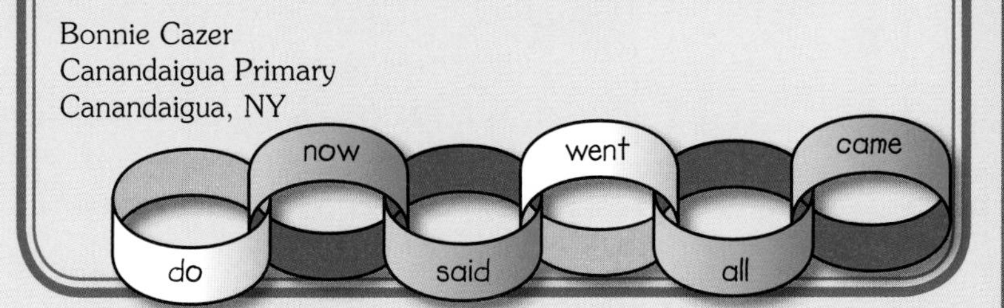

Festive Pages

This class book idea is easy to adapt to any holiday. I give each youngster a sheet of story paper. Then I ask her to draw holiday sights and traditions and write about them. I stack students' completed papers between two covers. Then I punch two holes at the top of the stack, thread a ribbon through the holes, and tie the ribbon into a bow. The resulting book looks like a holiday gift!

Helaine Rooney
Georgian Forest Elementary
Silver Spring, MD

Our Readers Write

Word Wall Alternative

I cover a small empty tissue box with decorative Con-Tact covering. Then I make word cards with vocabulary from a story and attach them to the box. I use different boxes for different stories. They're a great alternative to word walls since they're portable and fun to display.

Sister Kathleen Leary
St. Augustine School
Andover, MA

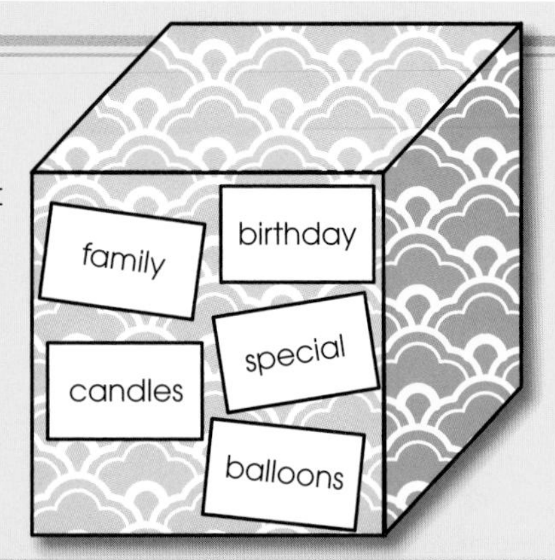

Consonant or Vowel?

For a quick, focused lesson, I write a student's name on the board. Then I ask the youngster to use a pointer to direct her classmates' attention to each letter in turn. As she points to each letter, I have the youngsters identify it as a consonant or vowel. Every child looks forward to having her name in the spotlight!

Rebecca Watkins
Columbia County Christian School
Bloomsburg, PA

Great Graph

Don't throw away old blank calendars. Use them to make large graph grids! I cut off the days of the week from two large blank calendars. I tape the calendars together to make one grid and then post it on a wall. After I designate the graph topic and headings, I have students complete the graph. It's a quick and easy activity. Plus my students enjoy it!

Sara Miller
All Saints Episcopal School
Lubbock, TX

Reusable Graphic Organizers

I use a permanent marker to draw graphic organizers on small whiteboards. My students and I use wipe-off markers to complete them. When we wipe off the information later, the organizers stay intact. Since the organizers are always ready to use, I can use them on the spur of the moment!

Diane Billman
McKitrick Elementary
Lutz, FL

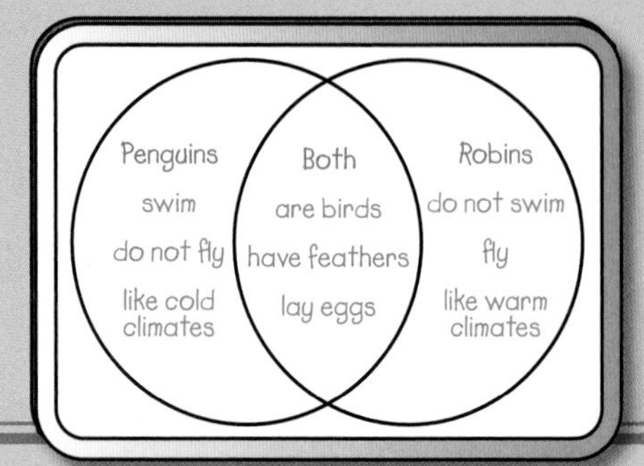

Honored Student Writers

To keep my students' writing motivation high during the second half of the year, each day I choose a youngster to read her writing to the class over the school intercom. The other students in my class eagerly wait to hear their classmate, and the honored youngster feels like a star. I give her a copy of the special note on page 124 to mark the occasion.

Betsy Charbonneau
Bristol Grade School
Bristol, IL

Textured Cabins

I found a really fun way for my students to make illustrations of Abraham Lincoln's log cabin. Each youngster draws a log cabin on the smooth side of brown corrugated paper. After he cuts out the cabin, he makes a door and one or two windows. He glues the cabin to a sheet of paper so the textured side is faceup. Then he adds background details such as trees. My students love the textured artwork!

Heather E. Graley
Grace Christian School
Blacklick, OH

Friendly Fridays

Every Friday morning, I have students pair up. Then I give the students time to study or read together. They might reread a recent reading selection, go over spelling words, review vocabulary words, or get ready for a test. My students enjoy working with their friends, so they always look forward to reviewing in this way.

Brooke McGrath
West Corinth Elementary
Corinth, MS

February Author Studies

During National Black History Month, I tell my students about different African American authors and read some of their books aloud. It not only helps youngsters connect with African-American achievements, but it also exposes them to great literature.

Jen Goldman
Sol Feinstone Elementary
Newtown, PA

Donald Crews: *Sail Away*
Patricia C. McKissack: *Goin' Someplace Special*
Faith Ringgold: *Tar Beach*

Hundred Highlights

Here's how I emphasize number patterns with a pocket hundred chart. I cut colorful plastic notebook dividers into squares that are the same size as pocket chart number cards. I display the number cards as usual. Then I have students put a colorful square in each of several pockets to highlight a chosen number pattern. Since the numbers show through the plastic, the patterns really stand out!

Rosemary Cliburn
Christian Home and Bible School
Mount Dora, FL

Beautiful Butterflies

For a supereasy spring project, I set out a container of cellophane grass or paper confetti. (To control static cling, I put fabric softener sheets at the bottom of the container or use antistatic spray above the container.) I have each child stuff a resealable plastic sandwich bag with cellophane grass or confetti. Then I help him twist a pipe cleaner around the middle of the bag to form wings and antennae. The butterflies look fantastic tacked to a bulletin board or suspended in my classroom!

Diane L. Flohr-Henderson
Kent City Elementary
Kent City, MI

Snack Surprise

I combine donated snack items—such as cereal, pretzels, and animal crackers—to make a snack mix. I mix in a few gummy worms and then offer each child a serving. I give the youngsters who receive gummy worms a small reward or special privilege. It adds excitement to the day and makes our snacks go further.

Sheila Criqui-Kelley
Lebo Elementary
Lebo, KS

Just for Mom

With this Mother's Day idea, each child's gift is unique. I give each child a blank puzzle. I ask her to write and illustrate on the puzzle a message for her mother. Then I have her take the puzzle apart and put it in a decorated envelope or box to prepare it for delivery.

Jannelle Weiss
Carousel School
Rancho Cordova, CA

Namely, Alphabetical

To determine the lunch count for my students, I post the headings "Cold Lunch" and "Hot Lunch" on a magnetic board. I have each youngster put a personalized magnet below the appropriate heading. Later, I ask a student to prepare the display for the next day by moving the names to the side and arranging them in alphabetical order. (I have him check his work against a class list.) It saves me time. Plus it gives students real-life skill practice!

Sarah Gregory
St. Gabriel School
Kansas City, MO

Our Readers Write

School of Readers

Here's one way I motivate my students to read. I give each child a paper with several fish illustrations. Each time the youngster reads at home for a designated amount of time, she colors a fish. After all the fish are colored and a parent signs the paper, I invite the child to put a sticky dot (scale) on a fish cutout. The more she reads, the more colorful the cutout becomes!

Cathy Adamek
Dr. S. G. Knight Elementary
Randall, MN

Read It Again!

To make a class book of the educational newspapers my class receives, I connect two covers with metal rings. After I go over an issue of the newspaper with students, I secure a copy of it between the covers. Youngsters enjoy rereading the newspapers since they're familiar with them!

Georgia Hayes
Christian Center School
Sioux Falls, SD

Words I Spy

This literacy activity requires no advance preparation. I simply set a timer for a few minutes and have each student write words he sees around the classroom. When the time is up, I invite the student with the most words to read his list aloud while classmates mark the corresponding words on their lists. Then I ask a different student to read any other words she wrote. We continue until all the words are read.

Sara Cohen
Chabad School
Brooklyn, NY

✓after ✓art
✓because ✓music
✓brother class
people ✓window
there ✓April
Thursday library

Roll a Vowel!

For a fun spelling review, I give each student a list of words that have blanks in place of the vowels. Students roll a die and use the code shown to complete the words. For a game version, I pair students. The first player in each twosome to complete all the words wins!

Jennifer Johnson
Dr. Nathan Cohen Elementary
Elmira Heights, NY

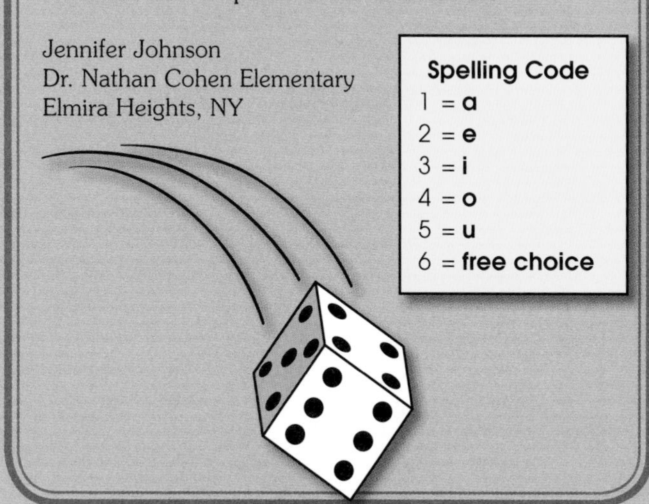

Photo Fun

I love to use a digital camera to complement my teaching! For math, I take photos of objects and have students name the corresponding solid figures. For science, I take photos of plants and trees. They're perfect for class discussions about similarities and differences. I also incorporate photos of class activities into computer-generated presentations that I show students.

Heather Minter
Meadville Elementary
Nathalie, VA

Summer Birthdays

Near the end of the school year, I post a jumbo cake cutout on a bulletin board. I decorate the cake with candle cutouts, one for each student who has a birthday in the summer. I lead the class in singing a birthday song for each honored youngster. Then I serve all the students special snacks.

Marie E. Cecchini
West Dundee, IL

Staple-Pulling Pal

I discovered a great alternative to staple removers: fingernail clippers! They work well in places that are too small for staple removers.

Sharon Isner
East Elementary
East Waynesville, MO

Stamp of Appreciation

Here's a gift idea for classroom volunteers that's easy enough for my students to help with. To make one gift, use fabric paint and stamps to decorate a white cotton kitchen towel (not terry cloth). If desired, add details with fabric crayons. Follow the directions on the craft supply packaging to set the colors. Then gift-wrap the towel and present it to the volunteer along with a class thank-you note.

Pamela Berry
St. Croix Catholic School
Stillwater, MN

Pleasing Present

My students enjoy making these bookmarks for Father's Day, but they are great gifts for any occasion. I give each youngster a bookmark like the one shown. I have him write his name on the bookmark and use paint to make a colorful fingerprint on each point of the starburst. After the prints are dry, I attach a photo of the youngster to the starburst. Then I laminate the bookmark for durability.

Barbara Cohen, Horace Mann School
Cherry Hill, NJ

Our Readers Write

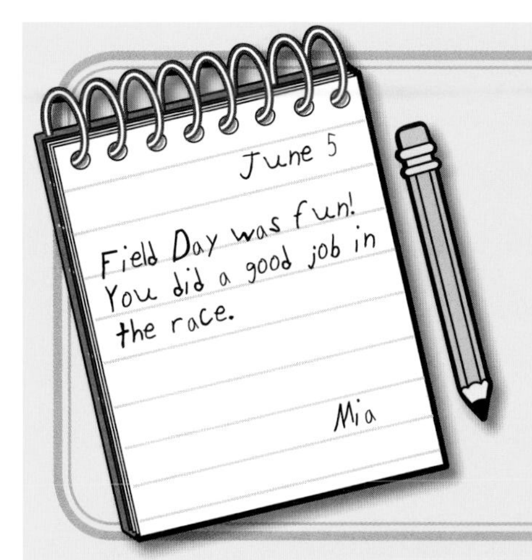

Friendship Fridays

Each Friday, I pair students for a variety of activities. For example, partners might read books to one another, read two-part readers' theater scripts, or write and illustrate stories together. Each student might also make an entry in her partner's friendship journal—a small personalized notebook. The journals are wonderful keepsakes for students!

Kathi Rogers
Maxwell Air Force Base Elementary
Maxwell Air Force Base, AL

Authors' Lunch

To promote writing and family involvement, I have my first graders take story paper home at the beginning of the week. I encourage each student to write a story at home and bring it to school by Friday. At the end of the week, I invite each student who wrote a story to join me for lunch. I invite their families and other staff members too. Students love to read their stories aloud during lunch, and their families enjoy the opportunity to hear them!

Teresa A. Thomas
Roberson Elementary
Granbury, TX

Word Wall Tag

To prepare this fun spelling review, I instruct each student to write on a small blank card a word from our word wall. Then I have students take their cards outdoors or to the gym. Students play the traditional game of Freeze Tag except that to unfreeze a classmate, a student must spell the youngster's word correctly.

Bethany Ficks
Cornerstone Christian Academy
Bloomington, IL

D-o-w-n.
Down.

Manipulative Solution

When my students work with manipulatives—such as imitation coins, dice, and pattern blocks—I have each youngster use a sheet of craft foam as a workmat. It cuts down on the noise. Plus it helps prevent the manipulatives from sliding off the desks and tables.

Colleen Bernhardt
Norwalk Catholic School
Norwalk, OH

Gameboards for Groups

File-folder games are too small for large groups, so I make big gameboards that I can display on an easel. To make one, I cut a sheet of posterboard in half. Next, I tape the two halves together, leaving ¼" between them so the gameboard can fold easily. Then I complete the gameboard with illustrations, a sticky dot game trail, or game pieces that I attach with Velcro fasteners.

Karen Smith
Pace, FL

 Note to the teacher: Use with "Honored Student Writers" on page 118.

Seasonal Activity Cards

Seasonal Activity Cards

Cut out a copy of the cards and have students complete the activities.

Counting coins

Cool Deal

Rex Reindeer got a hat for 50¢. Draw two different sets of coins that equal 50¢.

TEC40040

Addition combinations

Yum!

The jars have 12 cookies in all. Write addition sentences to show how many cookies could be in each jar.

TEC40040

Synonyms

Just for You!

Gift has almost the same meaning as **present.** Write words that have almost the same meaning as these words:

little   begin
glad   say
fast   tug

TEC40040

Action words

On the Move

Imagine Snowman Sam can dance, sing, and run. Write 10 more action words that tell what he might do.

TEC40040

Cut out a copy of the cards and have students complete the activities.

Problem solving

Roll Them!

It takes three snowballs to make one snowman. How many snowmen could you make with 12 snowballs?

TEC40040

Patterning

Super Scarves

Draw a scarf with an **AAB** pattern. Then draw a scarf with an **ABB** pattern.

TEC40040

Alliteration

Mitten Mania

Marty Moose makes mittens for many mice.

Write more silly sentences about Marty Moose. Use lots of **m** words!

TEC40040

Consonant blend: *sl*

Playful Penguins

Penguins can **slide** on the ice. Write two different words that begin with **sl.** Then write sentences with them.

TEC40040

Seasonal Activity Cards

Cut out a copy of the cards and have students complete the activities.

Number sense

That's the Date!

Valentine's Day is February 14. Use addition or subtraction to show 14 in different ways.

TEC42041

Problem solving

From the Heart

Digger wants to give each friend 2 hearts. He has 12 friends. How many hearts does he need?

TEC42041

Consonant blend: *gr*

Perfect for Groundhogs

Greta Groundhog likes **gr** words. Write 6 **gr** words. Then use 2 words in sentences about Greta.

TEC42041

Writing to explain

A Sweet Treat?

Would you like to work in a candy factory? Why or why not?

TEC42041

Counting coins

Coins for Cake

The cake costs 55¢. Mr. Rabbit has 6 dimes.
Can he buy the cake? Why or why not?

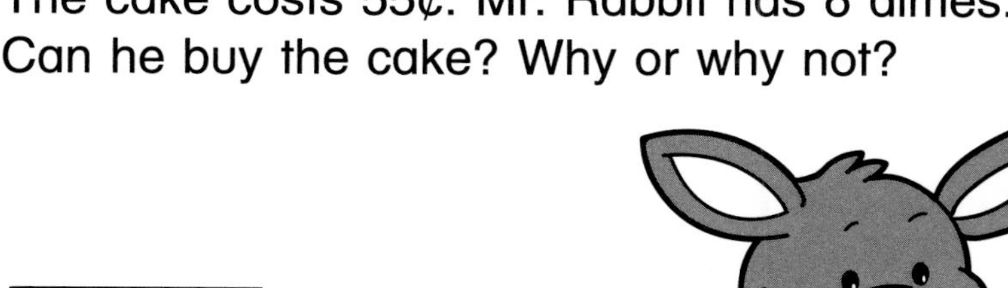

TEC40042

Subtraction

Ducky Swimmers

There are 14 ducks.
Eight of the ducks are swimming.
How many are not swimming?
How do you know?

TEC40042

Writing to explain

Just Imagine!

Would you rather be a caterpillar or a butterfly?
Why?

TEC40042

Consonant digraph: *ch*

Choosy!

Charlie Chick likes only words that begin with **ch.** Write four **ch** words. Then use them in sentences.

TEC40042

Seasonal Activity Cards

Cut out a copy of the cards and have students complete the activities.

Problem solving

Lots of Spots

Lucy Ladybug has the same number of spots on each wing. She has 12 spots in all. How many spots are on each wing?

TEC40042

Addition with three addends

Fly Feast

Three frogs eat 12 flies in all. Write two different addition sentences to show how many flies each frog could eat.

5 + 5 + 2 = 12

TEC40042

Silent *e*

Jump to It!

Read the words below. Then use each word in a sentence.

hop
hope
cut
cute

TEC40042

Alphabetical order

Word Garden

The words are in ABC order. Write 5 words that could be on the third flower.

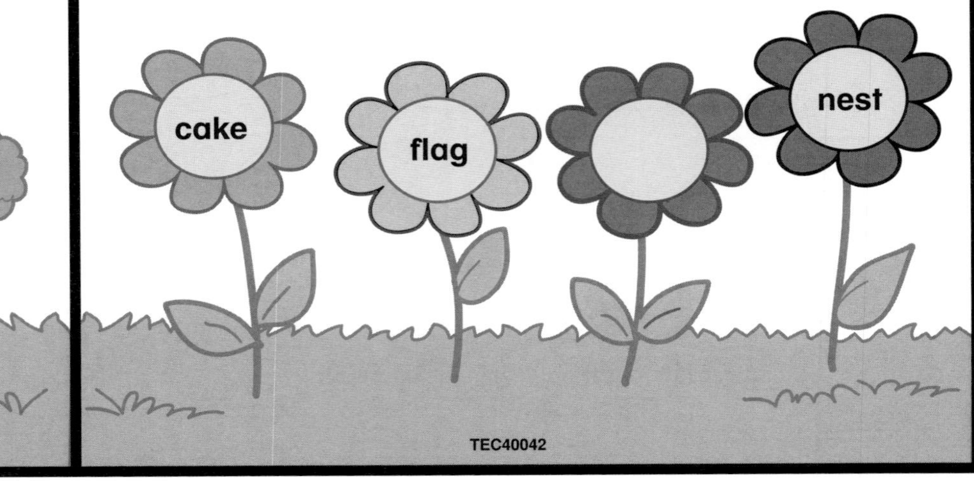

TEC40042

Cut out a copy of the cards and have students complete the activities.

Counting coins

Shopping for Shades

Draw a set of 4 coins that equals 55¢.
Then draw a set of 5 coins that equals 55¢.

TEC40043

Problem solving

Double-Decker Cones

Imagine that each person in your family eats 2 scoops of ice cream. How many scoops would that be? Explain.

TEC40043

Describing words

Summer Scene

Draw a summer picture. Then write 10 describing words.

TEC40043

Writing

Callie Camps Out

One day, Callie Cat went camping. She set up a tent. Then...

Finish the story.

TEC40043

Seasonal Activity Cards

Cut out a copy of the cards and have students complete the activities.

Simple Science

Simple Science

Colorful Combinations

Making predictions, mixing colors

Getting ready:

- Set out three small clear plastic containers of water. (Baby food containers work well.)
- Gather three craft sticks or plastic spoons for stirring. Also get yellow, red, and blue food coloring.
- Make a class supply of the recording sheet on page 140.

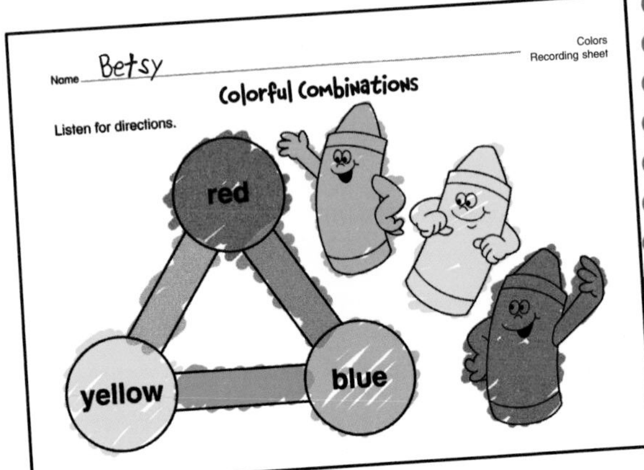

Activity: Instruct each youngster to color the circles on her recording sheet as indicated. Next, add a drop or two of yellow food coloring to one container of water and stir it. After students observe that the water turns yellow, have them predict what will happen if you add red food coloring to the same container of water. Test their predictions. Then ask each youngster to record the results on her paper by coloring the band that connects the yellow and red circles orange. Repeat the predicting and testing process with the remaining color combinations and have students complete their papers as described.

Sue Lein
St. Jude the Apostle School
Wauwatosa, WI

"Sound-sational" Pairs

Matching and identifying sounds

Getting ready:

- Collect ten empty black film canisters. Put in each canister pair a material or group of items that will make noise when the canister is shaken—such as soil, paper clips, or marbles—so each canister pair has the same material or items. Scramble the canisters and label each one with a different letter.
- Write the name of each different material or group of items on a separate blank card. Illustrate the cards if desired.
- Place the cards and canisters at a center.

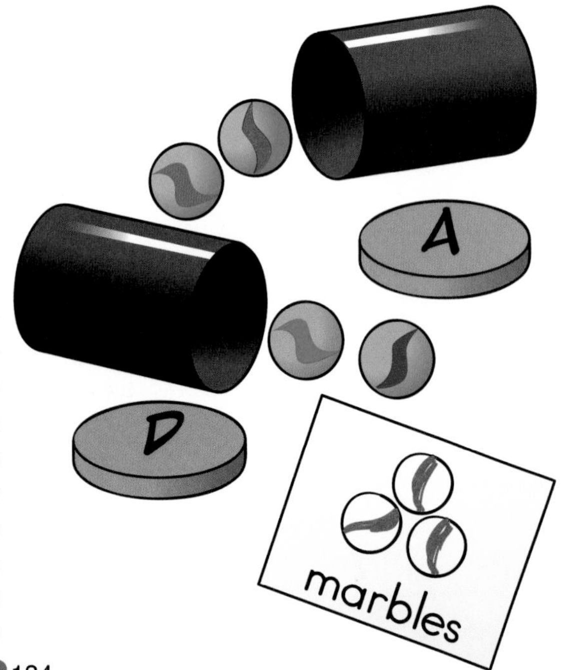

Activity: A student shakes each canister, in turn, and pairs the canisters with like sounds. He puts each card near the pair of canisters he thinks has the corresponding contents. Then he opens the canisters and checks his work.

Carol Moynihan
Smyser Elementary
Chicago, IL

3-D Tree

Understanding seasonal changes of a tree

Getting ready (for each student):

- Make two tagboard tree cutouts like the one shown. Cut one cutout from the bottom to the middle of the trunk. Cut the other cutout from the top of the trunk to the middle of it.
- Gather green, pink, orange, red, and white scrap paper.

Activity: Help each student insert one cutout into another cutout to make the tree self-standing. Secure the cutouts with clear tape. Point out the four main sections of the tree. Then instruct the youngster to glue torn paper to the tree to make green leaves on one section, orange and red leaves on the next section, white snow on the next section, and pink blossoms and green leaves on the last section. After she completes her project, ask her to turn it to display each section, in turn, and describe the corresponding seasonal changes.

adapted from an idea by Michelle Combs
Lemm Elementary
Spring, TX

Milk Mystery

Making and testing predictions

Getting ready: Get two large, shallow clear plastic containers; whole milk; skim milk; two or more colors of food coloring; and liquid dish detergent.

Activity: Pour whole milk into one container to cover the bottom of it. Then squeeze a drop of each color of food coloring on the milk near the sides of the container. Next, have students predict what will happen when you pour some detergent in the center of the milk. Record their predictions and then add the detergent to the milk. Encourage students to observe the food coloring move as the detergent breaks up the fat in the milk. Then repeat the experiment with skim milk. For further investigation, guide youngsters to ask questions such as the ones listed on this page. Have them predict the answers and then test their predictions.

Debra Eubanks
Flowery Branch, GA

SIMPLE SCIENCE

From Damp to Dry

Understanding evaporation

Getting ready:

- Set out one or more shallow containers of water.
- Cut several kitchen sponges to make two equal-size pieces for every two students.

Activity: Pair students. Give each twosome two sponges on a personalized disposable plastic plate and a resealable plastic bag. Then have the youngsters wet the sponges and squeeze out the excess water. (Encourage them to make the sponges equally wet.) Instruct them to put one sponge in the bag, seal the bag, and then put the bag and uncovered sponge on the plate. Have each youngster complete the first half of a recording sheet like the one shown.

The next day, ask students to observe their sponges and finish their recording sheets. Then invite youngsters to tell about their observations. Guide them to realize that water from the uncovered sponge evaporated causing the sponge to become dry, while the water from the sealed sponge could not escape into the air.

Marie E. Cecchini
West Dundee, IL

Name Sam

Which sponge will dry faster?

My Prediction	What Happened
I think the one in the bag will dry faster.	The sponge in the bag stayed wet. The other sponge dried out.

Ready, Set, Melt!

Observing changes in matter

Getting ready (for each small group): Make two ice cubes, each with a small novelty eraser inside it. Place the ice cubes in separate bowls. Gather two eyedroppers, a cup containing a strong saltwater solution, and a cup containing plain water.

Activity: Tell students that they will race to free the erasers from the ice. Explain that the students in each group will use drops of saltwater to melt one ice cube and drops of plain water to melt the other ice cube at the same time. Have students begin melting the ice as shown. After the students in each group free at least one eraser, invite youngsters to share their observations. Lead them to conclude that salt makes ice melt faster—a fact that's especially meaningful for youngsters who live where the roads are icy in the winter!

Christine Young
Prune Hill Elementary
Camas, WA

Simple Science

On the Go!

Exploring forces and motion

Getting ready:
- Put a metal toy car, some magnets, a length of string, some blocks, a book, and some paper at a center.
- Display a poster like the one shown.

Can you find two ways to move the car without pushing it with your hand?

1. Write a plan.
2. Test your plan.
3. Write what happened.

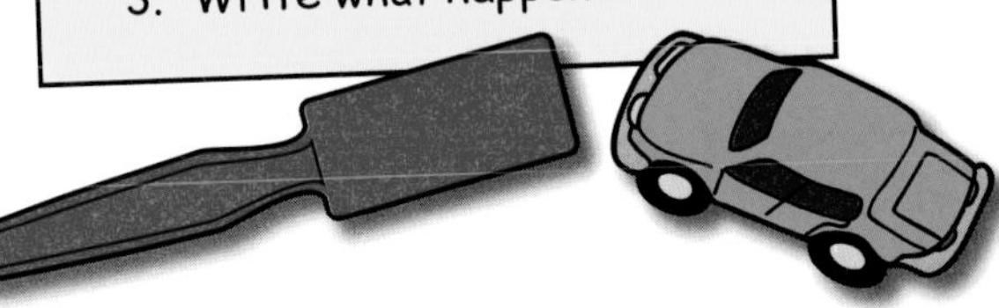

Activity: Have each center visitor answer the question on the poster by following the directions and using the materials as desired. For example, he might use the blocks and book to make a ramp for the car or he might use the string to pull the car.

Sunny Heater

Knowing the sun is a source of heat

Getting ready (for each student):
- Make a five-inch construction paper sun.
- Cut three 3" x 4¼" strips of white paper.

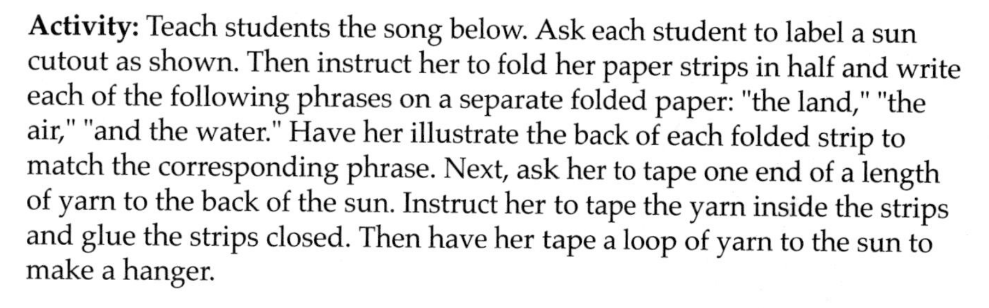

Activity: Teach students the song below. Ask each student to label a sun cutout as shown. Then instruct her to fold her paper strips in half and write each of the following phrases on a separate folded paper: "the land," "the air," "and the water." Have her illustrate the back of each folded strip to match the corresponding phrase. Next, ask her to tape one end of a length of yarn to the back of the sun. Instruct her to tape the yarn inside the strips and glue the strips closed. Then have her tape a loop of yarn to the sun to make a hanger.

Suzanne Moore, Tucson, AZ

(sung to the tune of "The Farmer in the Dell")

The sun warms the land,
The soil, the hills, the sand.
It heats our planet every day.
The sun warms the land.

The sun warms the air
At home and everywhere.
It heats our planet every day.
The sun warms the air.

The sun warms water too,
The oceans deep and blue.
It heats our planet every day.
The sun warms water too.

Simple Science

Pour and Observe!

Comparing soils

Getting ready:
- Gather three types of soil, a pitcher of water, a spoon, a measuring cup, and a ruler.
- Secure a coffee filter to the top of each of three identical clear containers, allowing each filter to droop into its container and form a pocket.

Activity: Ask the students to describe the different soils. Then have youngsters put the same amount of each soil in a separate filter pocket. Next, invite students to predict what will happen when water is poured on the soil. Then help students pour the same amount of water on each soil sample. Have students measure the height of the water that collects in each container and compare the measurements. Guide them to realize that different types of soil hold different amounts of water. They're sure to understand it's an important factor in plant growth!

Marie E. Cecchini
West Dundee, IL

Plant Power

Identifying the functions of plant parts

Getting ready:
- For each student, fold a 4½" x 12" piece of paper in half (to 4½" x 6"). Trim the paper to make two flowerpot shapes and then staple them, as shown, to make a booklet.
- Cut kitchen sponges into small pieces.

Activity: Each student puts a yellow adhesive dot in the center of a die-cut flower. She tapes the flower to a drinking straw (stem). Next, she tapes the free end of the stem to the right-hand page of her booklet. She draws roots at the bottom of the stem. Then she glues pieces of sponge to the roots. She cuts two leaves from paper scraps and tapes them to the stem.

After each child makes a flower, write "absorb," "holds," and "carries" on the board. Explain that a plant's roots absorb water much like a sponge does. Also explain that a stem is like a tube that holds a plant up and carries water from its roots to its leaves. Then ask each youngster to write about the functions of roots and stems on her left-hand booklet page.

adapted from an idea by Susana Poppe
Jordan Community School
Chicago, IL

Simple Science

Six and Three

Knowing parts of insects

Getting ready:
- Gather individual pictures of a spider and two different insects.
- Write the rhyme on a large sheet of paper.

Activity: Post the spider and insect pictures on the board. Poll students to find out which pictures they think show insects. Record the number of votes near the corresponding pictures. Next, teach students the poem. Explain that an insect has six legs and three body parts (head, thorax, and abdomen). Then revisit the pictures and poll students again. To follow up, have each youngster use arts-and-crafts materials to make a model of an insect. Then display students' work around the poem.

What two numbers are key
To knowing it's an insect I see?
Whether it's a grasshopper, ant, or bee,
Just remember six and three!

Puddle Puzzler

Understanding evaporation

After it rains, take students outdoors and have them find some puddles. Instruct volunteers to place a length of yarn around the edge of each puddle to show its size. When the students return to the classroom, ask them to predict what will happen to the puddles over a few days and have them explain their reasoning. Record the predictions on a sheet of chart paper. Revisit the puddles with students on the following days and invite them to share their observations. Guide youngsters to realize that heat from the sun causes the puddles to shrink, or evaporate. Then have each child write on a separate puddle cutout what he learned from observing the puddles. If desired, display students' writing with raindrop and umbrella cutouts.

Marie E. Cecchini
West Dundee, IL

Name ____________________

Colorful Combinations

Listen for directions.

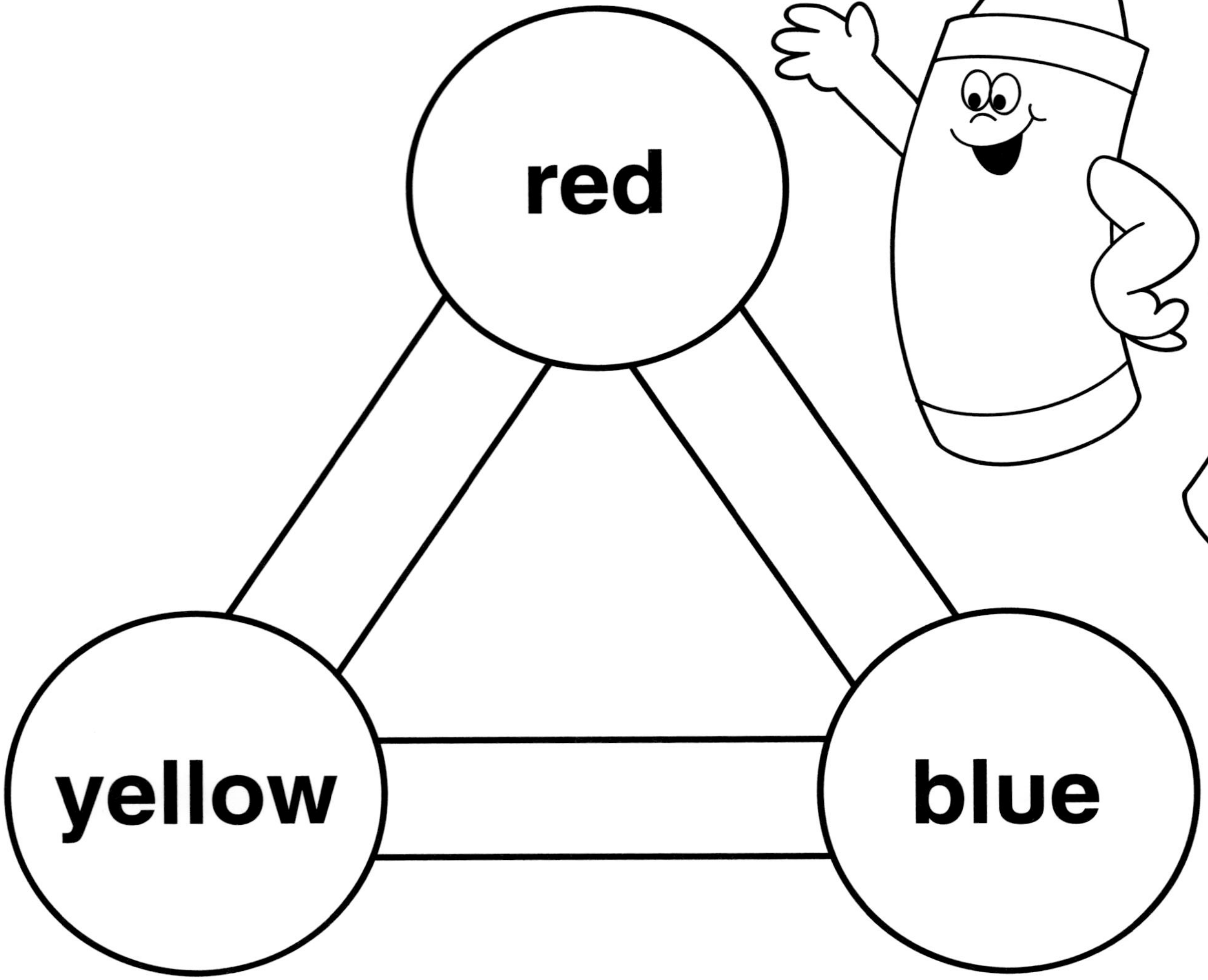

red

yellow

blue

Note to the teacher: Use with "Colorful Combinations" on page 134.

Name ____

On the Go

Read.

What can swim, dive, and slide? Penguins can! Penguins can move fast. They cannot fly as most other birds do, but they can swim well. They can dive deep into water. Penguins can swim faster than people can. Penguins can move fast on ice too. They lay on the ice and push with their feet and wings. They can slide fast on their bellies!

Circle **yes** or **no.**

1. Penguins can fly fast. yes no
2. Penguins are birds. yes no
3. Penguins can dive into water. yes no
4. Penguins can swim fast. yes no
5. Penguins are always slow on the ice. yes no

Name______________________

Deep Sleepers

Read.

Would you like to sleep most of the winter? That is what groundhogs do. A groundhog eats a lot in the summer and fall. That way it does not have to eat in the winter. It can stay in its den and sleep. You might think groundhogs wake up on Groundhog Day. Most of them do not wake up then. They wake up later when it is warmer.

Write.

1. When do groundhogs **eat** a lot? ______________________
2. When do groundhogs **sleep** a lot? ______________________
3. Why do groundhogs eat a lot at some times of the year? ______________________

   ____
4. When do groundhogs wake up from their long sleep? ______________________

Name ______________________________

Dance to Tell!

Read.

Bees dance to tell other bees about places they find. They find places for hives. They find places with flowers. Bees like flowers because they get food from them. How a bee dances tells where a place is. If a bee dances in a circle, the place is near. If a bee dances in a figure eight, the place is far away. Bees can say a lot without talking!

Circle **yes** or **no.**

1. Bees dance only for fun. yes no
2. Bees tell other bees things by dancing. yes no
3. Bees like to find places with flowers. yes no
4. Bees dance in only one way. yes no
5. Sometimes bees dance round and round. yes no

Name ______________________________ Octopuses Comprehension

Eight Is Great!

Read.

What if you had eight arms? How would you use them? An octopus has eight long arms. The arms help it move. The arms help it catch food too. An octopus is also special in another way. It can make a big cloud of dark ink. The ink hides the octopus. No one can see it behind the ink. That is a good thing if the octopus is being chased!

Write.

1. An octopus has ________________ arms.

2. An octopus moves with its ________________.

3. An octopus can catch ________________ with its arms.

4. An octopus might ________________ so no one can see it.

5. An octopus can hide behind dark ________________.

SKILLS FOR YOUNG READERS

Skills for Young Readers

Puppy Prints

Color words

Looking for a way to jump-start students' reading confidence? Try this booklet idea! Give each student one copy each of pages 156 and 157. Instruct her to write her name where indicated. Then read the cover and pages with students and have them color the illustrations to match the text. Next, ask each student to cut out the cover and booklet pages. After she sequences the pages behind the cover, staple them together. She's sure to be thrilled with the resulting booklet since she can read it on her own!

Which Letter?

Initial or final consonants

To prepare this lively game, choose whether to reinforce initial or final consonants and then post a different consonant in each of four areas of the classroom. Program a supply of blank cards with corresponding words, writing one word per card. Stack the cards facedown.

To play one round, have students stand in a circle. Play some lively music and invite students to dance or walk around the circle. After a few moments, stop the music. At this signal, each youngster goes to a posted letter. Once each child is standing near a letter, take the top word card and read it aloud without showing the word to students. Ask students to name the corresponding initial or final consonant. Have any students at the named letter sit out the next round and clap in time to the music. Then invite them to return to the game. **For a word-family variation,** post rimes and program cards with corresponding words.

adapted from an idea by Colleen Keller
Hubbard-Radcliffe Elementary
Radcliffe, IA

Pop and Stop!

Letter identification or high-frequency words

For this small-group review, decorate a container and a few blank cards with popcorn clip art. Make a supply of letter or word cards. Put all the cards in the container and sit with a group at a table. To take a turn, a child takes a card at random. If the card shows a letter or word, he identifies it and sets the card aside. If the card shows popcorn, he "pops" up out of his chair and returns to the container any cards that he and the other players have set aside. Then he sits back down. Students take turns as described for the allotted time.

Donna Follett, Kids Inn, Amherst, NH

Sentence or Song?

Letter-sound associations, concepts about print

Tune up several skills with this one activity! Gather five pictures whose names begin with one or more familiar letters and a card labeled "ABC." Mount the card and each picture on different sides of a small tissue box. To begin, ask a youngster to roll the box. If the box lands with a picture on top, have her name the picture, identify the corresponding initial letter, and use the word in a sentence. Write the sentence on chart paper and guide students to count the words. If the cube lands with the ABC side on top, ask students to sing the alphabet. To continue, invite a different youngster to roll the box.

Sadie Day, Carbondale Attendance Center, Carbondale, KS

Please Peek!

Word recognition

What makes these lift-the-flap books perfect for young children? They're self-checking! Choose an option below and make pages as described. (To conceal an illustration with a flap, place a paper rectangle on it and secure just the top of the rectangle.) Bind the pages between two covers and title the resulting book. After a youngster reads a page, he lifts its flap to check his reading.

Student names: Write each student's name on a separate sheet of paper and illustrate it with a corresponding photo. Conceal each photo with a flap.

Consonant-vowel-consonant words: Glue clip art for several CVC words on separate sheets of paper and write the corresponding word below each picture. Conceal each picture with a flap.

Lorena Gonzales,
Dalton Early Childhood Center, Uvalde, TX

Skills for Young Readers

Vowel Vases

Short-vowel sounds

To prepare this interactive display, post on a bulletin board the poem below. Write a different vowel on each of five vase cutouts. Then staple the vases in a row on the board within student reach so only the sides and bottoms are stapled. Cut out a copy of the blossom pattern and picture cards from page 158. Use the pattern to make 15 blossom cutouts. Glue each picture card on a different blossom and tape a pipe cleaner to the back of each blossom. To begin, say the poem with students. Then have student volunteers, in turn, "pick" a flower, name its picture, and put the flower in the vase with the corresponding vowel.

Roses are red.
Violets are blue.
The vowels are
A, e, i, o, and *u!*

adapted from an idea by Kathryn Davenport
Partin Elementary
Oviedo, FL

Word Search

High-frequency words

Students team up for this game! Give each small group of students several high-frequency word cards, a basket of books, and paper for keeping score. In each group, students stack their word cards facedown. Then one youngster turns over the top card and reads it aloud. Next, each student looks in a book for the word. When a youngster finds the word, she puts the card in the book to mark the corresponding page and the group earns a point. Then she turns over the next card in the stack and reads it aloud. Play continues for the allotted time or until one group finds all its words. At the end of the game, each group tells how many points it earned and volunteers read aloud the sentences in which they found selected words.

Katie Zuehlke, Bendix Elementary, Annandale, MN

Catch!

For, from, family, friend.

Word wall

This word review is perfect for whenever you have just a few minutes. Toss a foam ball to a youngster and say a letter. Have him read aloud the words on your word wall that begin with the letter. Next, invite him to toss the ball to a classmate. Then name a different letter and ask the classmate to read the corresponding words. Continue as time allows. **For an easier version,** ask the youngster who catches the ball to name a letter and then have all the students read the corresponding words together.

Janine Vieira
Chenoweth Elementary
Merced, CA

Sum It Up!

Beginning, middle, and end of a story

Help youngsters recap stories with handy bookmarks and this graphic organizer. To make bookmarks, label three index cards as shown. After a child is familiar with a storybook, have her place each card in the corresponding section of the story. Next, instruct her to write her name and the book title on a copy of the graphic organizer from page 159. Then ask her to refer to the book as she sums up the beginning, middle, and end of the story on the graphic organizer.

Lauri Christopher
Socrum Elementary
Lakeland, FL

Dozens of Words

Onsets and rimes

Program several identical plastic eggs as shown with consonant blends and rimes, using different-colored markers for the blends and rimes. Then separate the egg halves. Arrange the shells with the blends in one row and the shells with the rimes in a different row, concealing the letters from students.

To take a turn, a youngster takes a shell from each row, puts them together, and reads the resulting word. If he forms a real word, he takes the egg. If he forms a nonsense word, he takes apart the egg and returns the shells. Students takes turns until no eggs are left in play.

Kish Jefferson
Southside Elementary
Blairs, VA

Skills for Young Readers

Seuss-o!

Reading motivation

Here's a winning way to celebrate the anniversary of Dr. Seuss's birthday (March 2). Showcase several Dr. Seuss books in your classroom library. Explain to students that *Dr. Seuss* is a pen name and *Theodor Seuss Geisel* was the author's given name. Familiarize students with the books as desired.

To follow up, cut out one copy of the cards from page 160 to use as caller's cards. Ask each child to color and cut out a copy of the gameboard and cards from page 160. Instruct him to glue each card on a randomly chosen board space. Then give each student 12 game markers. Have students play the game like traditional lotto until one or more players mark four spaces in a row and call out "Seuss-o!" After students play a few rounds, count on them to revisit the books for more reading fun!

Terri Wells
Indian Fields School, Dayton, NJ

Valuable Vocabulary

Word recognition

This small-group reading game doubles as a coin-counting activity. Put word cards in a small paper bag and set out imitation pennies, nickels, and dimes. The players shake the bag and pour out the cards. To take a turn, a player takes a card and reads aloud the corresponding word. If she reads it correctly, she takes one cent per letter. She takes an additional cent if the card was originally facedown. If she does not read the word correctly, she returns the card. The players take turns, trading the coins they earn for equivalent coins of larger denominations whenever possible. After no cards are left in play, each player determines her total money amount. The player with the greatest amount wins.

For an easier version, instead of the players comparing their money amounts, they compare the number of dimes and nickels they each have. The player with the most dimes and nickels wins.

Gale Steward
Highland Park Elementary
St. Paul, MN

A Slice of the Story

Comprehension

Looking for a creative way to follow up a reading selection? Try this! Divide a pizza cutout into six pieces. Write each of the following words on the back of a different piece: *who, what, when, why, where, how.* Assemble the pizza. Next, ask a youngster to take a piece of pizza and read aloud the corresponding word. Then have him use the word in a story-related question. Invite the first student who answers the question correctly to take a different piece of pizza. Continue until students successfully ask and answer six questions.

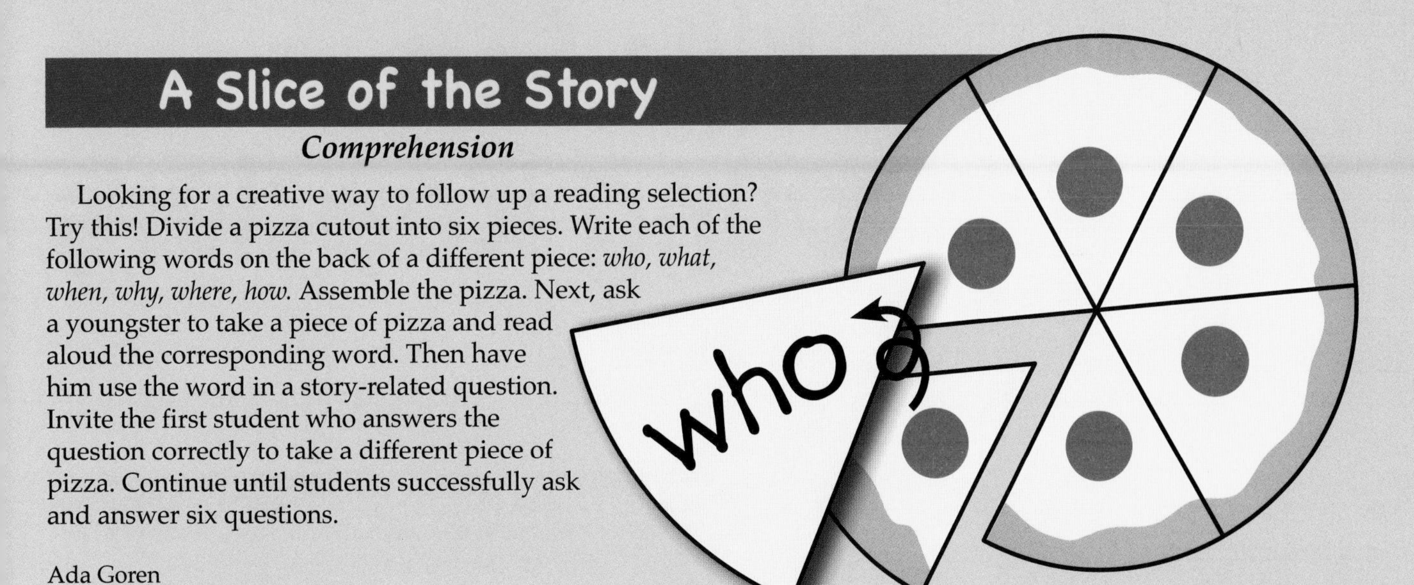

Ada Goren
Winston-Salem, NC

Begging for Bones

Long-vowel and short-vowel words

Put a colorful copy of each dog card from page 161 in the top row of a pocket chart. Program bone cards (patterns on page 161) with long-vowel and short-vowel words. To begin, give each child a sheet of paper. Instruct her to divide it into two columns, one labeled "Long" and the other labeled "Short." Next, have a child take a bone card, read it aloud, and then put it below the appropriate dog card. Instruct each youngster to write the word in the correct column on her paper. After students sort and write the remaining words, ask them to read their lists aloud.

Mary Ruth Downs
Community Christian School
Metcalfe, Ontario, Canada

Pleasing Posters

***Consonant digraph:* sh**

Make two posters like the ones shown, but without flowers and bubbles. Have students name words that begin or end with *sh.* Write each word that begins with *sh* on a flower cutout and each word that ends with *sh* on a bubble cutout. Ask students to glue the cutouts to the appropriate posters. Whenever youngsters come across different words that begin or end with *sh,* invite them to add the words to the display.

Skills for Young Readers

Add Chocolate Chips!

***Consonant digraphs:* ch, sh**

For this partner game, cut out a copy of the picture cards and answer key on page 162. Put the picture cards in a paper lunch bag. Laminate two brown paper circles (cookies). Place the cookies, bag, and two black wipe-off markers at a center.

The first player takes a card at random, names the picture, and identifies the initial consonant digraph. The second player uses the answer key to check her response. If the picture name begins with *ch,* the first player draws a chocolate chip on her cookie. If the picture name begins with *sh,* she puts a finger to her lips and says, "Shhhh!" Then she puts the card in a discard pile. The players take turns until all the cards are discarded. Then they compare the number of chocolate chips on their cookies.

Teamwork Timeline

The bears come back from their walk.

Sequencing story events

This comprehension activity is a perfect follow-up to a read-aloud. In advance, write several story events on separate sentence strips and then scramble the strips. To begin, give each strip to a different student. Direct the students who have strips to stand in front of the class and read the sentences aloud. Then encourage the seated classmates to help the youngsters line up side by side so the events are in chronological order. Once the events are in the correct order, have students read the sentences together. For extra practice, put the strips at a center along with writing paper. Instruct students to sequence the strips and write the events in order.

Joanna Davis
Hobbton Elementary
Newton Grove, NC

Story Pizza

Main idea and details

Here's a comprehension prop that can be used over and over! Write "Title" and "Main Idea" on a large pizza cutout. Laminate the pizza and separate topping cutouts. To begin, write the title of a familiar storybook on the pizza. Then write the main idea with student input. Next, ask a youngster to name a story detail. Write the detail on a topping cutout and then have the child put the cutout on the pizza. Point out that the detail helps tell the main idea just as one topping contributes to the flavor of a pizza. Then help students add the remaining cutouts to the pizza as described.

Karen Buhnerkempe
Teutopolis Grade School, Teutopolis, IL

Reading Reminders

Word analysis

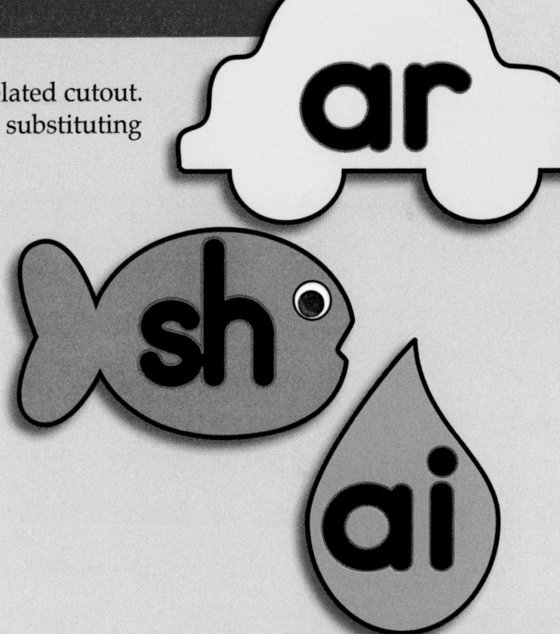

When you introduce a two-letter phonics element, write it on a related cutout. Post the cutout in a designated area. Then lead students in the song, substituting the letter combination and a corresponding word.

(sung to the tune of "If You're Happy and You Know It")

If you see [an *a* with an *i*],
Then say, "[/ā/]." *Clap, clap.*

If you see [an *a* with an *i*],
Then say, "[/ā/]." *Clap, clap.*

If you see [an *a* with an *i*],
Then think of the word *[rain]*.
If you see [an *a* with an *i*],
Then say, "[/ā/]." *Clap, clap.*

adapted from an idea by Kerri White
Ogletree Elementary
Auburn, AL

Find the Flowers!

Long-vowel words

To prepare this word sort, write each long vowel on a different flower cutout. Then glue the flowers to separate sheets of paper. Label each of several bug cutouts (patterns on page 163) with a different long-vowel word. Instruct students to read the words and sort the bugs as described below.

Interactive display: Post the papers and have students use reusable adhesive to attach each bug to the correct paper.

Floor activity: Spread out the papers in a row on the floor and instruct students to sit in front of them. Ask students to place each bug on the correct paper.

Amy Roby
Holm Elementary
Pensacola, FL

Skills for Young Readers

Word Hunt

Can you find a word that

has five letters house

has two vowels goat

begins with **bl** black

has a **short a** sound bat

has a **long a** sound cake

ends with **-ing** going

has double consonants little

has the letters **ow** brown

Word Hunt

Skill review

This versatile activity is perfect for the end of the year. Give each student a paper similar to the one shown for a reading scavenger hunt. Invite youngsters to look in books and around the classroom for words that match the descriptions. When a youngster finds a word, have him write it on his paper. At the end of the allotted time, ask students to tell the class the words they found.

Amy Roby
Holm Elementary
Pensacola, FL

Super Sorting

Long e: ea, ee

This word sort is so cute, you'll want to keep it on display for student reference. Use colorful markers to write "ice cream" and "green" on separate blank cards. Attach the cards to a cone cutout and a crayon cutout, as shown, and then post the cutouts within student reach. Use a black marker to program blank cards with long *e* words that contain *ea* or *ee*. Then make one ice cream scoop cutout per *ea* word.

To begin, ask a student to take a card at random and read the word aloud. If the word contains *ea*, have her attach the card to an ice cream scoop and post the scoop above the cone. If the word contains *ee*, instruct her to attach the card to the crayon. After students sort the remaining cards, ask them to read each group of words.

Picture This!

Vocabulary

Use this comprehension-boosting idea with either fiction or nonfiction text. After students read a selection or listen to a read-aloud, have each child write the title on a copy of page 164. Next, ask her to write a word from the selection in the bottom section of each blank box. Have her draw an illustration above each word to convey its meaning. Then invite her to color the bear illustration. Once each student completes her paper, pair students and ask each youngster to tell her partner about her work.

Jennifer Goldman
Sol Feinstone Elementary
Newtown, PA

Stuck on Words

Say is a synonym for your word.

Tell

Antonyms or synonyms

Large sticky notes are all you need for this activity. Write on a sticky note a word that has a familiar synonym or antonym without revealing it to students. Ask a volunteer to stand with his back to his classmates. Then put the sticky note on his back. Next, have a student name a corresponding synonym or antonym. Invite the volunteer to guess the word. If he is correct, remove the sticky note, post it on the board, and have the youngster return to his seat. If he is not correct, ask a youngster to give a different meaning-related clue. Continue as time allows. **To extend the activity,** have students use the words on the board in sentences.

Blair Schoenvogel
Edgewood Elementary
Homewood, AL

Shining Work

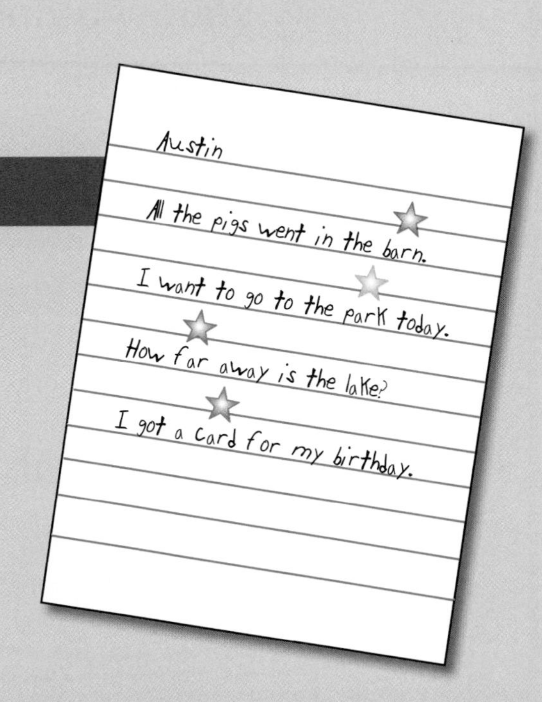

ar *words*

Pair reading and writing with this kid-pleasing idea. Enlist students' help to program star cutouts with *ar* words. Post the stars on a bulletin board. Later, give each student a sheet of writing paper. Have him write sentences with the words, leaving one line above each sentence blank. Then invite him to put an adhesive star above each *ar* word. Showcase students' work with the star cutouts.

Heather Minter
Meadville Elementary
Nathalie, VA

Booklet Cover and Pages 1–3

Use with "Puppy Prints" on page 146.

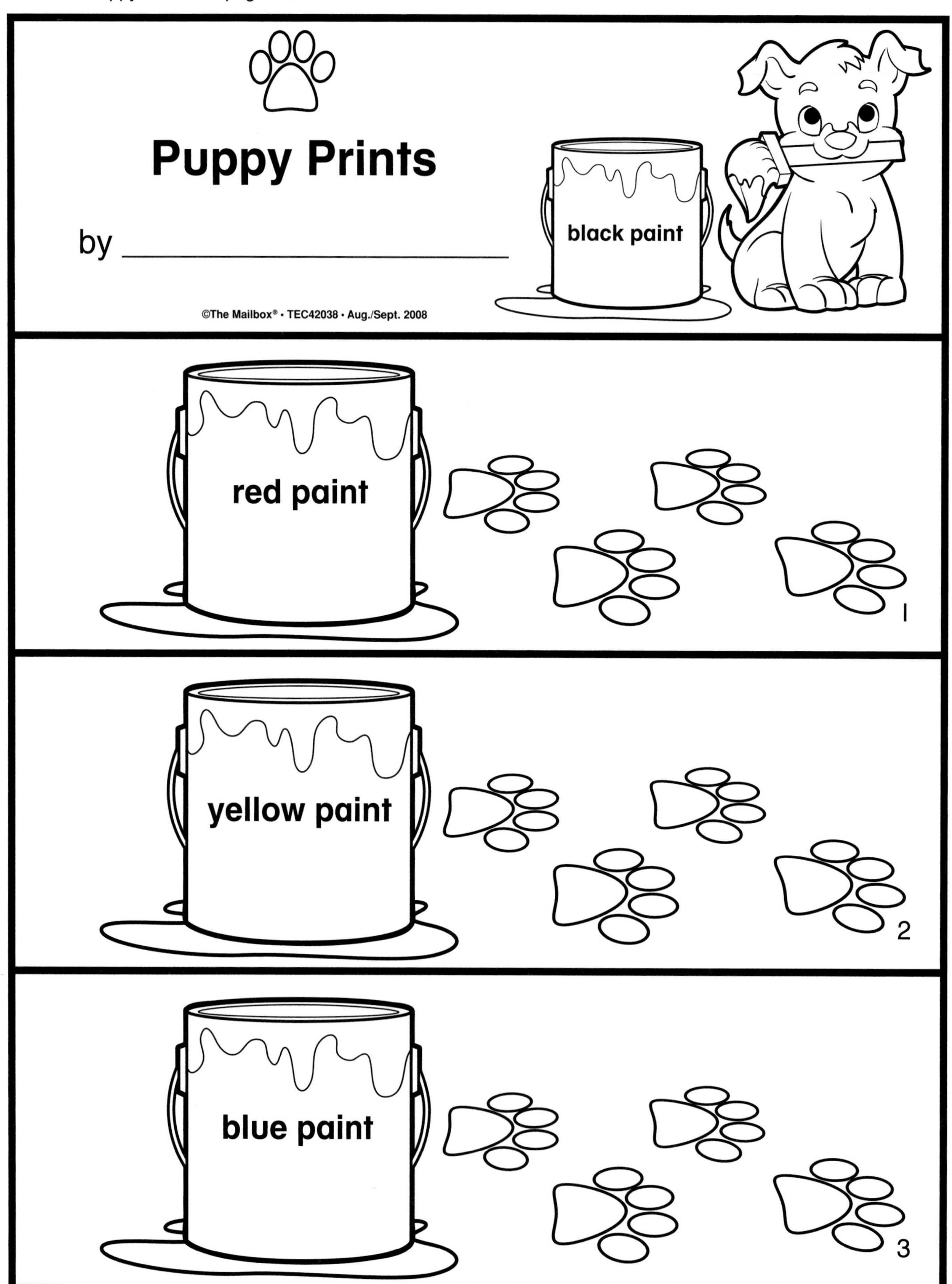

orange paint
4
green paint
5
purple paint
6
Wet paint!
7

Blossom Pattern and Picture Cards

Use with "Vowel Vases" on page 148.

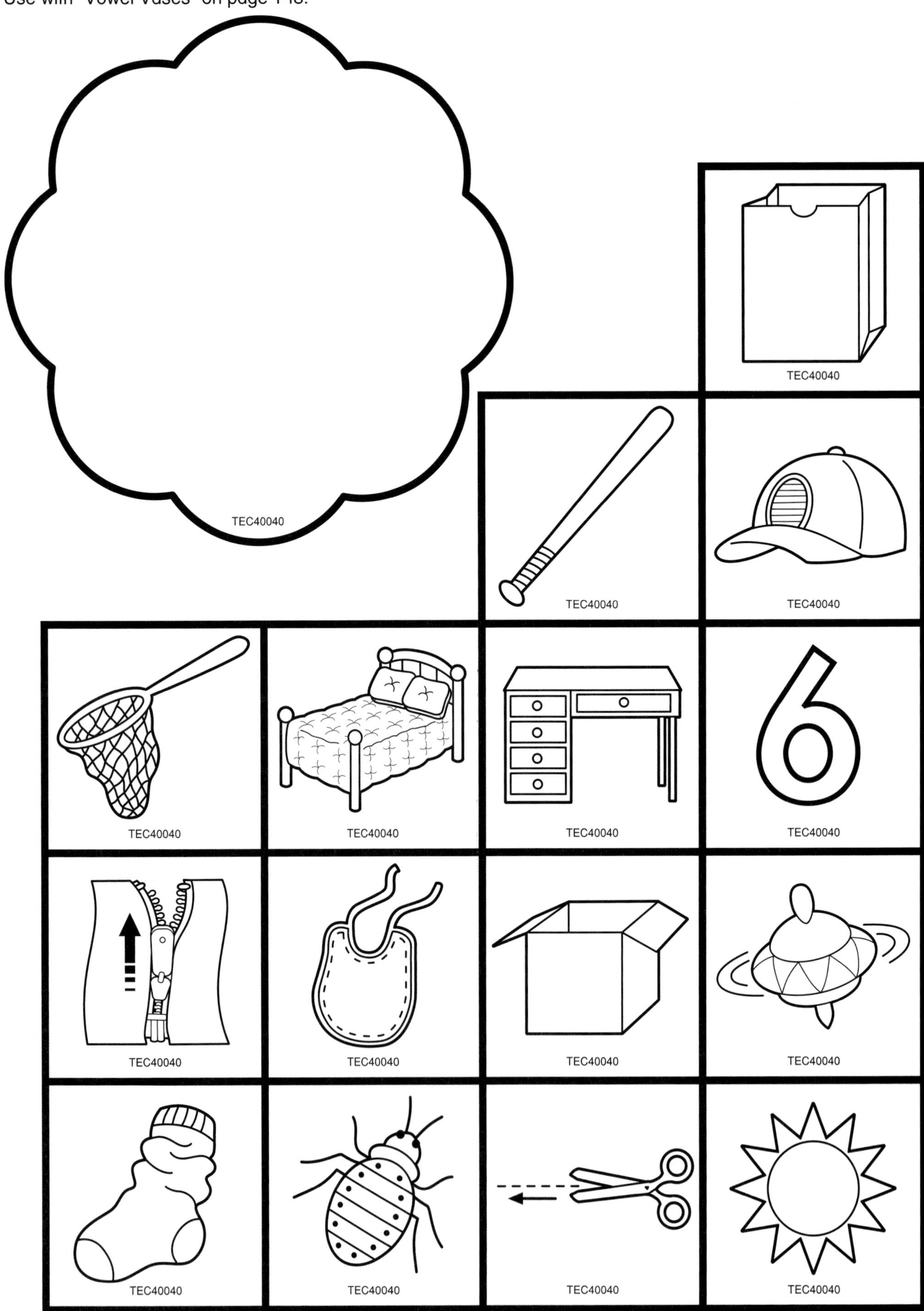

Name ______________________________ Graphic organizer

Story Wall

Title: ______________________________

Beginning	Middle	End

Note to the teacher: Use with “Sum It Up!” on page 149.

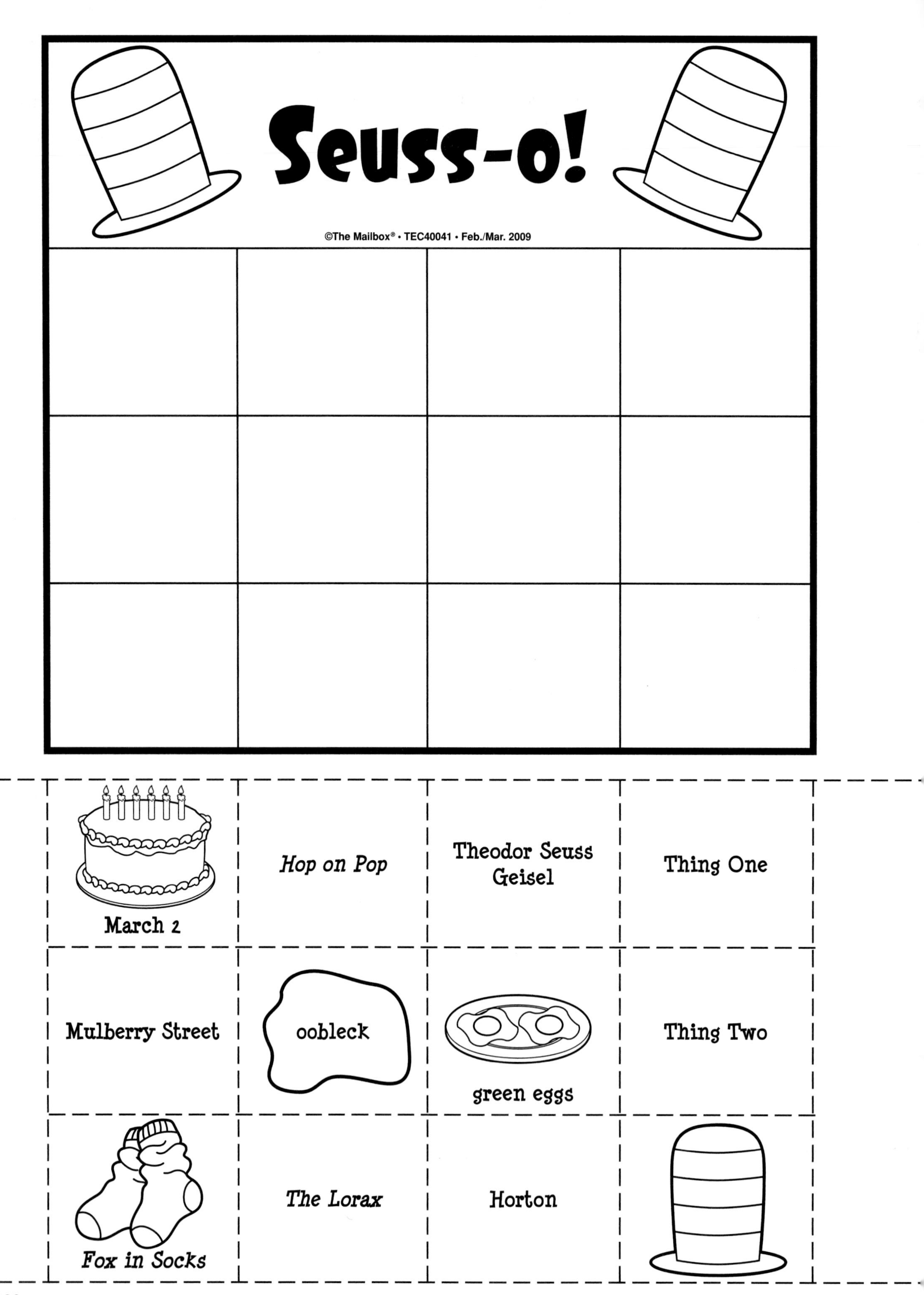

 Note to the teacher: Use with "Seuss-o!" on page 150.

Use with "Begging for Bones" on page 151.

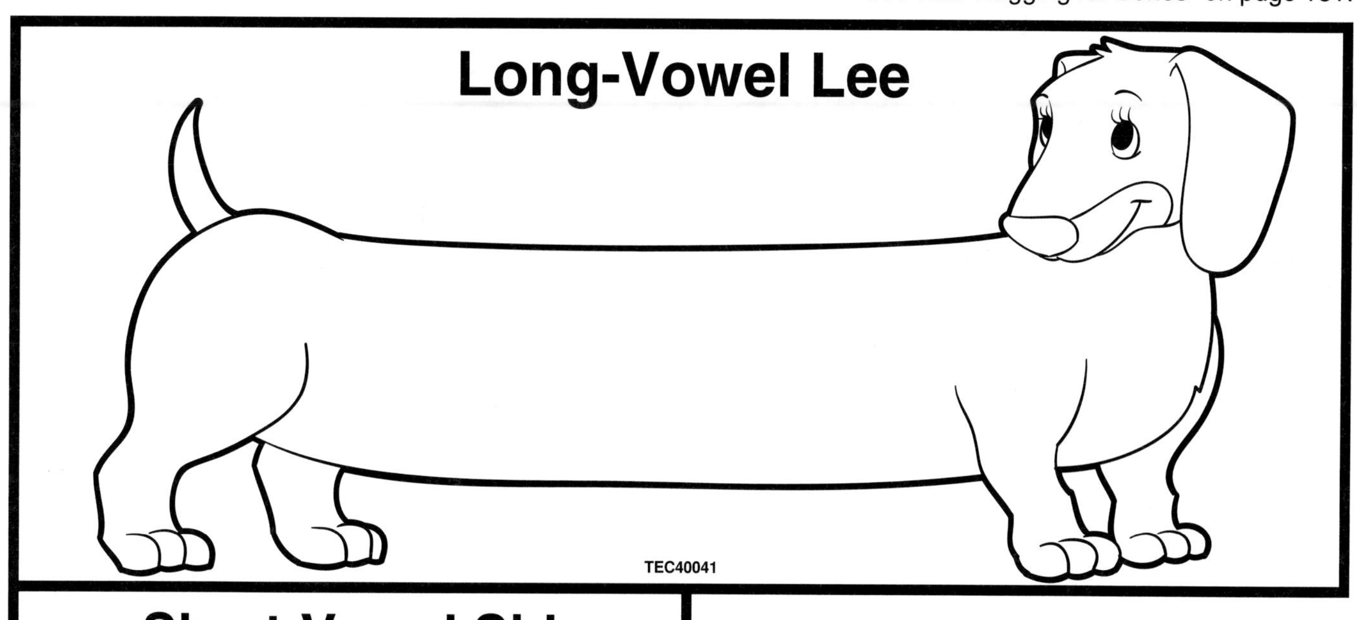

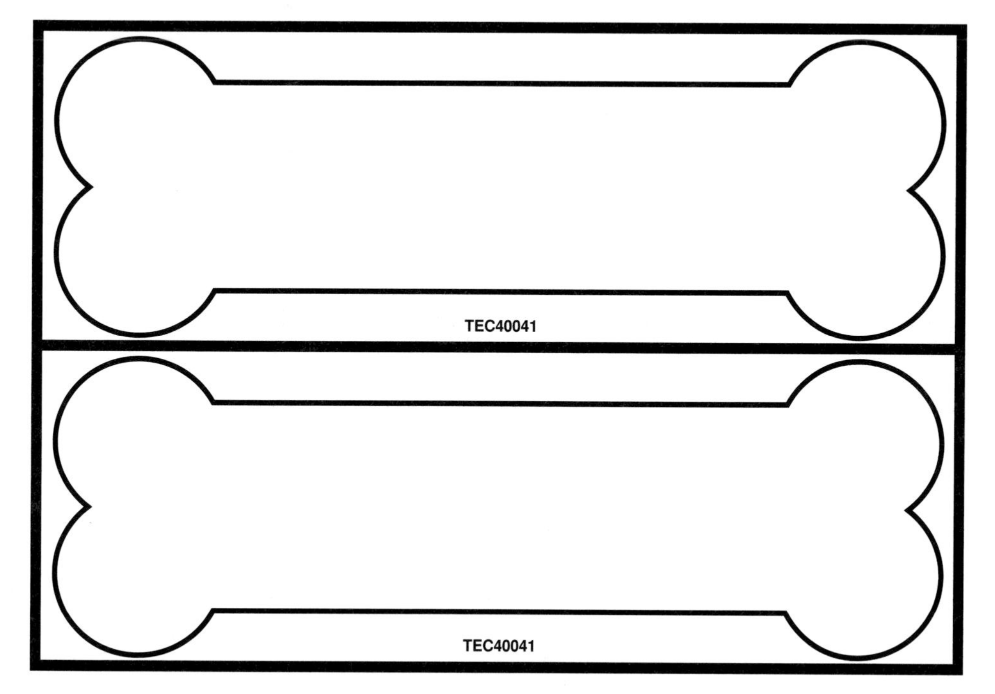

Picture Cards and Answer Key

Use with “Add Chocolate Chips!” on page 152.

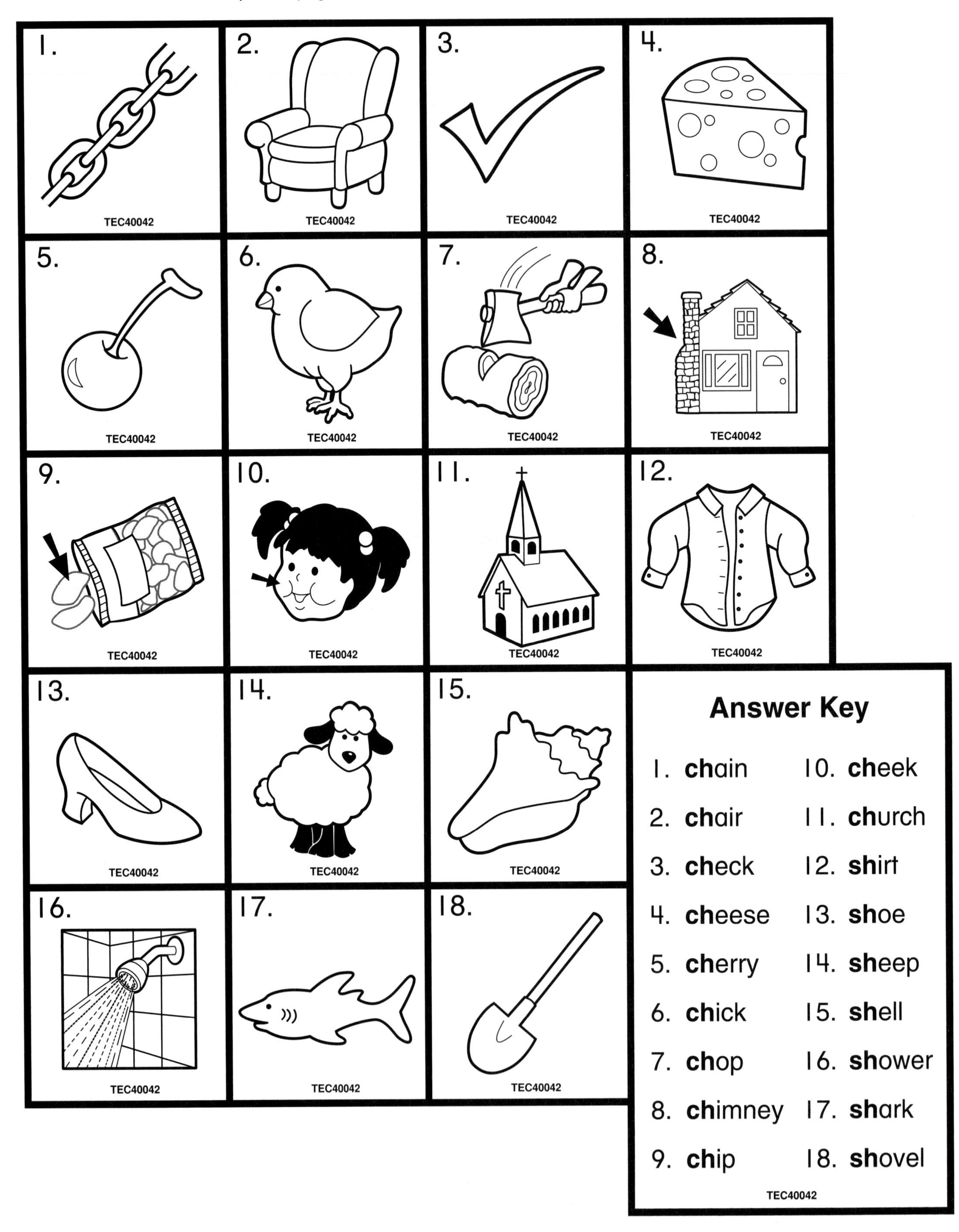

Bug Patterns

Use with "Find the Flowers!" on page 153.

Name ____________________

Picture This!

Listen for directions.

Title: ____________________

 Note to the teacher: Use with "Picture This!" on page 155.

Word Sort: sk, sl, sn Each child colors and cuts out a copy of the label below and the cards on page 166. Then he glues the label to the front of a legal-size envelope. Next he sets out the word cards that have pictures, sorts the other word cards below them, and then completes a copy of the recording sheet from this page. For additional practice, he take his cards home in the envelope.

Name_______________________________________ Recording sheet

Skate, Sled, and Snow!

Sort the cards.
Write. Read each group of words.

 **skate**	 **sled**	 **snow**
____________	____________	____________
____________	____________	____________
____________	____________	____________
____________	____________	____________
____________	____________	____________

Word Cards

Use with the word sort on page 165.

skate TEC40040	sled TEC40040	snow TEC40040
skin TEC40040	slam TEC40040	snack TEC40040
skip TEC40040	sleep TEC40040	snail TEC40040
skirt TEC40040	slide TEC40040	snake TEC40040
skunk TEC40040	slip TEC40040	snap TEC40040
sky TEC40040	slow TEC40040	sniff TEC40040

Word Sort: Long and short *a* Each child colors and cuts out a copy of the label below and the cards on page 168. Then he glues the label to the front of a legal-size envelope. Next, he sets out the cards that have pictures, sorts the other cards below them, and then completes a copy of the recording sheet from this page. For additional practice, he takes his cards home in the envelope.

Name______________________________ Recording sheet

Train and Tracks

Sort the cards.
Write. Read each group of words.

Word Cards

Use with the word sort on page 167.

Long **a** as in TEC40041	Short **a** as in TEC40041	
map TEC40041	ask TEC40041	paint TEC40041
rake TEC40041	pan TEC40041	day TEC40041
that TEC40041	name TEC40041	glad TEC40041
rain TEC40041	nail TEC40041	place TEC40041
fast TEC40041	stay TEC40041	flag TEC40041

Word Sort: *sh-* and *-sh* Each child colors and cuts out a copy of the label below and the cards on page 170. Then he glues the label to the front of a legal-size envelope. Next, he sets out the cards that have pictures, sorts the other cards below them, and then completes a copy of the recording sheet from this page. For additional practice, he takes his cards home in the envelope.

Name______________________________ Recording sheet

Shark and Fish!

Sort the cards.
Write. Read each group of words.

shark

fi**sh**

____________	____________	____________	____________
____________	____________	____________	____________
____________	____________	____________	____________
____________	____________	____________	

Word Cards

Use with the word sort on page 169.

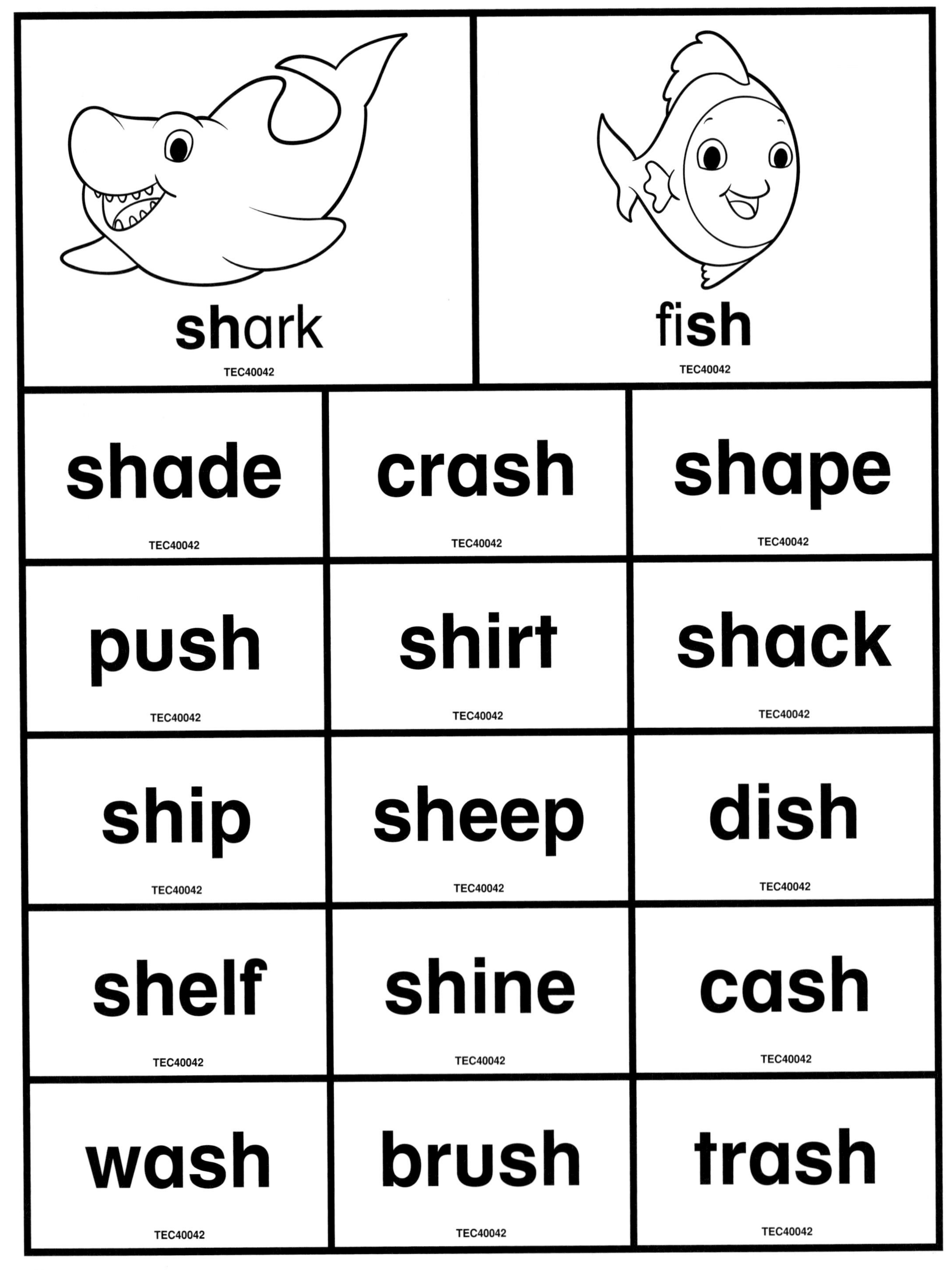

Word Sort: ar, ir, or Each student colors and cuts out a copy of the label below and the cards on page 172. Then he glues the label to the front of a legal-size envelope. Next, he sets out the cards that have pictures, sorts the other cards below them, and then completes a copy of the recording sheet from this page. For additional practice, he takes his cards home in the envelope.

Name______________________________ Recording sheet

Feeding Time!

Sort the cards.
Write. Read each group of words.

 **barn**	 **bird**	 **corn**
________	________	________
________	________	________
________	________	________
________	________	________
________	________	________

Word Cards

Use with the word sort on page 171.

barn TEC40043	bird TEC40043	corn TEC40043
farm TEC40043	horn TEC40043	dirt TEC40043
chirp TEC40043	yard TEC40043	fork TEC40043
for TEC40043	girl TEC40043	first TEC40043
sort TEC40043	hard TEC40043	storm TEC40043
dark TEC40043	stir TEC40043	car TEC40043

Name________________________________

Read and Do!

On the Go

I can ride in a car or take a train.

I can ride a sailboat or fly in a plane.

I can take a bus or ride a bike,

Or I can use my feet and go on a hike.

By land, by sea, or through the air,

I can travel almost anywhere!

Follow the directions.

1. What word in the poem rhymes with **train?** ____________________
2. How many times is the word **or** in the poem? _______
3. **Anywhere** is one compound word in the poem. What is the other compound word? ______________________________________
4. Underline each silent *e* word. Write each different word below.

_______________ _______________ _______________

_______________ _______________

Name______________________________________ Reading

Read and Do!

March Winds

Sometimes March winds blow hard.
They are strong and noisy too.
They sound like great big lions
Roaring at the zoo.

Other times March winds blow softly
Like lambs on little feet.
They come in very quietly,
So nice and soft and sweet.

1. What word rhymes with **zoo?** Circle it.
2. What word rhymes with **feet?** Draw a line under it.
3. Find four describing words. Write them.

__________ __________ __________ __________

4. Do you think the weather today is like a lion or a lamb? Why?

____

____

____

Name ______________________________

Read and Do!

Rainy Day

The rain taps on my window
This gloomy April day.
It's good for grass and flowers
But not for outdoor play.

Later when there is sunshine
And the raindrops go away,
I'll go outside and have some fun
And hope the sun will stay!

1. Circle **It's** and **I'll** in the poem. Write the words they stand for.

   It's: ______________________ I'll: ______________________

2. Circle the word **gloomy.** Circle the word below that tells what it means.

   nice dark pretty

3. **Outdoor** is a compound word. Find two other compound words.

   Write them. ______________________ ______________________

4. Do you think the bear likes rainy days? Why or why not?

   ____

   ____

Name ______________________________

Read and Do!

Along the Shore

In the summer, I really like
To walk along the shore.
I look around and find seashells,
And then I go explore.

I also like to make sand castles.
I make them big and tall.
But when the ocean waves rush up,
They make the castles fall!

1. Write the word that means almost the same as **beach.**

___ ___ ___ ___ e

2. Circle the compound word.

3. Write two words that describe the castles.

______________________ ______________________

4. Do the waves move fast or slow? ______________________

'Tis the Season

Story and Safety

Back-to-school means back to buses! Arrange for a bus driver to have your students sit with her on a bus as she reads aloud a picture book version of "The Wheels on the Bus." Have her encourage the students to join in during a second reading. Then ask the driver to review bus rules and discuss what students should do if they just miss the bus, drop papers near the bus, or have other bus-related concerns.

Sandra O'Connell, Margaret M. Pierce Elementary, Remington, VA

Brief Introductions

These booklets help you get acquainted with students. Plus, they are great projects to share during open house! Help each child complete a paper with sentence starters like the ones shown. Then have him cut the sentences apart, glue each sentence on a separate sheet of paper, and add illustrations. Bind the papers between two covers and title the resulting book "A Snapshot of Me." Then mount a camera cutout to the front cover and a photo of the child to the inside of the book.

Andrea Patnaude
Anna McCabe Elementary
Smithfield, RI

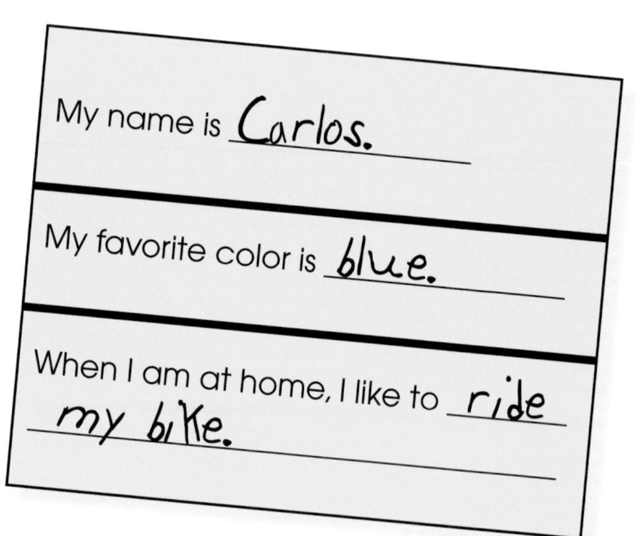

Fall Domino Fun

For this small-group game, choose an option below and make game cards as described. To begin a round, one player deals three cards to each player. She stacks the remaining cards facedown and sets the top card faceup on the playing surface. To take a turn, a player places a card beside a card in play so the adjacent domino sections match. For example, she may match the type of objects, the numbers, a number and a set of objects, or a number and a number word. If she does not have a matching card, she takes the top card from the stack. If she does not get a matching card, the next player takes a turn. Players take turns until they cannot play any more cards and no cards are left in the stack.

J. J. Markle, Hanover, PA

Numbers: Color and cut out two copies of the cards from page 184.
Number words: Color and cut out two copies of the cards from page 185.
Numbers and number words: Color and cut out one copy each of the cards from pages 184 and 185.

Tuneful Pumpkin

Display the song shown. After you teach it to students, program blank cards with chosen high-frequency words and ask youngsters to find the matching words in the song. Or instruct each youngster to draw a pumpkin like the one described. Then have him glue a copy of the song on his paper and point to the words as he reads them.

Faith Shiver, Camilla, GA

(sung to the tune of "I'm a Little Teapot")

I'm an orange pumpkin, big and round.
Here is my vine that trails on the ground.
If you come and pick me, I will say,
"Please decorate me for Halloween day!"

Chain of Thanks

For this Thanksgiving project, make a class supply of fall-colored paper strips. Ask each child to name something for which she is grateful; then write the information on an individual strip and have her write her name on the back of it. Instruct students to make a chain with the programmed strips. Display the completed chain as desired.

Rebekah Elder, University United Methodist Child Development Center, Fort Worth, TX

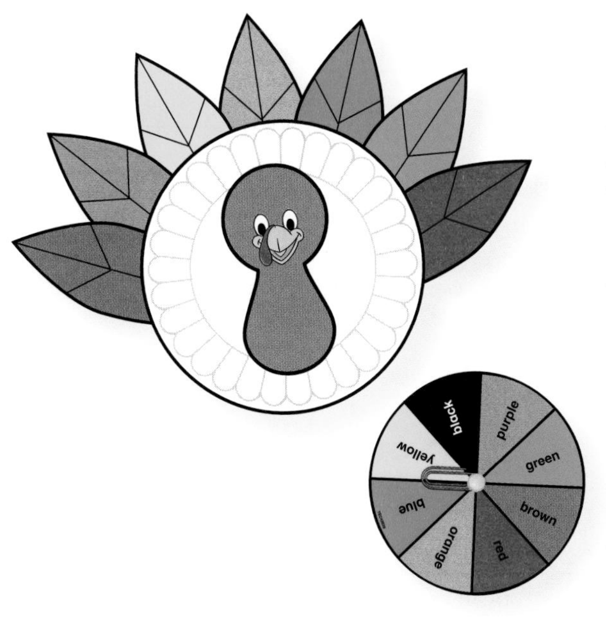

Find the Feathers!

To prepare this small-group game, cut out a copy of the spinner pattern on page 186. Then attach a paper clip to it with a brad. For each player, glue a turkey head to a small paper plate and make one feather of each of the eight basic colors. (See the patterns on page 186.) Put the feathers in the center of the group.

To take a turn, a player spins the spinner and reads the word on which it lands. If his turkey does not have a feather of the corresponding color, he tucks the end of a matching feather under his plate. If his turkey already has a matching feather, he does nothing. The players take turns as described for the allotted time or until one player's turkey has eight feathers. Then the players compare how many feathers their turkeys have. **For an easier version,** color each section of the spinner the corresponding color.

Andrea Singleton, Waynesville Elementary, Waynesville, OH

Wintry Estimations

Display a clear nonbreakable container of white cotton balls (snowballs). Have each youngster write an estimate of the number of snowballs in the container on a sticky note. Then help students place the sticky notes in a row on the board, arranging them from the smallest to the largest number. After all the notes are in order, count the snowballs. Then invite students to compare the actual number of snowballs with the estimates. For more wintry estimations, put a different number of snowballs in the container or stock the container with different ice or snow look-alikes, such as clear rock candy or white foam packing pieces.

Rebecca Brudwick
North Mankato, MN

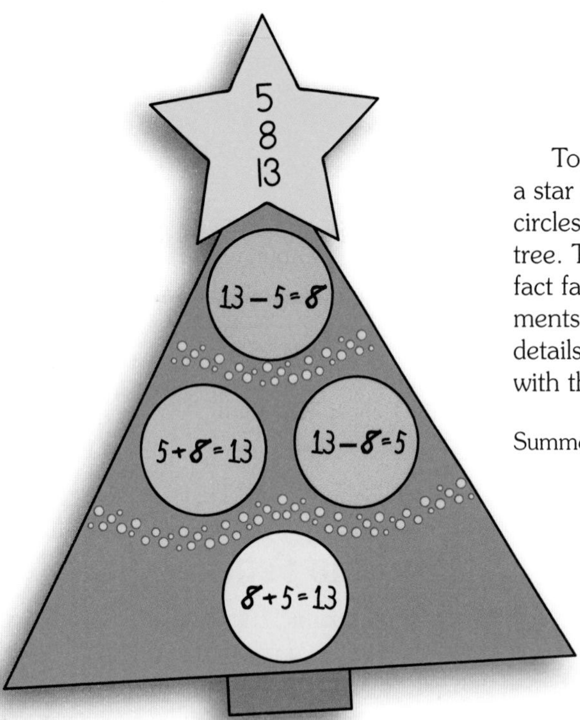

Adorned With Facts

To begin this festive project, give each child a tree cutout, a star labeled with the numbers of a fact family, and four circles (ornaments). Have him glue the star to the top of the tree. Then instruct him to write each number sentence in the fact family on a separate ornament. After he glues the ornaments on the tree, invite him to embellish the tree with crayon details, confetti, or glitter. Display students' completed trees with the title "Festive Facts."

Summer Andrus, Draper Elementary, Draper, UT

Before It Melts!

There's no doubt that students will be enthusiastic about this version of the traditional hangman game! Draw a snowpal on the board and draw one line for each letter of a secret word. Then play the game with students as you would play the traditional game except erase one part of the snowpal for each incorrect guess. If students correctly guess the word before the snowpal is erased, they win!

adapted from an idea by Virginia Zeletzki
Whispering Pines Elementary
Boca Raton, FL

'Tis the Season

Shadow Watcher

Do your students want six more weeks of wintry weather? Find out with this writing activity! Discuss the tradition of Groundhog Day with students. Next, have each youngster write whether he hopes Punxsutawney Phil will see his shadow. Then ask each student to mount his writing on a sheet of brown paper, leaving the top one or two inches of the brown paper blank. Have him color and cut out a copy of the groundhog pattern from page 190. Instruct him to glue the groundhog above his writing and then draw grass around the groundhog's burrow.

Beth Marquardt, St. Paul's School of Early Learning, Muskego, WI

Place Value Treasure

For this small-group activity, make several black pots and nine yellow coins (patterns on page 190). Give each youngster an individual whiteboard and writing supplies. To model a two-digit number, set out a number of pots to represent the tens and a number of coins to represent the ones. Have students identify the number of tens and ones. Then instruct each youngster to write the corresponding two-digit number on her board. After you check students' answers and guide them to make any needed corrections, model a different number for students to identify and write.

That's "Sum" Rainbow!

Give each youngster a white nine-inch half circle. Have him draw rainbow-colored arcs on it and cut a small arc from the bottom of it as shown. Then instruct him to write on the rainbow different addition facts for an assigned sum. After he completes his work, ask him to glue the rainbow on a larger piece of blue paper. Then invite him to glue cotton to the bottom of the rainbow to make clouds.

Jacqueline Budansky
P.S. 29
Staten Island, NY

Wing Wonders

To review silent *e* words, have each child color and cut out a copy of the ladybug booklet patterns from page 193. Instruct her to stack the wings with words on the left-hand side of the bug. Staple them in place and then staple the wordless wing to the right-hand side of the bug. Next, ask each youngster to read the words on the left-hand wings. Then have her lift the wordless wing and read the resulting silent *e* words. For additional practice, give a clue for a word and have each youngster show the word. Then ask a student to identify the word and spell it aloud.

Awesome Adjective Alphabet

Here's a class book sure to stretch students' thinking skills! Write a student-generated list of insects on the board. Then have the class brainstorm several corresponding describing words. Next, assign each student a different letter. Help him write on drawing paper an insect-related sentence with an adjective that begins with the letter. Then instruct him to underline the adjective and illustrate his paper. Ask early finishers to complete papers for any unassigned letters. Bind the papers in alphabetical order between two covers.

Amy Roby, Holm Elementary, Pensacola, FL

Flowerpot Problems

For this cute center, write a number sentence on each of several sentence strips, leaving blank space in place of the second number. Cut the ends of the strips as shown. Write each missing number on a separate sticky note and then place all the sticky notes on a sheet of paper. Attach a construction paper flower to each flowerpot and write the corresponding answer on the back of each flower.

A student completes the number sentences using the sticky notes. Then she reads the number on the back of each flower to check her work. After she makes any needed corrections, she writes the number sentences on a sheet of paper.

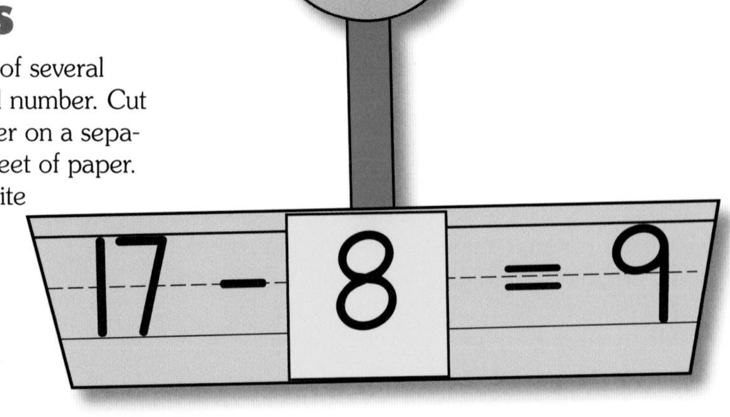

Beach Ball Blast

Write spelling words on a beach ball and post a sheet of chart paper. Have students sit facing the paper. To begin, toss the ball to a youngster. Ask him to read a word on the ball and toss the ball back to you. Then have him go to the chart paper, write the word, and quickly return to the group. Once he is seated, toss the ball to a different student. Continue, encouraging students to avoid repeating words, until each student has had a turn.

Melinda Casida, Crowly Elementary, Visalia, CA

Buggy Probability

Secretly put three red pom-poms (ladybugs) and seven yellow pom-poms (bees) in a paper lunch bag. Post a tally table labeled as shown. To begin, instruct each student, in turn, to take a pom-pom at random, draw a tally mark to show whether she took a ladybug or a bee, and then return the pom-pom. After students make at least 15 tally marks, write the totals. Invite students to tell whether they think the bag contains more ladybugs or bees and why. Then empty the bag and have students compare the number of ladybugs and bees.

Insects		Totals
Ladybugs	IIII	4
Bees	~~IIII~~ ~~IIII~~ I	11

adapted from an idea by Bonnie Gaynor, Franklin, NJ

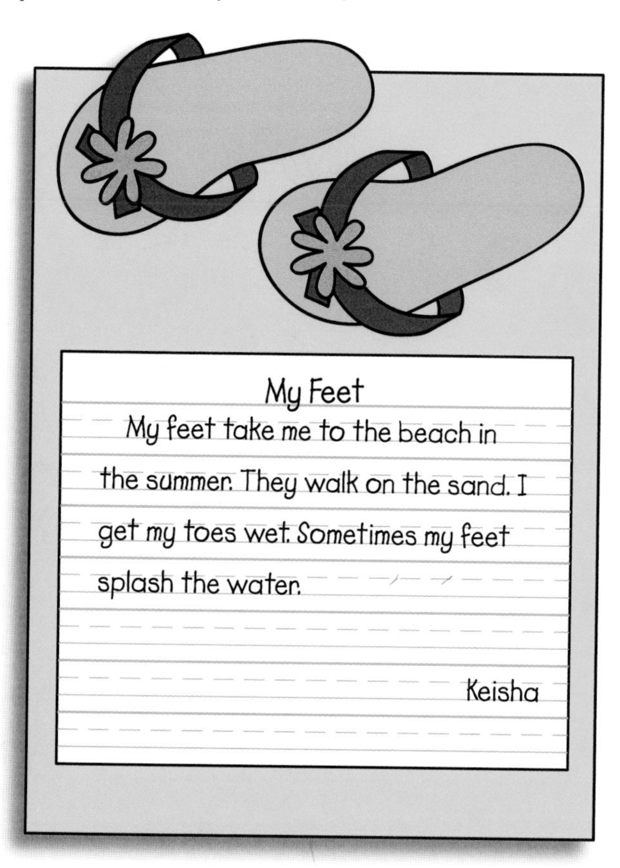

Step Into Summer!

Have each student write a response to the following prompt: "Where do your feet take you in the summer?" Then ask her to trace her shoe on a sheet of paper folded in half and cut out the tracing through both layers. Next, instruct her to stack two ½" x 5" paper strips. Staple the stack about one inch from one end. Then fan out the ends of the strips and help the youngster tape them to one of her shoe cutouts so it resembles a flip-flop. Attach paper strips to the other cutout in the same manner. After the student decorates the flip-flops, display them with her writing.

Johanna Litts
Holy Spirit Central School
Norway, MI

Domino Cards

Use with "Fall Domino Fun" on page 178.

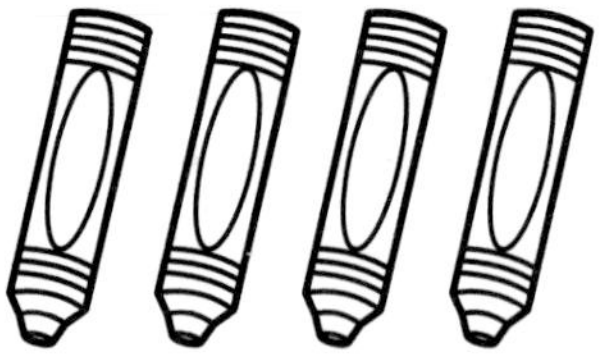 TEC42038	1	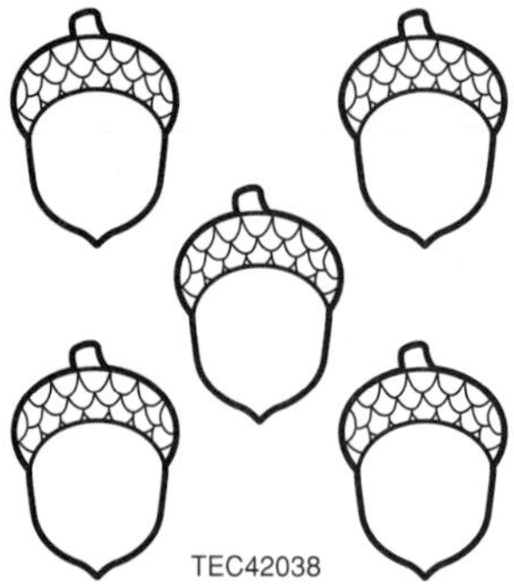 TEC42038	
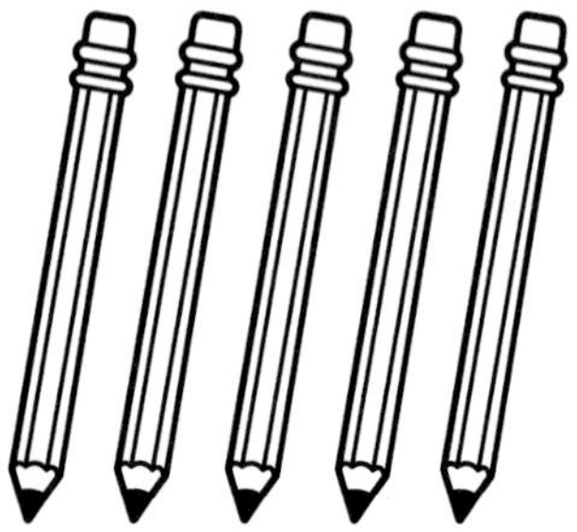 TEC42038	2	5 TEC42038	5
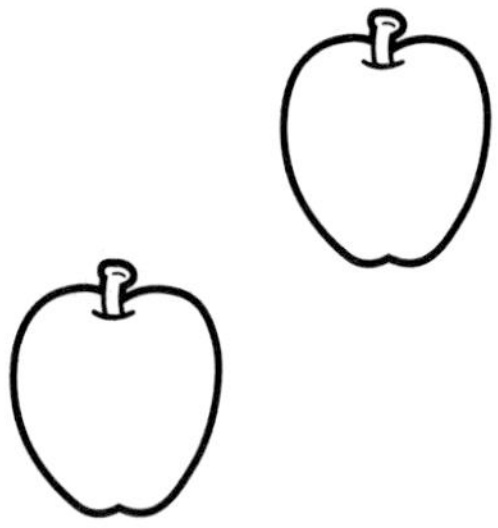 TEC42038	3	3 TEC42038	
 TEC42038	4	2 TEC42038	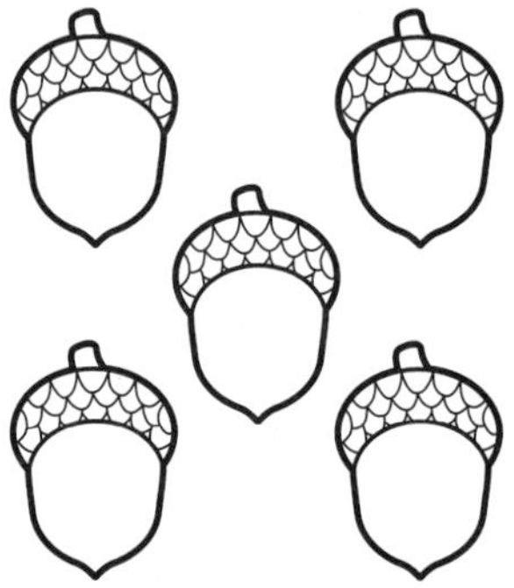
 TEC42038	5	1 TEC42038	

Domino Cards

Use with "Fall Domino Fun" on page 178.

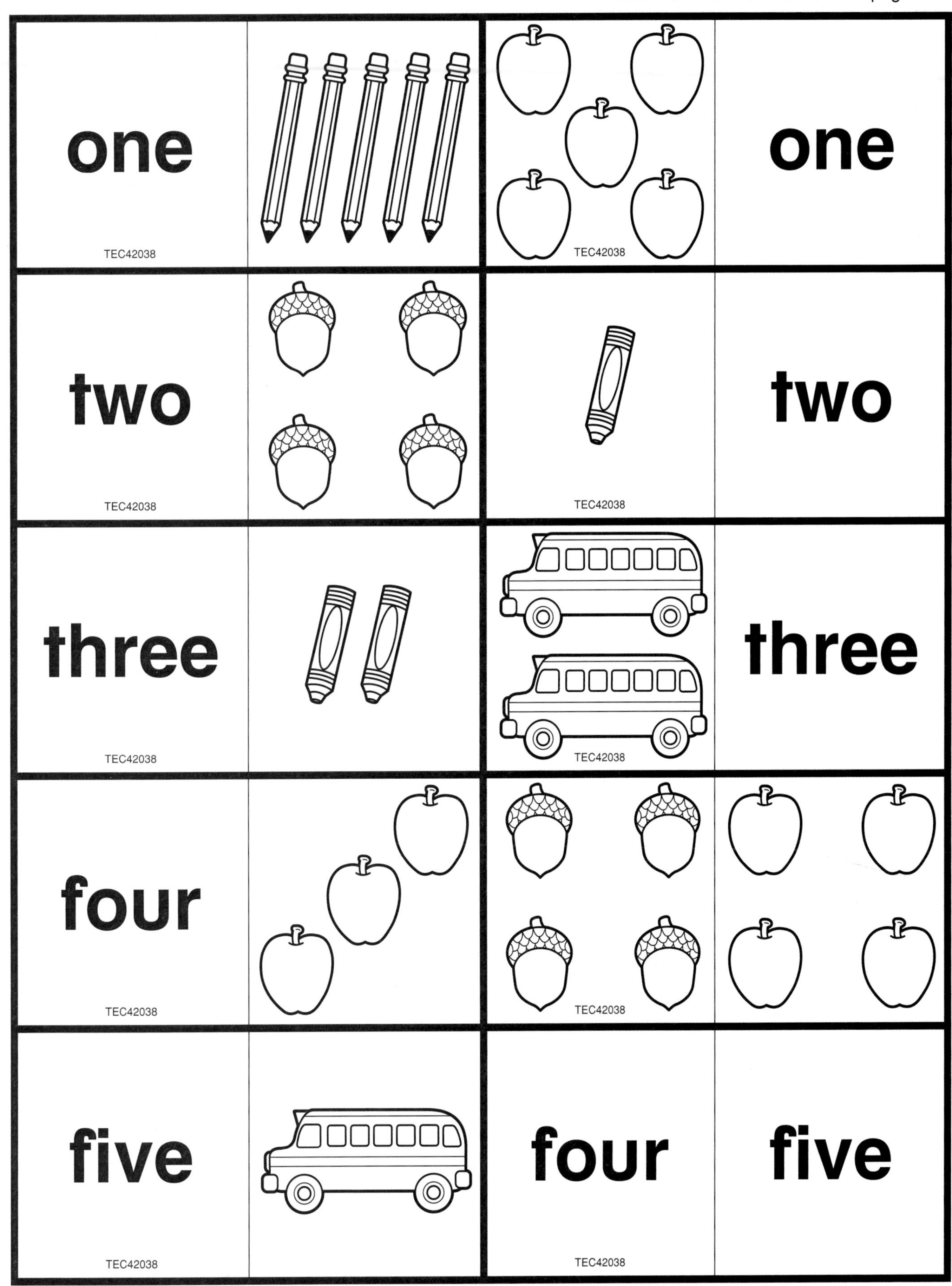

Spinner, Turkey, and Feather Patterns

Use with "Find the Feathers!" on page 179.

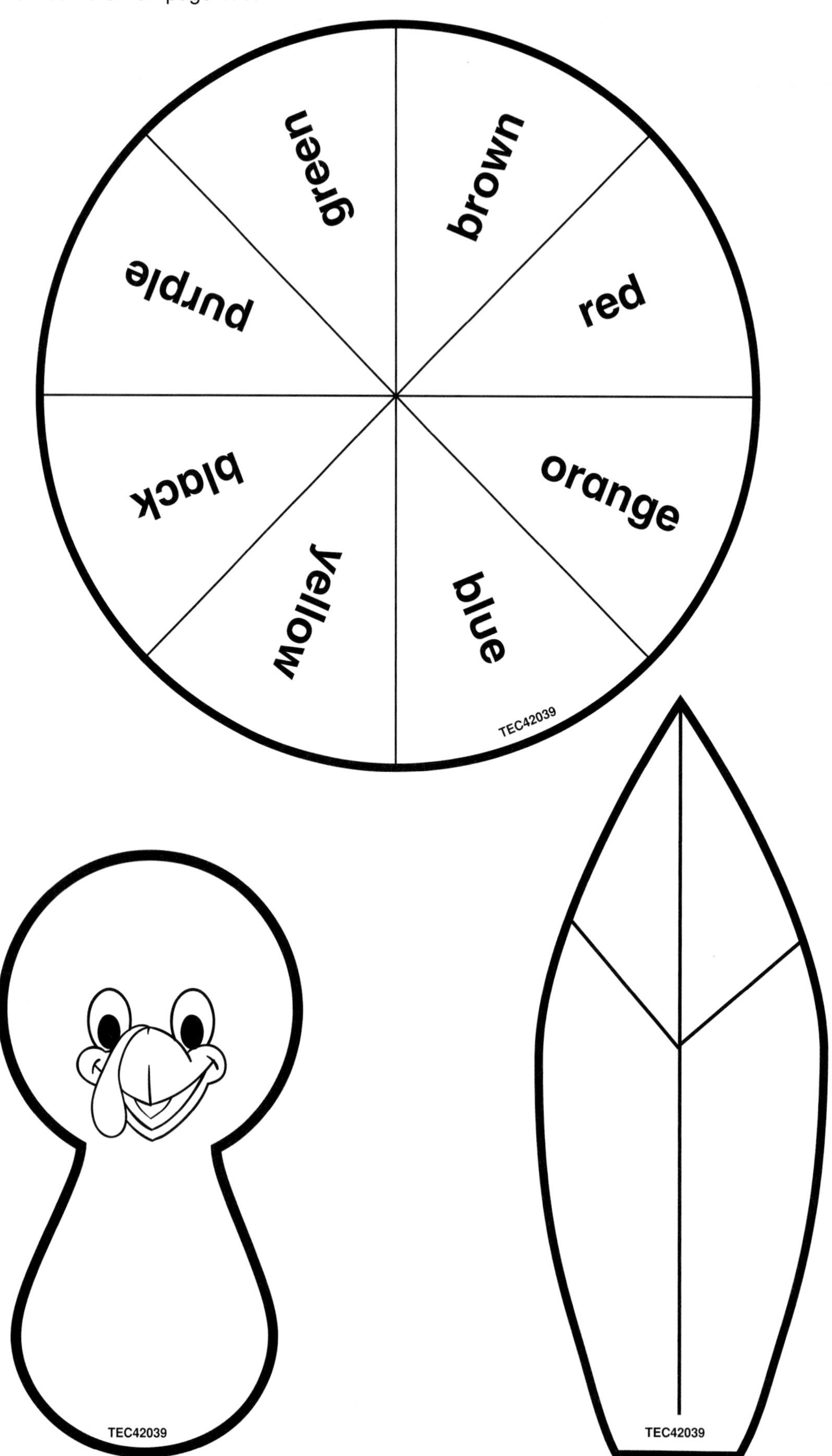

Name ____________________

Fractions
Equal and unequal parts

As Sweet as Can Be!

Color by the code.
Then write how many equal parts each yellow shape has.

Color Code
equal parts—yellow
unequal parts—brown

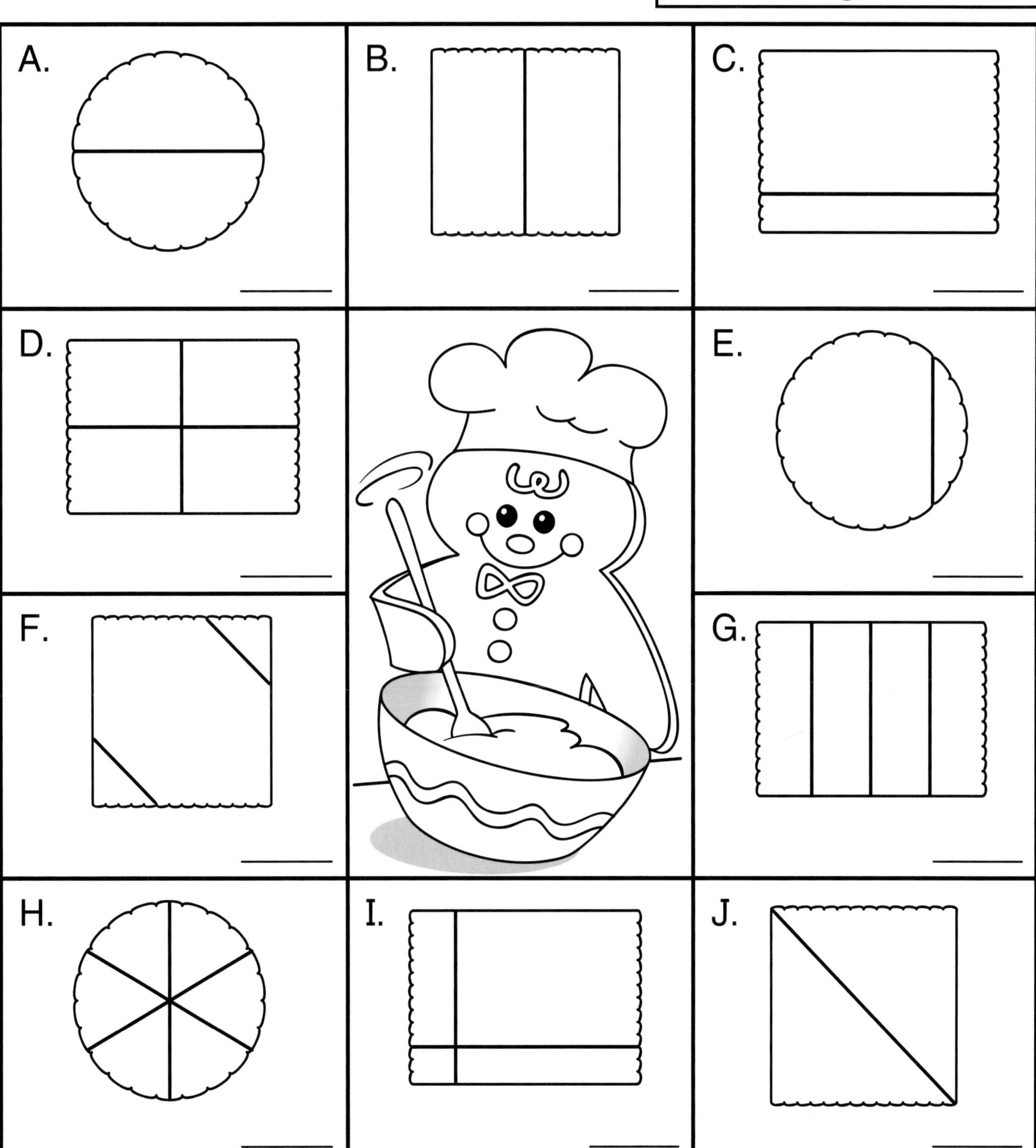

Name ____________________

Get Ready!

Write each matching word.

1. hat hats	2. sled sleds	3. coat coats	4. sock socks
5. boot boots	6. skate skates	7. mitten mittens	8. glove gloves

Name________________________________ Consonant blends *dr, fr, tr*

Candy Construction

Complete each sentence.
Use the word bank.

Word Bank			
from	drip	friend	draw
treat	Friday	try	tray

1. I will make a candy house on ________________.
2. My ________________ Cal is going to help me.
3. We will ________________ not to eat too much candy.
4. I will ________________ a plan for the house.
5. We will put the house on a little ________________.
6. I got the tray ________________ my mother.
7. I hope the frosting will not ________________.
8. Our candy house will be a very sweet ________________!

Groundhog Pattern

Use with "Shadow Watcher" on page 181.

Coin Patterns

Use with "Place Value Treasure" on page 181.

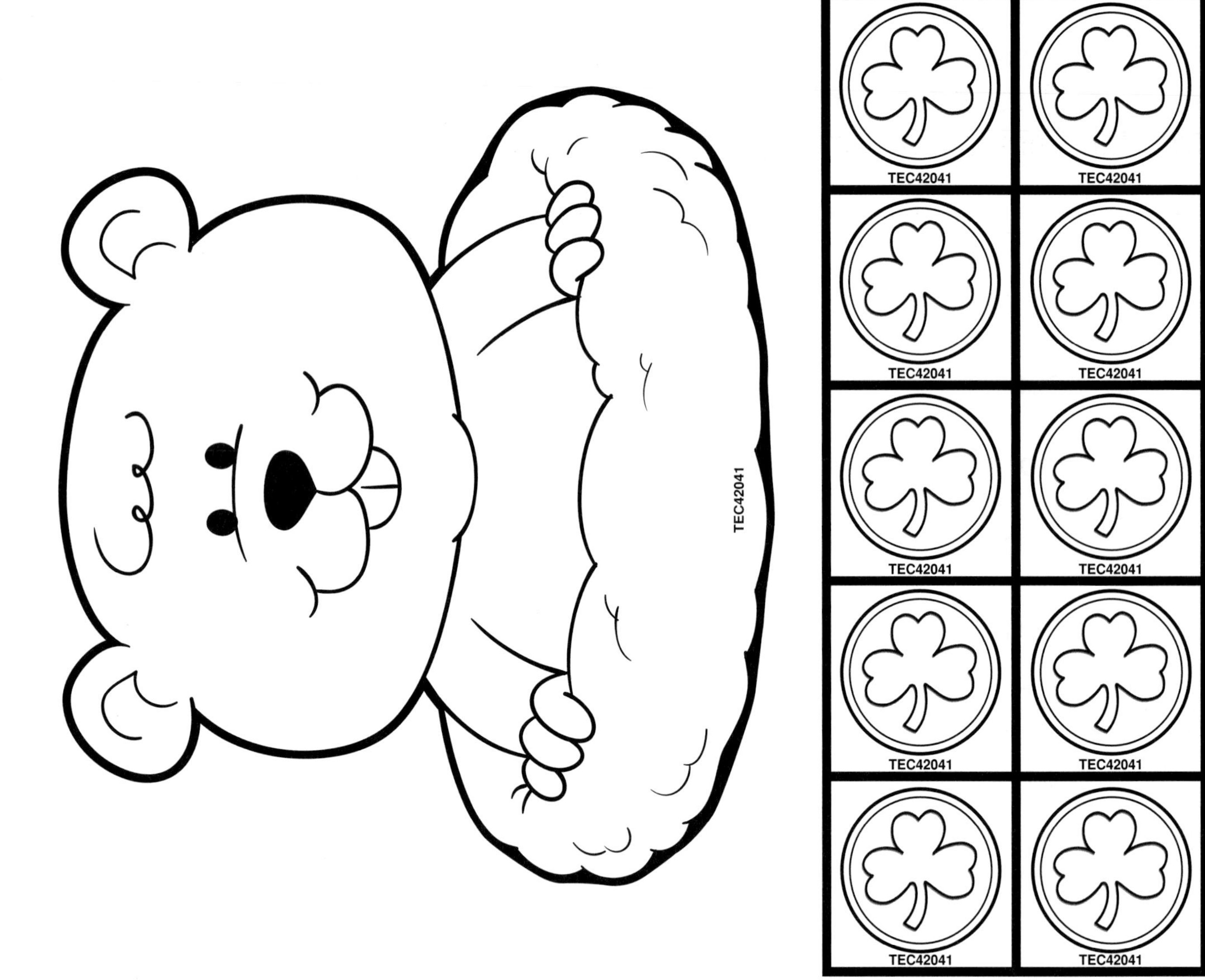

Pot Patterns

Use with "Place Value Treasure" on page 181.

Name ____________________

Party Plans

Circle each word that is missing a capital letter.
Write **.** or **?** for each sentence.
Write the sentences correctly.

There are 9 missing capital letters.

1. our party will be on friday
2. bess and i will bring punch
3. who will bring cupcakes
4. can ted bring the candy
5. bring your cards on monday

1. ____________________
2. ____________________
3. ____________________
4. ____________________
5. ____________________

Name ____________________

Sweet Hearts

Read.

A **small box** has 2 candies.
A **big box** has 4 candies.
Show how many boxes there could be for 12 candies.

Solve.

Write.

There could be _____ small boxes and _____ big boxes.

Ladybug Booklet Patterns

Use with "Wing Wonders" on page 182.

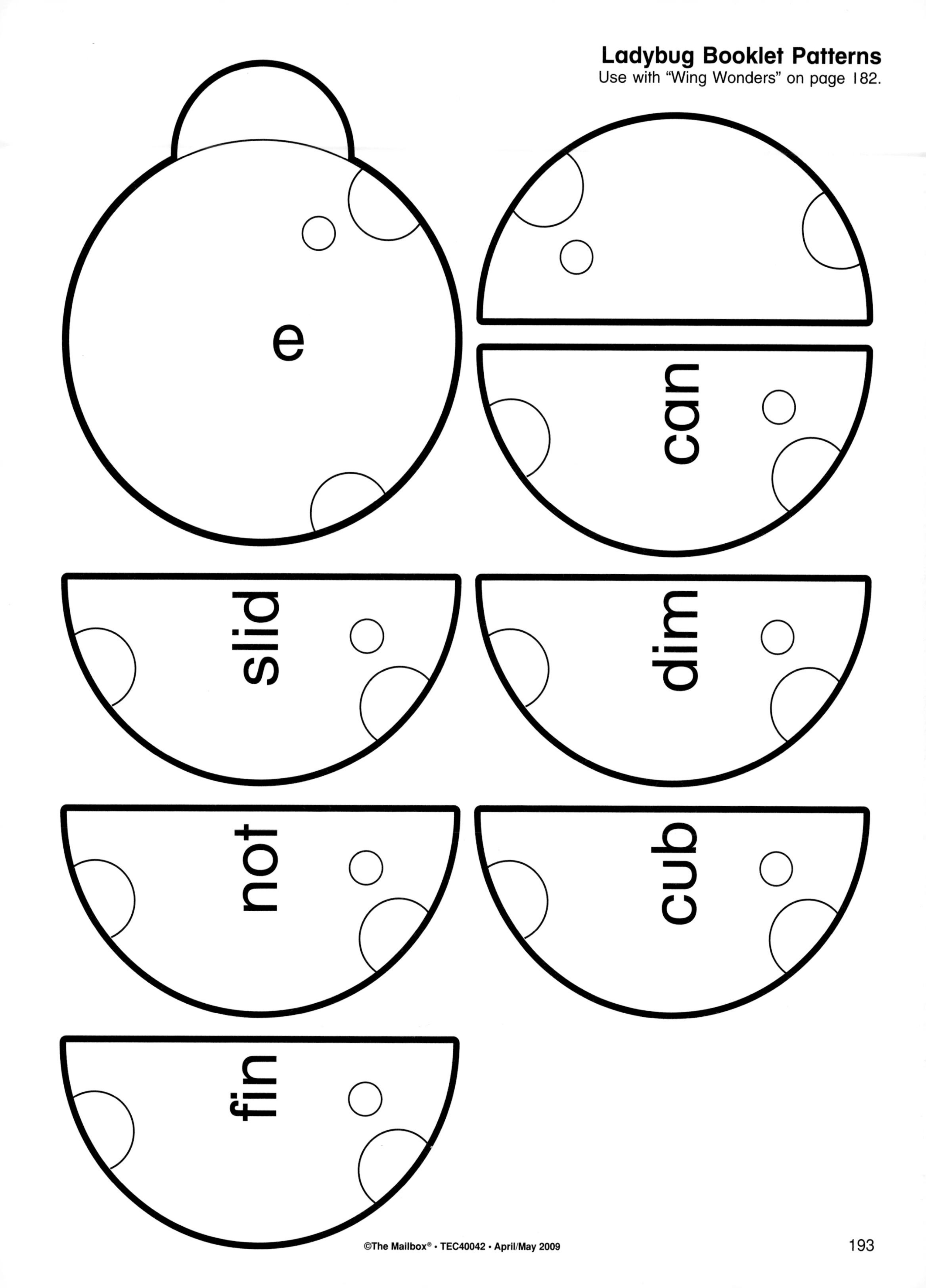

Name ______________________________

Look Who's Here!

Lotto Game (*-er* and *-ur* words or time to the half hour): To make caller's cards, cut out a copy of one set of cards from page 195. Give each child a copy of this page and a copy of the appropriate game cards. Ask him to cut out the cards and glue each card to a randomly chosen board space. Then give students game markers and have them play the game like traditional lotto.

Game Cards

Use with the lotto game on page 194.

Word Cards

baker	curl
better	fur
river	hurt
ruler	nurse
shower	turn
water	turtle

Time Cards

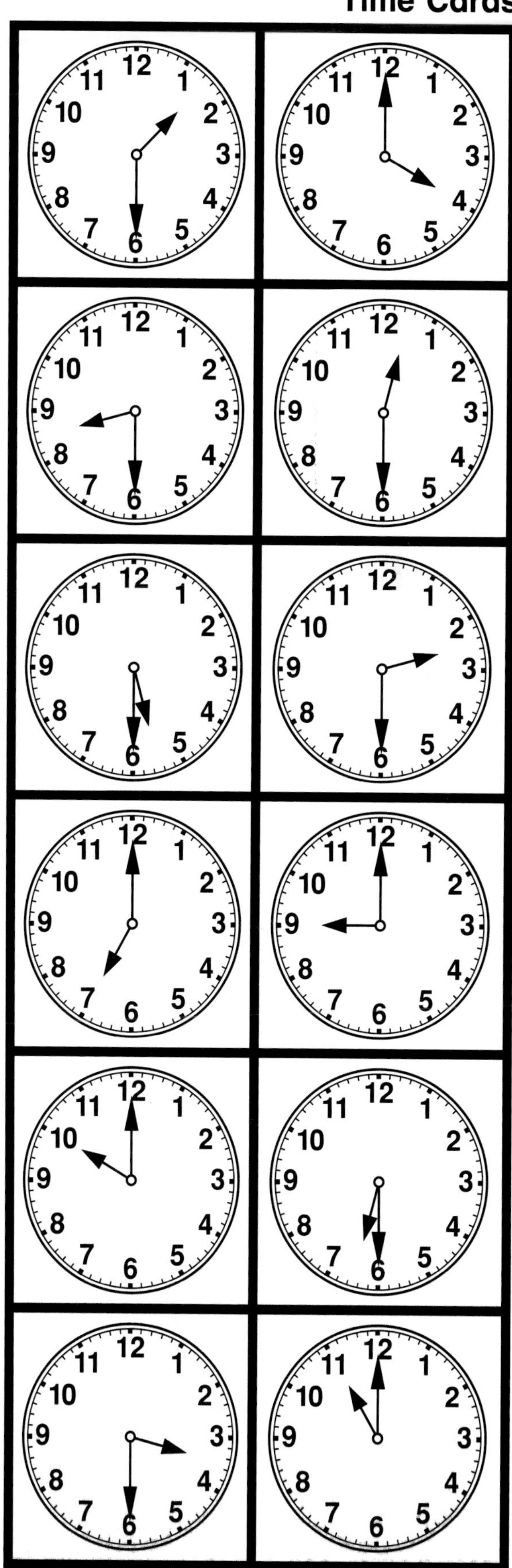

Name ____________________

Ladybugs and Lemonade

Lotto Game (addition and subtraction or *-ed* and *-ing* words): Cut out a copy of one set of cards from page 197 to make caller's cards. (For math, call the problem's answer. For an *-ed* or *-ing* word, say the word and then ask a student to spell its base word.) Give each child a copy of this page and a copy of the appropriate game cards. Instruct her to cut out the cards and glue each card to a randomly chosen board space. Then have students play the game like traditional lotto.

Game Cards

Use with "Ladybugs and Lemonade" on page 196.

Math Cards

18 – 9	7 + 8
11 – 4	12 – 9
9 + 9	6 + 5
8 + 8	14 – 6
13 – 7	6 + 6
5 + 9	12 – 8

Word Cards

walking	swimming
jumped	sitting
clapping	stopped
eating	cooked
played	running
talked	skipped

Name ____________________

Day at the Beach

Circle the correct words.
Write.

1. This morning Rex __________ to the beach.	walk walked
2. Then he __________ into the water.	jump jumped
3. Rex likes to __________ around a lot.	splash splashed
4. Bess __________ for some pretty shells.	look looked
5. Rex __________ her find many shells.	help helped
6. Bess will __________ the shells later.	wash washed
7. Bess __________ a very good place for lunch.	pick picked
8. Now all the seagulls __________ it too!	like liked

What Works for You?

Instead of trying to read and respond to every student's journal each day, I use colored sticky dots to divide students' journals into five groups. I review a different group of journals each day. *Carol Stillings, Colorado Springs, CO*

I display a photo of each student in a pocket chart titled "Writing." When a child finishes a first draft, he moves his photo to a pocket chart titled "Read to Edit" and begins a new piece of writing. It keeps things running smoothly and quietly! *Sheila Criqui-Kelley, Lebo Elementary, Lebo, KS*

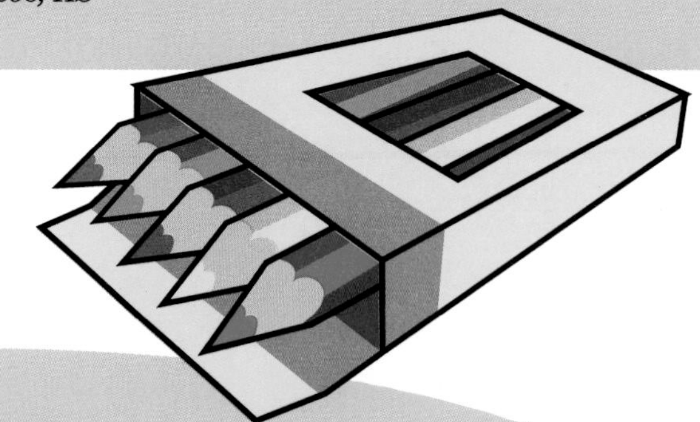

My students edit their work with colored pencils so I can easily see the changes they made. *Jennifer Lashbrook, Mary Carrico Memorial School, Philpot, KY*

To make the most of writing time, I designate a supply of plastic cups as writing cups. When a child begins writing, he stands a cup right-side up on his desk. When he needs my help, he turns the cup upside down and either illustrates his work or starts another piece of writing as he waits. *Stacie Dorin, Wagoner Elementary, Sauk Village, IL*

Publishing student work can be time-consuming, so I use a three-then-one rule. After a child writes three stories, he takes them home in a special envelope. (For an envelope label pattern, see page 204.) His family helps him select the story that he is most proud of, worked hard on, and wants to share. Then he returns the story to school and we publish it. *Kelly MacCall-Carter, Pine Run Elementary, New Britain, PA*

I use sticky notes to divide a blank journal into sections such as bulletin boards and learning centers. Whenever I see a great idea, display, or project, I record it in the journal with a brief note or a photo. *Molly Lynch, Arundel School, San Carlos, CA*

As I read a new issue of *The Mailbox*® magazine, I flag the pages that I want to refer to later. Also, I keep all my issues organized by months in magazine holders. That way, ideas for a certain time of year are all together, and it's easy to find particular activities. *Shelly Fales, Whittemore-Prescott Early Childhood Center, Whittemore, MI*

To make sure I don't forget what games I have for my first graders, I divided a notebook into different subject and skill areas. Whenever I make or find a new game, I list it in the correct section. *Sheila Criqui-Kelley, Lebo Elementary, Lebo, KS*

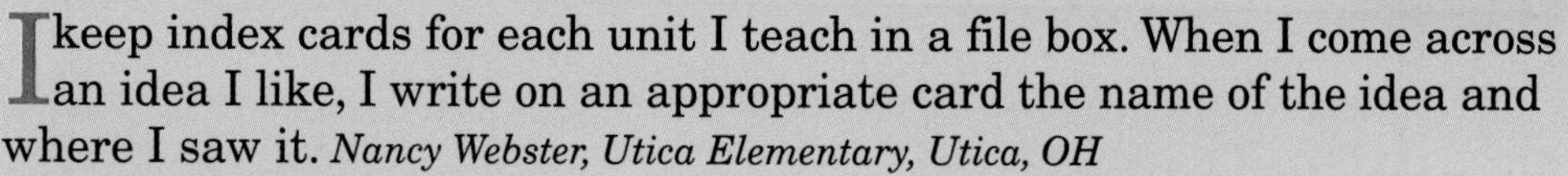

I keep index cards for each unit I teach in a file box. When I come across an idea I like, I write on an appropriate card the name of the idea and where I saw it. *Nancy Webster, Utica Elementary, Utica, OH*

When I get a new issue of *The Mailbox*® magazine, I put three large sticky notes, labeled as shown, on the front cover. I write the appropriate items and page numbers on the sticky notes for easy reference. *Barbie D. Bauman, Pasadena Fundamental Elementary, St. Petersburg, FL*

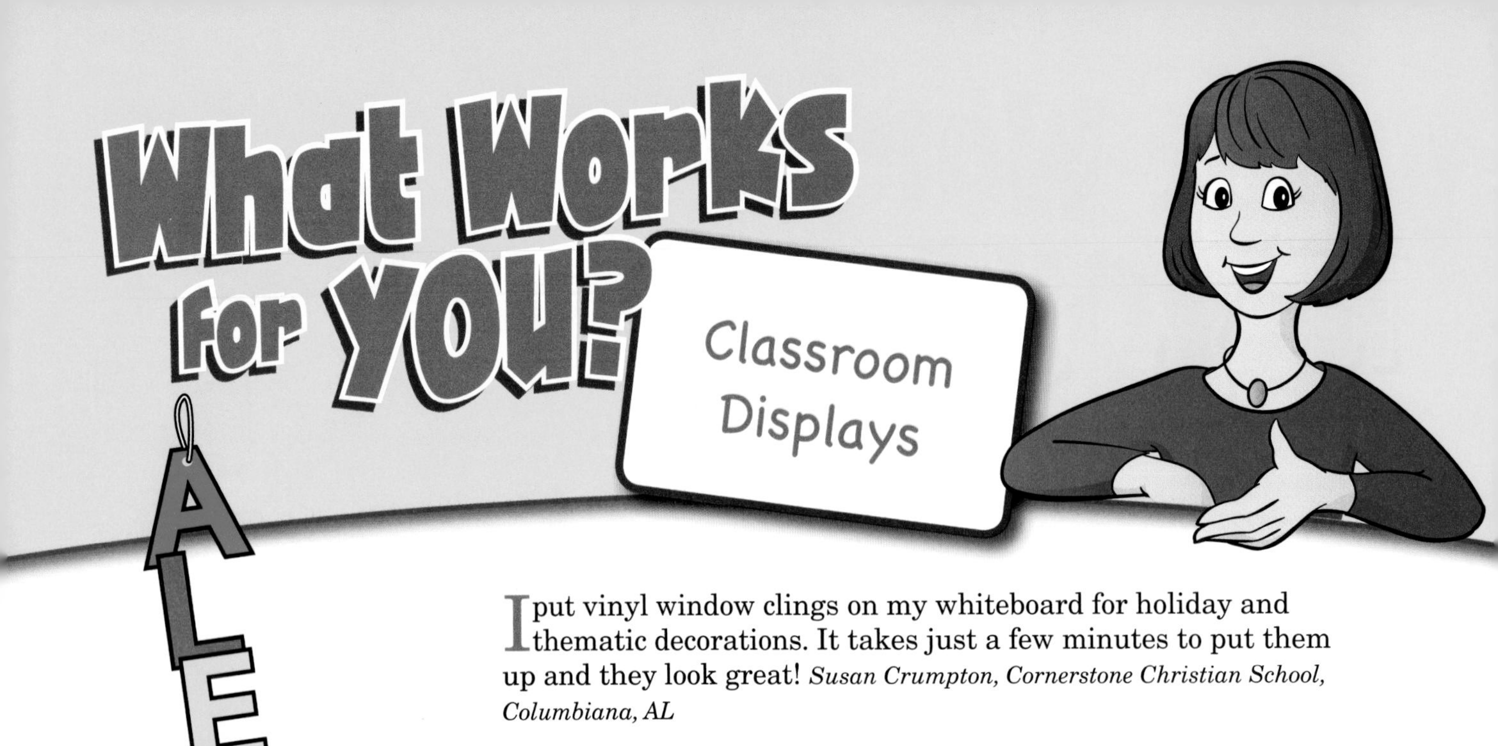

I put vinyl window clings on my whiteboard for holiday and thematic decorations. It takes just a few minutes to put them up and they look great! *Susan Crumpton, Cornerstone Christian School, Columbiana, AL*

For each child, I make letter cutouts that spell his name. Then I glue the letters together vertically and laminate them. I suspend each name and attach a sample of the corresponding youngster's work to the bottom of it. It's clear who did each work sample, and it's easy to update the papers on display. *Amanda Rau, Northwestern Lehigh School District, New Tripoli, PA*

To jazz up poems and songs that I write on chart paper, I decorate the paper with coordinating bulletin board border. *Karen Potter, Red Oak-Sturgeon Elementary, Alberta, VA*

The bulletin board above my sink often gets wet, so I back it with a plain-colored shower curtain liner and post laminated decorations. That way nothing gets ruined! *Trish Berk, Hopewell School, Glastonbury, CT*

A pocket shoe bag is perfect for storing bulletin board border. Simply hang the bag on a door, roll up the border, and then put the border in the pockets. *Brandi Jones, Red River Elementary, Coushatta, LA*

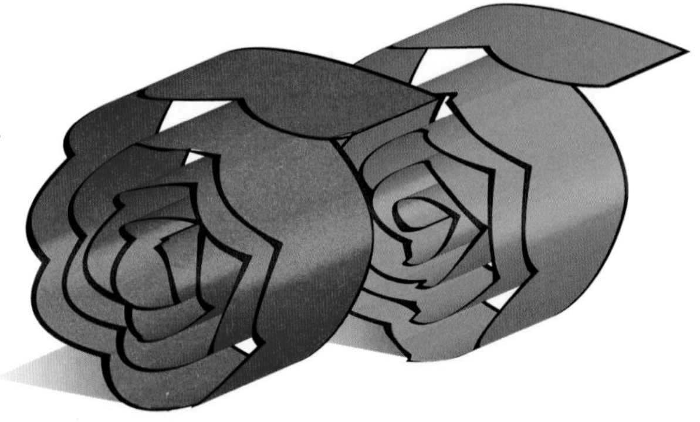

To ease my students' upcoming transition to second grade, I invite each second-grade teacher, in turn, to read her favorite storybook to my class. The storytime visits reduce youngsters' anxiety and create anticipation for fall. *Randi Austin, Lebanon, MO*

I have each of my students make an autograph book. Then I put one of my address labels in each student's book and encourage youngsters to write to me during the summer. It's a great way to promote writing! *Cathy Wroten, Bear Branch Elementary, Magnolia, TX*

My colleagues and I designate a different theme for each of several days to keep students excited about school. We have a special event each day, such as reading outdoors with beach towels on Beach Day and blowing bubbles on Bubble Day. *Cyndi Stumpf, Ellen T. Briggs School, Lake Hopatcong, NJ*

On the last day of school, I give each student a book from a book club. (Bonus points are a good resource for collecting books.) The books are wonderful mementos and they encourage students to read during the summer. *Marie E. Cecchini, West Dundee, IL*

I clear out classroom items I no longer need with a year-end give-away. I ask each student to draw a number. Then I call each number in sequential order and have the corresponding student choose an item to keep. *Jennifer Kresicki, Perquimans Central School, Winfall, NC*

Envelope Label
Use with "Managing Writing Time" on page 200.

WRITE ON!

On the Way

Here's a **prompt** to which every child can respond! Invite students to tell what they observed on the way to school. Guide them to describe details, such as color, size, and location. Then give each child a copy of page 211. Instruct her to illustrate her response to the question, encouraging her to include details like the ones discussed. Have her complete the sentence and then color the rest of the paper as desired.

Nancy Strout, Greater Portland Christian School, South Portland, ME

Drawing Stories

To encourage students to include **details in their illustrations**, tell them that you want to write a story about a student. Then use one crayon to draw a simple illustration of a secretly chosen youngster. Invite students to guess who the youngster is. After they share several guesses, wonder aloud whether a more detailed illustration would help tell the story. Then draw a similar illustration, this time using crayons that match the colors of the youngster's clothing and adding significant details. Guide students to identify the youngster if they did not already do so and have them compare the two drawings. Afterward, instruct each child to picture in his mind a story he would like to share. Then ask him to draw a corresponding illustration and write about it.

Rebecka Spence, Greensboro, NC

Dear Boys and Girls,
Today we will paint with sponges. Do you like red paint?
Sincerely,
Ms. Cochran

yes Angelica
yes Liam
no Maggie
yes Marco
no Eric
yes Raelyn

Variety at Group Time

Make the most of **morning messages**! Have students help you write a message each day as appropriate for their skills. Extend their learning with the options below.

Friday Find: Save the messages from the first four days of the week. Reread the messages on Friday and instruct students to draw different shapes around designated words.

Question Day: Include a yes-or-no question and ask students to write responses.

Puzzle Time: Cut the sentences apart. Have students cut the sentences between the words and then arrange the words in the correct order.

Marcia Cochran, Kalamazoo Christian West Preschool, Kalamazoo, MI

Write On!

Colorful Clues

When you write a **morning message**, use a different-colored marker for each sentence. It's a simple way to help youngsters distinguish between words and sentences! For reinforcement, have students count the number of words in each sentence. Then ask youngsters to point out the beginning and end of each sentence and identify the corresponding uppercase letter and end mark.

Sara Miller, All Saints Episcopal School, Lubbock, TX

Over and Under

This "spider-rific" booklet is great for helping youngsters understand that their **illustrations and writing should match**. For each child, make one copy of page 212 and two copies of page 213. Cut out the cover and pages. Then staple the *over* and *under* pages between the cover and last page. To complete his booklet, have each youngster write his name on the cover. Instruct him to complete the sentence on each page and illustrate it. Then give him a length of string to which you have tied a plastic toy spider or spider ring. Ask him to tape the free end of the string to the web on the cover. When the child reads the booklet, have him use the spider to point to the words and act out the story.

Patsy James, Eisenhower Elementary, Boulder, CO

"Sense-ational" Apples

Observation skills are the key to this **poetry idea**. Divide students into groups and place an apple in the center of each group. Then have students name words that describe how the apples look. List the words on the board. Next, cut the apples and give each child a slice. As the youngsters eat the apples, guide them to name different words that describe how the apples look. Also have them name words that tell how the apples sound, smell, feel, and taste. Add the words to the board. The next day, help each child write an apple poem similar to the one shown, using two or three describing words per line. Then have her mount the poem on an apple cutout.

Toni Walker, Southern Elementary, Lexington, KY

Write On!

Reindeer Pal

This supercute booklet is perfect for responses to **winter and holiday prompts.** For each student, staple a few sheets of writing paper between a seven-inch brown circle and a sheet of brown paper. Then trim the paper to make a circular booklet. Have each child write in his booklet a response to a prompt below. Next, ask him to illustrate a reindeer face on the front cover. Then instruct him to use the patterns on page 214 to make two antlers, a collar, and a bell. Have him glue the resulting cutouts to the booklet as shown.

- Imagine that Rudolph the Red-Nosed Reindeer has a cousin with a different-colored nose. Write about him.
- What are three things you like about this time of year? Write about them.
- Write about the best winter day ever!

Cindy Barber, Fredonia, WI

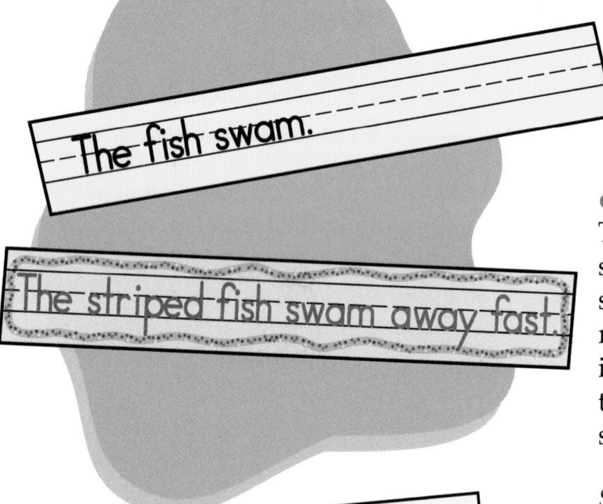

New and Improved

Here's a simple way to give students a visual reminder to include **details** in their writing. Title a board "Sentence Makeovers." Make a T chart on the board and then title the first column "Before" and the second column "After." Write a sentence without details on a sentence strip and post it in the first column. On a separate sentence strip, rewrite the sentence with student input so it includes more specific information. Decorate the revised sentence with glitter glue and then post it in the second column of the chart. Add several pairs of sentences to the display.

Suzanne Gerczynski, Glen Burnie Park Elementary, Glen Burnie, MD

This Is the Place!

Invite your young writers to focus on one element of a story, the **setting!** Ask each child to cut from a magazine a picture of a person, an animal, or a thing. Have her glue the picture on a sheet of drawing paper and incorporate it into an illustration of a setting. After she completes her artwork, instruct her to write a description of the scene.

Barbara Flynn, St. Ambrose School, Bridgeport, CT

Dates to Celebrate

Count on your students to enjoy this approach to writing dates! Review proper capitalization and punctuation of dates with students. Then pair students and give each youngster a sheet of writing paper. Have him write the dates of his next birthday and his partner's next birthday. After you check each twosome's work, instruct the pair to decorate a sheet of colorful paper and write their birthday information on it as shown. Display students' resulting gift boxes with the title "Mark the Dates!"

Michelle Woyshner, Millbridge Elementary, Delran, NJ

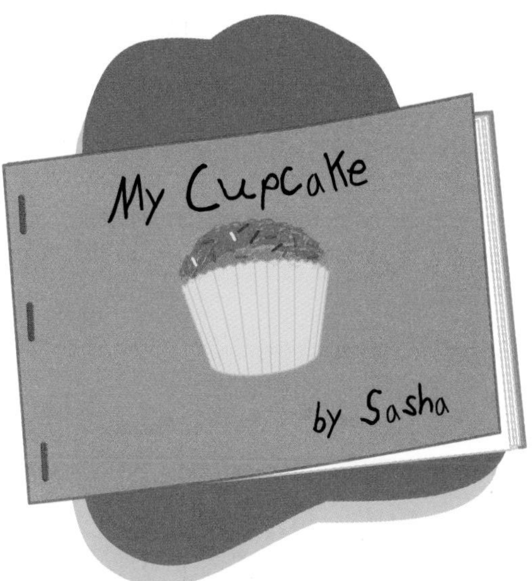

Step by Step!

Incorporate skill reinforcement into snacktime with this idea for writing how-to sentences. Get a class supply of cupcakes without frosting. Set out whipped topping or frosting and decorations such as sprinkles. Post a list of the items for a spelling reference. Then invite each child to decorate a cupcake. As students eat their cupcakes, give each youngster a blank booklet. Instruct her to explain how she decorated her cupcake by writing and illustrating each step on a separate page. Then have her title the booklet and illustrate the front cover with a relevant picture or a photo of her with her cupcake.

Sandra Shelton, Stout Field Elementary, Indianapolis, IN

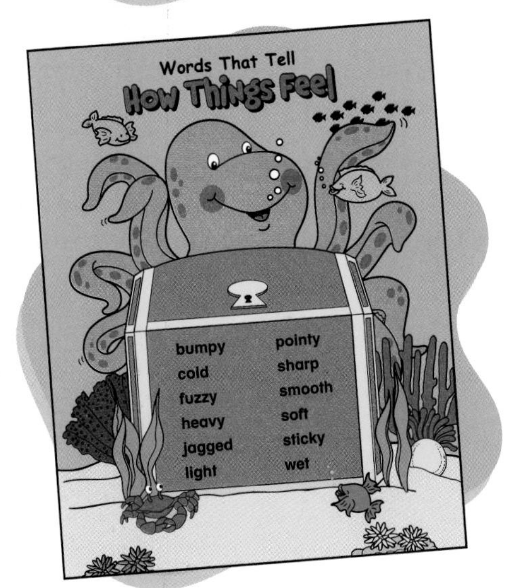

Writing Center Helper

Color a copy of the word bank on page 215 and post it at a center. Then choose an option below.

Adjectives: Give each youngster a blank booklet. Over several days, have him write and illustrate in the booklet a sentence for each word.

Descriptions: Ask each child to write about a classroom object, using describing words such as the ones on the poster.

Riddles: Place several objects at the center. Have students use words from the poster to write riddles about the objects. Post the riddles and invite youngsters to guess the answers.

Write On!

On Topic

What makes this booklet unique? It doubles as a planning tool! For each student, stack two sheets of paper and position them vertically. Slide the top sheet upward about one inch. Fold the papers forward to create a cover and three graduated pages. Staple along the fold. To complete a booklet, a youngster titles it with the name of a season and writes her name on the cover. Next, she labels the bottom of each page with an activity she does during that season and then lightly colors it. Finally, she writes about each activity on the appropriate page and illustrates her work.

S'mores, Step by Step

For this how-to writing activity, illustrate two tan craft foam squares so they resemble graham crackers and one brown craft foam square so it resembles a chocolate bar. Gather one large cotton ball (marshmallow) and one craft stick (skewer). To begin, use the items to pantomime making a s'more over a campfire. Next, ask students to brainstorm words they might use to write instructions for making s'mores. Then put the resulting spelling reference and the props at a center stocked with writing paper. Encourage each center visitor to pantomime making a s'more and then have him write and illustrate the corresponding steps.

Laura Wanke, Pecatonica Elementary, Pecatonica, IL

Writing Center Helper

Promote descriptive writing with this word bank. Color a copy of page 216 and post it at a center. Then choose an option below.

Responding to a prompt: Have each child write a journal entry that begins "I am [feeling word] when…"

Writing with details: Ask each child to write about a personal experience, encouraging him to include words from the word bank. Then instruct him to use a colored pencil to underline the feeling words in his work.

Character analysis: To follow up a reading selection, instruct each child to illustrate a character. Then invite him to write how the character feels and why.

Name ______________________________ Responding to a prompt

What Did You See?

Draw and write.

On the way to school, I saw ______________________________

Note to the teacher: Use with “On the Way” on page 206.

Booklet Cover and Last Booklet Page

Use with "Over and Under" on page 207.

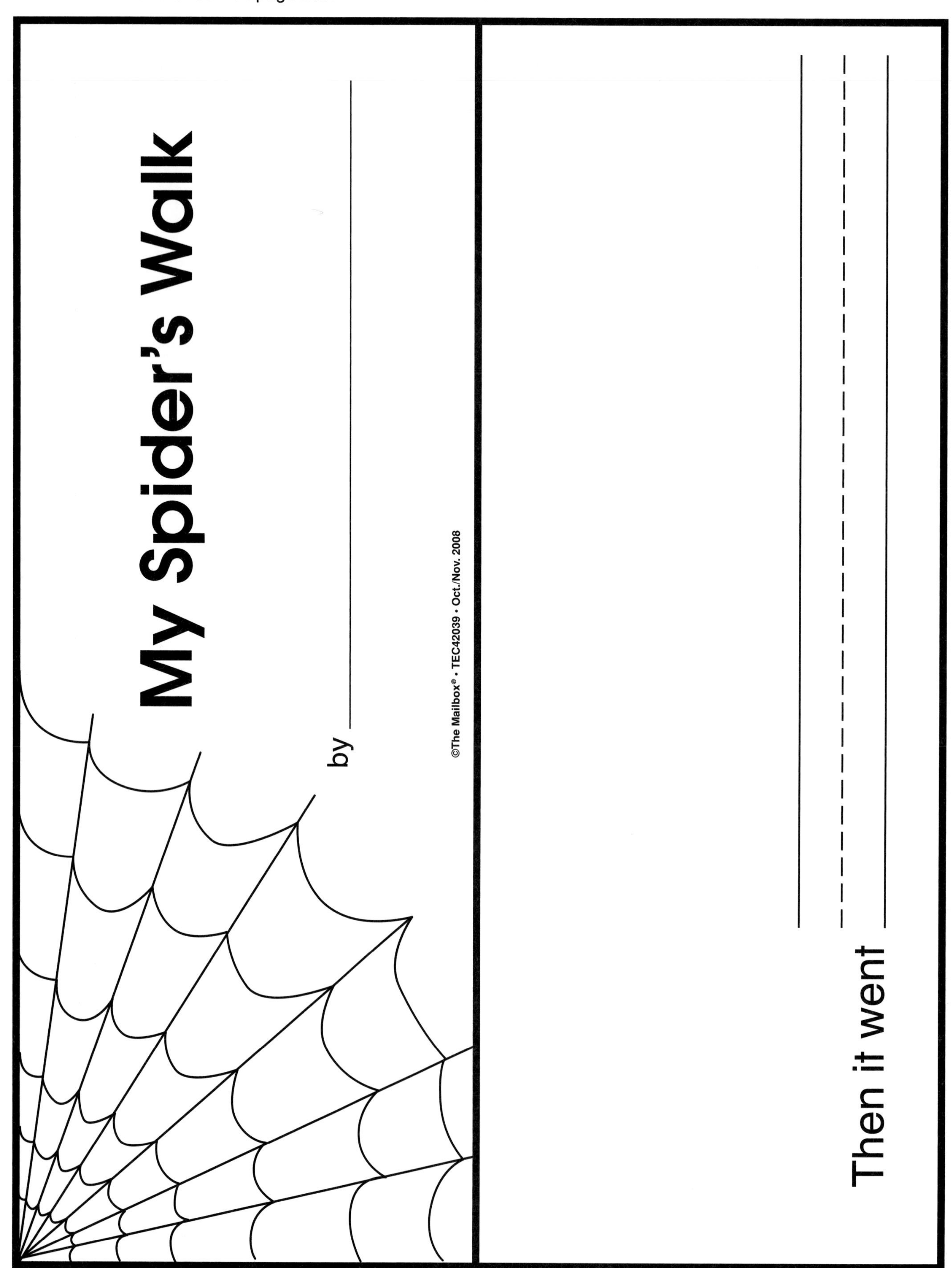

Use with "Over and Under" on page 207.

My spider went over the ________

My spider went under the ________

Antler, Collar, and Bell Patterns

Use with "Reindeer Pal"
on page 208.

Words That Tell
How Things Feel
bumpy
cold
fuzzy
heavy
jagged
light
pointy
sharp
smooth
soft
sticky
wet

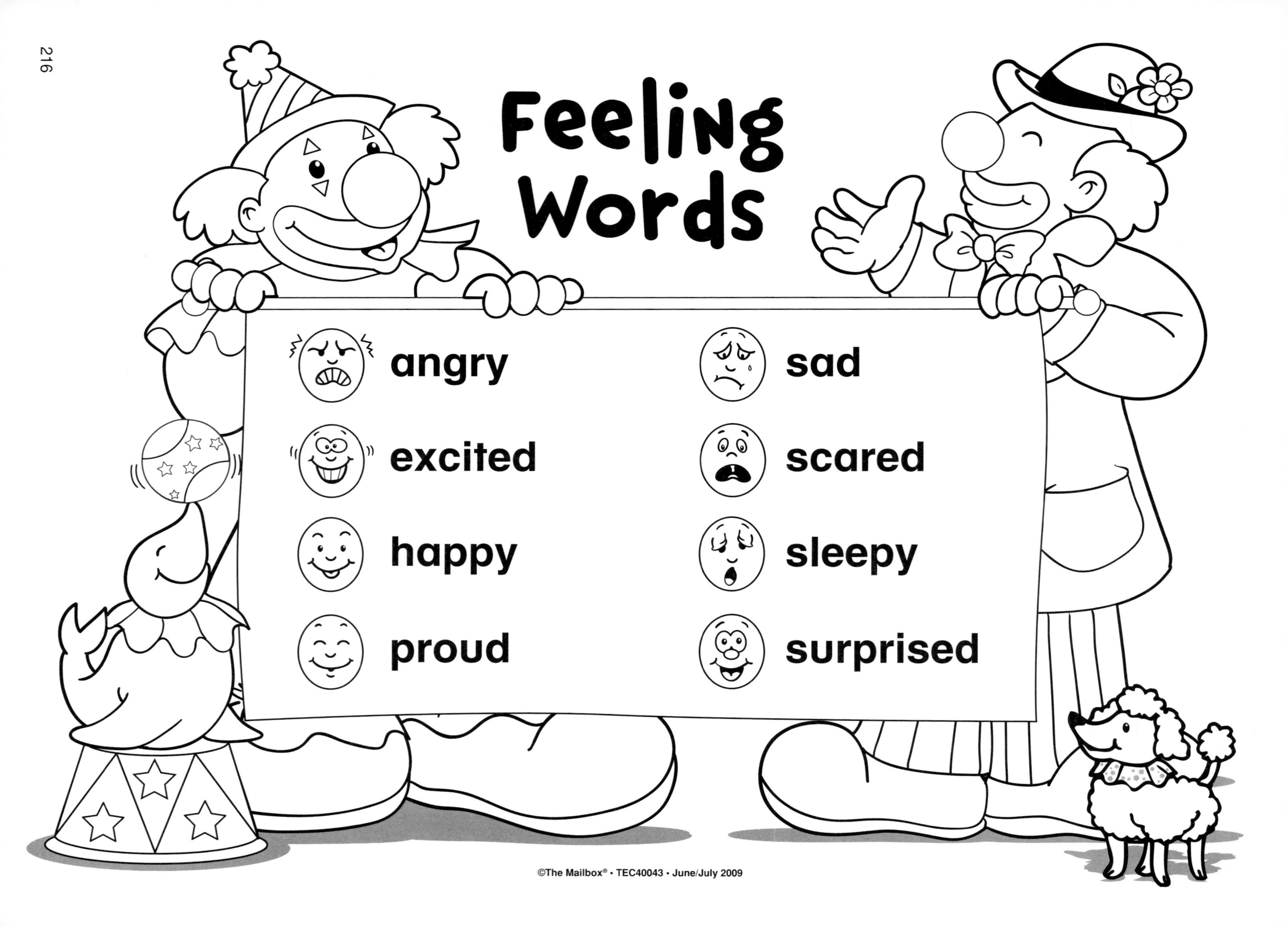
Feeling Words
angry
excited
happy
proud
sad
scared
sleepy
surprised

Name____

Writing Helper

Note to the teacher: Give each child a copy of this page. After you review the words and reminders with him, have him put the paper in a writing folder or journal for reference.

Name ____________________ March word bank

Writing Helper

Note to the teacher: Give each child a copy of this page. After you review the reminders and words with him, have him put the paper in a writing folder or journal for easy reference.

Name ______________________

Writing Helper

Spring Words

bird	leaves
bloom	puddle
butterfly	rainbow
flowers	seeds
grow	sunny
hatch	warm

WELCOME

Home, "Tweet" Home

Don't forget!
Use order words such as **first, then, next,** and **lastly.**
Check your **spelling.**

Note to the teacher: Give each child a copy of this page. After you review the words and reminders with him, have him put the paper in a writing folder or his journal for reference.

Writing Helper

Don't forget!
Use **exact verbs.**
Check your **spelling.**

Pond Words

cool	float	leap	splash
deep	frog	leaves	swim
dive	duck	lily pad	turtle
fish	jump	plants	water

Note to the teacher: Give each child a copy of this page. After you review the writing reminders and words with him, have him put the paper in a writing folder or journal for easy reference.

Name____________________

Wow!

Prompt: Think about a time you were surprised.

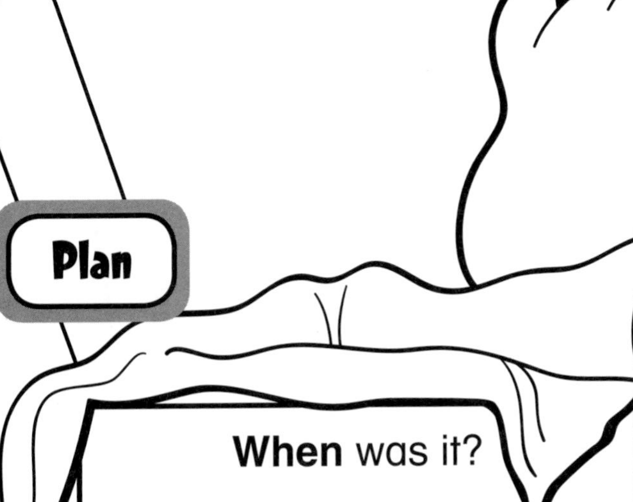

Plan

When was it?	**Where** were you?
Who was there?	**What** happened?

Write: Write about a time you were surprised. Be sure to tell when it was and where you were.

Good Morning!

Prompt: Think about how you get ready in the morning.

Write: Write how you get ready in the morning. Use words such as **first, next, then,** and **last.**

Name ______________________________

Splish, Splash!

Prompt: Think about a day it rained.

Plan

List two things you liked about the day.

1. ______________________________

2. ______________________________

List two things you did **not** like about the day.

1. ______________________________

2. ______________________________

Write: Write about the rainy day. Be sure to include details from your plan.

Name______________________________

Busy at the Beach

Prompt: Imagine you are at a sandy beach on a hot, sunny day.

Plan

What do you **see?**

What do you **hear?**

What do you **feel?**

Write: Write about a day at a beach. Write what you might see, hear, and feel.

Literacy Units

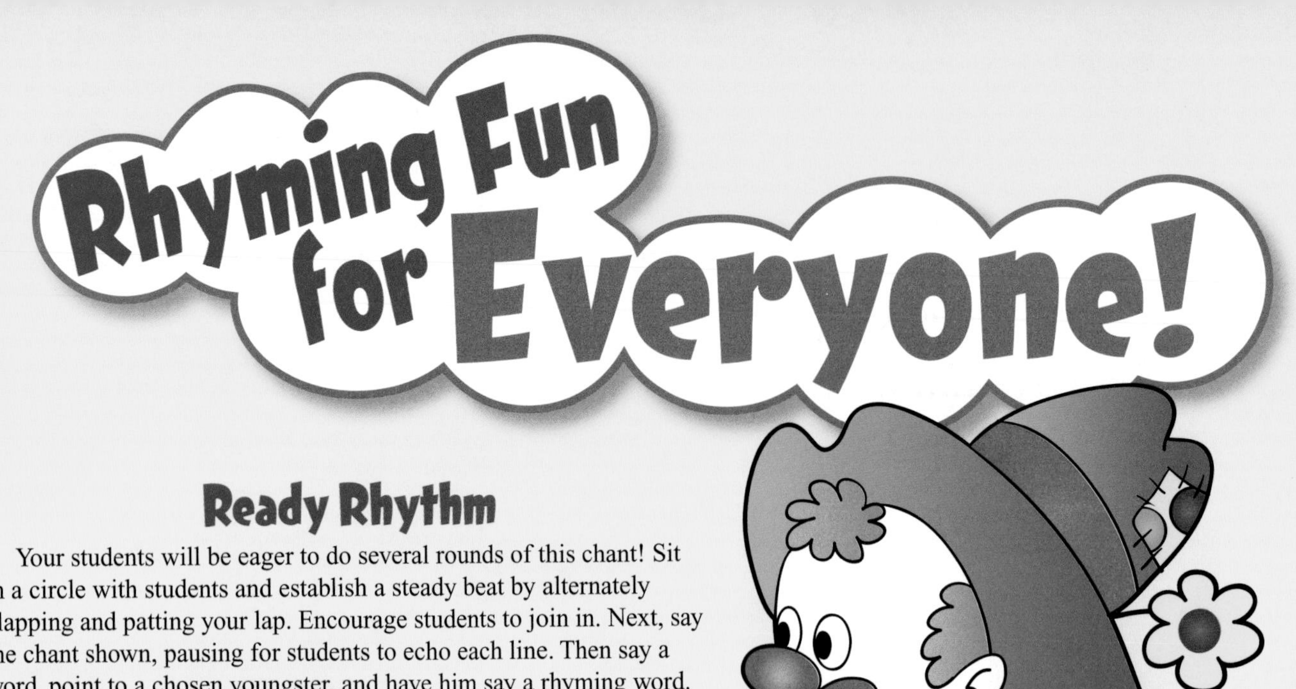

Rhyming Fun for Everyone!

Ready Rhythm

Your students will be eager to do several rounds of this chant! Sit in a circle with students and establish a steady beat by alternately clapping and patting your lap. Encourage students to join in. Next, say the chant shown, pausing for students to echo each line. Then say a word, point to a chosen youngster, and have him say a rhyming word. Repeat the chant to begin another round.

We're going on a rhyming hunt.
I know what to do.
I need to listen well
And rhyme that word for you.

Heather E. Graley, Grace Christian School, Blacklick, OH

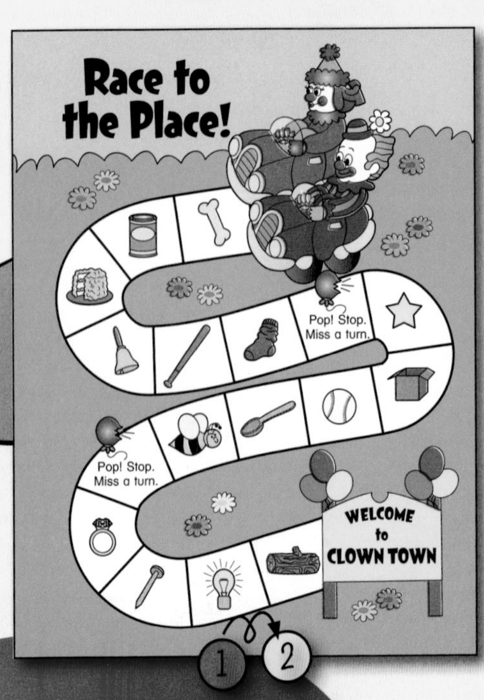

Race to the Place!

To prepare this partner center, color a copy of the gameboard on page 228. Label one side of a plastic math chip "1" and the other side "2." Then put the math chip in a disposable cup and set out two game markers. Have each player place her game marker on a different car. To take a turn, a player shakes the cup and spills out the math chip. Then she advances the corresponding number of spaces and follows any instructions where she lands. If she lands on a space with a picture, she names the picture and a rhyming word. (Encourage players not to repeat rhymes.)The players take turns as described until they reach Clown Town.

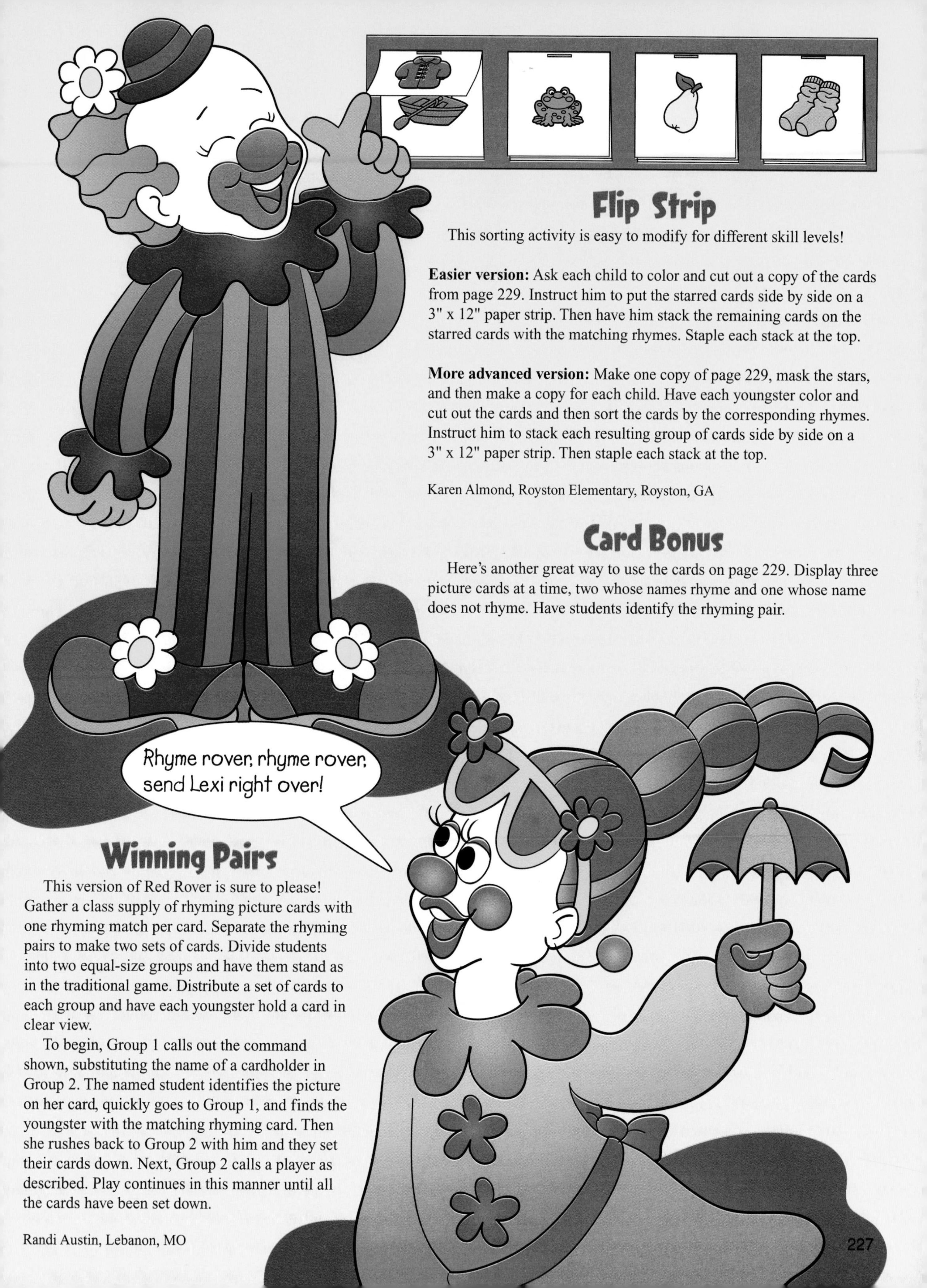

Flip Strip

This sorting activity is easy to modify for different skill levels!

Easier version: Ask each child to color and cut out a copy of the cards from page 229. Instruct him to put the starred cards side by side on a 3" x 12" paper strip. Then have him stack the remaining cards on the starred cards with the matching rhymes. Staple each stack at the top.

More advanced version: Make one copy of page 229, mask the stars, and then make a copy for each child. Have each youngster color and cut out the cards and then sort the cards by the corresponding rhymes. Instruct him to stack each resulting group of cards side by side on a 3" x 12" paper strip. Then staple each stack at the top.

Karen Almond, Royston Elementary, Royston, GA

Card Bonus

Here's another great way to use the cards on page 229. Display three picture cards at a time, two whose names rhyme and one whose name does not rhyme. Have students identify the rhyming pair.

Winning Pairs

This version of Red Rover is sure to please! Gather a class supply of rhyming picture cards with one rhyming match per card. Separate the rhyming pairs to make two sets of cards. Divide students into two equal-size groups and have them stand as in the traditional game. Distribute a set of cards to each group and have each youngster hold a card in clear view.

To begin, Group 1 calls out the command shown, substituting the name of a cardholder in Group 2. The named student identifies the picture on her card, quickly goes to Group 1, and finds the youngster with the matching rhyming card. Then she rushes back to Group 2 with him and they set their cards down. Next, Group 2 calls a player as described. Play continues in this manner until all the cards have been set down.

Randi Austin, Lebanon, MO

Race to the Place!

Picture Cards

Use with "Flip Strip" and "Card Bonus" on page 227.

Name____

Hold Tight!

Name the pictures.

Color the balloons by the code.

Color Code

rhyme—yellow

do not rhyme—orange

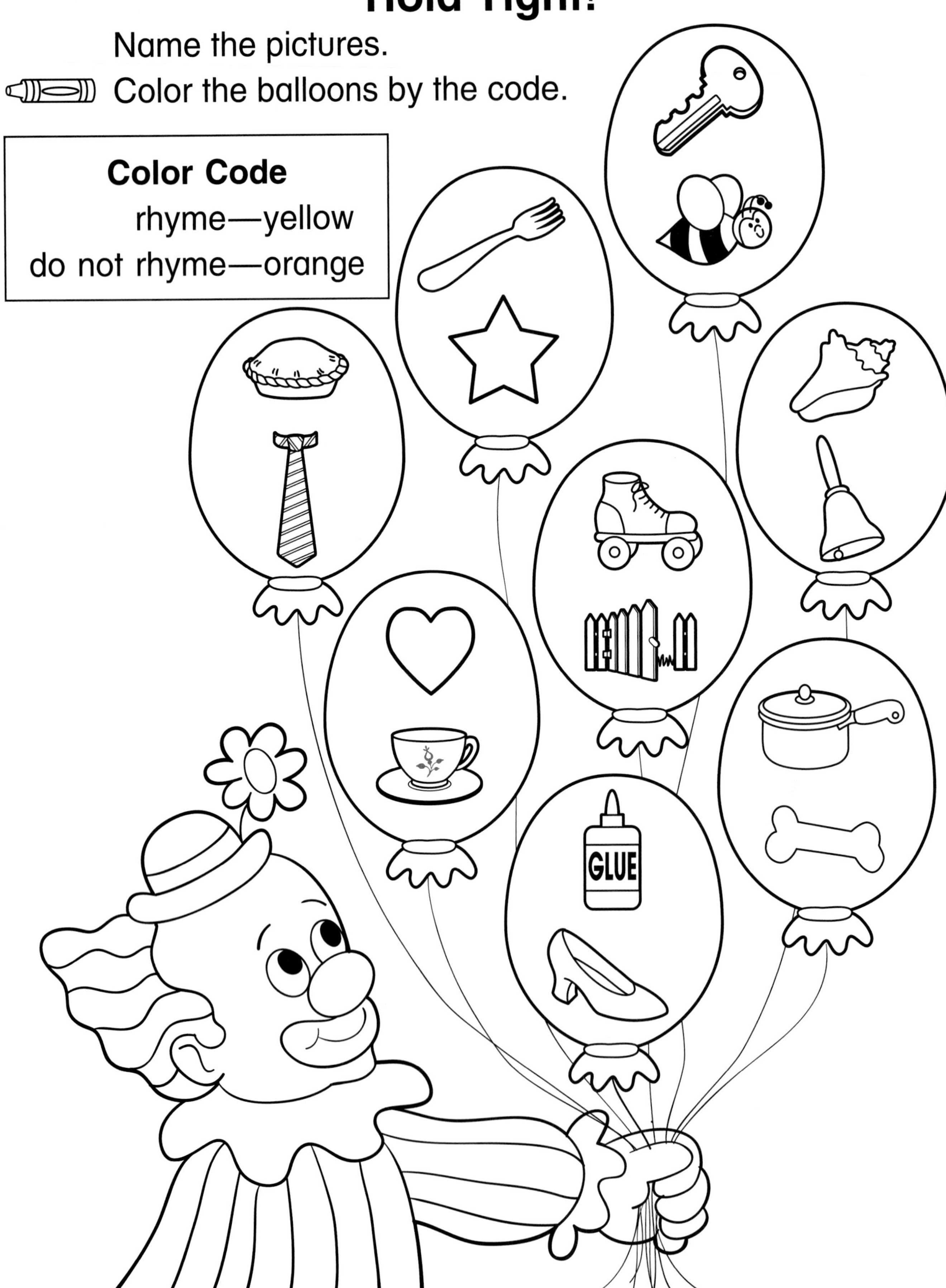

It's Time for Journals!

Spark students' enthusiasm for writing with these creative ideas.

Lovable Ideas

Choosing writing topics

What's a simple way to get students on the "write" track? Help them choose topics that are near and dear to their hearts! Give each child a copy of page 233. Have him illustrate each section of the heart to match the text, and encourage him to label his artwork. Invite him to color the rest of the paper and then instruct him to put it in his journal. When it's time for students to write, ask each youngster to refer to his paper for writing ideas or designate a chosen section of the heart and have students write about the corresponding topic.

Amy Rodriguez, P. S. 212, Brooklyn, NY

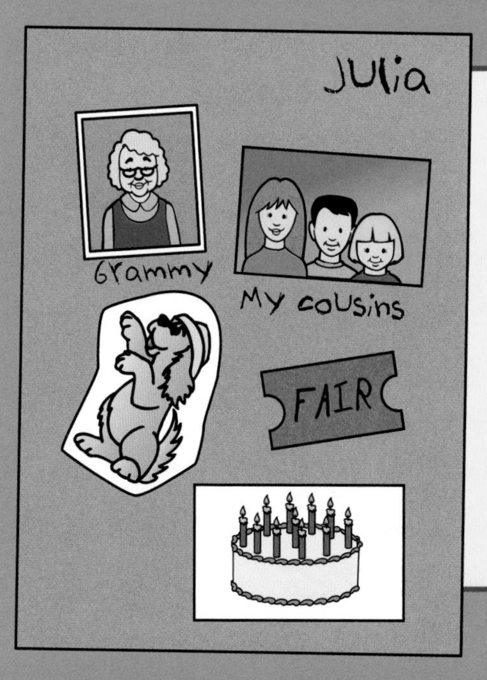

Photos and Such

Choosing writing topics

If a picture is worth a thousand words, these scrapbook pages are sure to give young writers lots to write about! Send a colorful sheet of paper home with each student along with a note asking an adult to help the youngster make a scrapbook page that shows people, activities, and occasions that are important to the child. (Explain that the scrapbook page will be returned.) After the youngster completes the page, have her return it to school. Put each child's scrapbook page in a separate top-loading page protector and then ask her to keep it in her writing folder for inspiration. To keep students' writing ideas fresh, have each youngster and a family member make a different scrapbook page each season.

Audrey Vohs, Homestead-Wakefield Elementary, Bel Air, MD

Ready Reference

Using an alphabet chart

To make this letter-perfect writing tool, list the uppercase and lowercase alphabet letters on a vertical half sheet of paper, leaving at least one inch blank at the bottom. Attach a colorful copy of the list to the back cover of each child's journal, as shown, and then fold down the list. When a child is ready to write in the journal, he unfolds the list and turns to the first blank journal page. He refers to the list as needed for help with letter formation. When he is finished writing, he folds the list down.

Bernadette Todaro, Grand Island, NY

Good Morning!

Writing to communicate

Since students often arrive at school eager to share news, why not channel that enthusiasm into writing? For each student, make a good morning journal by stapling several sheets of writing paper between two sheets of construction paper. Personalize the front cover and decorate it with a sun cutout or illustration. At the beginning of each day, have each youngster make an entry in her journal. At the end of the writing time, arrange for pairs or small groups of students to sit together and greet one another. Then invite them to share their journal entries. There's no doubt it will promote purposeful writing and build a positive classroom community!

Tina Buckley, Theodore Roosevelt School, Buffalo, NY

Tuneful Reminders

Establishing a writing community

Start your writing time with this pride-boosting song.

(sung to the tune of "I've Been Working on the Railroad")

I'm a first grade writer here at school today.
I'm a first grade writer; I have so much to say!
I can choose a good topic—
A topic just right for me.
I can draw and write great stories.
Take a look and see!

adapted from an idea by Kathy Brand
Cornerstone Christian School
New City, NY

Name ____________________

What Can I Write About?

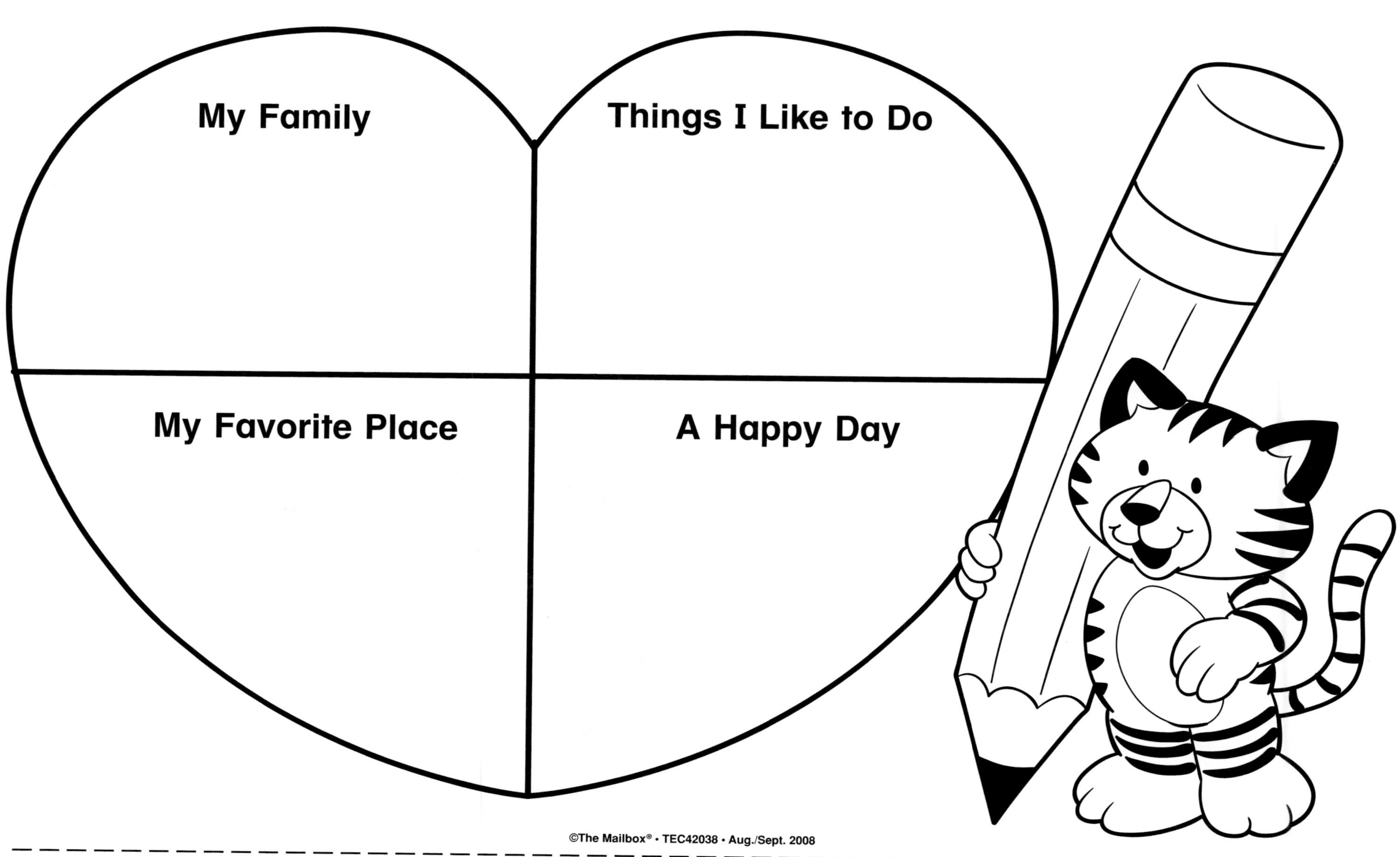

Note to the teacher: Use with "Lovable Ideas" on page 231.

Letter-Perfect Ideas

Switch!

Letter recognition

For this fun-filled game, gather a supply of matching uppercase and lowercase letter cards so there is one card per student. Have students arrange their chairs in a circle and sit down. Give each student a card at random. To play one round, name a letter. Then lead students in the song shown and have the two students with the named letter try to change places before the end of the song. For added fun, every few rounds say, "Alphabet soup!" instead of a letter. Then have all the students switch places as you sing the song, changing the first, second, and fourth lines to "If you have a letter card."

adapted from an idea by Linda Gordetsky
Boynton Creek Elementary
Delray Beach, FL

On the Lookout

Letter recognition

This letter-hunt activity is easy to adapt for different skill levels! In advance, gather one uppercase letter card per student. Post the cards around the room within students' reach. To begin, give each youngster a lowercase letter card that corresponds with a posted letter. Then instruct each student to look around the room for the card that matches her card. When she finds it, ask her to take the pair of cards to your large-group area and sit down. After each child is seated, have each youngster, in turn, show her cards to the group and name the corresponding letter.

For an easier version, post fewer different letters, repeating letters as needed.

For a more advanced version, instead of uppercase letter cards, post picture cards. Have each youngster find the picture whose name begins with the letter on her card.

Marlene Borysiak, Weston Elementary, Schofield, WI

Wipe Away Errors

Handwriting

Try this confidence-building idea whenever you teach students how to write a different letter. After you model the correct letter formation, give each student a handwriting paper in a plastic page protector. Then have him complete the paper with a wipe-off marker. Since the wipe-off format allows him to erase his writing, it's sure to alleviate any concerns he has about making mistakes. Plus, it allows for repeated practice. When the youngster is ready to complete the paper with a pencil, simply remove it from the page protector.

Jana Murphy, Primavera School, Prescott, AZ

Full Steam Ahead!

Letter recognition, handwriting

This center is just the ticket for reinforcing your choice of letters. Make one copy of page 236. Write a different letter on each train engine. Then place student copies of the paper at a center along with old magazines, scissors, glue, letter stampers, and ink pads. When a youngster visits the center, she cuts from the magazines one or two examples of each featured letter and glues them on the appropriate train cars. Then she stamps and writes the letters where indicated.

Angie Kutzer, Garrett Elementary, Mebane, NC

Artsy Alphabet

Letter-sound associations

Here's a fun way to incorporate literacy into your art center. Draw a large block letter on a sheet of paper. Arrange for each student to decorate a copy of the letter with illustrations or items whose names begin with the letter. For example, you might have students make red fingerprint apples on the letter *A,* illustrate balloons on the letter *B,* make corncob paint prints on the letter *C,* and make dots with a bingo dauber on the letter *D.*

If desired, have each youngster complete a paper as described for each letter of the alphabet. Then bind his papers in alphabetical order between two covers. No doubt he'll enjoy reviewing the pages and recalling how he decorated them! **For more advanced students,** ask each youngster to write captions with the letters and corresponding words.

Deborah Provencher, West Brookfield Elementary
West Brookfield, MA

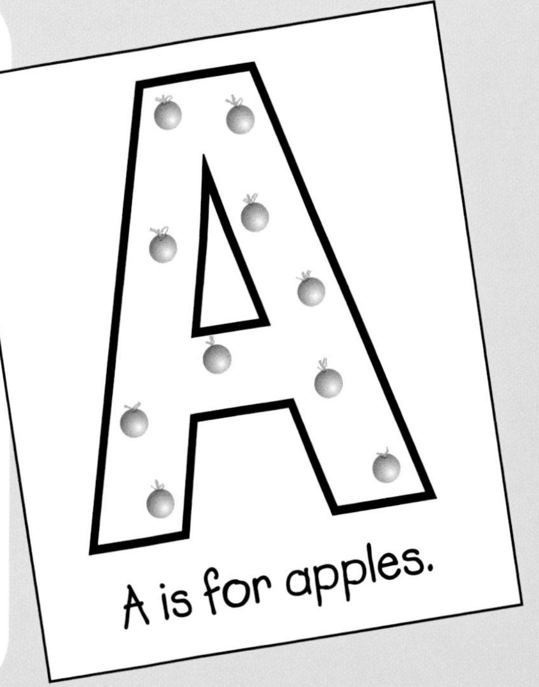

Name________________________________

Full Steam Ahead!

Cut and glue.

Stamp.

Write.

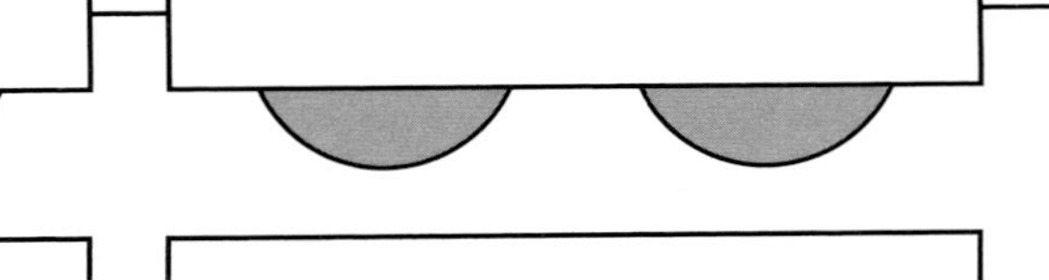

Note to the teacher: Use with "Full Steam Ahead!" on page 235.

Custom-Made for Literacy

Build your students' reading and writing skills with these ideas.

That Was Fun!

Writing about a personal experience

Use this supersimple idea to help youngsters choose writing topics. Have each child think of a fun experience she had with a friend. Ask her to give you a thumbs-up when she pictures the experience in her mind. After she signals you in this manner, give her a copy of page 239. Have her illustrate the experience and then write about it, using additional paper if necessary.

Name N. Keela

Custom-Made for Literacy
Writing about an experience

That Was Fun!

Think about a fun time you had with a friend.

Draw a picture.

Bird Club

Write.

Jordan cam to see my dog. We tk him for a wk.

Under Construction

Word families

Try this creative approach to sorting words! For a small group, gather three white cards (foundations), a supply of colored cards (walls), and three triangles (roofs). Write a different rime on each roof. Write a key word for each rime on a separate white card. Program each colored card with a word that contains a featured rime, programming a different number of cards for each rime. To complete the activity, the youngsters spread out the white cards to "set" the foundations. After they finish building the houses as shown, they read each group of words. Then each youngster lists on provided paper the words from the tallest house.

For an initial consonant variation, write a consonant on each white card and leave the roofs blank. Program each colored card with a picture whose name begins with a featured consonant.

sip hip lip dip -ip

pin fin win tin bin -in

-ig wig pig

Shellie Miller, Cessna Elementary, Wichita, KS

Brick by Brick

Concepts about print or word order

For these pocket-chart ideas, program red rectangles (bricks) with sentences, writing each word and any punctuation on a separate brick.

Concepts about print: Display the sentences, leaving space between the words to help students develop one-to-one correspondence between oral and written words. Have youngsters take turns wearing a pair of work gloves and pointing to the words as students read them.

Word order: Instruct students to "build" a wall by using the bricks to form sentences in separate rows of a pocket chart, beginning with the bottom row.

Shellie Miller, Cessna Elementary, Wichita, KS

Punctuation Playhouse

End marks

To prepare this variation of lotto, have each child color a copy of page 240. Then instruct him to cut out the punctuation cards and glue them on the grid in random order. Give each player eight counters to use as game markers. To play one round, display a sentence without ending punctuation and read it aloud. Ask a volunteer to identify the correct punctuation and add it to the sentence. Then have each player put a counter on a corresponding card on his gameboard. Continue as described until one or more players marks four cards in a row. **For an easier version,** use punctuated sentences. Have students point out and identify the ending punctuation before marking their gameboards.

adapted from an idea by Shellie Miller

Home Base

Initial or final consonants

Here's a lively phonics activity! Make six or more house cutouts and then write a consonant on each house. Arrange the houses in a large circle on the floor. To begin, instruct students to walk around the circle as you play some music. After a few moments, stop the music and have each youngster go to the house that is closest to him. Next, say a word. Have students identify either the initial or final consonant. Then ask each youngster at the house with the named letter to sit out the next round. Resume the music to continue.

Shellie Miller

Name ____________________

That Was Fun!

Think about a fun time you had with a friend.

Draw a picture.

Write.

Note to the teacher: Use with "That Was Fun!" on page 237.

Name ______________________________

Custom-Made for Literacy
End marks

Punctuation Playhouse

 Note to the teacher: Use with "Punctuation Playhouse" on page 238.

Wintry Mix

Initial consonant blends

The chance of having a blend blizzard keeps anticipation high with this small-group game! To prepare, gather a supply of blank cards. Decorate a few cards with snowflake stickers or clip art. Write on each remaining card a word that begins with a consonant blend. Shuffle the cards.

The players spread out the cards facedown. To take a turn, a player picks up a card. If it shows a word, he identifies the consonant blend and reads the word. If the card shows snowflakes, he says "Blend blizzard!" and each player who has any cards drops them back into the pool of cards. Then the player with the snowflake card sets it aside and mixes up the cards in play, making sure they are flipped facedown. Players take turns as time allows or until no cards are left in play.

Katie Zuehlke, Bendix Elementary, Annandale, MN

Pair the Mittens!

Initial consonant blends

For this partner game, make a supply of identical mitten cutouts. Write "Brrr!" on a few mittens. Program each remaining pair of mittens with words that begin with a different consonant blend, writing one word per mitten.

The students scramble the mittens and arrange them in rows facedown. Then they play as in the traditional game of Concentration except that if a player turns over a mitten that shows "Brrr!" she sets it aside and turns over two more mittens so there are three mittens faceup. Then she tries to make a pair with any of the words that are showing. The game continues until no mittens are left in play. The player with more mittens wins.

Word Wonders

Changing the last letter of a word

Have each child color the hat and cards on a copy of page 243 and cut them out. Next, name the first word in a word pair. (See the suggestions on this page.) Ask each youngster to use the letter cards to form the word on the hat brim and then have him write the word on a sheet of paper. Next, instruct him to change the last letter on the hat to form a new word of his choice. (The words may vary.) After he writes the newly formed word on his paper, have him clear his hat to prepare for the next word.

Suggested Word Pairs

flag—flat
ham—hat
mad—mat
man—map
pan—pat
tan—tag

Build a Snowpal!

Sorting by rimes

Who can build a snowpal the fastest? That's what students find out with this small-group game! Make one snowpal head and hat per player. Label each hat with a different rime. Write on each of four white circles (snowballs) a word that contains a featured rime so there are four words per rime. Put the snowballs in a container. To begin, each child puts a hat on her snowpal head. Next, each player, in turn, takes a snowball at random and reads the corresponding word. If the word contains the rime on her hat, she adds the snowball to her snowpal. If the word does not contain the rime, she returns the snowball. Alternate play continues until one player adds four snowballs to her snowpal.

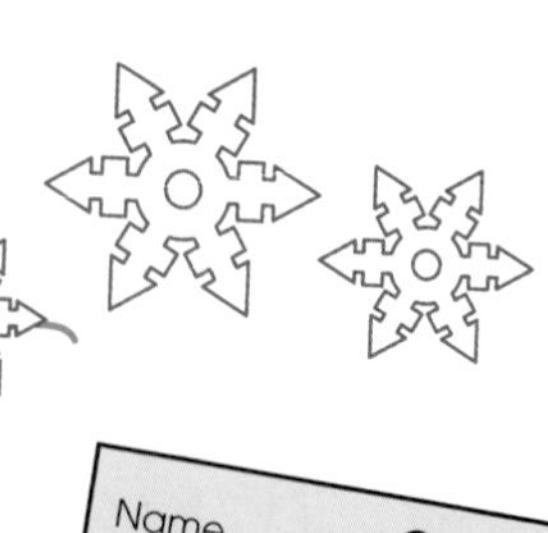

Snowball Toss

Categorizing by rimes

To prepare this beanbag game, choose three rimes. Program a supply of white circles (snowballs) with words that contain the rimes, writing one word per snowball. Spread out the snowballs facedown on the floor. Give each child a corresponding recording sheet like the one shown. To play, a child tosses a beanbag on a snowball. He turns the snowball over and reads its word aloud. Each student writes the word on his recording sheet. Then the child who tossed the beanbag sets the snowball aside. Play continues until students clear all the snowballs.

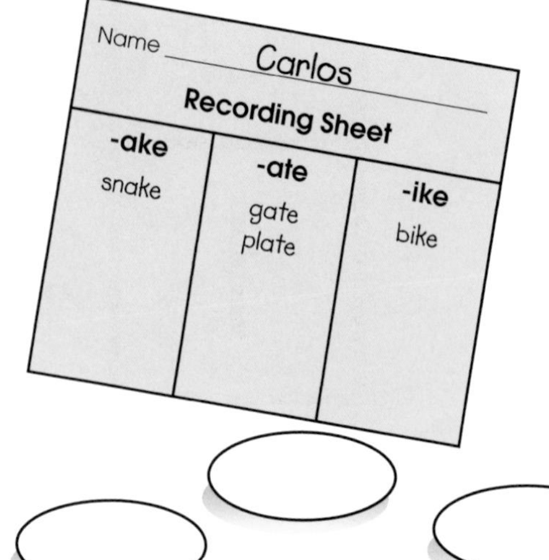

Katie Zuehlke, Bendix Elementary, Annandale, MN

Hat Pattern and Letter Cards

Use with "Word Wonders" on page 242.

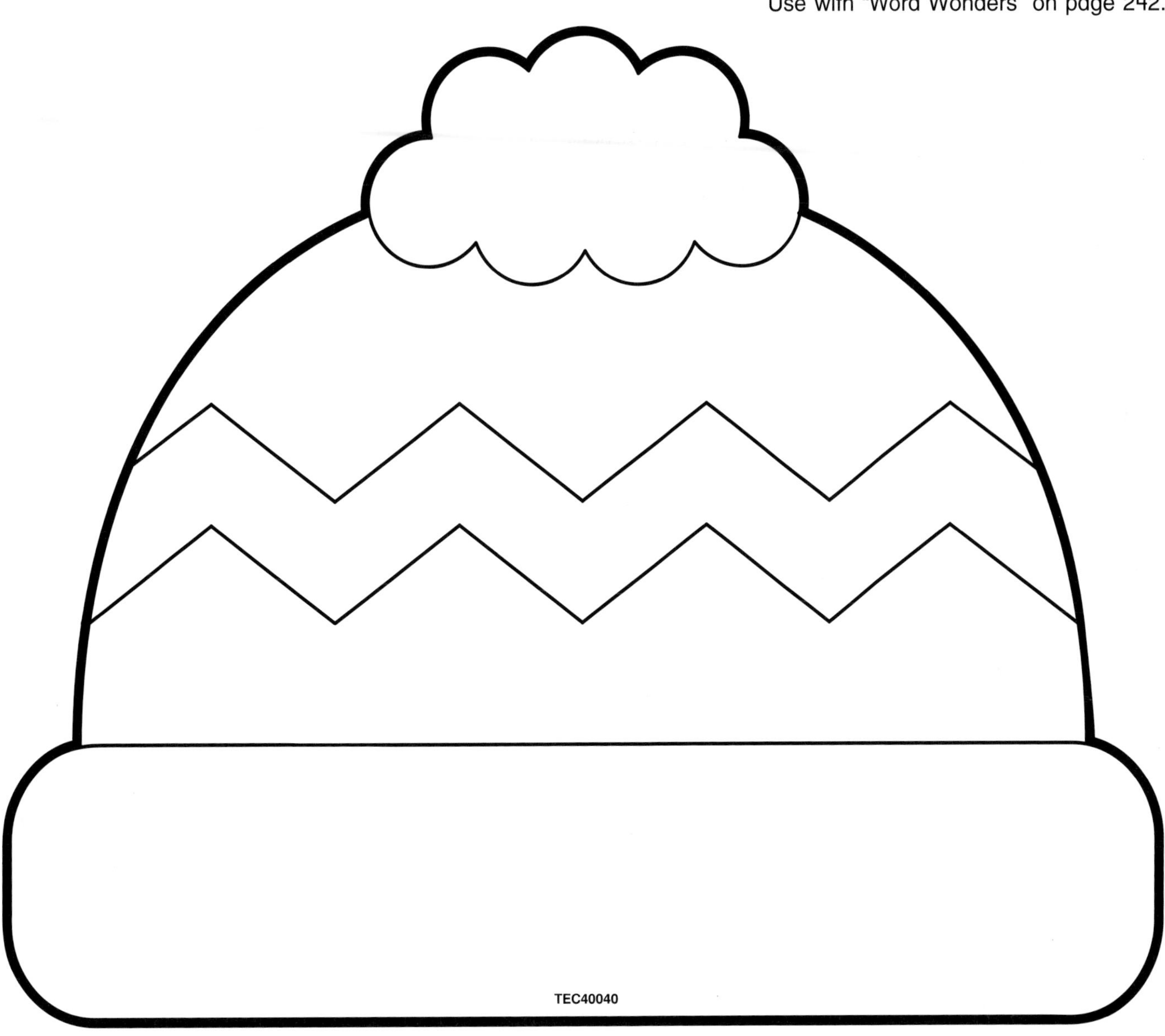

a	d	f	g	h
l	m	n	p	t

Revving Up Reading Skills

Stop, Think, and Read!

Prereading

Display a construction paper traffic signal like the one shown. As you point to each part of the signal, in turn, read its label. Explain to students that before they begin reading a book, it is a good idea to read the title and briefly look at the book, observing features such as a table of contents or illustrations. Then they should make predictions based on their observations and prior knowledge. Finally, they should give themselves the green light to read!

Tip: For reinforcement, invite each student to make a small traffic signal with a black rectangle and colorful adhesive dots. Have him put the traffic signal on the corner of his desk.

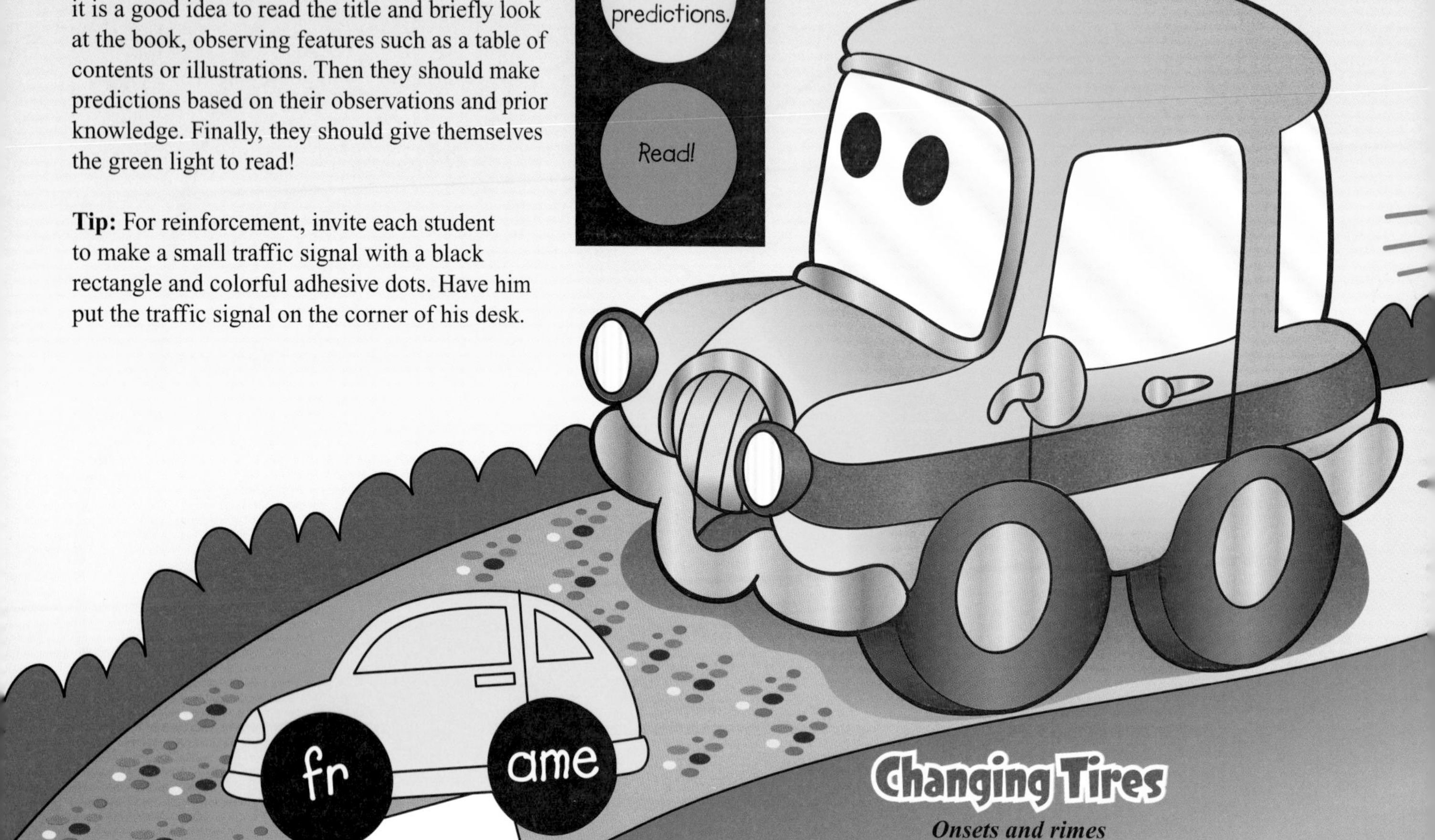

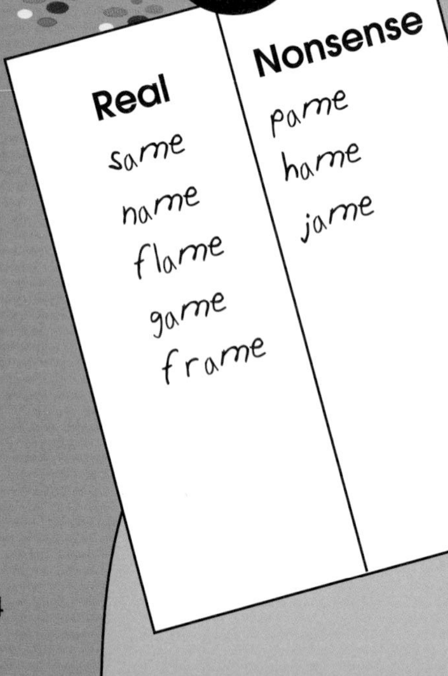

Changing Tires

Onsets and rimes

For this center activity, cut out a copy of the large car pattern on page 246 and make several two-inch black circles (tires). Program one tire with a rime and each remaining tire with an onset. Put the tires and the car at a center, along with copies of a recording sheet like the one shown. Then choose an option below.

Individual activity: A child places the tire with the rime on the right car wheel. Then she places each remaining tire on the left car wheel in turn. She writes each resulting word in the appropriate column on a recording sheet.

Partner game: The players put the tire with the rime on the right car wheel. They spread out the remaining tires facedown. In turn, each player takes a tire with an onset. She puts it on the left car wheel, reads the resulting word, and writes it on her recording sheet. The players continue with the remaining tires. The player who forms and writes more real words wins.

Courtney Pate, Burlington, NC

Watch the Speed!

Fluency

Attach a small car cutout (pattern on page 246) to one end of a pointer. Display several sentences on chart paper. Then have students read the sentences as you hurriedly point to each word without pausing. Comment that speeding through the sentences makes it hard to understand them. Then lead students in reading the sentences again, this time pointing to the words more slowly but at an uneven pace. No doubt students will agree that choppy reading is also difficult to understand.

To follow up, have each child cut out a copy of the bookmark on page 246. After you review the tips with students, explain that knowing words by sight is a key to reading fluently. Then have each child write high-frequency words on the back of his bookmark and encourage him to practice reading them.

Courtney Pate, Burlington, NC

License to Change

Changing the end of words

This activity is so quick and easy, it's perfect for a reading group warm-up. To begin, draw a blank license plate on a magnetic whiteboard. Then use magnetic letters to form a word on the license plate. (See the first word in each word pair on this page.) Put different magnetic letters nearby. After students read the word you formed, ask a student to change the end of the word to form a different word. Clear the license plate to prepare it for another word pair.

Word Pairs

cake, came
flag, flash
snap, snack
stop, stay
swim, swing
that, this

Moving Along

Word recognition

Here's a game for teams or two players. Make a supply of word cards. For each team or player, make a car cutout and divide a strip of paper into an equal number of sections to make a road. To begin, the players stack the word cards facedown. Each player or team places a car at the beginning of a different road. In turn, each player or team takes the top card from the stack, reads the word aloud, and determines how many syllables it has. Then the player or team advances the designated car the corresponding number of spaces. Alternate play continues until one car reaches the end of the road.

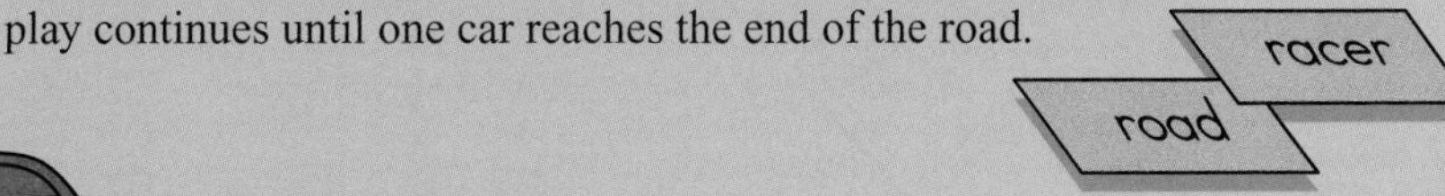

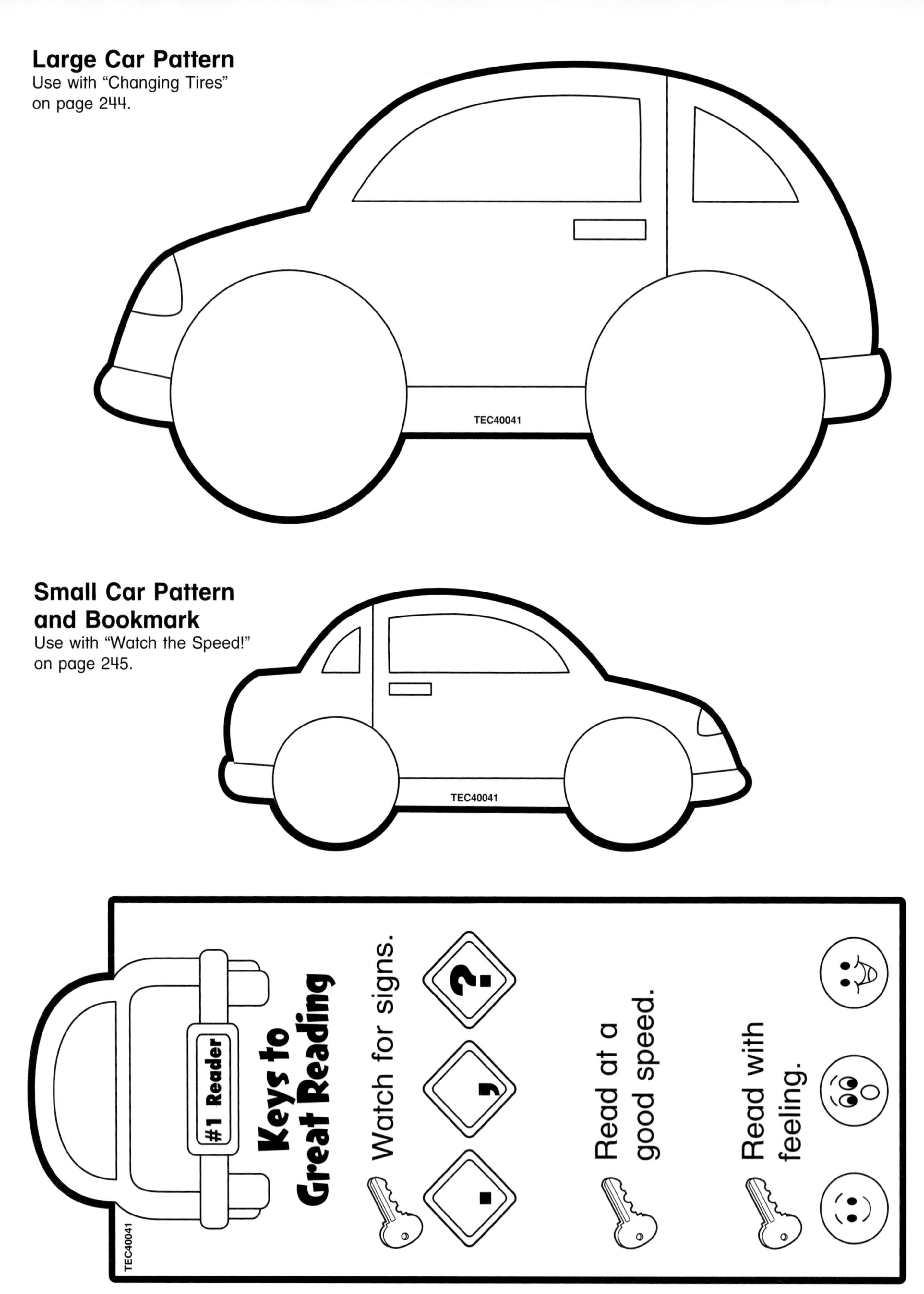
Large Car Pattern
Use with "Changing Tires" on page 244.
TEC40041
Small Car Pattern and Bookmark
Use with "Watch the Speed!" on page 245.
TEC40041
#1 Reader
Keys to Great Reading
Watch for signs.
Read at a good speed.
Read with feeling.
TEC40041

Recipe for Colorful Writing

One simple snack lends itself to three different skill-building activities!

ideas contributed by Kathryn Lane
Frederick, MD

Start With a Snack!

What better way to inspire your young writers than with a mouthwatering treat? Have students help you make Jell-O gelatin or Jell-O Jigglers in rainbow-colored flavors. (See a package of Jell-O gelatin for directions.) Give each youngster a serving with whipped cream (clouds). Then choose from the ideas below.

Writing how-to directions: Have students dictate the steps to make the snack; then write the steps on separate sentence strips. Scramble the strips and then ask youngsters to put them in order. **For a variation,** instruct each youngster to illustrate and write the steps on one or more copies of page 248.

Using sensory words: Have each youngster write about the color, flavor, and texture of his snack. Then ask him to mark the sensory words and phrases with a highlighter.

Writing with details: Write on the board the first sentence below. Rewrite the sentence with student input so it includes an additional detail. Then revise the newly written sentence with students to include one more detail. Continue until several sentences are displayed. Youngsters are sure to agree that the details create a vivid image!

I like Jell-O.
I like to eat Jell-O.
I like to eat red Jell-O.
I like to eat red Jell-O with whipped cream.
I like to eat red Jell-O with lots of whipped cream.

Name ______________________________ Writing how-to directions

How to Make a Rainbow Snack

____
____
____

____
____
____

____
____
____

 Note to the teacher: Use with "Start With a Snack!" on page 247.

Handpicked for Young Writers

Blossoming Ideas

Responding to a prompt

Here's a cute way to make sure your students always have fresh writing topics. Color several craft sticks green and then tape a construction paper blossom to each stick. Attach a sticky note with a writing prompt to the back of each flower. Stand the flowers in a foam block or a flowerpot containing rice. Whenever a student needs a writing idea, ask her to pick a flower and respond to the prompt. Periodically replace the sticky notes with new prompts. It's guaranteed to cultivate youngsters' interest in writing!

Seeds for Stories

Generating writing topics

Use this ongoing idea to help students recognize that everyday experiences are potential writing topics. For each student, cut an $8\frac{1}{2}$" x 11" sheet of paper into quarters ($4\frac{1}{4}$" x $5\frac{1}{2}$") and then staple them together to make a booklet. Instruct each youngster to title his booklet as shown, write his name on it, and illustrate the front cover to look like a seed packet. If desired, ask him to label each page with a different topic—such as "School," "Home," and "Other Places"—to organize the notes he will write.

A few mornings each week, set aside time for each student to jot down in his booklet notes about recent experiences. Have him refer to the booklet whenever he's ready for a new writing topic. He's sure to discover that when he writes details about a tiny topic, it grows into a story!

Write and Rotate

Naming adjectives

For this whole-group activity, gather several pictures from calendars or magazines. Glue each picture to the top of a different sheet of chart paper. Display the papers around your classroom and set out markers. Next, divide students into as many groups as there are posters. Instruct each group to go to a different poster and list on the paper words that describe its picture. After a few minutes, have each group move to the next poster. Encourage students to add to each list without repeating any words on it. Continue until each group has visited each poster. Then read the lists with students. Over a few weeks, display each poster at a writing center. Encourage center visitors to use each list to write about the corresponding picture.

Shellie L. Miller
Woodland Health and Wellness Magnet Elementary
Wichita, KS

How Handy!

Using a graphic organizer

Planning and great writing go hand in hand with this idea. Give each student a copy of page 251. Instruct her to write her name and the main idea of her writing topic where indicated. Then encourage her to note a relevant detail on each finger of the glove. After she finishes her work, ask her to cut out the glove and refer to it as she writes about the topic. Display each student's completed work with her glove.

Courtney Pate
Burlington, NC

Whose?

Using possessive pronouns

To prepare this center activity, label each of three flower cutouts as shown. Glue each flower to a separate flowerbox cutout. Type sentences with words that can be replaced by the possessive pronouns and underline those words. Cut the sentences into strips. To make the activity self-checking, write the corresponding pronoun on the back of each strip. A student sorts the sentences onto the correct flowerboxes. He checks his work and corrects any errors. Then he rewrites a group of sentences with the appropriate possessive pronouns.

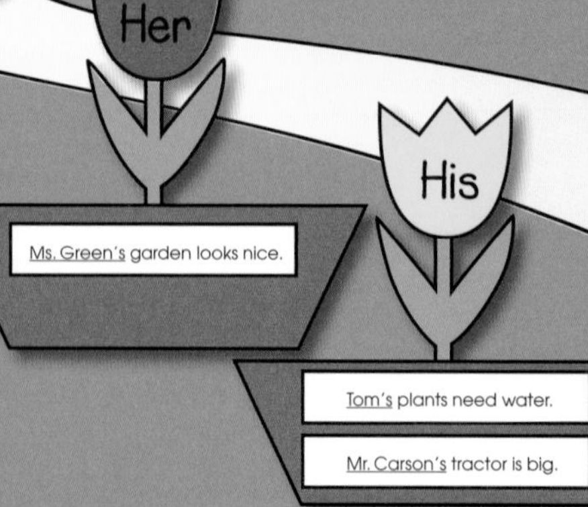

Glove Pattern

Use with "How Handy!" on page 250.

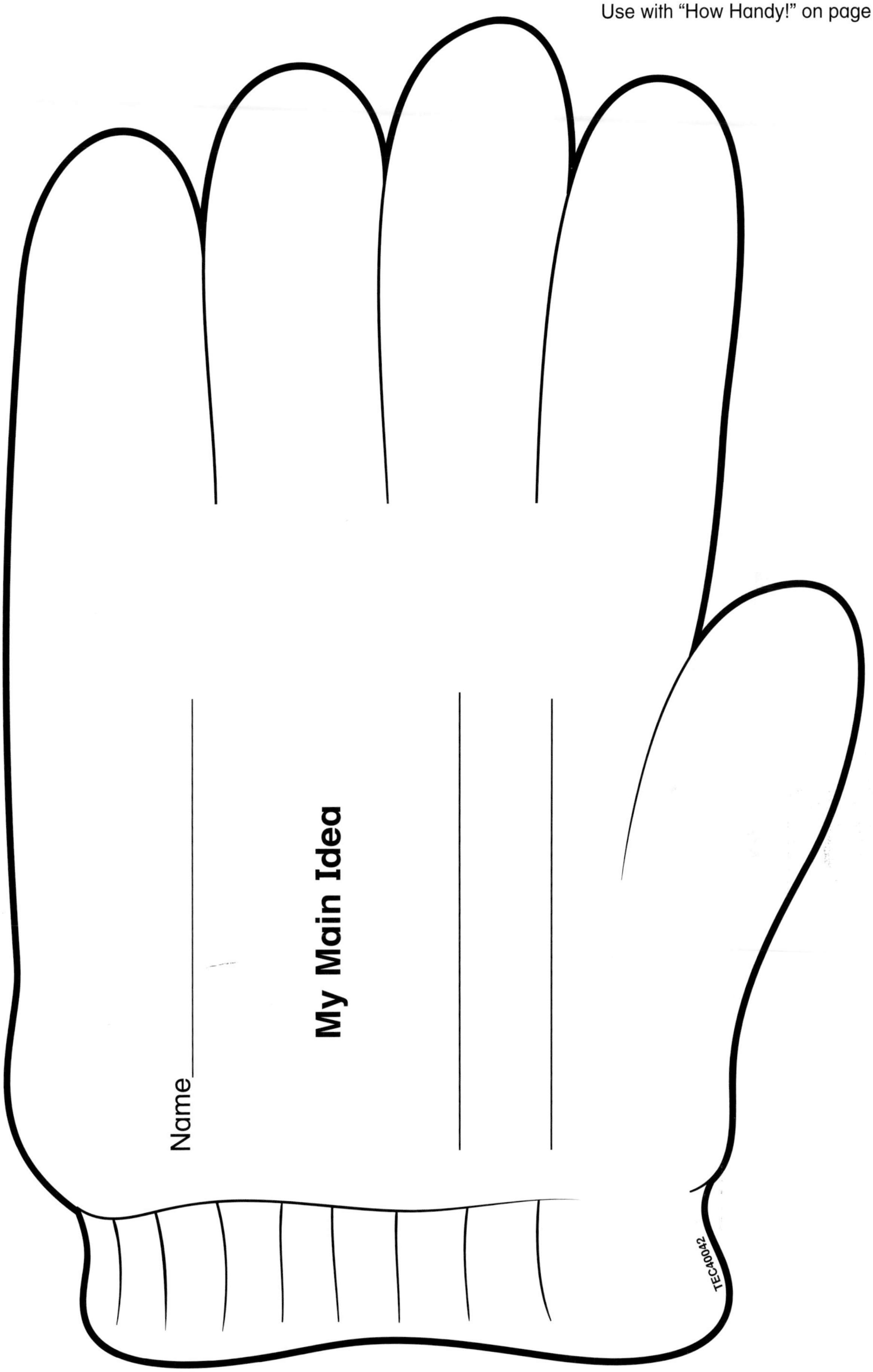

My Main Idea

Name______________

TEC40042

Comprehension Gems

Sum It Up!

Beginning, middle, and end of a story

Here's a clever little project for recapping a story. Give each child a 6" x 18" strip of white paper. Help him fold the ends inward so they meet in the middle. To complete the project, he writes the title and author of the book on the left flap as shown. He draws a story-related illustration on the right flap. Then he unfolds the paper and labels the first section "Beginning," the second section "Middle," and the third section "End." He writes about each part of the story in its appropriate section and adds any desired illustrations.

Inquiring Minds

Asking and answering questions

Use this ongoing idea with read-alouds or books that students read on their own. Give each student a small spiral-bound notebook or a blank booklet. Ask her to write "[Name]'s Reading Journal" on the front cover. At the beginning of a reading session, give each child a card programmed with a question word *(who, what, when, why,* or *how)*. Instruct her to write in her journal a book-related question that contains the word. At the end of the reading session, ask her to write a response to the question, either writing the answer or sharing relevant ideas if the reading does not provide an answer.

Tip: This idea works especially well with chapter books. It's great for nonfiction too!

Erin Minick, West Creek Hills Elementary
Camp Hill, PA

Pick a Pocket!

Story elements

To prepare this handy storytime prop, color and cut out a copy of the story element labels on page 254. Glue the "Parts of a Story" label to the front of a file folder. Glue each remaining label to a library pocket. Attach the pockets to the inside of the folder and gather seven index cards. After you read a story aloud, ask a volunteer to take an index card, put it in a library pocket, and then tell about the corresponding part of the story. Continue until each pocket contains a card.

Kelsea Wright, Seal Elementary, Douglass, KS

Book Box

Story elements

Looking for an alternative to book reports? Try this! Ask each child to bring an empty box, such as a cereal or cracker box. Have him tape the box closed and then help him cover the box with white paper. Ask him to decorate the front of the box so it resembles the cover of a familiar book. Next, instruct him to give the book a rating of one, two, or three smiley faces by sticking the appropriate number of adhesive dots to the top of the box and drawing faces on them. Then ask him to describe and illustrate the setting on one side panel, the main characters on the other side panel, and the story events on the back of the box. To showcase students' work, stand the boxes on a shelf or table.

adapted from an idea by Brandi Pearson
Thomastown Attendance Center, Carthage, MS

Right on Track

Main idea

This ongoing display is perfect for following up read-alouds. To prepare, post a train engine cutout titled as shown. After you read a book to students, write its title on a horizontal paper rectangle. Guide students to identify the main idea; then write it below the title. Invite volunteers to add an illustration and attach two wheel cutouts. Then post the resulting train car behind the engine. **For a variation,** write a main idea on the engine and the supporting details on separate train cars.

Courtney C. Pate
Burlington, NC

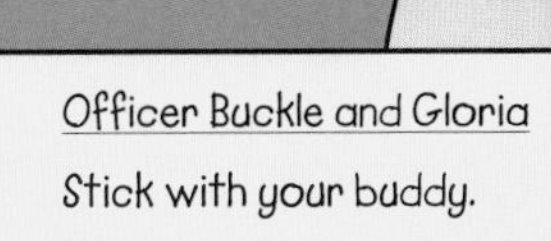

Story Element Labels

Use with "Pick a Pocket!" on page 253.

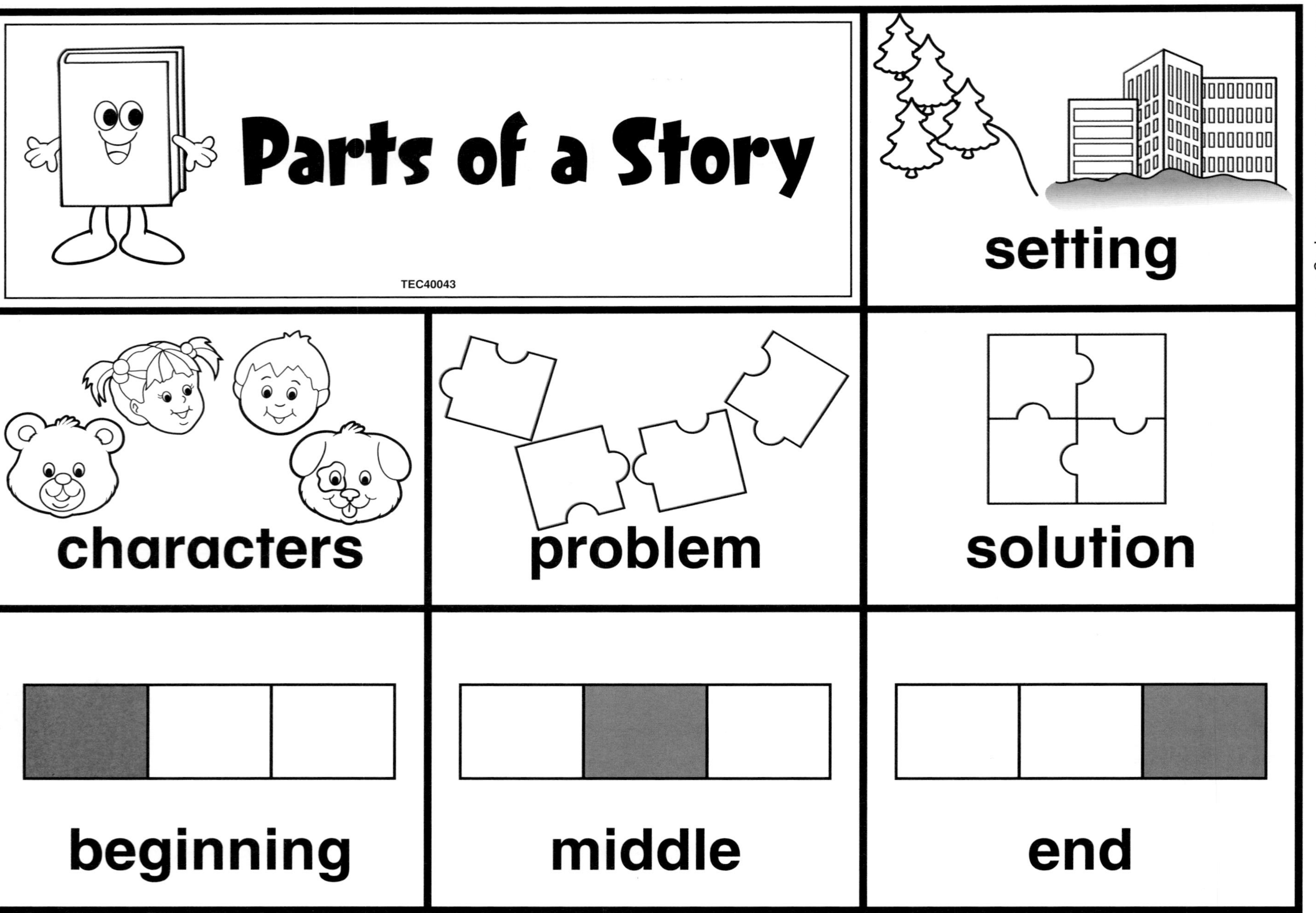

Literature Units

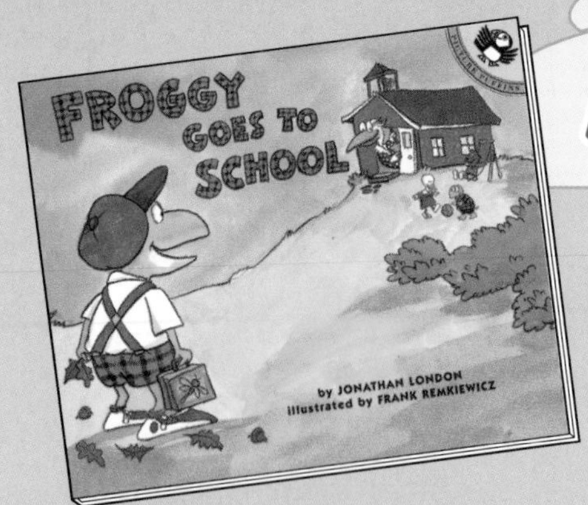

Froggy Goes to School

Written by Jonathan London
Illustrated by Frank Remkiewicz

Froggy is so worried he will be late his first day of school that he dreams he gets on the bus wearing only underwear! Fortunately, the day begins much more smoothly than Froggy imagines and leaves him in high spirits.

ideas contributed by Ada Goren
Winston-Salem, NC

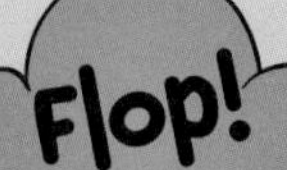

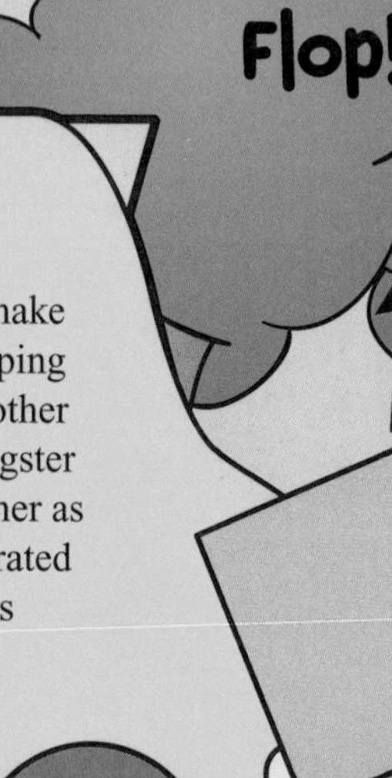

Flop, Flop, Flop!

Participating in a read-aloud

Engage your students in this "sound-sational" story by having them make sound effects! After a first reading, hold an index card in each hand, keeping one end of each card free. Flap the free ends of the cards against one another to imitate the sound Froggy makes when he walks. Next, give each youngster two index cards and invite students to practice flapping their cards together as you did. Then reread the book, prompting students to make the demonstrated sound whenever Froggy walks. For added fun, have students imitate Miss Witherspoon's clapping at the appropriate point in the story.

Getting There

Reading a predictable book

Whether or not your students ride a bus to school as Froggy does, count on this class book to get them on the road to reading! To prepare, make a supply of transportation cards (patterns on page 258).

Have each youngster color a transportation card that represents how she usually gets to school. Instruct her to incorporate the card into an illustration on a horizontal sheet of paper. As students work, invite each youngster, in turn, to dictate a sentence similar to the one shown to match her illustration. Write the sentence and her name on her paper. To make the last page of the class book, program a sheet of paper with the Froggy-related sentences shown and have a volunteer illustrate them. Then stack students' completed papers on the last page. Bind the stack between two covers and title the resulting book "Going to School." The picture clues and predictable format are sure to build students' confidence in reading!

Hop to It!

Story recall

Careful listeners are bound to learn a lot about Froggy and his family. To recap the information, bring in a toy stuffed frog or decorate a green beanbag to look like a frog face. Sit with students in a circle. Then have the frog "hop" to a youngster by gently tossing it to the student. After the child tells the group one thing he learned from the story about Froggy or his family, instruct him to toss the frog back to you. Continue as described, encouraging students not to repeat previously shared information, until each youngster has had a turn.

Wonderful Words

Reading names

Froggy adores his nametag. After all, it shows the only word he knows how to read! Help your students read lots of words with this pocket chart name activity. Write each student's name on a separate blank card. Display several cards in a pocket chart. Color and cut out a copy of the frog pattern on page 258. Then attach it to one end of a ruler or craft stick to make a pointer. To play one round, point to different name cards as you say the chant shown. When you say the last word in the chant, stop moving the pointer and keep it directed to a chosen card. Then have students read the corresponding name. To continue, invite the named student to use the pointer as described as you lead the class in saying the chant. Substitute different name cards as needed to ensure that each youngster's name is displayed during at least one round.

Hop, hop, hop.
Where will
Reading Frog stop?

Summer Reflections

Responding to literature

Froggy and his classmates had fun during the summer and no doubt your students did too! After students recall what Froggy did in the summer, have volunteers tell the class about their summer activities. Then give each youngster a large blank index card and a slightly larger yellow circle. Have her illustrate on the card an activity she enjoyed during the summer. Help her add a caption and glue the card to the circle. Then ask her to glue yellow crepe paper streamers to the back of the circle to make sun rays. Display students' completed work with the title "Bright Vacations."

Transportation Cards

Use with "Getting There" on page 256.

Frog Pattern

Use with "Wonderful Words" on page 257.

A Beasty Story

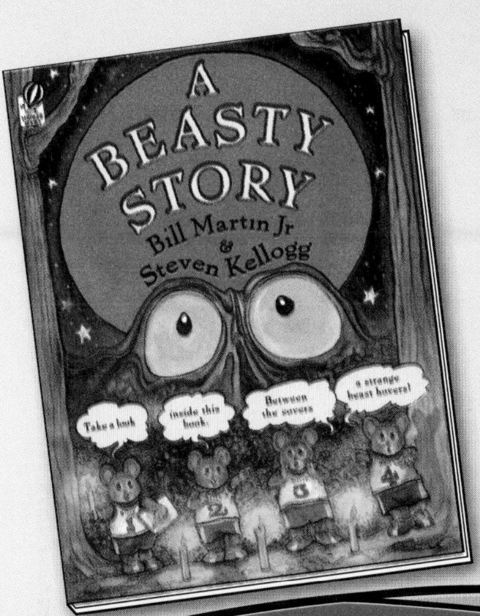

Written by Bill Martin Jr. and Steven Kellogg
Illustrated by Steven Kellogg

Four curious mice explore a dark, dark house in a dark, dark wood. All of a sudden, a beast appears and the rodents' exploration takes a decidedly spooky turn. But in the end, the mice happily discover that things aren't always what they seem!

ideas contributed by Courtney C. Pate
Burlington, NC

Light the Way!

Color words, reading and writing motivation

Battery-operated candles make these follow-up activities irresistible to young learners!

Color words: Stack a class supply of color-word cards facedown. Dim the lights and hand a battery-operated candle to each of two students. Have each youngster with a candle take a card, read it aloud, and then attach it to a classroom item of the corresponding color. As the seated students wait their turns, ask them to record the colorful sightings on provided paper just as the mice in the story do!

Reading and writing motivation: Put the book, small spiral-bound notepads, and one or more battery-operated candles at a center. Invite students to use the candles as they revisit the book and jot down colorful observations.

Outfitted for Retelling

Recalling story events in order

The numbered shirts in the story help readers distinguish the characters, and with this idea, they help youngsters retell the story! Ask each youngster to illustrate individual T-shirt cards (pattern on page 261) to represent the main story events. Next, instruct him to arrange the cards in the order the events occurred and number them accordingly. If desired, have him color the trim on the shirts. After he completes his work, punch a hole in each card. Then secure the cards in order by threading a pipe cleaner through the holes and twisting the ends of it to make a ring. Encourage the youngster to refer to the shirts as he retells the story.

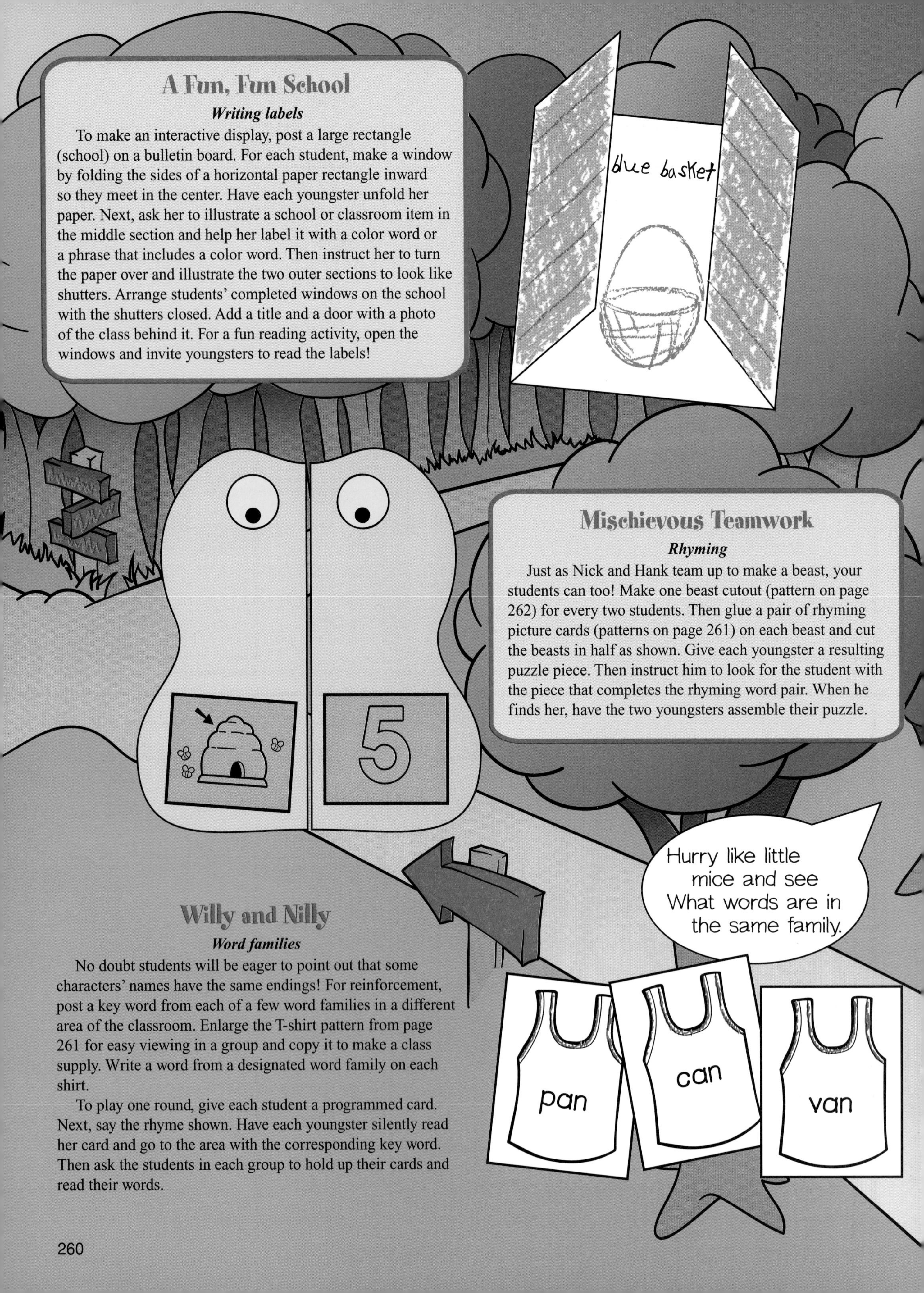

A Fun, Fun School

Writing labels

To make an interactive display, post a large rectangle (school) on a bulletin board. For each student, make a window by folding the sides of a horizontal paper rectangle inward so they meet in the center. Have each youngster unfold her paper. Next, ask her to illustrate a school or classroom item in the middle section and help her label it with a color word or a phrase that includes a color word. Then instruct her to turn the paper over and illustrate the two outer sections to look like shutters. Arrange students' completed windows on the school with the shutters closed. Add a title and a door with a photo of the class behind it. For a fun reading activity, open the windows and invite youngsters to read the labels!

Mischievous Teamwork

Rhyming

Just as Nick and Hank team up to make a beast, your students can too! Make one beast cutout (pattern on page 262) for every two students. Then glue a pair of rhyming picture cards (patterns on page 261) on each beast and cut the beasts in half as shown. Give each youngster a resulting puzzle piece. Then instruct him to look for the student with the piece that completes the rhyming word pair. When he finds her, have the two youngsters assemble their puzzle.

Willy and Nilly

Word families

No doubt students will be eager to point out that some characters' names have the same endings! For reinforcement, post a key word from each of a few word families in a different area of the classroom. Enlarge the T-shirt pattern from page 261 for easy viewing in a group and copy it to make a class supply. Write a word from a designated word family on each shirt.

To play one round, give each student a programmed card. Next, say the rhyme shown. Have each youngster silently read her card and go to the area with the corresponding key word. Then ask the students in each group to hold up their cards and read their words.

T-Shirt Card
Use with "Outfitted for Retelling" on page 259 and "Willy and Nilly" on page 260.

Picture Cards
Use with "Mischievous Teamwork" on page 260.

Beast Pattern

Use with "Mischievous Teamwork" on page 260.

Math Units

ideas contributed by Ada Goren
Winston-Salem, NC

Count Your Chicks!

To prepare these fine-feathered activities, have each youngster color and cut out a copy of the chick cards and rhyme on page 266. Give each youngster a 6" x 9" piece of paper that you have trimmed to make a henhouse. Ask her to glue her rhyme to it. Then choose an option below.

Counting: Instruct each youngster to put a designated number of chicks on her henhouse. Next, say the chant with students, inserting the appropriate number, and have each youngster touch her chicks one by one as she counts them. Then ask each youngster to clear her henhouse to prepare for another number.

Comparing numbers: For this partner game, write a different number on each of 20 blank cards. To play one round, the partners stack the cards facedown. Then each player takes a card. The player with the greater number puts one chick on her henhouse. The game continues as described until all the cards have been played. Then each player counts the chicks in her henhouse and says the rhyme with the corresponding number. The player with more chicks wins.

Pigs in Puddles

Choose an activity below for just-right independent skill practice!

Counting: Set out a supply of pink pom-poms (pigs) and several mud cutouts, each labeled with a different number. A student reads the numbers and puts the appropriate number of pigs on each puddle.

Addition: Place at a center a class supply of the recording sheet on page 267, a mud puddle cutout, and a die. Also set out six pink and six brown pom-poms (pigs). A youngster rolls the die and puts the corresponding number of pink pigs on the puddle. He rolls the die again to determine how many brown pigs to put on the puddle. Then he writes the corresponding addition sentence on a recording sheet. He clears the puddle and continues as described to complete the paper.

Farm Favorites

Graphing

This simplified graph is not only cute, but it is also reusable! Write the question shown on a poster-size barn cutout. Post the cutout and use reusable adhesive to display a farm animal card on each side of the door (patterns on page 266). Have each youngster put a personalized sticky note above the animal she likes more. (Help youngsters align the sticky notes horizontally.) Then guide students to discuss the results using words such as *more, fewer,* and *equal.* Repeat the activity on each of several days with different pairs of animals.

Gathering Eggs

For these center activities, gather 12 small plastic eggs and an empty sanitized egg carton. Position the carton horizontally and draw an arrow inside it to remind students to work from left to right. Roll down the sides of a brown paper bag to make a nest. Store the eggs in the nest.

Number order: Label each egg with a different number in a desired counting sequence. Draw a star on the first egg in the sequence. To complete the activity, a youngster arranges the eggs in the carton in order.

Addition: A student rolls a die and puts the corresponding number of eggs in the top row of the egg carton. He rolls the die again to determine how many eggs to put in the bottom row. He writes the corresponding addition sentence on provided paper. He models and writes additional number sentences as described.

Guess the Rule!

Sorting

Stretch students' thinking and observation skills! Color and cut out a copy of the farm animal cards on page 266. Make several identical barn cutouts. Sit with students in a circle and put the barns in the center of it. Without telling students your sorting rule, sort the cards on the barns by size. After students correctly guess your sorting rule, sort the animals by a different attribute, such as color or number of feet. Then have students guess how you sorted the animals.

Chick Cards and Rhyme

Use with "Count Your Chicks!" on page 264.

Farm Animal Cards

Use with "Farm Favorites" and "Guess the Rule!" on page 265.

Name____________________

Pigs in Puddles

Follow your teacher's directions.

Note to the teacher: Use with "Pigs in Puddles" on page 264.

Name ______________________

Duck, Duck, Goose?

Cut. Glue to complete the patterns.

A.

B.

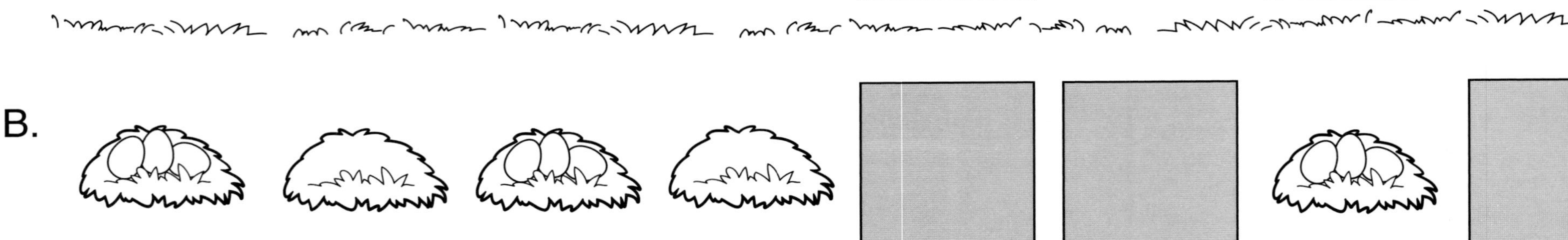

C.

"Whoooo's" Ready for Math Fun?

Watch students' skills soar with these simple ideas.

"Tree-mendous" Lineup

Ordinal numbers

For this group activity, draw a long tree branch on the board within student reach. Then arrange several owl cutouts (patterns on page 271) side by side on the branch. Next, ask a volunteer to draw a designated shape above an owl of his choice. Then have him point to the owl and ask his classmates to identify the owl's ordinal position. After a youngster correctly identifies the owl's position in the bird lineup, invite her to draw a shape above a different owl. Continue as described until students have identified each bird's ordinal position.

Where?

Positional words

Here are two more ways to use the owl patterns from page 271!

Top, Bottom, or Middle? Draw a tree on the board. Post three different-colored owls so one is at the top of the tree, one is at the middle of the tree, and one is at the bottom of the tree. Have students use the word *top, bottom,* or *middle* to describe the location of each owl. Then rearrange the owls and ask youngsters to describe the owls' new locations.

I Spy: Have each student color and cut out a copy of an owl pattern and then write her name on the back of it. Instruct students to put their owls in clear view in various places around the room. Next, invite a student to say, "I spy an owl…" and then use a positional word to describe the location of a classmate's owl. After your young birdwatchers point out the described owl, have its owner take it to her seat and then describe a different owl's location.

Angie Kutzer, Garrett Elementary, Mebane, NC

Give a Hoot!

Odd and even numbers

For student reference, display a number line on which you have marked each odd number with a sticky dot. Label an owl cutout (patterns on page 271) as shown and post it above an odd number. Randomly arrange several odd and even number cards near the number line. To begin, dim the lights. Tell students that Odd Owl lands only on odd numbers and they need to let him know which numbers are odd. Then shine a flashlight on a card. If the corresponding number is odd, the students say, "Hoot!" If the number is even, the students pantomime an owl flapping its wings. Continue with the remaining cards in the same manner.

Angie Kutzer, Garrett Elementary, Mebane, NC

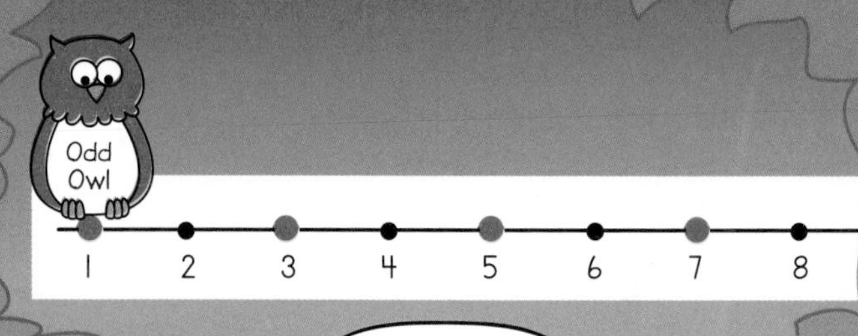

Owl and Mouse

Counting backward

Count on this variation of Duck, Duck, Goose to spark students' enthusiasm for math! Have students sit in a circle, and ask one child to be the mouse. To play one round, the mouse walks around the outside of the circle, tapping each classmate's head as she counts backward from a designated number. When she taps a child and says, "One," the tapped youngster becomes the owl and chases the mouse around the circle. If the owl tags the mouse, the mouse sits in the middle of the circle for the next round. If the mouse reaches the space where the owl was sitting without being tagged, she sits down. Then the player who is the owl becomes the mouse for the next round.

Angie Kutzer

Fine-Feathered Facts

Addition

Display several of these spotted owls to showcase math facts! To make a spotted owl, a youngster glues a circle, a large oval, and two smaller ovals together as shown. Then he adds facial details with provided arts-and-crafts supplies. Next, he puts a designated number of two-color counters in a cup and then spills them out. He records how many counters there are for each color by putting corresponding sets of sticky dots on the owl's wings. Then he writes the matching addition fact on the owl's body.

Angie Kutzer

Owl Patterns

Use with "'Tree-mendous' Lineup" and "Where?" on page 269 and "Give a Hoot!" on page 270.

Name ____________________

Starry Night

Write each group of numbers from the **least** to the **greatest.**

A.

______, ______, ______

B.

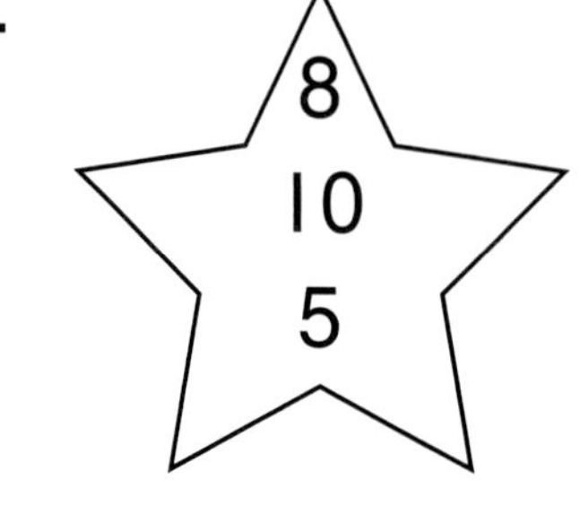

______, ______, ______

C.

______, ______, ______

D.

______, ______, ______

E.

______, ______, ______

F.

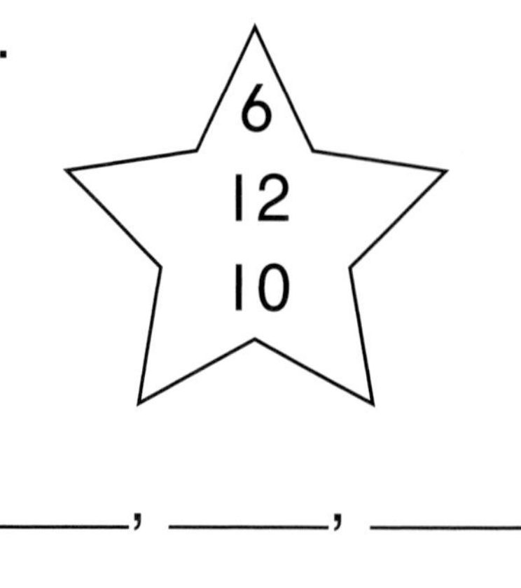

______, ______, ______

Great for Graphing!

Quick and Easy

Use colored masking tape to make a blank graph on a large sheet of paper or poster board. It's faster than drawing a graph. To save even more time, laminate the graph for reuse!

Lucia Botello, Early Childhood Center, Eagle Pass, TX

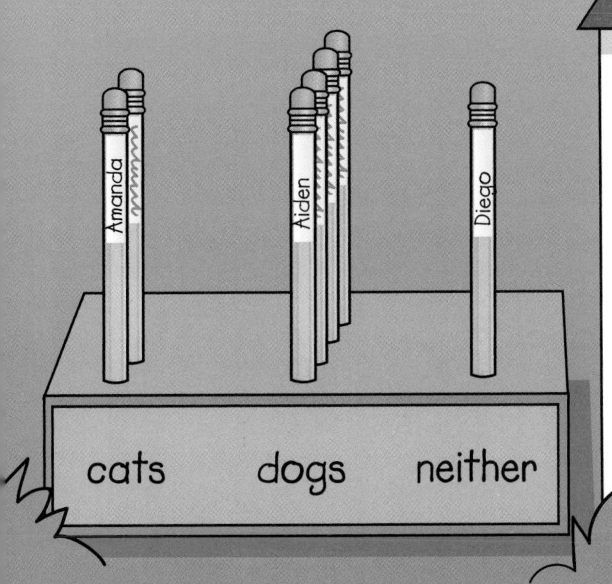

Fun Formats

Try these alternatives to traditional graphs. They're practical, creative, and just right for young learners!

Foam block: Label one side of a foam block with choices about which you would like to poll students. Have each youngster stand a personalized sharpened pencil in the block to indicate his choice. Then tilt the block to give students a clear view of the results.

Sticky notes: Instead of coloring a bar graph, instruct students to complete the graph with sticky notes.

Blocks: Have students make adjacent towers with LEGO blocks or similar blocks to make a three-dimensional bar graph.

Diana Meaney, Middle Village, NY

Day by Day

Get more skill practice out of completing a graph. Here's how! Post a blank graph for a topic about which you would like to poll students. Designate a different color for each response choice and cut a supply of matching paper squares. To begin, have each student take a paper square that corresponds with her response. Collect the squares in a paper bag. Then instruct volunteers to take a few squares from the bag and post them on the graph. Discuss the displayed data with students and pose relevant addition problems for them to solve. Continue as described over a few days until the graph is complete. No doubt students' anticipation for the results will build each day!

Jenny Lowe, Cooper Elementary, Loganville, GA

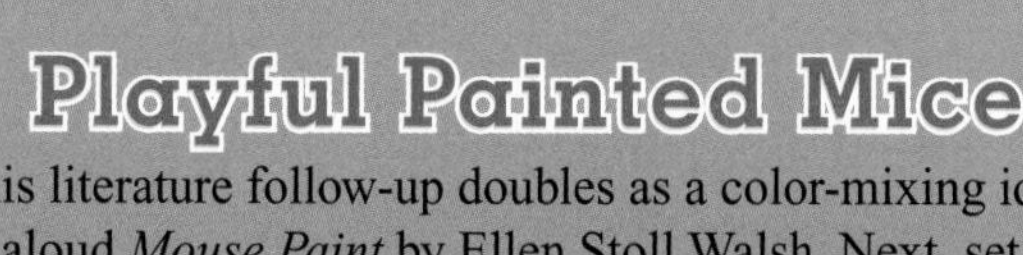

Playful Painted Mice

This literature follow-up doubles as a color-mixing idea. Read aloud *Mouse Paint* by Ellen Stoll Walsh. Next, set out red, blue, and yellow paint that you have thinned with water. Give each child a copy of the mouse pattern from page 275 and ask him to write his name on the back of it. Then instruct him to paint the front of the mouse a chosen color. Before the paint dries, have him paint the mouse a second color so the two colors mix together. Allow the paint to dry. The next day, display a graph grid like the one shown. Instruct each child to post his mouse on the grid. Then have students compare the number of mice in each column.

Vicki Altland
Florence Mattison Elementary
Conway, AR

Graphing in Season

Since this activity is so easy to prepare, you'll want to repeat it at different times of the year! Give each child a blank graph and a disposable cup containing seasonal confetti shapes of various colors or types. Have each youngster sort the confetti and then color the graph to show how many shapes she has of each type.

For an easier version, have her glue the confetti to the graph rather than color the graph.
For a more advanced version, ask each student to write about her completed graph.

Ruth Heckathorn, Oakland Elementary, Inman, SC

What a Harvest!

To prepare this fresh-from-the-garden activity, make copies of the vegetable cards from page 275 so there is one card for each student and the quantities of the different vegetables vary. Randomly spread the cards facedown on a large piece of brown paper (garden). Post a graph grid that you have titled and labeled as shown. Have each student, in turn, "pick" a vegetable, color the appropriate space on the graph, and put the vegetable in a basket. Once students have picked the entire crop, guide them to discuss the graph with words such as *more, fewer,* and *altogether.*

Ada Goren, Winston-Salem, NC

Mouse Pattern

Use with "Playful Painted Mice" on page 274.

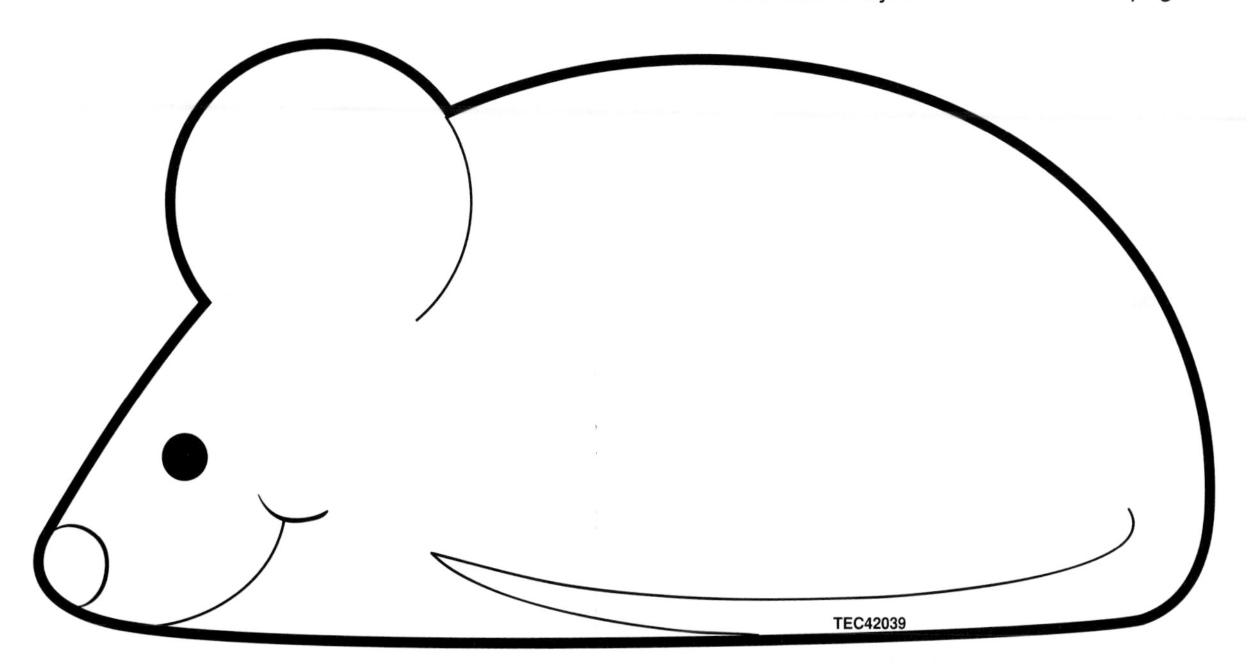

Vegetable Cards

Use with "What a Harvest!" on page 274.

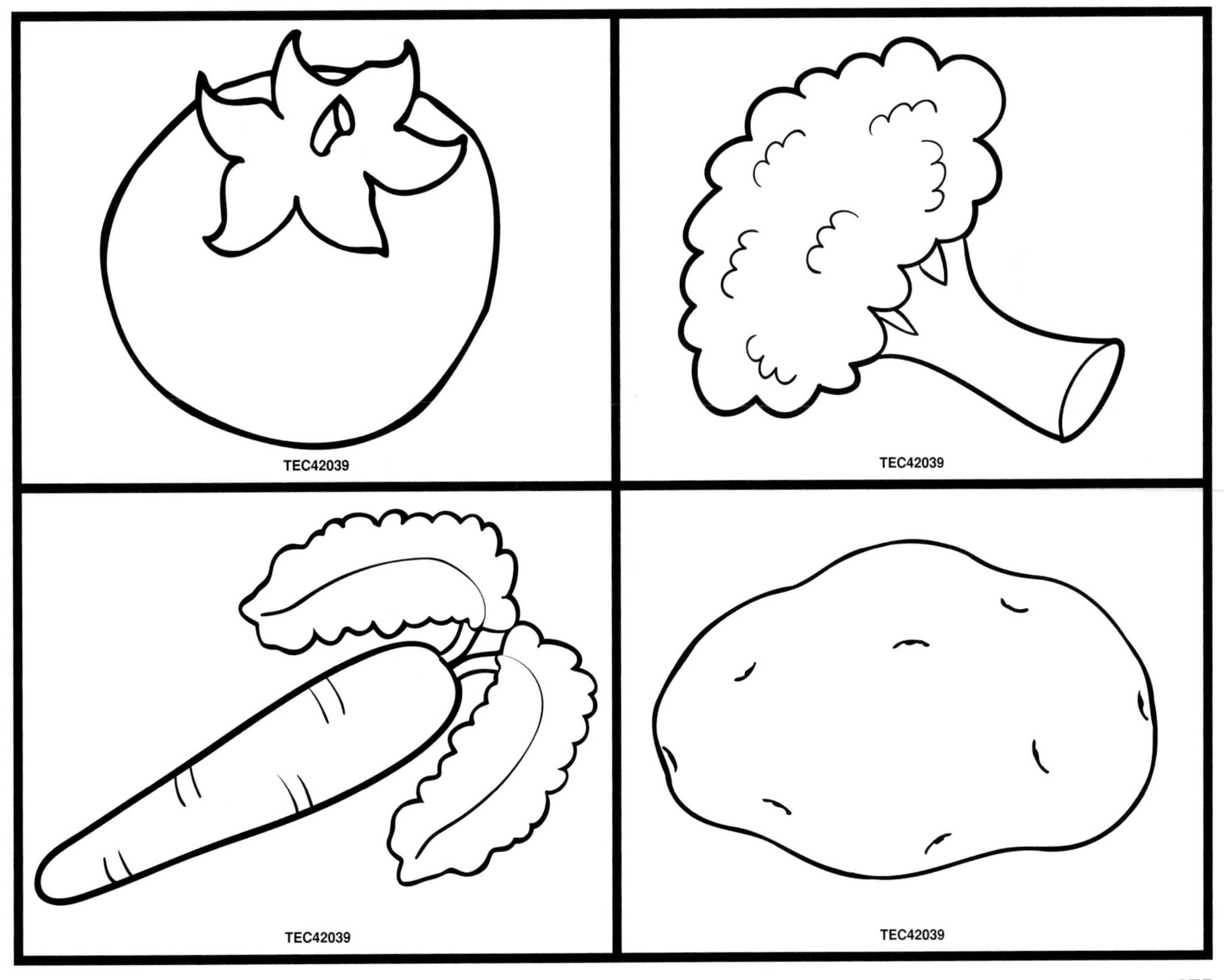

Plunging Into Place Value

Penguin Pal

This place-value mat is so cute that students will want to use it again and again! To make a mat, have a child divide a vertical 7" x 8" white rectangle into two columns and label them as shown. Instruct her to glue the rectangle on a vertical 9" x 12" sheet of black paper so the bottom edges are aligned. Then ask her to attach two white hole reinforcers for eyes, a triangle for a beak, and two small rectangles for feet. After each student makes a mat, have her use manipulatives to model various two-digit numbers on it.

Tens

Ones

The four is in the ones place.

6

4

Have a Seat!

Use this versatile idea with either two-digit or three-digit numbers. Depending on the desired number of digits, place two or three chairs side by side at the front of the classroom so the backs of the chairs face students. Loosely tape a different one-digit number card to the back of each chair. Then ask students to identify the resulting two-digit or three-digit number. Next, invite a volunteer to sit in one of the chairs. Ask his classmates to identify the place value of the corresponding number. Then say "Switch!" and have the volunteer move to a different chair. After students identify the corresponding place value, instruct the youngster to return to his own seat. Use different number cards for another round.

Heather E. Graley, Grace Christian School, Blacklick, OH

Missing!

Give each child a copy of a gameboard from page 278 and make one copy of each board for your reference. Have each youngster write the missing numbers to complete his board. Then guide students to notice that the numbers in each column have the same digit in the ones place and the numbers in rows 2–5 have the same digit in the tens place.

Next, give each child 12 Unifix cubes or paper squares for game markers. To play, call a number missing from one of your gameboards by naming the corresponding number of tens and ones. Have students identify the described number. Then ask each child who wrote the number on his board to put a game marker on it. Continue the game until one or more players mark all the numbers they wrote.

J. J. Markle, Rolling Acres Elementary, Littlestown, PA

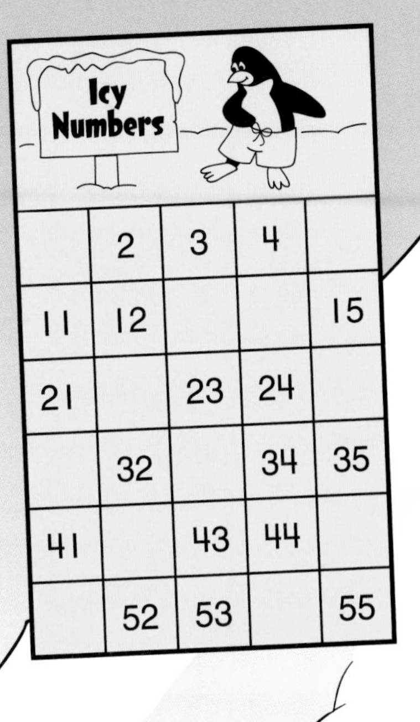

Domino Digits

Nearly no preparation is needed for this activity! Place several dominoes in a container, taking care not to include blank dominoes. Instruct each youngster to divide and label an individual whiteboard as shown.

Next, invite a student to take a domino and hold it horizontally. Ask her to say how many pips are on the left half of the domino and have her classmates draw the corresponding number of tens on their whiteboards. Then have the youngster tell how many pips are on the right half of the domino and instruct her classmates to draw the same number of ones. After each student finishes drawing, instruct her to write the corresponding two-digit number and hold up her board for you to see. Tell students the correct number. Then repeat the process with the remaining dominoes.

Clear Comparisons

For this partner center, place in several envelopes various quantities of paper strips (tens) and squares (ones) of two different colors. Letter the envelopes for easy reference. Then place the envelopes and two place-value mats at a center stocked with paper. To complete the activity, each student takes a mat. One youngster takes an envelope and writes the corresponding letter on a sheet of paper. Next, each partner takes a different color of the strips and squares and arranges them on his mat to model a number. The students write an inequality statement with the numbers. Then they continue with the remaining envelopes in the same manner.

Gameboards

Use with "Missing!" on page 277.

Icy Numbers

1	2			5
11		13	14	
	22		24	25
31		33	34	
	42	43		45
51	52		54	

Icy Numbers

	2	3	4	
11	12			15
21		23	24	
	32		34	35
41		43	44	
	52	53		55

Sweet Math Ideas

Perfect Purchase

Money

Use these tempting ideas for math warm-ups! Simply display a few different candy wrappers with prices and then choose an option below.

Equivalent coin amounts: Ask each youngster to select a candy to "purchase." Have her write its price on a sheet of paper. Then instruct her to draw and label two different coin combinations that match the price.

Problem solving: On each of a few days, give students the problem shown, using a different price each day. After students solve the problem, invite them to share their problem-solving strategies and answers.

Cathy Wroten, Bear Branch Elementary, Magnolia, TX

Bubble Gum Bliss

Addition or subtraction facts

For this small-group activity, label each of several colorful circles (gumballs) with a number (sum or difference). Put the gumballs facedown on a large construction paper gumball machine. Instruct students to sit in a circle around the cutout. Next, have the students pass a toy ball around the circle as you lead them in the rhyme below. Ask the youngster who is holding the ball when the rhyme ends to take a gumball and read the number on it. Then instruct students to name different addition or subtraction sentences that have the number for the answer. After they come up with two or more number sentences, say the rhyme to begin another round.

Bubble gum, bubble gum, round and sweet.
Doing math is such a treat!

Cathy Wroten

Tummy Ache!

Addition or subtraction

The element of chance makes this small-group game a favorite among first graders! Program cards with addition or subtraction problems, writing one problem on each card. Decorate each problem card with a candy sticker and make an answer key. On each of a few blank cards draw a sad face and write "Tummy ache!"

The students shuffle the cards and stack them facedown. To take a turn, a player takes the top card. If he draws a card with a problem, he reads it aloud and says the answer. If the answer is correct, he keeps the card. If the answer is not correct, he puts the card at the bottom of the pile. If the player draws a card that shows a sad face, he puts it in a discard pile and his turn is over. The players take turns until no cards are left in play. The player with the most cards wins.

Lots of Lollipops

Data analysis, fractions, or skip-counting

Have each student make a lollipop by taping a personalized construction paper circle to a craft stick. Then choose from the options below.

Colors	Tally Marks	Totals
purple	𝍸	5
red	𝍸 𝍷𝍷	7
green	𝍷𝍷𝍷𝍷	4

Data analysis: Ask students to complete a tally chart to show the colors of their lollipops. Then have them solve relevant problems, such as "How many purple lollipops and red lollipops are there altogether?"

Fractions: Display a group of one, two, or three like-colored lollipops and one different-colored lollipop. Have students tell what part of the group is the different color.

Skip-counting: Ask students to imagine that each lollipop costs two cents. Instruct them to count the lollipops by twos to determine how many lollipops they could purchase with a designated amount of money.

adapted from an idea by Cathy Wroten
Bear Branch Elementary
Magnolia, TX

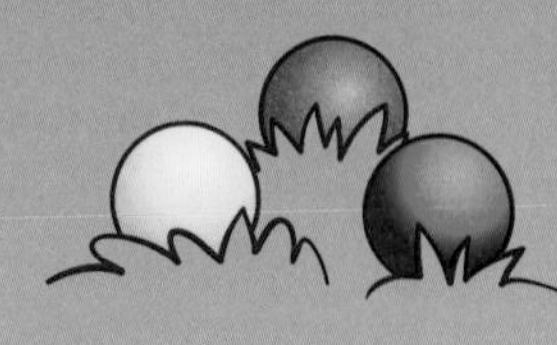

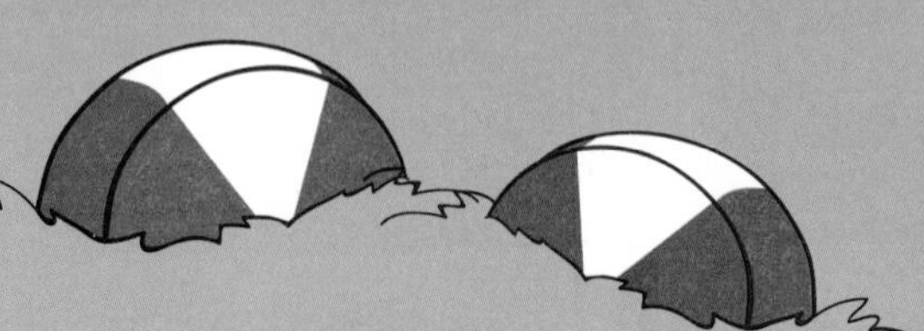

Name____ Coin combinations to 75 cents

Coins for Candy

Color the coins that match each price.

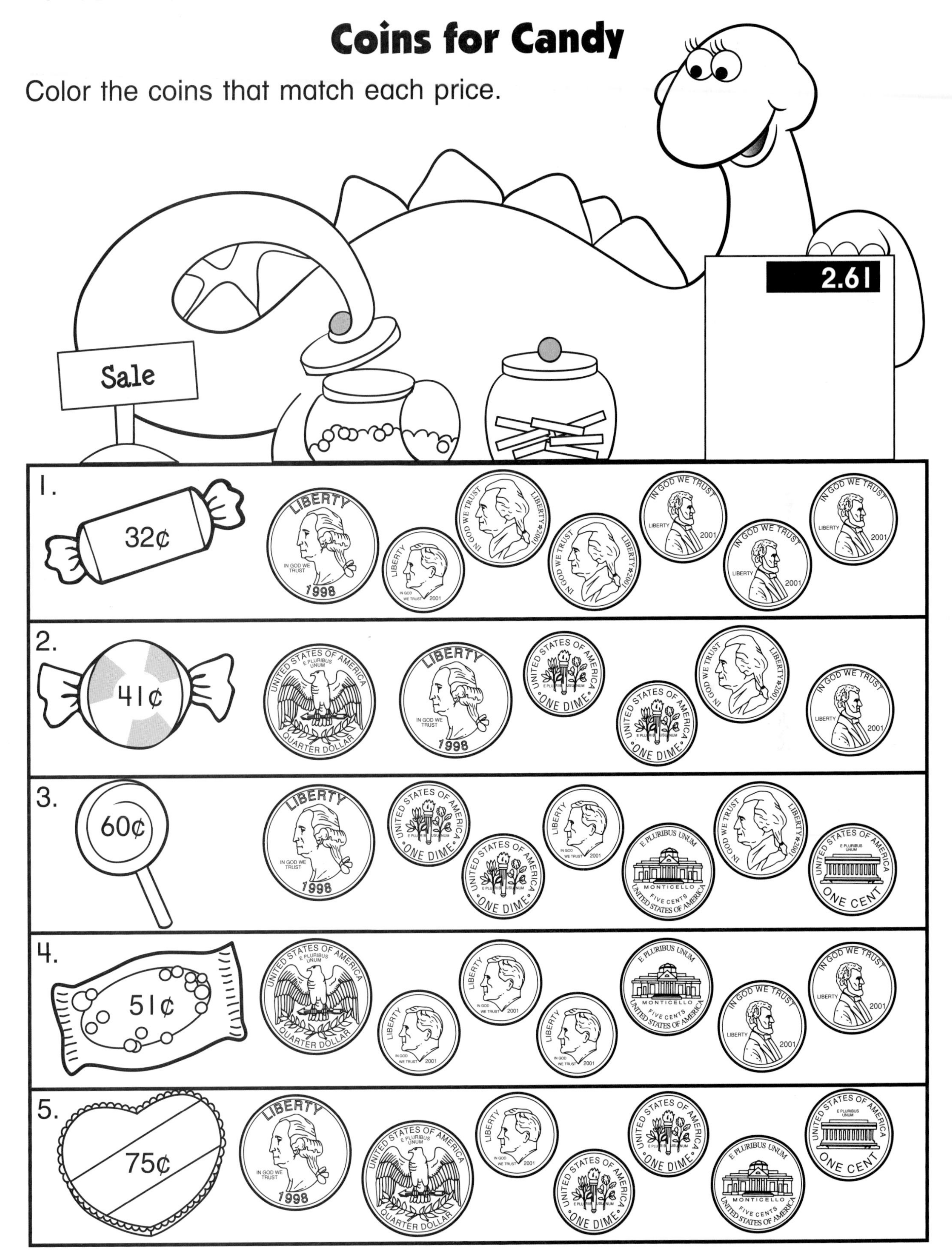

Digging Into Two-Digit Addition

ideas contributed by Gerri Primak
Charlotte, NC

Chow Time!

Adding groups of tens

Invite students to imagine they're feeding a dog as they model addition problems at this center. To prepare, make three white dog bowl cutouts and three blue dog bowl cutouts (pattern on page 284). Write the numbers 10, 20, and 30 on separate white bowls and the numbers 40, 50, and 60 on separate blue bowls. Put the bowls, tens rods, and paper at a center. For added kid appeal, also set out a toy stuffed dog.

To complete the activity, a student takes one bowl of each color. He puts the corresponding number of tens rods on each bowl. Then he writes and solves the corresponding addition problem, using the rods to check his answer. He continues to model and write different problems in the same manner.

Walking the Dog

Adding tens to two-digit numbers

Here's a "pet-acular" way to encourage students to use the counting on strategy. Color and cut out a copy of the dog card from page 284. Then tape it to a craft stick to make a pointer. Write a two-digit number on the board. Display in a row to the right of the number a few yellow paper strips (tens rods). Next, write the corresponding addition problem with student input. Instruct the group to read the number and count on by tens as a student "walks" the dog by pointing to each tens rod, in turn. Then have students identify the answer to the problem. There's no doubt students will be eager to solve more problems by "walking" the dog!

Catch!

Adding tens to two-digit numbers

Two programmed beach balls are all you need for this quick and easy activity. Write the numbers 10, 20, 30, 40, and 50 all over one ball and several numbers between 10 and 49 on the other ball. To begin, toss each ball to a different youngster and have her read aloud the number closest to her right thumb. Write on the board an addition problem using the two numbers. Then have each student in the class write and solve the problem on an individual sheet of paper. After you confirm the correct answer, continue until each youngster has had a turn catching a ball.

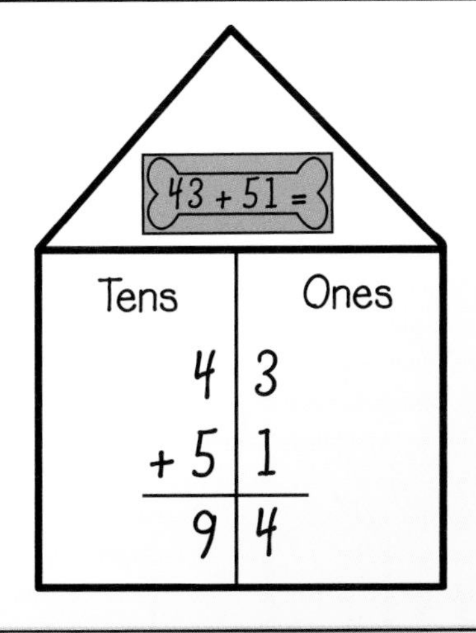

In the Doghouse

Using tens and ones columns

Help students bone up on place value! Program several dog bone cards (patterns on page 284) with horizontal two-digit addition problems. Draw and label a doghouse on the board, as shown, and ask each youngster to make a similar doghouse on an individual whiteboard. Then post a dog bone card on the board. Next, have a volunteer write the problem on the doghouse and instruct each youngster to write it on his own doghouse. After students solve the problem, think aloud as you solve the problem on the board. Guide students to solve different problems in the same manner.

Bones and Bowls

Two-digit addition without regrouping

For these activities, use copies of the dog bowl pattern and bone cards from page 284. Write on each of several bone cards a vertical two-digit addition problem that does not require regrouping. Write each answer on a separate bowl. Then choose an option below.

Small-group game: The players arrange the dog bowls and bones facedown. They play as in the traditional game of Concentration and match each problem with its answer.

Learning center: A student spreads out the bowls. She puts each bone on the matching bowl. Then she writes each problem and its answer on a sheet of paper.

Dog Bowl Pattern

Use with "Chow Time!" on page 282, "Bones and Bowls" on page 283, and *"The Stray Dog"* on page 28.

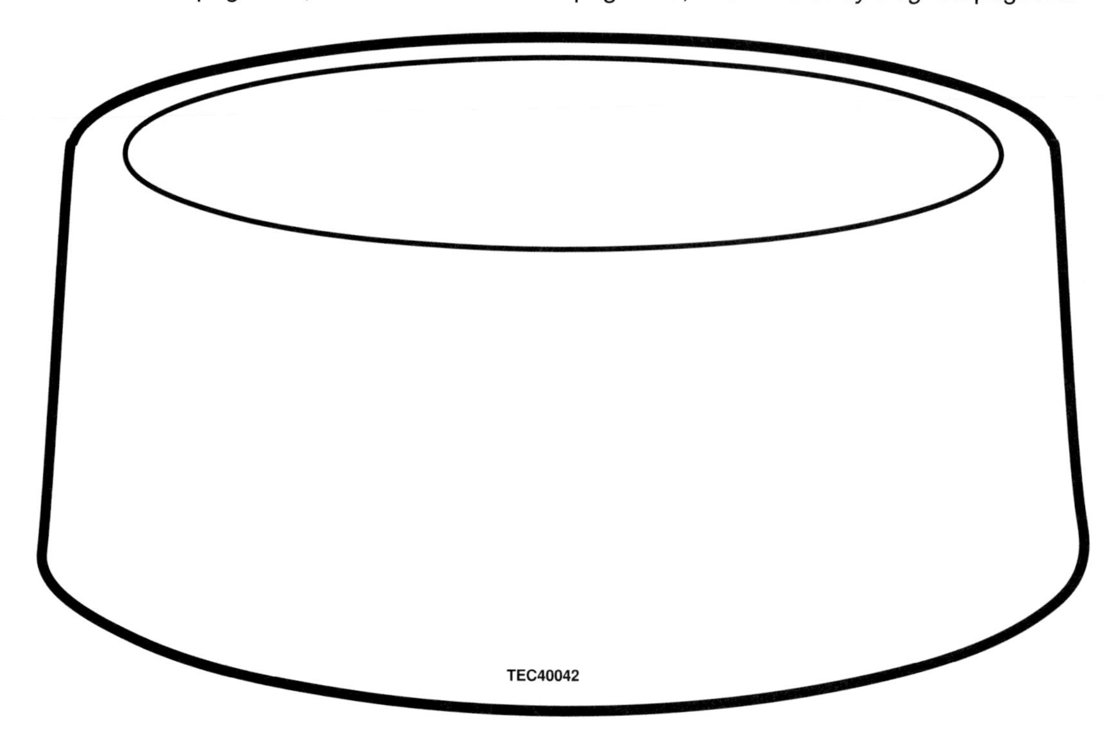

Dog Card

Use with "Walking the Dog" on page 282.

Bone Cards

Use with "In the Doghouse" and "Bones and Bowls" on page 283.

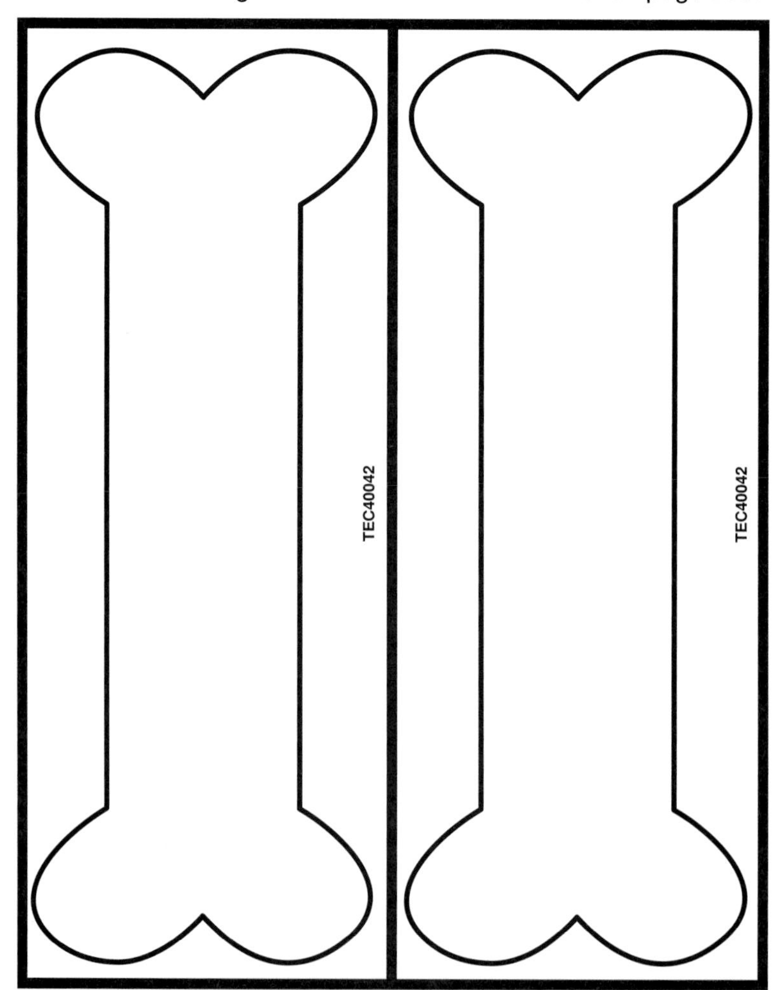

Math Picnic

Pairs of Plates

Place value

For this hands-on activity, write a one-digit number on each of several small paper plates. Put the plates in a picnic basket. To begin, ask each of four volunteers to take a paper plate at random. Pair the volunteers. Then have the students in each pair stand side by side to form a two-digit number. Next, instruct their classmates to tell how many tens and ones each number has. Have the youngsters tell which two-digit number is greater. Then ask each volunteer to change places with her partner. After students identify and compare the newly formed numbers, instruct the volunteers to return the plates. Continue until each student has a turn holding a plate.

Ada Goren, Winston-Salem, NC

Sandwich Fixings

Addition with three addends

The math problems at this center are made to order! Make an even number of bread slice cutouts. For each pair of bread cutouts, write a one-digit number on an orange rectangle (cheese), a red circle (tomato), and a green rectangle (lettuce). Put each set of programmed shapes and bread cutouts in a separate resealable plastic bag. Place the bags at a center stocked with paper. To complete the activity, a child takes a bag. Next, he arranges the programmed shapes in a row between the bread slices to show the order in which he wants to add the numbers. He writes the corresponding addition problem on a sheet of paper and solves it. Then he continues with the remaining bags.

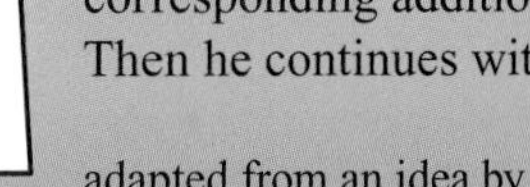

adapted from an idea by Ada Goren

Seed Need

Number sentences with unknown numbers

To prepare this fresh approach to addition and subtraction, make watermelon slice cutouts. Write a number sentence on each cutout, drawing a blank in place of the second number. Then write each missing number on a separate watermelon seed cutout. Place the seeds and watermelon slices at a center stocked with paper. When a youngster visits the center, he completes the number sentences using the seeds. Then he writes each number sentence on a sheet of paper. **For an easier version,** omit from each number sentence the sum or difference instead of the second number.

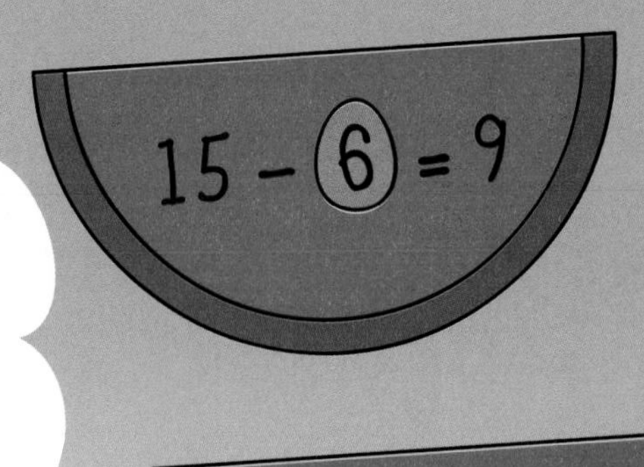

Basket Booklet

Story problems

Give each child a copy of page 287. Have her write her name where indicated and color the cover. Instruct her to cut out the cover and pages and then help her staple the pages in order behind the cover. Ask her to gently fold a narrow paper strip in half and then tape it to the back of the booklet so it resembles a picnic basket handle. On each of five days, read a booklet page with students. Invite them to share their ideas on how to solve the problem. Then have each youngster determine the answer and write it in her booklet.

Pie, Please!

Telling time

Here's a tempting review! In advance, use watercolors to paint a paper plate light brown. After the paint dries, write numbers and add marker details so the plate resembles a clockface on a pie. Use a brad to attach two clock hands to the plate. To begin, sit with students in a circle. Next, lead students in saying the chant below as the pie is passed around the circle. Ask the student who is holding the pie at the end of the chant to show a time on the pie. After a youngster correctly identifies the time, repeat the chant as students continue passing the pie around the circle.

For dessert, I must wait
Until I eat what's on my plate.
Apple, chocolate, cherry, plum.
Is it time to have some?

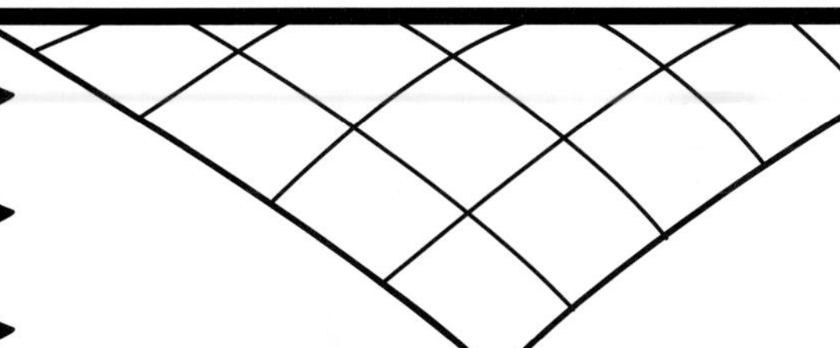

Picnic Problems

Name ______________________________

We packed 16 cookies.
We ate 7 cookies.
How many cookies are left?

There are 15 grapes.
9 of the grapes are red.
The rest are green.
How many grapes are green?

There are 2 apple pies.
There are 4 blueberry pies.
There are 6 lemon pies.
How many pies are there in all?

6 people went on a picnic.
They each ate 2 pieces of chicken.
How many pieces did they eat in all?

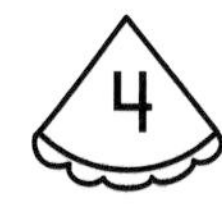

I ate 9 chips.
My mom ate the same number of chips.
How many chips did we eat in all?

Year-End Math Event

Looking for a way to spice up the end of the school year? Try these centers one day for an extra special math time!

ideas contributed by Laurie Diggins
Shamona Creek Elementary
Downington, PA

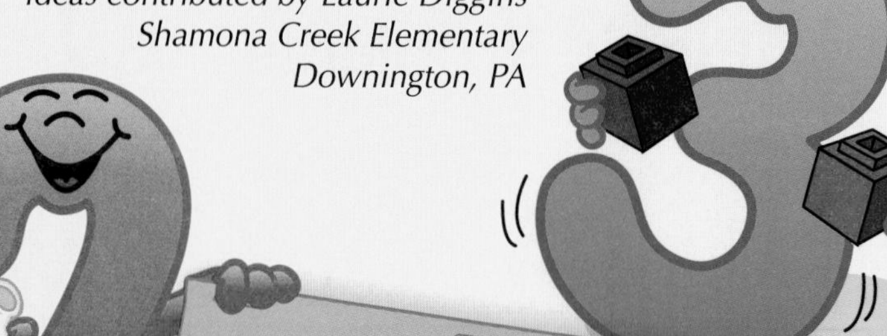

Here's What You Do

For each student, staple a cut-out copy of the booklet pages from pages 289 and 290 in order between two construction paper covers. Set out the center materials. Then divide students into five groups and arrange for each group to visit each center. To wrap up the event, invite each student to tell which activity she enjoyed the most and why.

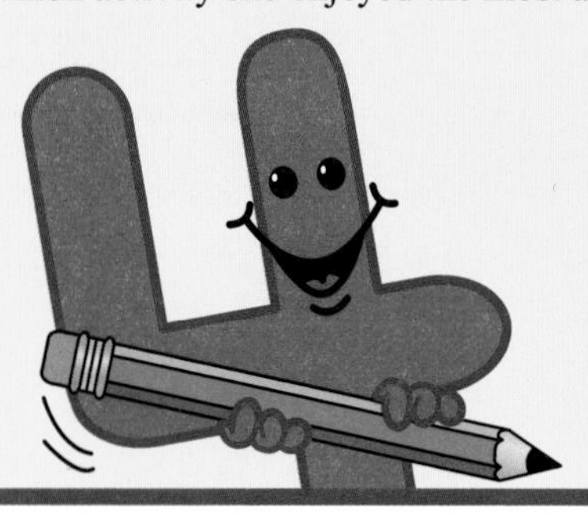

The Centers

Booklet Station

Materials: Arts-and-crafts supplies such as crayons, number stencils, number stamps, and ink pads
Activity: Each student personalizes her booklet cover.

Guess and Check

Materials: Uncooked macaroni pasta, dried beans, and imitation dimes and nickels
Activity: Each student completes his corresponding booklet page.

Mystery Numbers

Materials: Math cubes
Activity: Each student completes her corresponding booklet page.

Birds and Bears

Materials: Crayons
Activity: Each student draws and/or writes to solve the problem.

Read About Math!

Materials: Math picture books such as the ones listed below

Each Orange Had 8 Slices: A Counting Book by Paul Giganti, Jr.
Subtraction Action by Loreen Leedy
Eating Fractions by Bruce McMillan
One Hundred Hungry Ants by Elinor J. Pinczes
Math for All Seasons by Greg Tang

Activity: Each student writes about one book on his corresponding booklet page.

Guess and Check

How many fit in the circle?

Objects	Guess.	Check.
pasta		
beans		
dimes		
nickels		

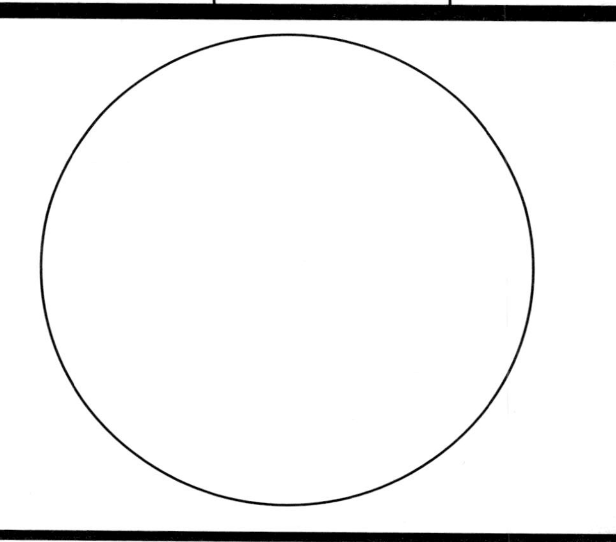

1

Mystery Numbers

Solve the problems.
Use cubes to help you.

A. _____ + _____ = 15

B. _____ + _____ = 18

C. _____ + _____ = 17

D. _____ + _____ + _____ = 12

E. _____ + _____ + _____ = 10

F. _____ + _____ + _____ = 14

2

Booklet Pages 3 and 4

Use with "Here's What You Do" on page 288.

Birds and Bears

There are birds and bears.
There are 12 legs in all.
How many birds and bears could there be?

3

Read About Math!

Title: ____________________

____

Write about the book.

____

____

____

____

____

____

____

4

Seasonal Units

Terrific Tools for Back-to-School

Welcome! Welcome!

Song

Help youngsters warm up to the new school year with this catchy tune! Teach students the song. Then post a different verse on each of three days and have students circle a designated high-frequency word—such as *at, and,* or *the*—each time it appears.

(sung to the tune of "London Bridge")

All the children are at school,
Are at school, are at school.
All the children are at school.
Welcome! Welcome!

Books and pencils, teachers and friends,
Teachers and friends, teachers and friends.
Books and pencils, teachers and friends.
It's time for learning!

This school year will be the best,
Be the best, be the best.
This school year will be the best.
We're so happy!

adapted from an idea by Julie Granchelli
W. P. Towne Elementary
Medina, NY

Treasured Sights

School tour

For this first-day activity, bring in a toy treasure chest and gather several small treasures, such as shiny beads, imitation gold coins, and seashells. Put a note with the message shown in the empty chest. Hide a treasure at each school location with which you would like students to become familiar.

To begin, direct students' attention to the treasure chest and read the note with mock surprise. Then take students on a school tour, stopping at each chosen location for youngsters to find and collect the hidden treasure. After you return to your classroom, have students recall the locations they visited as they put the treasures in the chest.

Sandra Bonny, West Irvine Elementary, Irvine, KY

Tour the school with a watchful eye
And the treasures you will spy.

Who's Who?

Class book

Reinforce concepts about print as you familiarize students with school staff members. Here's how! Collect an individual photo of yourself and of each staff member with whom students will interact regularly. Mount each photo on a separate copy of the booklet page from page 294. After students have met each staff member, complete each page as shown with students' input. Bind the completed pages between two covers and title the resulting book "School Workers, School Workers." When you read the book with students, point to each word, in turn, and encourage youngsters to chime in.

Elizabeth Newmark, Brick Mill Elementary
Middletown, DE

A Perfect Fit

Display

This name idea results in eye-catching projects that are ideal for an open house display. For each child, copy the puzzle pieces from page 295 so there is one piece for each letter in his first name plus one more. Write his name on the puzzle pieces, positioning the pieces so the dots are at the bottom. Have him color the pieces, cut them out, and glue a small photo of himself on the blank piece. Then ask him to glue the pieces on a strip of black paper so the lettered pieces spell his name and the piece with the photo is last. Display students' completed puzzles with the title "We All Fit Together!"

Tammy Willey, Pine Street Elementary, Presque Isle, ME

Special Someone

Group activity

To help youngsters get acquainted, sit with them in a circle. Secretly choose one youngster and sing the song below. Then give students a clue to the youngster's identity, such as "She is wearing pink." Once students successfully identify the youngster, ask her to stand. Then lead the class in greeting her by name. After she sits back down, secretly choose another student and sing the song again. Continue as described until the group has greeted each youngster.

(sung to the tune of "Mary Had a Little Lamb")

I am thinking of someone,
Of someone, of someone.
I am thinking of someone.
It's someone in this class.

Lucille Iscaro, P. S. 257, Bronx, NY

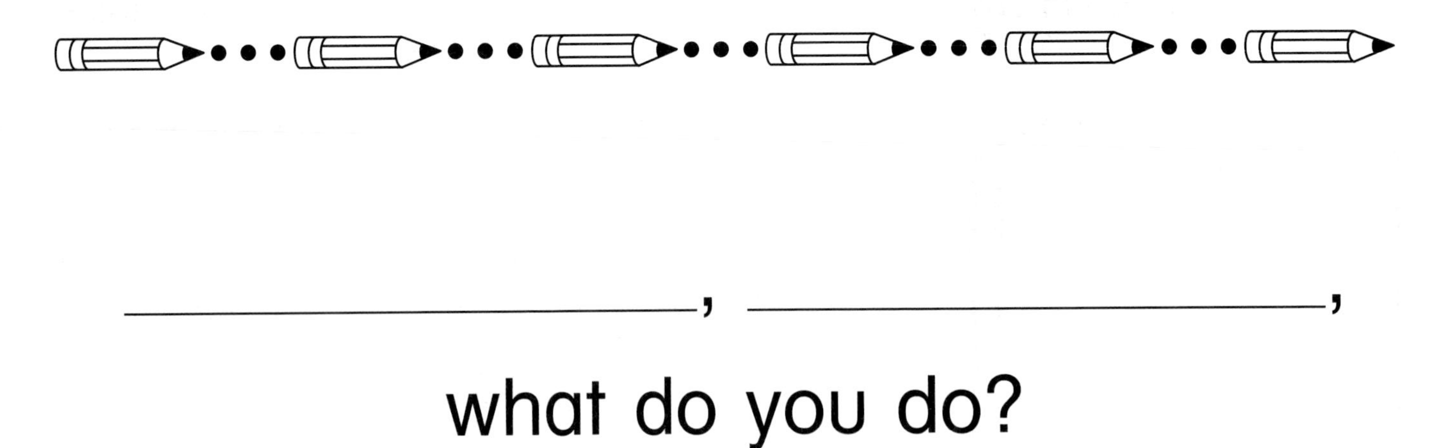

_______________, _______________,

what do you do?

I ____________________________

at our wonderful school.

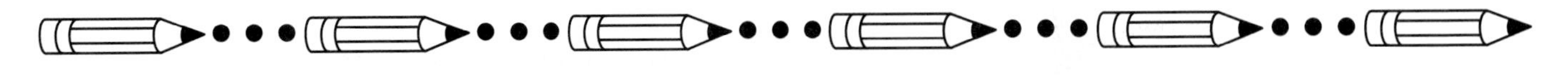

 Note to the teacher: Use with "Who's Who?" on page 293.

Puzzle Patterns

Use with "A Perfect Fit" on page 293.

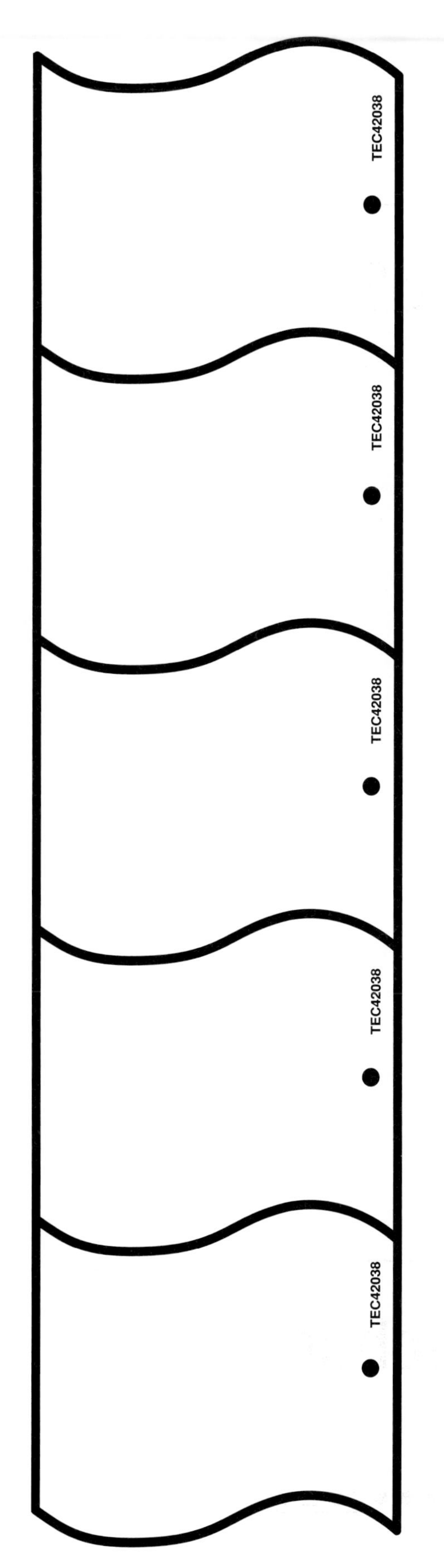

School Notes

Use copies of the notes below as desired to brighten each student's day.

Seasonal Skill Practice
Apples

LITERACY

Wormy Surprise

To make this adorable booklet, instruct each child to color, cut out, and sequence a copy of the booklet pages from page 298. Then fold a 4" x 10" paper strip in half and staple the pages inside. Ask the youngster to add his name and an illustration to the booklet cover. Next, give him a narrow four-inch green rectangle that you have trimmed to make a worm. Instruct him to draw a face on one end of the worm. Punch a hole in the opposite end and tie a 12-inch string through it. Tape the free end of the string inside the booklet on the back cover. Then reinforce skills as described below.

Print awareness: As you read the booklet with students, have them track the print with their worms.

Rhyming: Ask students to identify the rhyming words.

Word recognition: Instruct each youngster to highlight the word *apple* each time it appears. Or have him use different-colored crayons to underline high-frequency words such as *a, an, has,* and *is.*

adapted from an idea by Laura Wanke, Pecatonica Elementary, Pecatonica, IL

LITERACY OR MATH

Toss and Pick!

When it comes to being easy to adapt, these floor mat activities are the pick of the crop! Place a large tree cutout on the floor. Make a class supply of apple cutouts and choose an option below. (If the tree is too small to hold all the apples, set some apples aside and restock the tree after students "pick" several apples.)

Student names or high-frequency words: Program the apples with students' names or high-frequency words, writing one word per apple. Place the apples word side down on the tree. Invite each student, in turn, to toss a beanbag on the tree and then "pick" the apple nearest the beanbag. Ask the group to read the corresponding word and spell it aloud.

Number sense: Write a number on each apple (you may repeat numbers). Put the apples on the tree number side down. Have each youngster, in turn, toss a beanbag on the tree and then "pick" the apple nearest the beanbag. Instruct her to read the number on the apple and lead the group in clapping the corresponding number of times.

Kathryn Davenport, Partin Elementary, Oviedo, FL

SCIENCE

From Seed to Tree

Use this catchy song to teach students that apple trees come from seeds. After youngsters are familiar with the lyrics, have them recall from the song what the seeds need to grow. Explain that in addition to soil and water, the seeds also need air and sunlight. ***Understanding how plants grow***

(sung to the tune of "Sing a Song of Sixpence")

I took a little apple seed
And put it in the ground.
I filled the hole with soil
And poured water around.
The little seed soon sprouted;
It grew into a tree.
Now it has big red apples
Just right for you and me!

Deborah Garmon, Groton, CT

MATH

That's Tasty!

For this taste test, make a class supply of the recording sheet on page 299 plus one extra. Cut from one copy the illustrated boxes in the first column. Then glue each box at the top of a separate vertical sentence strip. Add simple face illustrations and labels as shown. To begin, arrange for each youngster to sample the foods listed on the recording sheet. Have him color the appropriate faces on his recording sheet. Then compile students' responses on the sentence strips as shown to make simplified graphs. Guide youngsters to compare the results. ***Completing a chart, graphing***

Jennie Cashman
Bennett Elementary
Bennett, IA

SCIENCE

What's Inside?

Do big apples have more seeds than small apples? That's one of several questions students may explore with this guess-and-check activity. Arrange three different apples in a row. Illustrate and label a separate blank card for each apple and then display the cards near the apples.

Have students predict how many seeds the first apple contains. Then cut the apple, count the seeds, and write the corresponding number on the appropriate card. Next, ask students to predict how many seeds the second apple contains. After you check the predictions as described, write the actual number of seeds on the matching card. Repeat the predicting, checking, and recording process with the third apple. Students may be surprised to learn that regardless of size, color, or variety, most apples have five to ten seeds! ***Making predictions***

Marie E. Cecchini, West Dundee, IL

Booklet Pages

Use with "Wormy Surprise" on page 296.

Name________________________________

Taste Test

Follow your teacher's directions.

What I Tasted	Did I Like It?	
apple juice	yes	no
apple jelly	yes	 no
 apple cereal	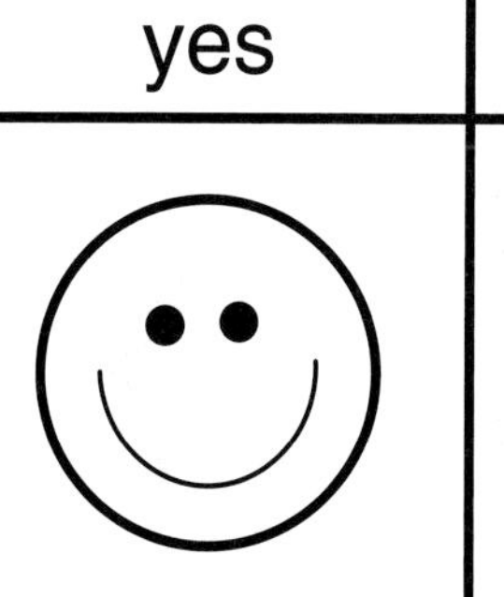 yes	 no
 applesauce	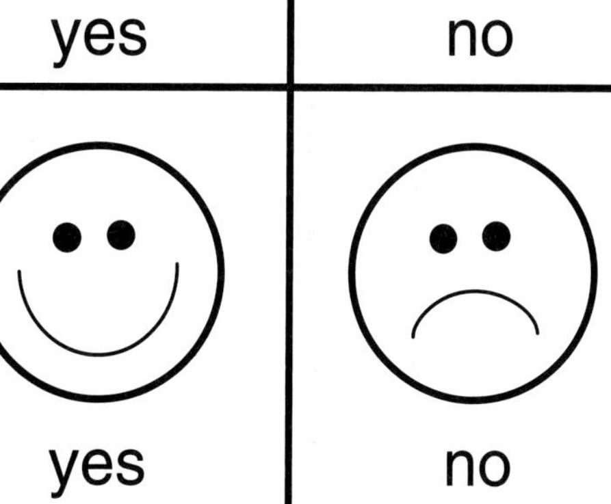 yes	 no

Note to the teacher: Use with "That's Tasty!" on page 297.

Reasons for Rules

What better way to introduce the topic of the U.S. Constitution than by discussing the importance of rules? Review with students why each of your classroom rules is important. Then ask students to imagine what a grocery store, a bank, and other locations in the community would be like without rules. After students share their ideas, point out that rules are important everywhere to help people get along and stay safe. Then show students a picture of the Constitution and explain that it contains rules, or laws, for the United States.

Freedom, Rights, and Laws

Post on chart paper the poem shown. Read the poem with students and choose from the ideas below.

Phonological awareness: Circle the word *Constitution.* Clap once for each syllable as you say the word and have students count the syllables. Then invite students to clap as they repeat the word with you.

Vocabulary: Discuss with students what the words *freedom, rights,* and *laws* mean to them.

Social studies: Give each student a paper with a sentence starter such as "I am glad our country has laws because…" Help him complete the sentence and have him illustrate his work.

Word recognition: Write each of the following words on separate blank cards: *freedom, rights,* and *laws.* Have students find the matching words in the poem and underline them.

High-frequency words: Give each student a copy of the poem. Have her highlight words such as *and, it, the,* and *we.*

The Constitution was written long ago;
We honor it today.
It gives Americans freedom and rights
And laws that lead the way.

ideas contributed by Ada Goren
Winston-Salem, NC

READING

Colorful Favorites

Use this idea over a few days for different skills! To prepare, write on sentence strips the poem shown, drawing blanks in place of the color words. Display the poem in a pocket chart, adding the color words on separate sentence strips. For each color word, put a matching leaf card (patterns on page 303) in the corresponding pocket. To begin, read the poem with students a few times. Next, invite student volunteers to rearrange the color words and change the leaf cards to match. Then ask students to read the revised poem. Follow up with the ideas below.

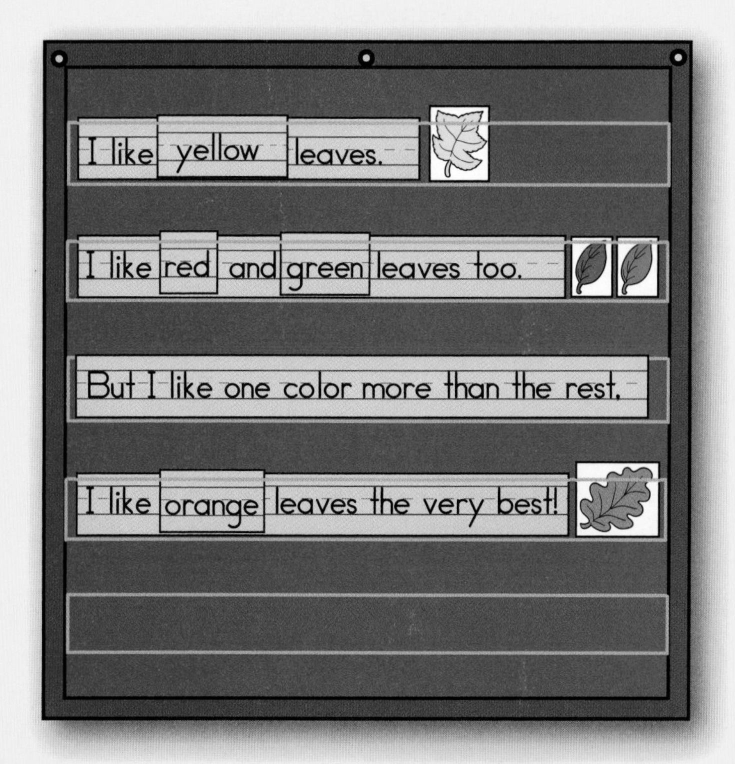

Letter recognition: Have students find the words that begin with the letter *l*.

Color words: Display the poem without the leaves. Make a second set of color word cards, writing the words with markers of the corresponding colors. Have students read the cards and place them on the matching words in the poem.

High-frequency words: Frame chosen words and ask students to read them.

SCIENCE

Paired to Compare!

Begin this observation activity by taking your students on a walk outdoors. Have each youngster collect a leaf that has fallen to the ground before he returns to the classroom. (Or give each child a colorful copy of a leaf card from page 303, ensuring that there is a variety of leaves among students.) Next, pair students and give each youngster a copy of the recording sheet from page 304. Have each child write his name and his partner's name where indicated. Ask him to illustrate their leaves in the corresponding boxes and circle the appropriate words to describe the leaves. Then guide him to write how the leaves are alike and different. ***Observing similarities and differences***

MATH

Fluttering Free

For this hands-on approach to subtraction, draw a large tree on a whiteboard. Use loops of tape to loosely attach to the tree a chosen number of oak leaf cards. (See the patterns at the bottom of page 303). To begin, say the poem shown, pausing after the second line to remove the appropriate number of cards. At the end of the poem, have students determine how many leaves remain on the tree. Model different subtraction problems in the same manner. **For more advanced students,** after you model a problem, have each youngster write the corresponding subtraction sentence on an individual white-board. ***Beginning subtraction***

[Eight] pretty leaves on the old oak tree.
[Two] pretty leaves flutter free.
How many leaves do you still see
Up in the branches of the old oak tree?

SCIENCE

Two-Sided Tree

This art project is a great avenue for explaining why leaves change colors in the fall! Give each youngster a large white tree cutout like the one shown. Instruct her to use a brown marker to color the tree trunk and draw branches. Then have her use green paint to make handprints or sponge prints on the treetop.

After the paint dries, tell students that the chlorophyll in a tree's leaves helps make food for the tree and makes the leaves green. Explain that as the tree gets ready to rest for the winter, the chlorophyll fades away. Guide students to realize that the green color disappears as this happens. Explain that the leaves then show colors (red, orange, and yellow) that the green color had hidden. Next, have each youngster color the trunk and draw branches on the blank side of her tree. Then ask her to make fall-colored paint prints on the treetop. The result will be a handy reminder of what she learned about leaves! ***Understanding seasonal changes of leaves***

Leaf Cards

Use with "Colorful Favorites" and "Paired to Compare!" on page 301.

Oak Leaf Cards

Use with "Colorful Favorites" and "Paired to Compare!" on page 301 and "Fluttering Free" on page 302.

My Name: ______________________

My Partner's Name: ______________________

My Leaf

My Partner's Leaf

Size: small medium large

Edges: jagged smooth

Size: small medium large

Edges: jagged smooth

Same: ______________________________________

Different: ______________________________________

Note to the teacher: Use with "Paired to Compare!" on page 301.

Colonial Kids

ideas contributed by Laurie K. Gibbons
Huntsville, AL

Different and Alike

Identifying similarities and differences

As you teach students this song, guide them to compare their lives with the lives of colonial children.

(sung to the first verse of "My Bonnie Lies Over the Ocean")

Colonial children were different
From the children today, we know.
They worked hard from sunup to sundown
And rarely to school could they go.

Colonial children did chores then
To help with their families' needs.
They cooked and they gardened and hunted
And did different household deeds.

Colonial children were also
Like so many children today.
They laughed and learned and they had great fun
With the games they liked to play!

Peek at the Past

Developing vocabulary

This cabin project holds reminders of how colonial children spent their time! Have each child place a copy of the cabin pattern from page 306 on a piece of corrugated paper and then do a crayon rubbing on it. After he adds any other desired crayon details, staple the top of the house to a blank sheet of paper. Then have the youngster cut out the house through both thicknesses. Next, ask the youngster to open the resulting booklet and glue an envelope facedown on the back cover, keeping the flap free. Then instruct him to color and cut out a copy of the picture cards from page 307 and store them in the envelope. Follow up with the ideas below.

Action words: Read the cards' captions with students. Then have students underline the action words and act them out.

Categorizing: Help students sort the cards by the categories of work, play, and school. *(Work: sampler, butter churn, and chickens; Play: hoop, top, and kite; School: hornbook and feather quill)*

Cabin Pattern

Use with "Peek at the Past" on page 305.

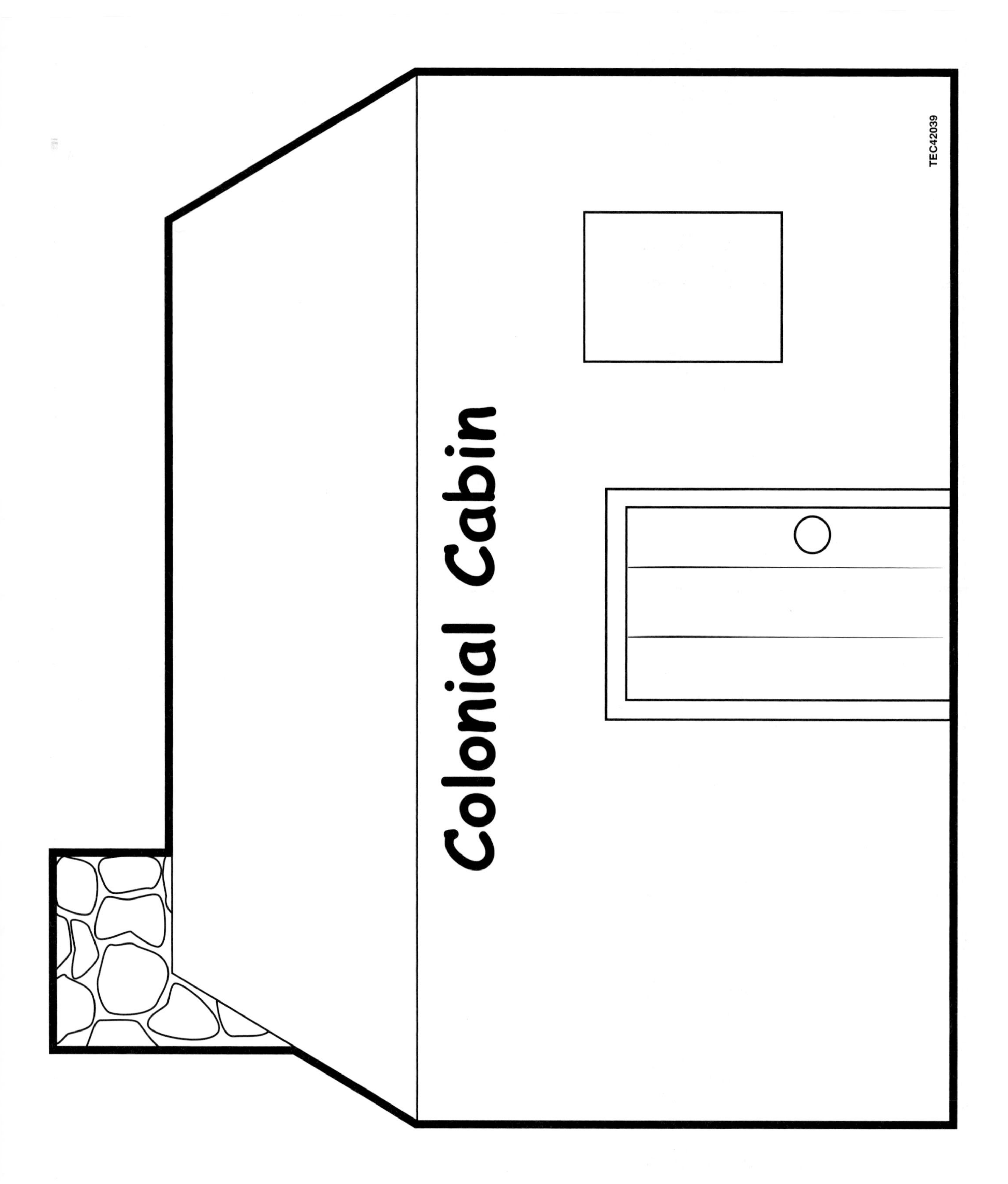

Picture Cards

Use with “Peek at the Past” on page 305.

Read a hornbook.

TEC42039

Sew a sampler.

TEC42039

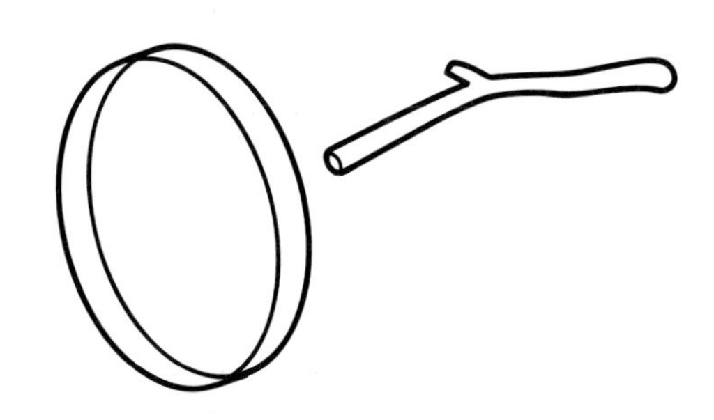

Roll a hoop with a stick.

TEC42039

Churn some butter.

TEC42039

Feed the chickens.

TEC42039

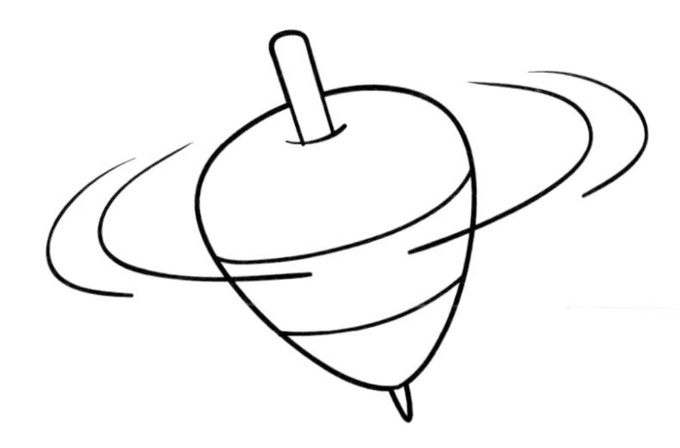

Spin a top.

TEC42039

Write with a feather quill.

TEC42039

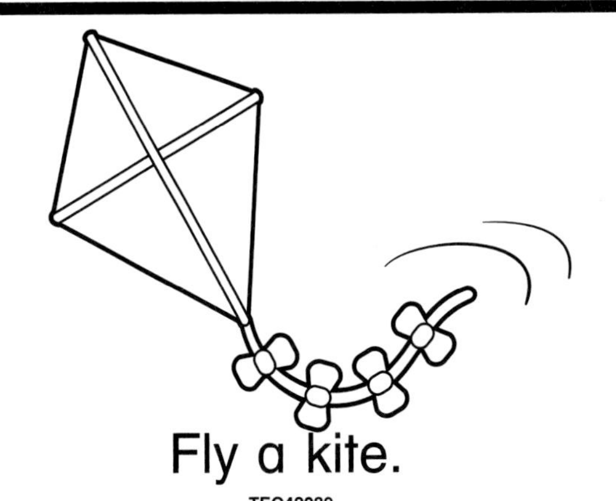

Fly a kite.

TEC42039

Seasonal Skill Practice

Hearts

MATH

Clear Columns

Here's a clever way to help students align two-digit numbers for vertical addition. Mask the five and six on two number cubes and then replace each masked number with a number from zero to four. Place the cubes, a heart tracer, construction paper, and scissors at a center.

A student uses the heart tracer to make a few heart cutouts. She folds each heart in half, firmly pressing the fold to make a crease, and then unfolds it. Next, she rolls the cubes and places them side by side to form a two-digit number. She writes the number on a heart so the crease separates the two digits. She rolls the cubes again and adds the resulting two-digit number to the number on the heart. After she writes and solves an addition problem on each heart, she staples the hearts together to make a booklet. ***Two-digit addition without regrouping***

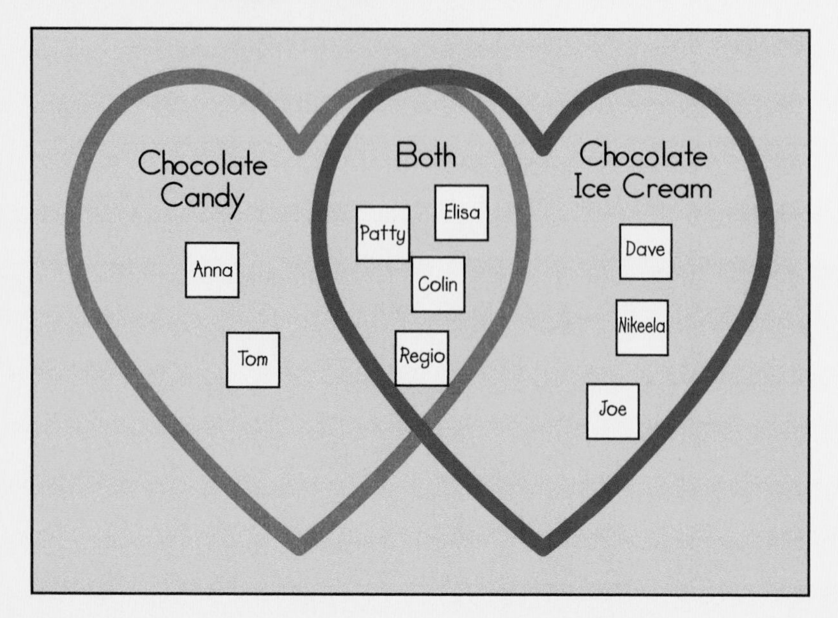

LITERACY OR MATH

"Heart-y" Comparison

Give a traditional graphic organizer a holiday twist! Draw two overlapping hearts on a poster-size piece of paper. Then choose an idea below. ***Using a Venn diagram***

Candy Hearts: Purchase some conversation heart candies. Label one heart in the diagram with a color of a candy and the other heart with a word shown on several candies. Place the diagram on a table. Then instruct students to place the candies on or outside the diagram.

Sweet Treats: Label the diagram as shown. Have youngsters write their names on sticky notes and then place the notes on or outside the diagram to show their food preferences.

adapted from an idea by Stephanie Aldrich
Halifax School, Halifax, VT

LITERACY OR MATH

Mending Broken Hearts

Make one identical heart cutout for every two students. For literacy, write a compound word on each heart. For math, write a pair of related addition and subtraction facts on each heart. Cut the hearts in half as shown. Next, give each youngster half a heart. Then instruct him to find the student who has the matching heart half and sit with her. After all the students are paired, ask the students in each twosome to read aloud their assembled heart. ***Compound words or related math facts***

Kathryn Davenport, Partin Elementary, Oviedo, FL

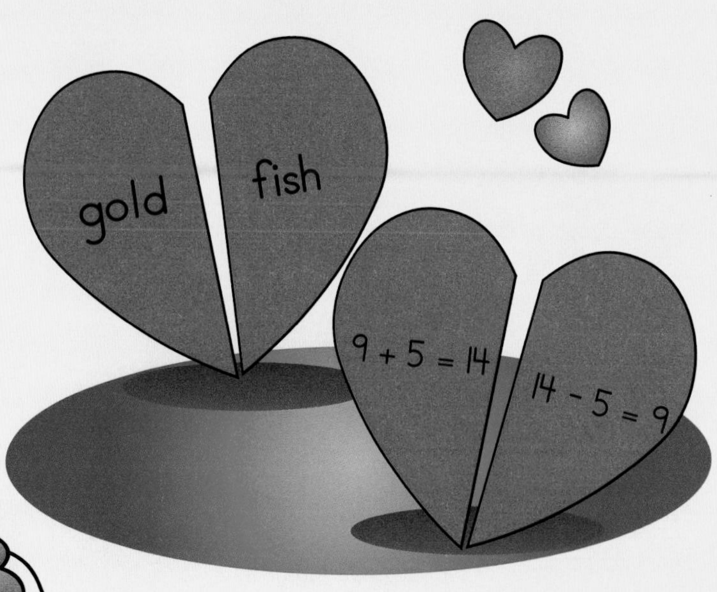

MATH

Twirling Facts

To make this project, a student folds a colorful sheet of paper in half. She draws two half hearts on the fold, as shown; cuts them out and then unfolds them. Next, she writes her name on the small heart. She uses a glue stick to mount the large heart to a different-colored paper. Then she trims the paper. She writes three numbers of a fact family in the heart center and the corresponding addition and subtraction facts on the heart frame. Then she glues the heart with her name to the back of the project. Finally, she punches a hole in the top of the project and ties a string through it to make a hanger. ***Fact families***

LITERACY

Vowel Valentines

Label each of five small heart cutouts with a different vowel. Display the hearts on the board. Next, write on the board a word from the list shown. Have youngsters read the word aloud. Then invite a youngster to tape a heart over the vowel to change the word. After students read the newly formed word, erase the board and write a different word for students to change. ***Changing the vowel in a word***

Suggested Words
cut
drop
pick
run
step
trap

adapted from an idea by Diane L. Flohr-Henderson
Kent City Elementary, Kent City, MI

Seasonal Skill Practice

Caterpillars and Butterflies

SCIENCE

Tell-All Wings

This clever butterfly is a great life-cycle prop or 3-D addition to a display. Give each child a light-colored copy of page 312. Explain that the illustrations on the wings represent the stages of butterfly development. Have each student color the eggs and leaves, the caterpillars, each chrysalis, and the butterfly body. After he cuts out the pattern, staple the butterfly body to a four-inch long cardboard tube. Instruct him to glue two narrow paper strips (antennae) and a pom-pom to the butterfly head. Then have him gently fold the wings up. ***Life cycle of a butterfly***

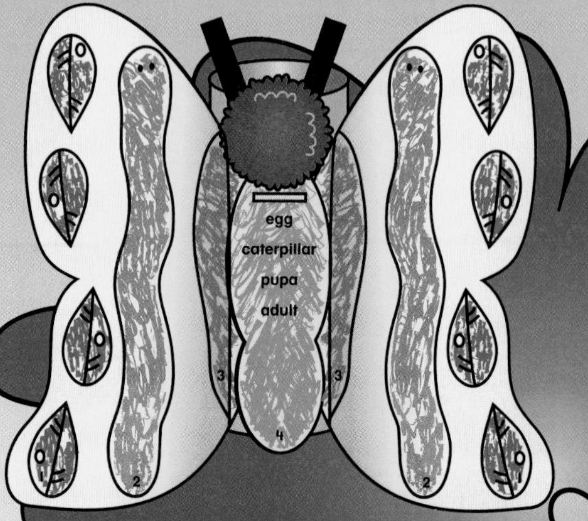

Oral follow-up: Have each youngster put two fingers in the tube of his butterfly to hold it. Ask him to refer to the illustrations on the wings as he tells about butterfly metamorphosis.

Written follow-up: Instruct each student to write about butterfly metamorphosis. Then post his writing with his butterfly.

Diane L. Flohr-Henderson
Kent City Elementary
Kent City, MI

LITERACY

Which Leaf?

Here's a springtime word sort for a small group. Label three leaf cutouts as shown. To make caterpillars, round the ends of several paper strips and draw a face on each. Program the caterpillars with short *e* words or long *e* words containing *ea* or *ee,* writing one word per caterpillar. To complete the activity, students put the leaves in a row. They read the words on the caterpillars and sort the caterpillars by vowel patterns. Afterward, each youngster lists the resulting groups of words on provided paper. ***Short and long*** **e** ***spelling patterns***

LITERACY OR MATH

Splendid Spinner

To make a butterfly spinner, fold a colorful sheet of paper into quarters. Trim the paper as shown, unfold it, and then trace the fold lines. Next, draw a circle in each resulting section. For reading, write a question word in each circle. For math, write a number in each circle. After you color the circles, use a brad to attach a paper clip to the center of the butterfly and tape two paper strips (antennae) to the back of the butterfly. Use the spinner as described below.

Reading: To follow up a reading selection, have a student spin the spinner and then ask his classmates a relevant question with the corresponding word.

Math: Ask two students to spin the spinner, in turn, and announce the two numbers on which the spinner lands. Then instruct each youngster to write a math fact with the numbers.

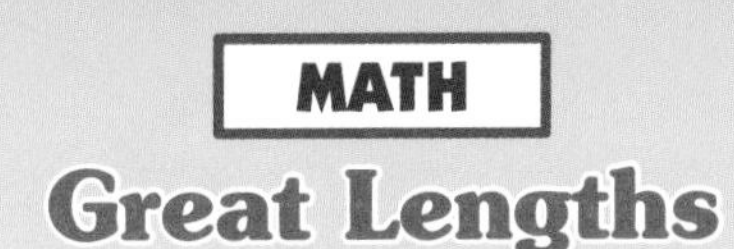

MATH

Great Lengths

Sticky dots make this activity easy to prepare. To make a caterpillar, put a row of sticky dots on a strip of paper and then draw a face on the first sticky dot. Make caterpillars in several lengths and letter each caterpillar for easy identification. Put the caterpillars at a center, along with rulers and paper. A student lists the letters on a sheet of paper, measures each caterpillar's length to the nearest inch or centimeter, and writes each measurement beside the corresponding letter on her paper. ***Linear measurement***

LITERACY

Word Metamorphosis

Give students practice changing words with this minibooklet. To begin, a student folds a half sheet of paper into quarters (to 2¾" x 4¼"). He cuts apart the quarters, stacks them, and then staples them together as shown. Next, he writes a title and his name on the front cover. He illustrates the front cover with a butterfly egg and the back cover with an adult butterfly. He writes each of the following words on a different page: *flower, fly, net, spot,* and *wing.* Then he changes the first letter or letters of each word and writes the resulting word below it. ***Changing initial letters to make new words***

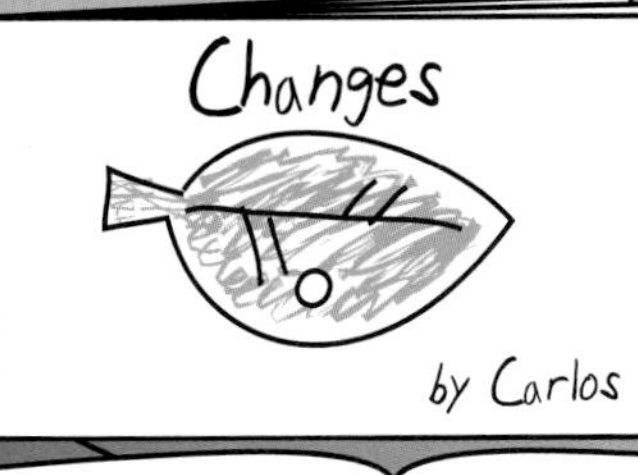

Butterfly Pattern

Use with "Tell-All Wings" on page 310.

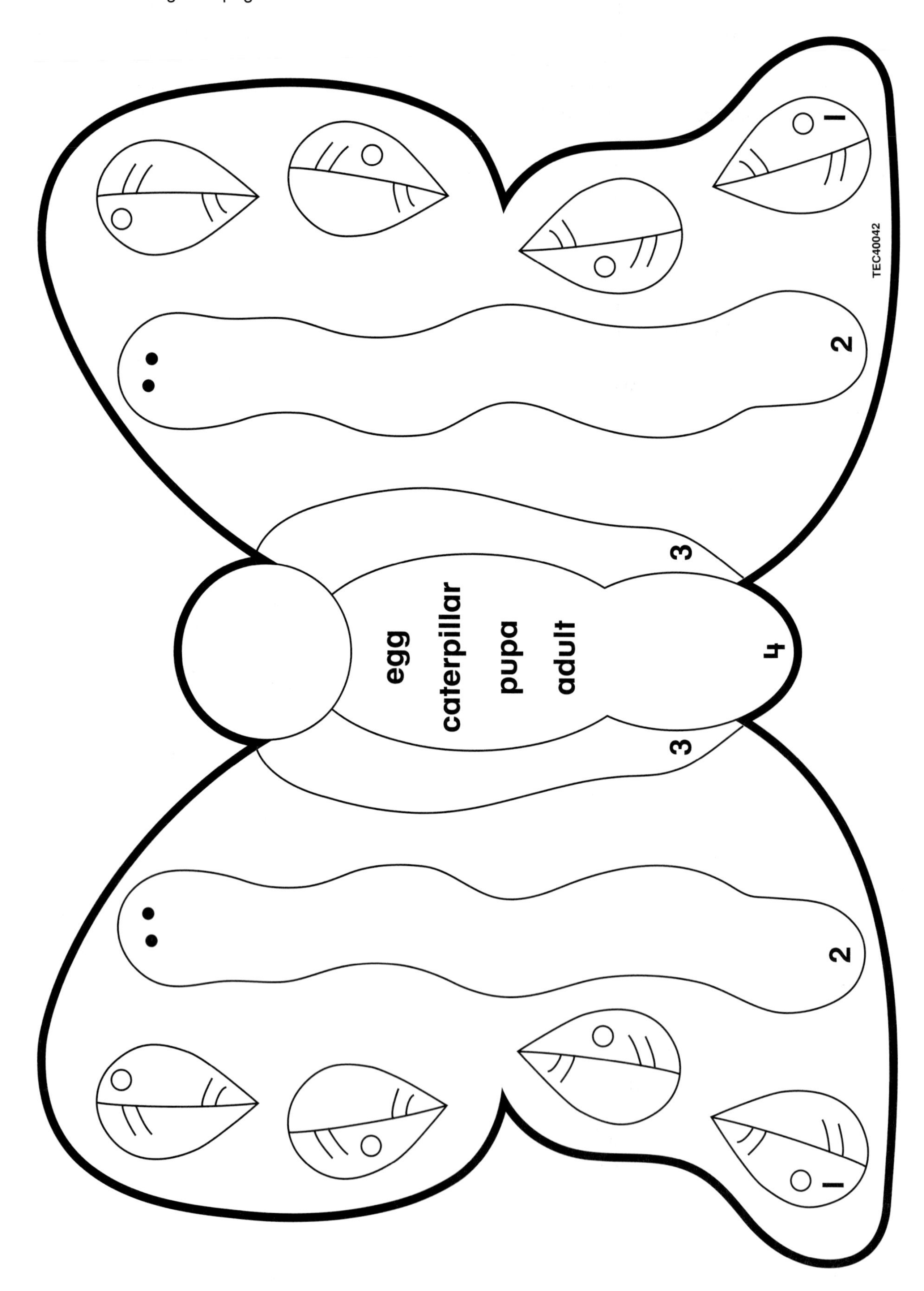

INDEX